Plans Unraveled

Plans
UNRAVELED
The Foreign Policy of the
CARTER
Administration

SCOTT KAUFMAN

NORTHERN ILLINOIS UNIVERSITY PRESS *DeKalb*

Published by the Northern Illinois University Press, DeKalb, Illinois   60115

Manufactured in the United States using postconsumer-recycled, acid-free paper.

Design by Julia Fauci

Library of Congress Cataloging-in-Publication Data

Kaufman, Scott, 1969–

Plans unraveled : the foreign policy of the Carter administration / Scott Kaufman.

   p.   cm.

Includes bibliographical references and index.

ISBN 978-0-87580-390-6 (clothbound : alk. paper)

1. United States—Foreign relations—1977–1981. 2. Carter, Jimmy, 1924– I. Title.

E872.K39 2009

327.73009'047—dc22

2008014039

To my father

CONTENTS

ACKNOWLEDGMENTS

★   I would like first to thank the staff of the Jimmy Carter Library, who were always ready to help me locate material and to keep me abreast of new documents about to become available. Having had numerous occasions over the past two decades to do research there, I feel like they have become members of my family. My appreciation goes out as well to my colleagues at Francis Marion University, who consistently have supported my research endeavors.

In addition to the anonymous readers who took time to look over and comment on the manuscript, I want to thank my father, Dr. Burton Kaufman, and Jackie Stanke, Associate Professor of History at Campbell University, who read over my work and made suggestions to improve it.

Completion of this monograph would not have been possible without the generous financial assistance of both the Francis Marion University History Department and the Francis Marion Foundation.

Thanks also go to the people of Northern Illinois University Press for their assistance as this project progressed: thanks go especially to Melody Herr, former Acquisitions Editor; Susan Bean, Managing Editor; and Alex Schwartz, Director.

Finally, I cannot express enough my appreciation to my mother, Diane, and sister, Heather, for their love and support.

Plans Unraveled

PRELUDE

★   In a poll held about two months after the 1980 election, respondents were asked to judge how Jimmy Carter would go down in history. Only 3 percent answered "outstanding," while nearly half rated him as "below average" or "poor." A survey of historians and policy experts taken just prior to Ronald Reagan's inauguration found a similar assessment. "The most common view," reported the *New York Times,* "is that while he can point to a few notable accomplishments, Mr. Carter will not bequeath a particularly distinguished legacy to the nation."[1]

With a few exceptions, most scholars of the Carter administration's foreign policy share these conclusions. Where they differ is in their explanation for Carter's diplomatic record. The most common reasoning focuses on the rivalry between National Security Adviser Zbigniew Brzezinski, the cold warrior who viewed Soviet machinations as the cause of instability worldwide, and Secretary of State Cyrus Vance, who wanted to downplay the Soviet threat. Like Vance, Carter—at least initially—favored redirecting the focus of America's foreign policy, with morality being the keystone of the president's diplomacy. Yet Carter never effectively reconciled the approaches of his secretary of state and NSC adviser, resulting in a policy that was inconsistent, incoherent, and even contradictory. Eventually, Brzezinski came out on top in this struggle for influence.[2] While other scholars have given less emphasis to the Vance-Brzezinski split or the perceived danger posed by Soviet-inspired communism, they agree that Carter did a poor job in confronting intra-governmental squabbles. The result was a confused foreign policy.[3]

Other critics of the thirty-ninth president point to how he viewed his role as chief executive. Regarding himself as both an outsider who owed nothing to members of his party, as well as a trustee whose job it was to do what he believed was right, Carter tended to snub lawmakers, creating unnecessary tensions between the executive and legislative branches. Consequently, he had a more difficult time accomplishing his goals than had he played the political game of give-and-take.[4]

A third interpretation is more forgiving. While acknowledging that Carter's diplomatic record was less than stellar, these scholars contend that the president was the victim of forces he could not control. At home, he faced a burgeoning neoconservative movement; divisions within his own Democratic Party, which was trying to recover from the shock of the Vietnam War; or unyielding bureaucratic or corporate interests that fought policies of his they opposed. Abroad, he had to contend with uncoopera- tive foreign leaders, such as those in Iran and Nicaragua; a Soviet Union that, unlike the United States, believed détente permitted challenges to the status quo; and revolutionary movements, like that in Iran, which Carter had no possibility of stemming.[5]

More recently, a revisionist analysis has appeared which is more sup- portive of Carter's record. Carter's human rights policy improved the standing of a United States that had been criticized for backing repressive regimes. He was not indecisive or weak; rather, he had a foreign policy that was necessarily pragmatic. And the president had some significant successes, including ratification of the Panama Canal treaties and the sign- ing of the Camp David Accords.[6]

This work acknowledges that Carter had some important foreign policy achievements. But it ultimately finds, as have many scholars of the presi- dent's diplomacy, that his record was mediocre. This book, however, offers an interpretation different from those of the other critics. Carter did come to office seeking to promote morality in U.S. foreign policy, but his moral- ism is often exaggerated; indeed, the president repeatedly demonstrated a preparedness to push aside morality in the name of protecting geopolitical or strategic interests. While Carter faced both external and internal con- straints, such is true of any president. Carter did do a poor job of con- fronting governmental infighting, and he did see himself as a trustee of the American people, which caused problems with Congress.

Yet none of this explains why Carter's foreign policy record ultimately was lackluster. The prime cause was his poorly designed management sys- tem. In addition to his trustee mentality, his spokes-in-the-wheel method of decision making failed to resolve disagreements among his advisers be- fore they reached him. He tended to stitch together alternatives rather than make choices, which caused confusion as to what his policies were. Instead of taking time to vet policies before trying to implement them, he sought to enact many initiatives at once. As a result, policies interfered with one another or had to be so revised that they became inconsistent in their implementation. Maybe most important, he saw himself as someone whose job it was to solve individual problems rather than to give the American people a vision of where he planned to take the country. The U.S. public thus saw more often than not contradictory and inconsistent policies. Had Carter had a better grasp of both the possible and of Washington politics, his foreign policy record might have proven more successful.

CONTINUITY *or* CHANGE?

One

★ It was something that neither Washington, D.C., nor the nation had ever seen before. On his way from the U.S. Capitol to the inaugural ceremony, the recently elected president, Jimmy Carter, his wife, Rosalynn, and their daughter, Amy, got out of their armored limousine and walked to the White House, the first couple holding hands while Amy jumped and danced at their side. "They're walking! They're walking!" exclaimed the surprised onlookers lining the parade route.[1]

While seemingly innocuous, the Carters' decision to walk to the White House was highly symbolic. The Vietnam War and the Watergate scandal had divided the American people from those they had elected to high office. By walking the route, the Carters suggested that it was time for a change: the president was neither special nor distant from those who had chosen him to lead the country. Rather, he was one of them.[2] He was, in short, someone whom average Americans could both relate to and trust.

This desire for new directions had ramifications for the nation's foreign policy. The Vietnam War had brought an end to the Cold War consensus that had viewed the United States as obligated to contain a monolithic communist threat directed from the Soviet Union. Moreover, Americans questioned the morality of their nation's diplomacy, let alone the moral standing of their own elected leaders. During the campaign Jimmy Carter had played upon these concerns, promising to deemphasize the East-West Cold War struggle, to bring honesty back to Washington, and to promote morality in U.S. foreign policy. The new president, however, was not clear on how he intended to accomplish these goals. More important, his top foreign policy advisers were split over policy making. Such division ultimately created serious problems for the new administration.

A Mainstream South, an East-West Détente

Since the early 1970s, the country had been changing, demographically, politically, and ideologically. For one thing, people were moving, physically. The Sun Belt, which referred to the states ranging from Florida to California, had seen its population grow by 9 percent during the first half of the decade, 7 percent higher than the rest of the country. Most of the cities in the North and East, in the meantime, had registered little population growth or had even had more people leave than move in.[3]

As the number of people residing in the Sun Belt grew, so did its political influence. This was especially true with regard to the South. Historically the South had been the target of criticism from individuals living in the North and West for its social conservatism, particularly when it came to race. By the 1970s, though, the states of the South had changed significantly. Racism by no means had completely disappeared. But more and more southerners understood that racial intransigence discouraged investment and the talent and money new businesses brought. The stage thus was set for racial moderates who could "bring the region into the national mainstream."[4]

In fact, the South in some respects was becoming the mainstream. If many Americans rejected racism, they began embracing other aspects of the social conservatism that had been particularly prevalent in the South. The 1960s, with its Great Society programs, "free love," increasingly violent civil rights and student protests, feminists' demands for an Equal Rights Amendment (ERA) and the right to an abortion, and homosexuals' desire for equal rights, bred a backlash that would continue throughout the 1970s and beyond. This backlash came in the form of the New Right movement, which combined a religious evangelism with an opposition to the liberal activism of the 1960s and a belief that America had lost its moral compass. The problem with the New Right was its desire to create a nation based on Christian values, which turned off a large number of voters. But by the early 1970s, it had found a more acceptable voice via the broader-based neoconservative movement, which shared the New Right's social attitudes but lacked its determination to develop a Christian-oriented country. In general, neoconservatives were fiscally frugal with regard to social programs, which they believed represented a waste of taxpayer money, and morally opposed to abortion, homosexuality, unfettered sex, and the ERA.[5]

Although neoconservatives devoted most of their attention to social issues, they did not ignore foreign policy.[6] The neoconservative movement appeared at the same time Americans had turned against the Vietnam War and once-tense U.S.–Soviet and Sino–American relations had entered a period of improvement known as détente. President Richard Nixon, who has received credit for the establishment of détente, had a number of reasons to seek closer ties with America's communist adversaries. For one, while the Soviet Union and communist China had once been very close allies, by the late 1960s they had become enemies. Although there were a number of reasons for this, one of the more recent was the announcement in 1968 by Soviet General Secretary Leonid Brezhnev that as leader of the socialist world, the Soviet Union had the right to intervene in other socialist countries. The Kremlin used what became known as the "Brezhnev Doctrine" to justify an invasion of Czechoslovakia that August. The Chinese became apprehensive that they might be next. The two communist powers soon thereafter engaged in border skirmishes. Now seeing Moscow as a greater threat than Washington, Beijing turned to the United States. Nixon and his national security adviser, Henry Kissinger, saw an opportunity they could not pass up. They would seek détente with both China and the Soviet Union while playing off their differences. In so doing, they could keep the former communist allies at loggerheads, thus weakening the communist world, while using each to the advantage of the United States.

One of those possible advantages was Vietnam. The United States had sent combat troops to South Vietnam in the mid-1960s to defend that country from the communist North and Marxist-led Vietcong guerrillas fighting in the South. The Soviet Union and China had responded to the American presence in South Vietnam by sending economic and military aid to the North. As the war continued, its unpopularity in the United States swelled, and ongoing talks between U.S. and North Vietnamese officials made little progress. Nixon and Kissinger hoped to use better relations with Beijing and Moscow as a price for their cooperation in getting North Vietnam to bargain on ending the Vietnam conflict.[7]

Détente also could bring sanity to the arms race between the United States and the Soviet Union. By 1970, Moscow had achieved nuclear parity, or equality, with Washington. Yet the arms race continued, with both sides producing large numbers of intercontinental ballistic missiles (ICBMs), sea-launched ballistic missiles (SLBMs), and aircraft. The United States feared the Soviet Union might begin deployment of an antiballistic missile system (ABM), possibly inducing Moscow to feel protected enough that it could launch a preemptive nuclear strike against America. An anxious Washington began MIRVing its missiles. Multiple independently targeted reentry vehicles, or MIRVs, allowed the United States to place more than one warhead on a single missile; that single weapon could hit numerous targets and, hopefully, overwhelm any ABM defense.[8]

Controlling the arms race offered one other advantage: world stability. Treating the Soviet Union as an equal would provide Moscow with a vested interest in seeking to maintain the status quo. Here, the Nixon administration believed it possible to engage in linkage, tying American concessions, such as food shipments or most-favored-nation (MFN) status, to Moscow's cooperation on issues of concern to Washington.[9]

The Soviets shared the American interest in détente. They too did not want the arms race to spin out of control. Moreover, with nuclear parity now a reality, an arms control agreement between the superpowers would demonstrate to the world that the United States indeed saw the Soviet Union as an equal, thus bringing political prestige to Moscow.[10] But there were other reasons for seeking closer ties with the White House. Moscow did not want to see Sino–American collusion against it. Additionally, the Kremlin needed access to sophisticated Western industrial equipment to help it combat economic shortfalls at home, including difficulties in meeting its people's agricultural needs. Finally, détente could legitimize the status quo in Europe, where Soviet-inspired communist-led governments controlled much of the eastern half of the continent.

To the Soviets, détente did not mean that competition between the two superpowers for influence around the world would end. Rather, Moscow would seek to keep that competition from reaching a point where it spun out of control. As Brezhnev explained in 1972, "socialism and capitalism are opposite and irreconcilable. But we shall strive to shift this historically inevitable struggle onto a path free from the perils of war, of dangerous conflicts, and an uncontrolled arms race."[11]

Neoconservatives v. New Internationalists

It was Brezhnev's talk of irreconcilability between the superpowers that made neoconservatives generally less supportive of détente than Nixon and Kissinger. Neoconservatives believed that America's difficulties in Vietnam had weakened the nation's position in the world, and the effort to improve relations with the Soviet Union risked undercutting it even more. It was essential, they contended, that the United States increase spending on defense and adopt the more confrontationist anti-Soviet stance it had maintained during the earlier years of the Cold War.[12] Neoconservatives tended to be less skeptical about seeking closer ties with communist China, knowing that Beijing shared their concerns about the Kremlin's intentions.

In 1976, a group of those critical of détente formed the Committee on the Present Danger (CPD). Calling détente "one-sided disarmament," they included a number of influential persons from both political parties, among them Paul Nitze, the director of the State Department's Policy Planning Staff during the administration of Harry Truman; President Lyndon Johnson's head of the National Security Council (NSC), Walt Rostow; and Nixon's former defense secretary, James Schlesinger. They asserted that the Kremlin sought to dominate all of Europe, using adventurism in the Middle East and Africa to isolate America's European allies. Simply put, Moscow could not be trusted.[13]

Sharing the CPD's concerns was a Democratic senator from Washington state, Henry Jackson.[14] First elected to the upper house in 1952, Jackson developed a reputation as a liberal on domestic matters but as a conservative when it came to America's foreign policy. He was an ardent proponent of a strong U.S. military who was regarded as an expert on national defense policy and became a highly influential member of the Armed Services Committee. An avowed cold warrior, in 1972 he founded the Coalition for a Democratic Majority, a group of Democrats who called for strengthening the U.S. military to counter the threat posed by the Kremlin.

It is not surprising that both the CPD and Jackson had serious qualms about one of the hallmarks of détente, the Strategic Arms Limitations Treaty (SALT) with the Soviet Union, which President Nixon submitted to the Senate in 1972 for ratification. One part of the treaty, an accord of unlimited duration, restricted each superpower to the construction of two ABM systems. Both the United States and Soviet Union agreed that it was important to place caps on the building of ABM networks so that neither would feel safe enough from attack that it might launch a nuclear strike on the other. The other portion of SALT, an interim agreement with a five-year lifespan, placed caps on the building of nuclear missiles. Both of the superpowers promised to limit the number of ICBMs to those already deployed or under construction and to freeze the number of SLBMs. In both cases, the Soviets had the edge, with over 1,600 ICBMs and 740 SLBMs to 1050 ICBMs and 656 SLBMs for the United States. While it looked like SALT handicapped Washington, the treaty did not cover long-range strategic bombers or MIRVed missiles. In both categories of weapons (bombers and MIRVs), the United States had a sizeable advantage over its communist rival. Furthermore, SALT did not prohibit the development of new weapons systems, thereby allowing the White House to continue work on the Trident submarine and cruise missile. The Trident could carry two dozen SLBMs; the cruise missile was a guided, pilotless drone designed to hit targets as far as 1,500 miles (about 2,500 kilometers) away.[15]

To the White House's frustration, Jackson ignored these provisions favorable to the United States. Rather, as the price of his vitally important support for SALT, he added to the treaty prior to its ratification an amendment requiring that future arms limitation agreements guarantee the two superpowers the same number of ICBMs and SLBMs.[16] Two years later, Jackson cosponsored with Representative Charles Vanik of Ohio the Jackson-Vanik Amendment, which imposed economic sanctions on Moscow because of the Kremlin's refusal to let Jews emigrate. Using Jackson-Vanik, the Washington senator successfully fought the White House's desire to grant the Soviet Union MFN status.

The Jackson-Vanik Amendment received widespread endorsement from not just neoconservatives but from another group of lawmakers, the so-called new internationalists. If neoconservatives took from the Vietnam War era the need to combat America's weakness with higher defense spending and a return to anti-Sovietism, new internationalists determined that Washington had to refocus its foreign policy, giving more attention to human rights and the spread of democracy. To them, anti-Sovietism was dangerous. It had been a desire to stop the spread of Soviet-inspired communism that had dragged the United States into the mire of Vietnam. It was imperative to avoid another such mistake.

Moreover, explained the new internationalists, the focus on Moscow ignored a changing world. Numerous former colonies in the Third World had achieved their freedom since the end of World War II and had begun to demand international respect for their interests. Meanwhile, older nations, such as Japan and those in Western Europe, had recovered from the ravages of war and were challenging America's worldwide economic supremacy. Transnational corporations and banks had their own ability to impact international politics and economics. "What is needed today," commented Harvard University's Stanley Hoffman in 1977, "is a new international system that goes beyond past forms of . . . balance of power eras."[17]

Finally, anti-Sovietism had driven the White House to support repressive regimes and even engage in assassination. New internationalists pointed particularly to the Church committee reports that appeared between 1975 and 1976. Headed by Democratic Senator Frank Church of Idaho, the committee found that former presidents, including John F. Kennedy and Nixon, had issued orders to oust or murder such persons as Congolese Prime Minister Patrice Lumumba, Cuban President Fidel Castro, and Chilean President Salvador Allende. Simultaneously, the White House had supported regimes that violated the rights of their people, including those of Philippine President Ferdinand Marcos; Iran's shah, Muhammad Reza Pahlavi; and General Augusto Pinochet Ugarte, who led the 1973 military coup that overthrew Allende. The Church committee reports prompted President Gerald Ford in 1976 to issue an order barring the United States from assassinating foreign leaders.

Congress also sought to require the United States to take human rights into account when providing aid to other countries. In 1973, Representative Donald Fraser (D-Minnesota), the chair of the Foreign Affairs Subcommittee on International Organizations and Movements, held a series of hearings that examined the human rights situation in, and U.S. policy toward, eighteen different nations, including Argentina, Chile, Brazil, Nicaragua, and Uruguay.[18] While Fraser succeeded in getting through Congress several pieces of legislation designed to apply human rights criteria to American military and economic aid to foreign countries, none of them were binding. That changed in 1975, when the United States, Soviet Union, Canada, and numerous European countries signed the Helsinki

Accords, in which they agreed to respect the rights of their people. Using the momentum from the Church reports and the Helsinki Accords, Fraser and his supporters passed legislation between 1975 and 1976 that required the president to cut economic and military aid to countries that violated human rights (though these laws permitted economic aid for the needy).

One must be careful, of course, not to place too much emphasis on the neoconservative–new internationalist dichotomy. Some of those on Capitol Hill, such as Senator Howard Baker (R-Tennessee), were not easily labeled; others, such as Senator Church, appeared to shift from one camp to the other. But the division among lawmakers demonstrated two things. First, the Cold War consensus had broken down. Whereas the majority of the members of Congress, and indeed most Americans, in the 1950s and well into the 1960s strongly supported a confrontationist, anticommunist foreign policy, that consensus no longer existed. Neoconservatives wanted to keep the focus on the Soviet Union, while new internationalists wanted to broaden it to include any country, communist or not, that violated human rights. Second, while Democrats held the majority vote in both houses of Capitol Hill throughout the 1970s, they had serious divisions over the direction of U.S. diplomacy and offered potential difficulties for any incoming president, even if that person was a Democrat.

On top of all this, Congress had begun to reassert itself. The "imperial presidency," in which much of the U.S. government's power rested in the hands of the chief executive, had begun to disappear. Americans reacted not just to Vietnam but to the Watergate scandal by electing 75 new faces to Congress in 1974. These "Watergate babies," who included Patrick Leahy of Vermont, Massachusetts's Paul Tsongas, and Tom Harkin of Iowa—all of them Democrats—tended to align themselves with the new internationalists on foreign policy.[19] But they also aligned themselves with an effort that had begun prior to their election to reform government and curtail presidential power. In addition to the aforementioned provisions regarding foreign assistance to repressive regimes, lawmakers passed the 1973 War Powers Act, which restricted the ability of the White House to send troops overseas and, Capitol Hill hoped, would prevent a replay of Vietnam; imposed restrictions on the Central Intelligence Agency; created, under the Budget and Impoundment Control Act of 1974, committees in the House and Senate to give Congress more authority over appropriations; and that same year amended the Freedom of Information Act to allow Americans greater access to government documents about themselves.

Jimmy Carter

Jimmy Carter tapped into these changes occurring in the United States. He was a racial moderate from the Sun Belt. He was a religiously devout, born-again Christian, which appealed to the New Right. He was fiscally frugal, which neoconservatives found attractive. His strong sense of morality enticed not just new internationalists but those Americans upset by Watergate. Finally, during the 1976 campaign he was fuzzy on the issues. This allowed him to draw upon both conservative and liberal sentiment while leaving unclear exactly what his specific plans were when it came to directing the foreign policy of the nation.

Carter was one of America's shorter presidents, standing five feet, nine inches tall. His height appears to have been a sore point for him throughout his life. He was boyish-looking with an oval face, and those who knew him tended to comment on his steely blue eyes and smile; his advisers came to realize that while the smile in particular sometimes indicated happiness, it might act as a mask for his anger.[20]

The new president had been born in 1924 in Plains, Georgia. His father, Earl, was a successful small businessman who ran a local peanut warehouse, a supporter of segregation, and an anti–New Dealer who regarded Franklin Roosevelt's domestic programs as a waste of taxpayer money. While Jimmy was not as parsimonious as his father, it was from Earl that he developed his fiscal conservatism. Morally, the future president rejected his father's attitude on race; rather, he found inspiration from his mother, Lillian, a trained nurse who had more liberal racial views and who offered medical care for African-Americans in the area surrounding Plains when many others refused. Indeed, a number of Jimmy's childhood companions were African-American, including his closest friend, A. D. Davis.

Carter, who as a child had desired to go into the navy, achieved his dream in 1942, when he received word of his admittance to the U.S. Naval Academy at Annapolis, Maryland. Because he would not actually begin his appointment until the following year, he took courses at Georgia Tech to prepare him for his naval education. In 1946, he graduated in the top 10 percent of his class. That same year, he married Rosalynn Smith, his sister Ruth's best friend and a fellow resident of Plains.

For the next seven years, the future president served in the navy, during which time he became a qualified nuclear engineer. In 1953, he resigned his post following his father's death. After successfully rebuilding the family business, which had been in serious financial trouble, Carter decided to make a go at politics. In 1962 he ran for and won a seat in the Georgia state senate. Four years later, he attempted, but failed, to win the state governorship. In 1970, he ran for governor again and won.

Carter only served one four-year term as governor, for soon after his victory he began to give serious thought to taking a crack at the White House. After the 1972 Democratic National Convention, Peter Bourne, a psychiatrist, the head of Georgia's drug abuse program, and a friend of Mrs. Carter's, and Hamilton Jordan, an astute political adviser who had worked on both of Carter's gubernatorial campaigns, sent the governor a memorandum urging him to run for the presidency. Changes in the Democratic Party's nominating process, they pointed out, had given more power to voters than to party leaders in determining the party's nominee. Moreover, the questions Americans had asked of their elected leaders had opened to door to an outsider who promised positive change. The two men concluded that if he ran, Carter stood a good chance of winning.[21]

Carter concurred and launched his bid for the presidency in December 1974. Using lessons learned from his gubernatorial campaigns, he had established a well-organized network of contacts throughout the nation to help him spread his ideas. His major area of weakness was foreign policy. Consequently, he had taken the step in 1973 of joining the Trilateral Commission. Founded earlier that year, the commission's purpose was to strengthen political, economic, and strategic ties between the United States, Japan, and Western Europe. Carter, who was a voracious reader, took care to read the commission's reports. Furthermore, he used the commission to make contacts with individuals well known in the field of international affairs. Many of the future president's appointees were members of the commission.

Carter emphasized values during the campaign. He chastised Nixon and Kissinger for their secretiveness and deception. He also denounced the Kissingerian policy of realpolitik, which emphasized power in international relations over morality and which, Carter declared, led America to support corrupt, repressive governments in the name of containing communism. Carter promised an administration that was honest, moral, and open. No longer would U.S. officials hide secrets from the American people, involve themselves in scandalous activities, or support oppression abroad. Rather, he promised, his White House would consult closely with Congress and hold "periodic summit conferences and occasional meetings" with Western officials to promote closer ties and coordination between the United States and its allies.[22]

Human rights, the centerpiece of the new internationalist agenda, would also be a keystone of the future president's foreign policy. Interestingly, Carter had not been a strong proponent of human rights in American diplomacy. In 1975, he had declared his opposition to the Jackson-Vanik Amendment on the grounds that it interfered in the Kremlin's internal affairs. But as the campaign continued, he had a change of heart. As a born-again Christian, Carter came to see a link between his own religious beliefs and upholding human rights around the world. Furthermore, Senator Daniel Patrick Moynihan (D-New York) and Carter's own campaign strategists told him that human rights was "a 'no-lose issue.'" First of all, they pointed out, Americans questioned the ethics of their current officials in Washington, making them receptive to a candidate who promoted morality in his policies. Moreover, the 1968 and 1972 presidential campaigns had left the Democratic Party divided. Championing human rights, Carter's advisers explained, could unite Democrats: neoconservatives in the party could use human rights as a reason to attack the Soviet Union and other communist nations, while new internationalists could apply it as well against right-wing governments.[23]

Carter invoked the language of President Woodrow Wilson during the campaign. Wilson had talked of the importance of morality in American foreign policy. To him, the most moral form of government was democracy because it allowed the people of a nation to choose their leaders. Wilson therefore had envisioned a world based upon democratic values, in which all peoples would have a say in their national affairs, and in which international difficulties could be resolved via negotiation rather than conflict. Carter used similar rhetoric. America's leaders, he declared during the campaign, "have ignored those moral values that had often distinguished our country," with the result of weakening Washington's stature in the world. He later stated, "[O]ur greatest source of strength has come from those basic, priceless values which are embodied in our Declaration of Independence, our Constitution, and our Bill of Rights." Failure to uphold those principles in America's diplomacy had made "a mockery of [them]."[24]

Carter tied his promotion of human rights to another major campaign theme, arms control. For the candidate, this meant not just reducing the number of strategic nuclear weapons held by the United States and Soviet Union, but also curbing conventional arms sales to Third World nations and preventing the proliferation of nuclear technology. According to a 1947 report, only the United States and the Soviet Union had the ability to produce a large number of conventional weapons for sale abroad. The report continued that it was important for America to offer such arms as a means of gaining political influence and leverage elsewhere. Using that reasoning, the United States had increased its foreign conventional arms sales. Between just 1970 and 1975 those sales had gone up by 750 percent, to $15 billion.[25] Meanwhile, the number of nations that could complement nuclear weapons with their conventional arsenals had grown. The Soviet Union had tested its first atomic weapon in 1949, followed by Great Britain in 1952, France in 1960, China in 1964 and, most recently, India in 1974. The United States, Soviet Union, and Great Britain had signed the Nuclear Nonproliferation Treaty in 1968, under which they pledged to prevent the spread of atomic technology, but China and India had not. It was well known that other countries, such as Pakistan, sought to obtain their own nuclear capability.

Carter wanted to put a stop to the spread of conventional and nuclear technology and weaponry. They threatened U.S. security by giving enemy nations, if not terrorists, access to sophisticated equipment. But there was also a human rights component to his call for conventional arms control and nuclear nonproliferation. The arms race and diffusion of atomic technology endangered human life by giving more and more nations the potential to spread conflict abroad. And if governments spent money on conventional or nuclear devices, they would have less available to cure social ills at home, such as poverty. Poverty not only placed human beings in a terrible state of living, but it also bred frustration and instability, which jeopardized the well-being of the international economy and could lead to war if not checked.[26] In short, curbing military spending and the spread of nuclear information would open the door to a safer, more peaceful, and wealthier world.

To achieve this vision, Carter planned to move away from the Nixon-Kissinger policy of realpolitik. Although he agreed with Nixon that the United States had limits to its power, and while he supported continuing the policy of détente, the presidential candidate took a page from the new internationalists and played down the rhetoric of the Cold War. Carter understood that the Soviet Union was a repressive nation that posed a threat to America's interests. But he felt that by "downplaying the ideological differences that divided the two countries, and instead concentrating on problems that both powers had a mutual interest in solving, such as the nuclear arms race," then they could achieve "a more cooperative relationship." As he stated in his first major foreign policy address, at Notre Dame University in May 1977, "The unifying threat of conflict with the Soviet Union has become less intensive even though the competition has become more extensive."[27]

Therefore, cooperation with the Soviet Union was important to Carter, but he determined not to make it the centerpiece of his foreign policy. America's Cold War diplomacy had focused on the relationship between the East and West. Carter, influenced by the Trilateral Commission, intended to end America's fixation on the East-West conflict and switch its focus to the "partnership between North America, Western Europe, and Japan." He denounced Kissinger for ignoring Western Europe in his (Kissinger's) attempt to improve U.S.–Soviet ties. "To the maximum extent possible," Washington's relationship with communist nations "should reflect the combined view of the democracies."[28]

Aside from turning Washington's attention from the U.S.–Soviet conflict to U.S.–Japanese–West European relations, Carter also had plans to devote more time to North-South issues, referring to the relationship between the United States and the developing world. The presidential candidate had a long-standing interest in Latin America, having studied Spanish since college and visited Mexico and Brazil while Georgia's governor. Also, strong African-American support in the 1976 campaign and Carter's own interest in human rights moved him to give greater attention to the issue of black rule in Africa.[29]

Carter, however, never went into specifics on how he intended to achieve his goals. He did not explain how to curb arms sales or nuclear proliferation, or how to advance human rights abroad. Would he stop the transfer of weapons to countries vital to American interests even though those countries had repressive regimes? How would he contend with a resurgent Congress made up of lawmakers with divergent views over what the focus of U.S. foreign policy should be? Indeed, Carter appeared contradictory at times. He told the *New York Times* in June 1976 that he opposed the idea "of a limited nuclear war," yet a month later said he would launch a preemptive nuclear attack "if I was convinced that the existence or the security of our nation was threatened." He talked of continuing the policy of détente but accused his Republican opponent, Gerald Ford, of being soft on the Soviets. He declared his desire to cooperate with the Soviet Union to resolve world problems while denouncing Moscow for violating the Helsinki Accords.[30] His double message created problems for him as president almost from day one.

Adding to his difficulties was how Carter viewed his role as president. Trained as an engineer, the former governor saw himself as a problem solver who believed it possible to tackle each issue separate from the others. He thus never did something that is vital for a successful presidency, which is to provide the American people an overarching vision of where he plans to take the country. The ingredients for such a vision were there, but Carter never adequately expressed it. Human rights would be the "central moral" for the incoming administration. Yet that very issue, human rights, lacked the "ideological power" to bring the country together in a way that anticommunism had. Communism was seen as posing a direct threat to the United States itself; human rights supposed helping others, not defending the country. The president might have adopted a more Wilsonian tack. He could have made the argument that the focus on national security had actually made America less secure by promoting an arms race and confrontation with the Soviet Union that, if unchecked, could lead to war.[31] By extension, a world where democratic values flourished, and in which America's current or future enemies lacked the means to wage either a conventional or nuclear conflict, would promote not just world peace but America's safety. However, Carter's innate habit of compartmentalizing policy made that impossible.

In addition to seeing himself as a problem solver, the president conceived his role as that of a trustee of the American people, who knew what was right for them and their country. As such, he had little compulsion to play the game of give-and-take that is commonplace in Washington. Indeed, having run as an outsider who got elected without the support of established members of his party, he felt he did not owe members of Congress anything. Despite Carter's promise to consult with lawmakers, many on Capitol Hill criticized him for failing to return their phone calls or confer with them, which created an oftentimes tense relationship between the executive and legislative branches of government.[32]

Then there was Carter's managerial style of leadership. Upon taking office, he established a "spokes-in-the-wheel" system, by which each of his top advisers would have equal access to him. He would use the information provided by those advisers, make a decision, and then issue instructions to carry it out. This system, however, could only work if his advisers truly had equal access and if there was some means of making sure that those involved carried out the instructions they received.

The fact was that this system of advising and decision making had serious flaws. The assumption that cabinet officials would execute instructions as intended by the president left open the possibility that they would not be implemented as Carter had wanted. More important, there was infighting within the administration, particularly between the president's selections for secretary of state and national security adviser. The battle for influence between those two officials only compounded the White House's troubles.

Cyrus Vance

For secretary of state, Carter nominated Cyrus R. Vance. Standing about six feet tall, with a pale and almost rectangular face highlighted by rubicund cheeks, he looked younger than his years. Hard-working, quiet, and patient, he disliked political infighting, preferring to find an honorable way of resolving disputes and formulating policy.

A graduate of Yale Law School, Vance had served in the Pacific during World War II. After the war, he worked with a law firm in New York City; during that time, he became increasingly interested in foreign affairs and joined the Council on Foreign Relations. Following the Soviet launch in 1957 of *Sputnik,* the world's first unmanned space satellite, then-Senate Majority Leader Lyndon Johnson (D-Texas) established the Preparedness Investigation Committee to look into the state of America's space program. Vance served on the committee and, in the process, expanded his connections in Washington.

Vance quickly rose up the ranks of the Washington bureaucracy. After his election in 1960, President Kennedy appointed Vance general counsel to the Defense Department and then secretary of the army. In 1964, President Johnson promoted Vance to deputy secretary of defense. Johnson found Vance an able negotiator and, therefore, sent him on several diplomatic missions abroad and at home. In 1965, the deputy secretary went to Panama and the Dominican Republic to bring an end to violence in both nations. Two years later he traveled to Detroit, which had been the scene of a race riot, and then to Greece and Turkey to try to resolve their dispute over the island of Cyprus. In 1968, Johnson appointed Vance deputy chief negotiator at the U.S.–North Vietnamese ceasefire talks. After Nixon's victory in the presidential elections that same year, Vance returned to New York and his law firm.

Vance, like Carter, was a member of the Trilateral Commission, but it was more than that common experience that attracted them to each other. Although Vance's family had moved to New York City, he retained a love he had developed from his childhood years in West Virginia for fishing and hiking, pursuits shared by Carter. Both had served in the navy during World War II. Carter found in Vance someone good at solving problems, and the president, with his engineering background, was impressed with Vance's attention to detail. Vance, for his part, regarded Carter as "intelligent and hard working" and determined that the Democratic candidate's views were "in the centrist mainstream in which I felt comfortable. . . . As the weeks passed, it became increasingly clear that we agreed philosophically about the main elements of a fresh approach to foreign policy."[33]

What Vance meant by a "fresh approach" was a U.S. foreign policy that rejected the confrontationist, bipolar view of the Cold War. It was important for the United States to remain strong vis-à-vis the Soviets, he wrote Carter in October 1976, but "U.S./Soviet issues should not be permitted to so dominate our foreign policy that we neglect other important relationships and problems." While he realized that there were times when military force might be required, his experiences before and during the Vietnam War had convinced him that its use tended to cause more problems than it solved; the surest and safest way to promote peace and stability was through diplomacy, with force to be used only as a last resort.[34]

If he rejected the confrontationist approach toward Moscow of the Cold War consensus, so too Vance renounced its belief that foreign crises were the result of Soviet machinations. Instability might just as much be caused by indigenous nationalist groups and movements as it might arise from the activities of the superpowers. And while the Soviet Union could have influence upon those indigenous groups, it was possible to use their nationalism and desire for independence to draw them away from the Kremlin. "Except where the Red Army imposed itself," believed the secretary of state, "Soviet influence was reversible."[35]

Vance understood that the United States and Soviet Union had, and always would have, their differences. But he felt that they shared an overriding interest to avoid war between them. As proof, he pointed to negotiations that took place in 1974 at Vladivostok, in the Soviet Union, between Kissinger, Ford, and Brezhnev; those discussions had established the outline for a SALT II pact. Finalizing what had begun at Vladivostok was, for Vance, central to improving relations between the superpowers.

The question was how. For Vance, there were two keys to successful negotiations. The first was to use friendly diplomacy; Washington had to avoid intimidation unless all other diplomatic efforts had failed. Second, the White House had to refrain from using linkage. For instance, Nixon and Kissinger had tied the Soviets' interest in arms talks, technology, and trade to Moscow's preparedness to pressure North Vietnam to help resolve the Vietnam conflict. To Vance, linkage would only serve to anger Moscow; therefore, when seeking an arms agreement, it was important for Washington not to attach its desire for such an accord to Soviet actions elsewhere.

Zbigniew Brzezinski

Vance in a number of respects was the opposite of Carter's appointee as national security adviser, Zbigniew Brzezinski. Standing about Carter's height, with a triangular-shaped face, sharp nose, a smile that curved down at the end, a hairdo that looked like the prow of a ship— which led Hamilton Jordan to refer to Brzezinski as "Woody Woodpecker"[36] —and an accent he retained from his native Poland, Brzezinski was more vocal, self-promoting, and willing to engage in political battle than his counterpart in State. He had moved to Canada as a child when his father, a Polish diplomat, was posted there. He received his bachelor's and master's degrees from McGill in 1949 and 1950, respectively, and a Ph.D. in Soviet studies from Harvard in 1953. Brzezinski taught at Harvard from 1953 to 1961, during which time he received his American citizenship. In 1961, he became head of the new Institute on Communist Affairs at Columbia University in New York. During that time, he served as an adviser to both presidents Kennedy and Johnson. In 1966, he began a two-year stint as a member of the State Department's Policy Planning Council and worked as Vice President Hubert Humphrey's foreign policy adviser during Humphrey's 1968 bid for the presidency.

Like Vance, Brzezinski played down the centrality of the U.S.–Soviet conflict in America's foreign policy. "How to deal with the Communist world remains a key problem for the U.S.," he wrote in 1973, "but it may no longer be the *central* threat." The central threat was change, and it was vital for the United States to understand it and develop policies to meet it.[37] In 1970, Brzezinski had written *Between Two Ages: America's Role in the Technocratic Era,* in which he asserted that technological advancements required the United States and other industrially advanced countries to collaborate in promoting constructive programs worldwide. Three years later, David Rockefeller, the chairman of Chase Manhattan Bank, founded the Trilateral Commission; viewing the world in similar terms, he appointed Brzezinski as the new organization's first director.

Though he too believed in deemphasizing the East-West conflict, Brzezinski took a harder line toward the Soviet Union than did Vance. While the communist Chinese, like the Soviets, posed a threat to the United States and its interests, Moscow was the more dangerous of the two because, unlike Beijing, it could back its revolutionary ideology with enormous military might. Hence, during the 1962 Cuban missile crisis, Brzezinski had argued in favor of bombing the Soviets' missile sites in Cuba and against President Kennedy's decision to use the U.S. Navy to blockade the island. Moscow's achievement of nuclear parity with Washington by the end of the 1960s greatly worried Brzezinski. "Until now," he wrote in 1969, "peace was safeguarded through asymmetrical deterrence." But with the two superpowers' nuclear arsenals now essentially equal, "deterrence may just not work as well in the future." Though he approved of détente with the Soviet Union as a noble idea, he believed that Nixon and Kissinger had so desired it that they ended up giving a political and strategic advantage to the Soviet Union. Brzezinski charged that SALT offered "numerical superiority to the Russians on the spurious argument of U.S. technological superiority." As a result of the Nixon-Kissinger policy of improving trade ties between the superpowers, "we are not only helping the Soviet economy but we are also buttressing the Soviet political system."[38]

Clearly, Brzezinski did not support Kissinger's Soviet policy. He also placed less faith than Vance in the idea that Moscow embraced peaceful coexistence with Washington and would willingly sign another arms agreement. In 1964, he had coauthored with Samuel Huntington *Political Power: USA/USSR,* in which he concluded that a natural convergence of interests between the superpowers was unlikely. "[F]or the two systems to converge there would have to be a drastic alteration of course—in a historical sense, a revolutionary change of direction—in the path of development between them." This did not mean a future arms agreement with Moscow was impossible. The issue was timing. The only language the Kremlin understood, declared Brzezinski, was military might: if Moscow determined it was stronger than Washington, then it would demonstrate less willingness to make concessions than if it believed it was weaker. The problem with Kissinger's policy making was that Kissinger sought SALT at a time when the superpowers had nuclear parity. Consequently, the United States received too few concessions from the Soviet Union, and all the while the Kremlin continued to augment its military might. Following a line of thought that dated back to the early days of the Cold War, Brzezinski said that what America had to do was to build up its armed forces to the point that it could negotiate with the Kremlin from a position of strength.[39] Only then could America get from the Soviets the types of concessions required to make any future arms agreement worthwhile and effective. To put it another way, the only way to get the Soviets to negotiate in good faith was through intimidation.

Yet at the same time he criticized Kissinger, Brzezinski showed a willingness to use linkage. Moscow, he wrote, "could not have a free ride in some parts of the world while pursuing detente where it suited them." Détente had to be "both more *comprehensive* and more *reciprocal,*" meaning that if necessary, the United States should tie Soviet actions in one area to its actions in another.[40]

Thus, Brzezinski differed with Vance over whether to use coercion and linkage in negotiations with the Soviets. The two advisers also disagreed on the issue of nationalism. To Brzezinski, the Soviet Union's handiwork was involved in indigenous instability elsewhere in the world. Moscow, he argued, would use détente "to deter the United States from responding effectively to the changing political balance." This would leave the door open to the Kremlin to involve itself in affairs elsewhere when the opportunities afforded themselves. In short, while offering cooperation with the United States, the Soviet Union would also engage in "competition, not to preserve the status quo, but to transform it."[41] Rather than face the Soviet threat with the cautious diplomacy favored by Vance, Washington needed to adopt a more open, confrontational approach that, as noted, would incorporate the use of linkage when necessary.

Clark Clifford, who had served as an adviser to Harry Truman and as secretary of defense to Lyndon Johnson, and who had advised Carter during the presidential campaign, resisted the new president's choice for NSC adviser. When, after the election, Carter told Clifford of his selection, Clifford replied that he regarded Brzezinski as not having the type of personality necessary to be NSC adviser and would not get along with Vance. "Well, if we don't put Zbig there, what should I do with him?" asked the incoming president. "Make him the first American Ambassador to the Bermuda Triangle" was the reply. Carter laughed,[42] but he did not take the advice.

Jordan, who became one of President's Carter's key aides, shared Clifford's concerns. He reportedly quipped, "[I]f, after the inauguration, you find a Cy Vance as secretary of state and Zbigniew Brzezinski as head of National Security, then I would say we failed. And I'd quit."[43] Jordan did not quit, but his statement was most prophetic. The opposing views of Brzezinski and Vance with regard to confronting the Soviet threat would permeate their views of U.S. foreign policy, not only vis-à-vis Moscow, but elsewhere in the world.

As Jordan put it, Carter's intention was that "Zbig would be the thinker, Cy would be the doer, and Jimmy Carter would be the decider." Increasingly, though, Zbig gained the upper hand, becoming both the thinker and the doer. There were several reasons for this. One was the location and size of the National Security Council. Housed in the White House itself, the NSC had easier access to the Oval Office than did members of the State Department staff, and its small size allowed for better coordination than State, which had thousands of employees. Moreover, Vance was oftentimes out of the country on diplomatic missions, making it harder for him than Brzezinski to speak face-to-face with the president on matters of concern.[44]

Further helping Brzezinski was how the president and he envisioned the NSC's role in policy making. To the State Department, Brzezinski's job was solely to "coordinate" the views of Carter's foreign policy staff. But the spokes-in-the-wheel managerial system established by Carter assumed that Brzezinski would have the same access to the Oval Office as Vance. Accordingly, Vance would not be "the top," but "a top" foreign policy adviser. That the head of the NSC had received from Carter the same status as a cabinet secretary further attested to the president's determination to give Vance and Brzezinski equal status.[45]

Brzezinski shared this desire to act as a major player in policy making. He saw himself as being as much a foreign policy "advocate" as a "coordinator." He had little faith in the State Department, contending that "large bureaucracies do not produce strategies—they produce shopping lists." To help create those strategies, Brzezinski, with Carter's approval, established two committees within the administration. The first, the Special Coordination Committee (SCC), chaired by Vance, focused on matters of intelligence policy, arms control, and crisis management. The second, the Policy Review Committee (PRC), which Brzezinski headed, oversaw foreign policy, defense, and international economic issues. What perturbed Vance was that if the SCC or PRC proved unable to reach a conclusion, Brzezinski would put together the report for Carter summarizing what had occurred at the meeting; if the committee in question was able to reach a decision, the NSC adviser would present to the president a presidential directive (PD) for Carter to sign. "In neither case," Vance later wrote, "were the summaries or PDs to be circulated to the SCC or PRC participants for review before they went to the president." Consequently, Brzezinski "had the power to interpret the thrust of discussion or frame the policy recommendations of department principals." Vance raised his concerns with Carter, but the president, fearful of leaks that might result from circulating sensitive materials to PRC or SCC members for review, favored Brzezinski's approach.[46]

A third reason for the NSC adviser's preeminent role was his relationship with the president. Despite their similar personal interests and even commonalities in policy, Vance and Carter never developed more than an acquaintanceship. In fact, during the 1976 campaign, Vance had supported the candidacy of Sargent Shriver, the former ambassador to France, who made a short bid for the presidency. It was through some of Carter's advisers, among them Anthony Lake and Richard Holbrooke, that the former deputy secretary came to the governor's attention.[47]

Brzezinski had known Carter longer and had developed a closer relationship with him than had Vance. Upon his appointment as head of the Trilateral Commission, Brzezinski decided he wanted a governor from each party represented on it. One of those recommended to him was Carter. Carter impressed Brzezinski, who decided that the governor had a good shot at becoming president. From that point, the Trilateral Commission director supported Carter's campaign, acting as the governor's main foreign policy adviser. While other members of the Trilateral Commission served in the administration, "none threw their support to Carter so early or provided advice as extensively as Brzezinski."[48]

The president came to like Brzezinski. He found a lack of "innovative ideas" from the State Department and commented that Vance saw himself more "as a secretary of state than he did an aide or assistant to the President." Brzezinski, however, "was interesting" and "always thinking. . . . Next to members of my family, Zbig would be my favorite seatmate on a long-distance trip; we might argue, but I would never be bored."[49]

Harold Brown

A final reason for the NSC adviser's predominance over Vance was that the former could usually rely upon two other key individuals for support. One was Defense Secretary Harold Brown. Carter, who was fiscally conservative, had wanted someone who could increase the cost-effectiveness of the military. The president found in Brown, who was a trained scientist —and also a member of the Trilateral Commission—the knowledge necessary to bring about the changes he sought.

Slender, with a rectangular head and brownish hair that he parted off to the right, Brown was very much unlike the gregarious Brzezinski. Brilliant, serious, impatient, and in some respects a loner, he "spoke and wrote clearly, succinctly, and colorlessly," which reflected his personality. Israeli Defense Minister Ezer Weizman remembered his American counterpart being "almost incapable of small talk."[50]

Three years younger than Carter, Brown received his bachelor's and master's degrees and doctorate from Columbia. In 1950, a year after getting his Ph.D., he became a research scientist at the University of California's E. O. Lawrence Laboratory. Brown then worked for the Lawrence Livermore Radiation Laboratory after its establishment in 1952. During the next decade, he served on the Air Force Scientific Advisory Board and the President's Scientific Advisory Committee, and between 1958 and 1959 was Senior Scientific Advisor to the U.S. Delegation to the Conference on Discontinuance of Nuclear Weapons Tests. Brown's expertise convinced President Kennedy's defense secretary, Robert McNamara, to appoint him as the Defense Department's director of defense research and engineering. Brown's work on such issues as the modernization of weaponry and the coordination of weapons systems among the military branches so impressed McNamara and President Johnson that Johnson appointed Brown as secretary of the air force in 1965. In 1969, Brown left Washington and accepted the presidency of the California Institute of Technology, where he remained until Carter offered him the defense secretaryship.

As defense secretary, Brown maintained his preoccupation with military efficiency and cost-effectiveness. He also had an interest in arms control, having served as a member of the U.S. delegation that hammered out the 1972 SALT agreement with the Soviet Union. Even so, like Brzezinski, Brown held that the United States had to avoid any semblance of military inferiority toward Moscow. He thus called for maintaining the U.S. nuclear triad of ICBMs, SLBMs, and strategic bombers. Though he opposed expensive new weapons systems that did not appear cost-effective, he advocated upgrading America's B-52 bomber fleet and called for developing stealth weaponry—which could make an aircraft or ship invisible to radar—and the "Missile Experimental," or MX missile system, which, to protect it from a Soviet strike, would be moved periodically from one location to another via truck or train. In addition, Brown increasingly came to support Brzezinski's confrontationist approach in dealing with the Soviet Union. For instance, by the middle of 1978, Brown had endorsed Brzezinski's desire for closer defense ties with China, which Vance charged would undermine his efforts to reach a SALT II agreement. "Without Brown," the NSC adviser later wrote, "I would have been much more isolated on the critical issues during the more difficult phases of the Carter Presidency."[51]

Rosalynn Carter

The other person to whom Brzezinski could turn was the first lady, Rosalynn Carter. Four years younger than her husband, Eleanor Rosalynn Smith was shy but driven during her childhood. Her father passed away from leukemia when she was thirteen, which cast her into the role of taking care of her three younger siblings while her mother worked to help make ends meet. When she was old enough, she took up a job as a beautician to bring additional money to the family. She graduated as her high school's valedictorian, spent two years at Georgia Southwestern College, and then planned to attend Georgia State College for Women (GSCW), with the intention of becoming an interior designer.

Instead of going to GSCW, Rosalynn wed Jimmy Carter in 1946. There were close ties between the Smith and Carter families: Jimmy's mother, Lillian, had cared for Rosalynn's father in his last months, and, as mentioned earlier, his sister Ruth was Rosalynn's best friend. The future Mrs. Carter had developed a crush on her husband-to-be after seeing a photograph of him. With Ruth's help, the two began a whirlwind romance.

The Carters' marriage marked the beginning of what would become a full-fledged partnership between them. As the wife of a Navy officer, Rosalynn often found herself home alone, taking care of the bills and, by 1952, their three sons. After the Carters moved back to Plains, Rosalynn helped Jimmy run the family business. She took part in all of his campaigns, including his 1976 run for the presidency. Her work required her to go out on the stump, which obligated her to overcome her shyness. As time went on, she grew into an increasingly confident and impressive speaker.

A slender, attractive woman of five feet, five inches, with a soft southern accent, the first lady gave the impression of being charming and subdued. In fact, she was a tough, determined individual whom one reporter called "a Sherman tank in a field of clover," but who more commonly was referred to by the media as the "steel magnolia." Set on being more than White House hostess, Mrs. Carter became the most active first lady since Eleanor Roosevelt, and in some areas went even further. To get a better idea of what was happening in the administration, she attended cabinet meetings, sat in on many of the daily foreign policy briefings Brzezinski gave the president, and held a weekly lunch with her husband, during which they discussed a wide range of issues, including policy. The president used her as his personal representative on a number of missions abroad, including to Latin America and Southeast Asia. Carter later wrote that "aside from a few highly secret and sensitive security matters, she knew all that was going on." Although Mrs. Carter stated that she did not try to sway her husband's decision making on issues about which she had little knowledge—such as top-secret arms discussions—she did more than once note that she had influence in the administration, that the president oftentimes used her as a sounding board, and that she was willing to give him advice. Members of the administration observed that she could be key in getting the president's ear. One former White House official remarked, "She has more impact on policy than any other President's wife in this generation." Commented Jordan, "Whenever I think the President is pursuing an unwise course of action and I strike out with him, I try to get her on my side."[52]

Contemporaries reported that the first lady and Brzezinski were good friends who oftentimes saw eye-to-eye on issues, and more often than not, she shared his more hard-nosed diplomatic philosophy. The NSC adviser believed that his relationship with Mrs. Carter was critical to the influence he had within the administration. "A very important factor . . . was Rosalynn's attitude towards me," he said after leaving office. "She liked me, and in fact she told me when we were leaving the White House that I was her special person. That was not unimportant with him [the president]." As a result, continued Brzezinski, if he ended up in a fight with the State Department, "I felt pretty confident that I would win." Indeed, "[i]t was no secret Zbig was one of Rosalynn's favorites."[53] While there was no guarantee the president would follow the advice given him by his wife and Brzezinski, they could be assured that it would receive his attention.

Walter Mondale

At times, Brzezinski could also turn to Vice President Walter Mondale for support. Slightly taller than Carter, with a high forehead, brown hair—which was showing some signs of turning silver, and which he "slicked back in a pompadour"[54]—and a cordial personality, Mondale had grown up in Minnesota. His political activism began during his freshman year at Macalester College, when he volunteered to work on Hubert Humphrey's successful campaign for mayor of Minneapolis. Two years later, Mondale helped oversee Humphrey's triumphant bid for a seat on the U.S. Senate. After graduating from Macalester—which was delayed by a decision he made to move to Washington, D.C., and work for the liberal organization Students for Democratic Action—he attended the University of Minnesota, receiving his law degree in 1956.

Mondale continued his political activism after law school. In both 1958 and 1960, he managed Orville Freeman's successful campaigns for Minnesota governor. After his second victory, Freeman appointed Mondale state attorney general. In 1964, Mondale left Minneapolis for Washington, D.C., after the new governor, Karl Rolvaag, assigned him Humphrey's senate seat, which Humphrey had vacated to take up his new job as President Johnson's vice president. Senator Mondale developed a reputation for supporting a liberal agenda. He backed the 1965 Voting Rights Act, helped guide through the Senate a bill supporting open housing, and advocated consumer protection. Because of his loyalty to Humphrey, he refused to criticize the Vietnam War until after Humphrey received the Democratic nomination for president in August 1968.

Carter chose Mondale as his running mate for several reasons. Being from Minnesota, the senator could draw the Georgia governor votes from the Midwest. Mondale's liberal record would balance Carter's more conservative orientation and bring the campaign support from the left wing of the party. Additionally, the governor understood the benefit of having a running mate with years of experience within the Beltway. Finally, Mondale insisted that, as vice president, he play more than just a symbolic role; that desire matched Carter's own interest in having an activist and involved vice president.

Mondale would indeed play a significant role within the administration. He, along with Brzezinski and Vance, regularly attended the president's Friday morning foreign-policy breakfast. The breakfasts, which sometimes included Brown, Jordan, and Press Secretary Jody Powell, were begun by Carter in June 1977 to allow for deeper discussion of diplomatic matters. Mondale also traveled as Carter's representative to discuss substantive matters with foreign officials, played a key role in getting the Panama Canal treaties passed, partook in the Camp David negotiations on Middle East peace, and oversaw the administration's African policy. Although he disagreed with Carter on some matters—for instance, he thought that the president's foreign policy agenda attempted to do too much too quickly—he kept those disagreements private. Because of his extensive experience in Washington, much of the advice he gave the president focused on the domestic political impact of the administration's initiatives.[55]

Unlike Brzezinski and Vance, Mondale had a pragmatic foreign affairs philosophy. At times, he supported Vance. For example, he shared Vance's judgment that Brzezinski exaggerated Soviet influence in Africa. Yet, like the NSC adviser, Mondale believed that it was important to normalize relations with communist China.[56] With Brown and Mrs. Carter on his side, and with Mondale sometimes joining them, Brzezinski stood a good chance of influencing the direction of the Carter administration's diplomacy.

★   Jimmy Carter came to Washington at a time of transition. Concerns over the direction of U.S. foreign policy, the Watergate scandal, and a resurgent Congress threatened to place limits on what a chief executive might be able to accomplish. But none of this meant that Carter's foreign policy was doomed to fail. He had a Congress dominated by his own party. If prepared to play the game of give-and-take, he might get much of what he wanted adopted. Maybe most important, he had the components of a vision that foresaw the United States' mission as one of promoting a secure and peaceful world where the rights of all people were upheld. If properly sold to the American people and Congress, this vision stood a fighting chance of receiving their enthusiastic endorsement.

Carter brought traits with him, however, that severely complicated his diplomatic efforts. His failure to understand the complexity of the numerous issues he sought to address or to consult with lawmakers, his belief that it was possible to separate and solve each problem on its own, his view of himself as a trustee who knew what was best for America, and his error in not providing the country his vision for its mission repeatedly bred confusion and anger, and required the White House to expend enormous amounts of political capital to achieve its goals. His managerial style of leadership and internecine battles between the State Department and NSC only made matters worse. It was not the formula for a successful foreign policy.

The HUMAN RIGHTS,

ARMS CONTROL, *and* NON-

PROLIFERATION CONUNDRUMS

★   Both of them had urged him not to overstretch himself. It was vital, explained Vice President Walter Mondale, that the new president,
Jimmy Carter, avoid trying to do too much at once. Even Carter's wife,
Rosalynn, attempted to make him understand that there were limits to
what her husband could accomplish. The new chief executive ignored
them both. "[I]t was better to get 95 percent of something," Mrs. Carter remembered her husband telling her, "than it was to get just an awful 5 percent of what you really wanted."[1]

     Carter should have listened. Trying to achieve too much in a short
amount of time risked getting far less than the 95 percent he sought. Most
any initiative he undertook required working closely with Congress,
which for Carter proved a problem throughout his presidency. Given his
training as an engineer, the president believed he could resolve each issue
he confronted individually; he too often failed to realize the complexities
involved in finding a solution for each one, and there were times when
one initiative conflicted with another. Trying to achieve a lot at once,
moreover, limited the amount of time he and his subordinates could devote to each topic. Added to all of this was his spokes-in-the-wheel approach to management and decision making, which created battles within
the bureaucracy to influence administration policy. Consequently, on the
three foreign policy initiatives to which he devoted most of his attention
in his inaugural address—human rights, arms control, and nuclear nonproliferation—the White House found itself caught off guard, sending
contradictory and confused messages to friends and foes alike, as well as
angering both lawmakers and foreign allies.

Human Rights—Turf Wars

Politically and personally, human rights resonated with Jimmy Carter. Promoting respect for individual rights would not only bring him political points at home, but it meshed with his own religious values. Thus, during his inaugural address, he declared that the United States' "commitment to human rights must be absolute," thereby suggesting that any nation, friend or foe, would face punishment if it failed to uphold the rights of its citizens.[2]

The president clearly had suggested a preparedness to move U.S. foreign policy in a direction it had not previously traveled. Washington historically had avoided making human rights a centerpiece of its diplomacy. It was true that American officials had berated communist countries such as the Soviet Union for the treatment of their citizens, but that had not been done as part of any formal human rights initiative.

Pressure from Congress in the 1970s forced the White House's hand—to some extent. For instance, during a June 1976 meeting of the Organization of American States (OAS), Secretary of State Henry Kissinger attacked those governments in the Western Hemisphere that violated the rights of their citizens. Yet in general, Kissinger and President Gerald Ford were careful in how they applied human rights. Strongly believing in realpolitik, and fearful that publicly denouncing countries such as the Soviet Union and China for human rights violations might upset his efforts at developing and maintaining cordial relations with them, Kissinger more often than not leveled his criticisms at them privately. The Ford administration also approached anticommunist friends cautiously. As one example, after Kissinger gave his speech before the OAS, the White House, fearful it might have upset Chilean President Augusto Pinochet Ugarte, approved $9 million in new military funding for Santiago, despite Pinochet's repressive regime. Aid continued as well to Nicaragua, El Salvador, South Korea, and the Philippines. When Congress in 1976 tried to make the administration give more attention to human rights by establishing within the State Department a Bureau of Human Rights and Humanitarian Affairs (HA), Ford and Kissinger responded by largely disregarding the new agency.[3]

Carter had implied that he would not show the kind of leniency Ford and Kissinger had, but that was easier said than done. In addition to an "absolute" human rights initiative, Carter—though it was not mentioned in his inaugural statement—made clear he supported noninterference in the affairs of other countries. Yet for the United States to demand that other nations adhere to certain standards contradicted that policy of noninterference. As Anthony Lake, Carter's head of the Policy Planning Staff, explained, "Unhappily, in a complicated world and for any but the most simple of political philosophies, principles themselves—when put into

practice—may collide as often as they coincide. So it was with the principles of respect for the sovereignty of other nations and support for
human rights."[4]

Carter, simply put, had failed to understand the impossibility of separating human rights from other issues. And his style of leadership further
complicated matters. Viewing himself as a manager, he announced initiatives and then left it up to his cabinet officers and their subordinates to
carry them out. The problem, Secretary of State Cyrus Vance complained
years later, was the lack of direction allowed each cabinet officer to create
his or her own "empire" and combat with one another for influence
rather than cooperate and "advance the best interests of the country and
those of the President."[5] Such became clear in the case of human rights.

Determined to give new life to HA, Carter named as its head Patricia
Derian, a 1960s civil rights advocate and the deputy manager of his 1976
campaign. Not only was Derian an outspoken champion of human rights,
but her appointment helped fulfill a promise Carter had made during the
campaign to name women to high government posts. In April, with the
president's support, the National Security Council (NSC) ordered the establishment of the Interagency Group on Human Rights and Foreign Assistance, with Undersecretary of State Warren Christopher appointed as its
head. The "Christopher Group," as it became known, included representatives from all major government departments as well as the NSC, the Export-
Import Bank (Eximbank), and HA. Its purpose was to apply human rights
considerations to all foreign economic and military aid requests. In short,
HA received a voice on all matters of foreign aid. Then, in August 1977,
with the approval of Christopher and members of Congress, Derian's title
was elevated from "coordinator" to assistant secretary for human rights. It
seemed, therefore, that HA would have significant influence in the making
of U.S. foreign policy.[6]

But the reverse proved the case. Within the State Department, HA
waged war with its geographic counterparts. The officers of the geographic
bureaus believed that it was their duty to maintain cordial relations with
the nations they represented; to introduce questions of human rights
could upset those ties. Furthermore, the geographic bureaus, which were
manned by career officers, viewed the political appointees of HA as dangerous outsiders. Of the geographic bureaus, HA found itself most often in
battle with those of East Asian and Pacific Affairs, headed by Richard Holbrooke, and Inter-American Affairs, led by Terence Todman.[7]

But there was also opposition from outside State. The Defense, Agriculture, and Treasury Departments all resisted HA to varying degrees. In the
Defense Department, for instance, Undersecretary of State for Security Assistance Lucy Benson was the strongest opponent of both HA and the
Christopher Group and threatened to resign if she did not get what she

wanted. Realizing that her resignation would reflect poorly on the president's promise to appoint women to high office, Vance and Christopher allowed her to remove both military assistance and Security Supporting Assistance from the Christopher Group's purview. The former consisted of grants and credits to provide training and weapons to other nations; the latter provided money so other countries could beef up their militaries. Agriculture succeeded in exempting Title I of the Food for Peace program; it had to document that any aid going to repressive nations would be delivered to the needy, but that was generally easy. Commodity Credit Corporation export credits were also largely waived from the Group's coverage. The Treasury Department successfully kept the International Monetary Fund from the Christopher Group's purview. By 1978, human rights law covered the Eximbank and the Overseas Private Investment Corporation, but both succeeded in avoiding "systematic review by the Christopher Group for integration into human rights policy." Finally, HA agreed that the Group should exempt the Agency for International Development's Development Assistance program and assistance from the International Fund for Agricultural Development, as aid from those programs went to impoverished persons.[8]

What all of this meant was that the Group by the middle of 1978 found its purview limited primarily to assistance from the multilateral development banks (MBDs): the Asian Development Bank, the Inter-American Development Bank, the African Development Bank, and the World Bank. Even then, the administration did not effectively use its vote on the MBDs. Caleb Rossiter, who worked for the Arms Control and Foreign Policy Caucus, pointed out that representatives to the MDBs "cast negative votes as instructed, but it was little more than a pro forma exercise. No serious efforts were made to build the voting coalitions with other member nations that were necessary to ensure the defeat of loans to human rights violators."[9]

HA had few places to turn to make its voice heard. The human rights bureau did have a seat on Benson's Security Assistance Program Review Working Group and on that organization's parent, the Arms Export Control Board. However, commented Lincoln Bloomfield, a member of the NSC who worked on global issues, "[i]f the case was bumped up to higher levels, PM [the State Department's Bureau of Political-Military Affairs] or the regional bureaus (who usually advocated positive action) invariably won out and the sale would be approved."[10]

Turning to Congress did not guarantee success. Republicans tended to disapprove of actions that threatened U.S. relations with right-wing, anti-communist governments. Democrats could not agree whether the human rights policy was too tough or not tough enough. New internationalists, including Senators Edward Kennedy of Massachusetts and James Abourezk of South Dakota, and Representatives Donald Fraser of Minnesota and

Tom Harkin of Iowa, fell into the latter category; neoconservative-leaning Representatives William Moorhead of Pennsylvania, Joseph Minish of New Jersey, and Pennsylvania's Gus Yatron, as well as Senator Henry Jackson of Washington, fell into the former, charging the administration with unfairly targeting right-wing friends.[11]

Nor did HA and its supporters have the guarantee of a sympathetic ear from the White House. Carter, Vance, and National Security Adviser Zbigniew Brzezinski had other foreign—and, in the case of the president, domestic —matters about which to worry, a main reason why Christopher and not Vance or Brzezinski received the headship of the Interagency Group. More important, the president quickly realized that demanding other nations adhere to an "absolute" standard risked endangering relations with important allies. It was for that reason that by the end of February 1977, Vance had announced a more pragmatic human rights initiative that took into account U.S. strategic or geopolitical concerns before determining whether and what types of punishments would be exacted. The secretary's statement confused observers as to how extensive the administration's commitment to human rights was.[12] It also undoubtedly emboldened those within the administration who wanted to push human rights concerns to the side.

Human Rights in (In)action—The Philippines

The Philippines provided an excellent example where geopolitics usurped human rights. Regarding the Philippines as essential to the protection of American strategic interests in the Western Pacific, Washington and Manila in 1947 had signed an agreement by which the former received the right to use nearly two dozen Philippine air and naval facilities for 99 years. By the 1970s, however, President Ferdinand Marcos, who had been elected in 1965, demanded a revision of that arrangement. He contended that whereas other countries where the United States had bases retained sovereignty over the land used by Washington, the Philippines did not. In turn, he continued, it was difficult for him to promote the self-reliance of the Philippine military, which he asserted would buttress America's regional defense capabilities. Additionally, he wanted to make his nation a leader in the Third World, and one way of doing that was to challenge an example of American imperialism.[13]

It sounded like Marcos wanted the U.S. military presence out of the Philippines. But that was all bluster. In actuality, the main reason he wanted a new base agreement was that it could bring him money, and money meant power. In 1972, charging the existence of a communist conspiracy to overthrow him, Marcos imposed martial law. While there was a Marxist-inspired insurrection at that time, it was not nearly as extensive as the Philippine president portrayed it. He used his emergency powers to imprison not just revolutionaries but democratic-minded opponents. Meanwhile, he took money from the Philippine treasury and a variety of businesses (including casinos) owned by him and his wife, Imelda, to pay off friends, family, and the military leadership. One estimate was that Marcos, whose annual salary was supposed to be under $6,000 a year, was worth at least $1 billion by the mid-1970s. During a visit to New York, Mrs. Marcos, who loved to shop—she had an enormous collection of shoes—spent over $2 million in just one day. As it was, the bases brought $200 million each year into the Philippine treasury. A revised base deal could mean an even larger influx of dollars, thereby allowing the Marcoses both to stay in power and to continue their opulent lifestyle. The Philippine president thus asked for "some form of compensation for use of the bases, such as rent or a guaranteed level of military assistance."[14]

Marcos had every reason to believe that the White House would accommodate him. Among the bases Washington maintained in the Philippines were Clark Air Force Base—the fourth largest such facility outside the United States and the home of the 13th Air Force—and Subic Naval Bay, home of the U.S. 7th Fleet. That military might allowed the United States to make its presence felt in the western Pacific and Southeast Asia and reassured America's friends that the White House would not abandon them.[15] To draw down U.S. forces or close the bases on the heels of the recent American withdrawal from Vietnam could raise questions about Washington's trustworthiness and credibility.

It was with these considerations in mind that Kissinger opened discussions with the Marcos government on a new base agreement. But the talks had stalled by the time of the 1976 election. The Defense Department asserted that what Marcos essentially wanted was for the United States to pay "rent" to use Filipino land; the United States, declared Defense, did not pay "rent" to any country, as America's bases were there for the mutual benefit of both the United States and the host nation. (In actuality, providing military aid to another nation that has American bases amounts to rent, but the term is not used.) Kissinger proposed $1 billion in compensation—in essence, rent—for use of the bases for the next five years, but Marcos said it was not enough. Rather, he insisted on $1 billion in just military aid and millions more in economic assistance.[16]

The Carter administration first took a look at the base issue in April 1977 but decided to wait until Marcos showed a willingness to renew the discussions on a new agreement. That signal came in August when the Philippine leader called for their resumption. The White House had presumed that it could reach an accommodation with Manila, for Marcos had offered some concessions. He no longer insisted on Philippine sovereignty. He also dropped the demand for "rent," stating now that financial compensation for use of the bases would make his military more self-sufficient.[17]

As the White House prepared a package to offer, in January 1978 Derian arrived in the Philippines. She infuriated Marcos when she blasted him and Defense Minister Juan Ponce Enrile for human rights abuses. She then met Benigno Aquino, a leading opponent of the government whom the Filipino leader had jailed. Before departing, she urged the White House to curb its "commitment to Marcos on human rights/needs basis, at least until martial law is relaxed or preferably lifted."[18]

Despite his anger, Marcos understood the bases gave him leverage, and he realized he could gain even more if he appeared less repressive. He therefore announced the holding of legislative elections in April, the first to take place in the Philippines since the imposition of martial law. He refused, though, to release Aquino, despite requests by Vance and other U.S. officials to do so.[19]

Holbrooke feared the impact Derian's trip could have upon the base talks. Shortly after her departure, the White House offered Marcos $400 million for use of the bases until 1985. He rejected it. Rather, he wanted a proposal similar to that made by Kissinger; to even give the semblance that he would consider this new offer, he said, could cost him votes in the April election. Desirous to rebuild the trust between the United States and the Philippines he felt Derian had damaged, if not to bring the base negotiations to a successful conclusion, Holbrooke urged that Mondale travel to the Philippines. Brzezinski agreed, and both Vance and Christopher seconded the NSC adviser.[20]

In the April election, Marcos, through the use of fraud, guaranteed his New Society Party a sweeping victory. When angry protesters took to the streets, government forces arrested over 500 of them. Members of U.S. Congress and American reporters criticized Marcos's crackdown. One *New York Times* journalist "observed tally clerks not even bothering to count the ballots before recording all votes for the Government candidates; once discovered he was shoved down a flight of stairs." Commented the *Washington Post,* "Not since Muhammad Ali took on Joe Fraser has there been a 'thrillah in Manila' to match the elections that the Philippines' strongman president Ferdinand Marcos ran the other day." It was clear that Marcos did not want to "give his opposition a fair crack at power." Yet he also wanted "to sweeten up the Carter administration and, specifically, to put Congress in the mood to pay the Philippines heavy compensation for the military bases. . . . His purpose was, in brief, to run a phony election that looked good."[21]

The White House had no intention of allowing such criticism of the Philippine leader's human rights violations to derail the talks. "The base negotiations will provide the principal focus for my discussions with Marcos," Mondale wrote Carter prior to his departure, and he indicated his hope that he could get Marcos to compromise on that subject.[22] He said nothing about pressing the Philippine president to stop his repression.

Mondale did indeed smooth things over. Although he visited with opposition leaders, it became clear what his real purpose was. Mondale "sure tricked me," commented Diosdado Macapagal, Marcos's predecessor. "He misled us because he made us believe he was here in order to help the opposition in promoting democracy." Instead, Mondale "came here to assure President Marcos of the support of the Carter administration." With Carter's approval, the vice president offered to increase the base compensation package to $450 million, the maximum bid the administration was willing to make. He also signed several agreements that provided the Marcos regime with over $40 million in additional aid. Afterward, the Philippine president wrote Carter, praising the Mondale visit, justifying his decision to impose martial law, and calling the recent election a first step "to full popular participation in government." Rather than insist upon further progress on human rights, Carter in his reply simply expressed appreciation of Marcos's "frankness" and his "hope that, under your leadership, events will give us the opportunity to turn the corner of this difficult issue."[23]

The Inconsistency of Policy

Yet it was not just the Philippines where the administration downgraded human rights. It took a cautious approach as well toward Iran, South Korea, communist China, Cambodia, South Africa, Zaire, Egypt, North Yemen, Israel, Saudi Arabia, and Indonesia. Indeed, in January 1978, the White House was forced to admit to itself just how restricted its human rights policy had become. Looking at the application of human rights criteria to aid from the MDBs, Lake noted that the targets of cuts in assistance were more often than not in Latin America. There were a number of reasons for this, "some better than others," he explained, including U.S. leverage in the hemisphere, the smaller "security and economic stake" Washington had in the region as compared to "East Asia or the Middle East," and the fact that the countries of Central and South America were "ideologically disinclined to turn to Moscow."[24]

When it did punish human rights–violating nations, the White House did not always rely on cuts in assistance. It used, in addition to or instead of reductions in aid, symbolic gestures and private and public statements. One illustration was a trip Rosalynn Carter took to seven Latin American nations in May 1977. The purpose of her junket was to act as her husband's emissary to discuss substantive issues with foreign officials; it was the first time a first lady had ever assumed such a role. While most of her discussions focused on economic and military concerns, she did quietly raise the issue of human rights with the Peruvian leadership and, in Brazil, publicly agreed to take to her husband a letter written by university students complaining about repression in that country. As a symbol of concern, the

White House purposely did not have her make stops in the Southern Cone nations of Argentina, Chile, and Uruguay, because, while like Brazil they had repressive governments, the administration concluded that they, unlike Brasilia, had shown no willingness to restore democracy.[25]

The White House also cut aid to the Southern Cone countries. The Carter administration dramatically reduced new military aid to Argentina and economic assistance to Chile and Uruguay and completely cut off further military assistance to Santiago and Montevideo. Nicaragua and El Salvador saw decreases in aid as well. U.S. military assistance to Latin America fell from $233.5 million in 1976 to $54 million in 1979, a decrease of over 75 percent.[26] The focus on Latin America eventually became too much for Todman. In 1978, he publicly criticized the application of the human rights policy in the hemisphere; the White House subsequently reassigned him as ambassador to Spain.

Yet even in Latin America, there was only so much Carter could or would do. The White House could not stop other nations from providing aid to countries to which the United States refused to provide economic or military aid. Western Europe and Israel, seeing an opportunity to fill the gap left by U.S. cuts in assistance, sold Argentina over $1 billion in military aid each year.[27] Unwilling to anger allies who could use the money to purchase goods from the United States, the president made no serious attempt to stop such activity.

And Carter himself was prepared to make exceptions to his own policy of cutting off economic or military aid to hemispheric violators of human rights. For instance, in 1977 the administration overcame an effort by Senator Kennedy that would have eliminated all economic and military aid to Argentina, including aid in the "pipeline"—referring to goods already purchased but not delivered. Carter opposed the Kennedy bill, contending that it would prevent him from offering inducements to Buenos Aires to improve its behavior. With the help of Senator Hubert Humphrey (D-Minnesota), Congress passed legislation that freed up the pipeline assistance.[28]

Despite the more flexible legislation, Brzezinski was uneasy. He warned the president in March 1977 that the White House could find itself "having bad relations simultaneously with Brazil, Chile, and Argentina" because of its human rights initiative. Indeed, while speculative, this concern might explain why he advocated the establishment of the Christopher Group. On the one hand, having HA as a member of the Group pleased supporters of an active human rights policy. On the other, by giving a voice to the NSC, Defense, and other departments and bureaus that were less supportive of a tough policy, it might be possible to check the influence of HA and its allies. As Brzezinski himself noted, human rights was important, but "I put stronger emphasis . . . on the notion that strengthening American power was the necessary point of departure."[29]

The Soviet Union—Human Rights v. Arms Control

While reluctant to apply too much pressure on Latin America, Brzezinski was more than prepared to turn up the heat on Moscow. "I saw in human rights an opportunity to put the Soviet Union ideologically on the defensive," he later wrote. Both the president and Press Secretary Jody Powell agreed that the Kremlin should not be immune from criticism. Carter assumed that the Soviets would not link human rights to other aspects of U.S.–Soviet relations. Powell judged that Congress would look favorably upon criticism of the Soviet Union for its human rights abuses, making it easier to get lawmakers to support measures affecting East-West ties, such as arms control.[30] Thus, a week after the inauguration, the State Department criticized Czechoslovakia for its treatment of pro-democracy intellectuals. It then warned Moscow not to mistreat Soviet dissident Andrei Sakharov. The president followed by sending a personal letter to Sakharov, promising to support human rights around the globe.

When Malcolm Toon, the U.S. ambassador in Moscow until 1979, resigned in protest because the Carter White House largely ignored him, he observed, "The administration claim[s] that it want[s] a good relationship with the [Leonid] Brezhnev administration, but this [is] precisely the wrong way to go about it."[31] Certainly the Carter human rights initiative had a far different outcome than anticipated. An infuriated Soviet leadership charged the administration with breaking a fundamental, unwritten rule in superpower relations, which was not to comment publicly on the other's internal policies. The Kremlin retaliated by escalating its oppression, arresting dissidents such as Yuri Orlov and Alexander Ginsburg.

The USSR's unwillingness to respect the human rights of its citizens raised hackles among conservatives at home. Cognizant of Carter's interest in détente, the Committee on the Present Danger and neoconservatives asked how he reasonably presumed he could establish a working rapport with a repressive regime that he himself had denounced.[32] Such questions threatened to jeopardize another Carter initiative, that of signing a major arms control agreement with the Soviet Union. Moreover, Moscow's response to his human rights initiative forced the president to rethink to what extent he should press Moscow on human rights.

A year after the signing of the Strategic Arms Limitations Treaty (SALT) in 1972, U.S. officials learned that the Soviets had begun to test a new intercontinental ballistic missile (ICBM), the SS-9, with a payload far larger than anything the United States had. This new "heavy" missile, as it became known, greatly concerned Washington. During the Cold War, the United States relied upon the so-called triad of nuclear weapons for its protection: ground-launched ICBMs, submarine-launched ballistic missiles (SLBMs), and long-range strategic bombers. By 1970, Washington had developed a new type of ICBM called the Minuteman, which was more accurate than its predecessors. The trouble with the SS-9 was not only the size of its payload or the fact that some of them were MIRVed—had multiple independently targeted reentry vehicles, or more than one warhead per missile, each of which could hit a different target—but that it appeared Moscow intended to use it as a first-strike weapon designed to destroy America's Minuteman force and, hence, one-third of the triad. While it was highly unlikely that the Soviets would risk nuclear war, Washington could not ignore the Minuteman's potential vulnerability.[33]

To address both the subjects of protecting the Minuteman and SALT's failure to restrict certain types of weapons, and because the SALT I agreement on ICBMs and SLBMs was only temporary, talks began on a SALT II pact almost immediately after the ink had dried on SALT I. In 1974, President Ford and Soviet General Secretary Brezhnev reached an agreement at the Soviet city of Vladivostok by which they intended to place a limit, or "ceiling," of 2,400 launchers, or delivery vehicles—which referred to underground missile silos, missile-firing tubes on submarines, and heavy bombers—for each superpower and a "sub-ceiling" of 1,320 per nation for all MIRVed missiles. (In other words, of the 2,400 launchers, no more than 1,320 of them could carry MIRVed missiles.) The problem was that the two superpowers could not agree on all the weapons to include within the 2,400 limit. One was the Soviets' Tupolev Tu-26 "Backfire" bomber. U.S. officials claimed that the Backfire, first developed in 1969, had the capability of being a long-range, strategic bomber and should be included in the 2,400 ceiling; Moscow denied that the Tu-26 had a strategic potential or that it intended to give the aircraft such an ability and refused to include it. Meanwhile, the Kremlin contended that because it could travel over 600 kilometers, the cruise missile should be incorporated into the launcher ceiling. The White House rejected that argument. The cruise missile, which the United States had only recently begun to develop, would fly low over the ground to avoid radar detection rather than into the atmosphere like a ballistic missile. The ceiling on launchers, said Washington, referred only to ballistic missiles, and, therefore, the cruise missile was exempt.[34] Unable to reach an agreement on these topics, both sides continued their arms buildup. By the time Carter became president, the United States had 8,500 warheads and the Soviets about 4,000; Moscow, though, had more delivery vehicles: 2,440 to 2,059.

Seeing the arms race as a threat to world peace, President Carter pressed ahead with the SALT II talks. There were indications from the beginning that reaching an agreement would not be easy. One was the Senate's response to his nomination of Paul Warnke (another Trilateral Commission member) as chief SALT negotiator. To neoconservatives and the CPD, Warnke was a "dove" who would concede too much to the Kremlin.

While the upper house eventually voted 58–40 in support of his appointment, the fact that this was less than a two-thirds majority hinted at how much opposition SALT might face. Another omen appeared when Carter, shortly after the election, explained to Averell Harriman, the long-time diplomat who became a roving ambassador to the new president, that he had no intention of "be[ing] bound by past negotiations," meaning Vladivostok. Carter's comment made the Soviet ambassador in Washington, Anatoly Dobrynin, uneasy. Moscow's emissary cautioned that throwing out Vladivostok would create "serious complications for future negotiations."[35]

What Carter had in mind was even lower limits for weapons than agreed to at Vladivostok. There was pressure upon the new president to do just that. Within the cabinet, the strongest proponent of what became known as "deep cuts" in the U.S. and Soviet nuclear arsenals was Defense Secretary Harold Brown. Brown worried about the danger posed to America's nuclear deterrent by the expansion and technological improvement of the Soviet atomic arsenal and wanted to see it significantly reduced. In Congress, Senator Jackson led the charge for deep cuts. The White House knew that his reputation as an expert on national defense made the senator's endorsement of any SALT II agreement vital. "Jackson," Vance remarked, "would be a major asset in a future ratification debate if he supported the treaty, and a formidable opponent if he opposed it."[36]

The reason why Dobrynin disliked Carter's intention to reject Vladivostok was that the Soviet leadership liked what Brezhnev and Ford had worked out, as it did not require Moscow to destroy many of its missiles. Deep cuts, however, would force the Kremlin to give up many of its land-based ICBMs, which made up the heart of the Soviets' nuclear arsenal. Thus, the Soviet ambassador from the start made clear that his country would not admit any proposal that deviated from the 1974 accords. Brezhnev confirmed that position in a letter to Carter two weeks after the president's inauguration. Carter ignored them. He explained to the Soviet leader the need for "drastic limitations" in both countries' nuclear arsenals. He also suggested removing both the Backfire bomber and cruise missiles from any SALT discussions, with those two topics to receive attention at a later time. Brezhnev found those recommendations "deliberately unacceptable" and insisted that arms control talks had to take place "on the basis that was agreed upon in Vladivostok." Furthermore, he wrote, the United States had acquiesced to including cruise missiles in the 2,400 limit on delivery vehicles while the Backfire never was a part of any of the talks; hence, he refused to discuss the Soviet bomber as part of an arms agreement.[37]

Brezhnev had exhibited a case of selective memory. The United States viewed its long-range bomber, the B-52, as a pad for air-launched cruise missiles (ALCMs); since the B-52 could carry well over a dozen missiles, it could become a powerful weapon in the case of a superpower war.

Knowing that the Soviets shuddered at a U.S. B-52 fleet armed with cruise missiles, in 1976 Kissinger had proposed, and Foreign Minister Andrei Gromyko had accepted in principle, that the United States would include in the 1,320 MIRV sub-ceiling all bombers carrying ALCMs in return for Soviet acquiescence to place limitations on the Backfire. The Soviet leader had forgotten the second part of that agreement. When Carter reminded Brezhnev that the superpowers had reached no formal arrangement on either the cruise or Backfire, the general secretary insisted that they had. He also spurned discussion of the Tu-26, saying that it had a range of only 2,200 kilometers; he was willing to make that information part of the record of the SALT negotiations, though not part of the treaty, and only if the United States stopped trying to include it in any arms control agreement. He then turned to the cruise missile, calling for the banning of all sea- and land-based cruise missiles with a range greater than 600 kilometers and of ALCMs with a range of over 2,500 kilometers. The Soviet Union, he continued, would accept ALCMs that could travel 600 to 2,500 kilometers, but only if heavy bombers were permitted to carry them, and only if the United States agreed to count those ALCM-carrying bombers in the 1,320 sub-ceiling for MIRVed weapons. He let Carter know that this was the position he would take when Vance arrived in Moscow to discuss arms control.[38]

Despite this warning, the president and his advisers pressed ahead with formulating a comprehensive deep cuts proposal. It would reduce the Vladivostok ceiling from 2,400 to 2,000 launchers and the MIRV sub-ceiling to 1,200. It added a new sub-ceiling that would freeze Soviet MIRVed ICBMs at 550—the same number the United States had—and cut the number of Soviet "heavies" in half, to 150. (Thus, in the 1,320 sub-ceiling for MIRVed weapons, no more than 550 could be ICBMs.) The United States would not count the Backfire as a strategic bomber if the Soviets both promised not to give it a strategic capability and permitted all cruise missiles, not just ALCMs, to have a range up to 2,500 kilometers. The comprehensive proposal also would freeze the "creation and deployment of new types of ICBM" and ban mobile ICBMs. This last measure would require the United States to give up the missile experimental (MX), a mobile weapon then under development.[39]

In light of Moscow's insistence not to deviate from Vladivostok, Vance, seconded by Warnke, had legitimate concerns that Brezhnev might reject the U.S. plan; the secretary of state advised the preparation of a fallback offer. Accordingly, the White House decided that if the Kremlin rejected its comprehensive proposal, it would suggest a pact based on Vladivostok, minus the Backfire and cruise missiles.[40]

Carter should have known that these proposals were unacceptable to the Soviet Union. Neither met the Kremlin's demands regarding the cruise missile, and Moscow had eschewed any arms control plan that included the Backfire. Furthermore, Carter all but sealed the fate of both offers when, prior to Vance's departure, he publicized them and stated that if the Soviets rejected them, "we'll try to modify our stance." In so doing, he gave the Kremlin all the more reason to turn down both proposals in the hopes of getting something better.[41] Hence, when Vance arrived in Moscow and presented both formulas, Brezhnev and Gromkyo rejected them without making any counteroffers.

Even had Carter not publicized the two arms control schemes, it is unlikely that the Soviets would have accepted either of them and not just because they did not meet the Kremlin's demands. For one, Moscow was not pleased with the public criticism of the treatment of its citizens. Carter naively believed he could delink human rights from arms control. He was forced to admit a few months after Vance's return home, "There has been a surprising, adverse reaction to our stand on human rights. . . . That's provided a greater obstacle to other friendly pursuits of common goals, like in SALT, than I had anticipated." Had the president not pressed human rights as he did, Dobrynin wrote years later, "we probably could have finished the SALT talks and signed an agreement by the end of '77, or perhaps by the beginning of '78."[42]

Additionally, it appears that Brezhnev was under pressure from his military. According to Dobrynin, the Soviet leader had faced criticism from the minister of defense and members of the Politburo who accused him of giving up too much at Vladivostok. It behooved Brezhnev, therefore, not to accept additional cuts. The point was, argued the Soviet ambassador, that Carter early in his administration could have gotten signed a SALT agreement based upon the Vladivostok accords had he not been so vocal in his criticism of the Soviets' treatment of its citizens and had he not sought to alter the arrangement reached in 1974.[43]

Of course, there would still have been the issue of getting the Senate to approve an agreement with the 1974 provisions. More extensive consultation with members of the upper house might not have guaranteed ratification, but the president's failure to do so clearly made achieving such a goal all the more remote. Even Carter acknowledged he had erred in his handling of U.S. Soviet policy. "Had I known then what I know now about the Soviet Union," the president said after leaving office, "I would have approached it differently, in a little bit slower fashion and with more preparation before Vance's mission was publicized."[44]

With Vance to meet Gromyko again in two months, the White House reexamined its position. The administration decided to divide SALT into three categories. The first would meet the Soviets' desire to incorporate Vladivostok into any new agreement. The second would cover the most difficult subjects, including cruise missiles and new types of weapons, while the third would focus on goals to which the superpowers should give their attention after SALT II expired. These proposals eventually became, respectively, the SALT II treaty, which would remain in force until 1985, a three-year protocol to SALT, and a set of principles to establish a foundation for SALT III. Specifically, the president decided: to hold firm on reducing the MIRV sub-ceiling to 1,200 but offered to increase the overall ceiling to 2,200 rather than 2,000; to have the Soviets "limit the production and deployment of Backfires"; and to have both sides ban the testing and deployment of mobile ICBMs (like the MX) or the deployment of new ICBM types.[45]

In May, Vance and Gromyko met in Geneva, where U.S. and Soviet officials had been holding arms control talks for some time. The Russian foreign minister accepted the three-tier approach, but beyond that, the two officials accomplished little. Even so, the administration pointed to the Soviets' adoption of the three-tier strategy as a sign of progress. Significantly, as proof of its desire not to upset the discussions underway at Geneva, the White House ordered its delegates not to raise the issue of human rights.[46]

In an attempt to break the deadlock after the May Vance-Gromyko meeting, the administration chose to give up pressing the Soviet Union to reduce its stock of heavy missiles. This was largely the work of Brown and Marshall Shulman, a Soviet expert and adviser to Vance, who concluded that the SS-19 posed a greater threat to the Minuteman than the SS-9. While the SS-19 was a "light" missile, it was the most technologically advanced in the Soviet arsenal, and it was MIRVed. Therefore, the White House decided that rather than focus on heavies, it would seek to place limits on MIRVed ICBMs.[47]

The issue of capping MIRVed ICBMs became tied to another matter, one that eventually aroused controversy in the United States: Carter's decision to cancel the B-1 long-range bomber. Conceived in the mid-1960s, the B-1's purpose was to replace America's fleet of 330 older and slower B-52s. For years, officials in Washington had debated whether to build the new plane that, said some, had too high a price tag.

In June 1977, Carter canceled production of the aircraft. His announcement came as a surprise to many in the capital. The president had approved funding for the construction of five of the bombers in the Defense Department's budget for 1978, and Secretary Brown was known to have supported the B-1 program when he worked for President Lyndon Johnson. But Brown now stated that the plane was too expensive, and Carter, sharing his defense secretary's fiscal conservatism, agreed. Instead, he would use the savings to build ALCMs for the existing B-52s. This would allow the older aircraft to hit targets from hundreds of miles away, where they stood less chance of being hit by enemy fire. But the president's determination created serious problems for his administration. First, the decision to cancel the B-1 infuriated its proponents in Congress, including

Senators Alan Cranston (D-California) and Barry Goldwater (R-Arizona), Cranston because the plane would have been built in his state, Goldwater because he felt Carter's decision militarily weakened the United States. Even Vance believed that Carter could have insisted upon Soviet concessions at the SALT talks in return for giving up the B-1, which might have resonated well in the Senate. As it stood, senators' anger would come to haunt the president when SALT came up for ratification. Second, there was the matter of how to count the ALCM-armed B-52s within the ceilings established by SALT. To deal with this latter issue, the administration created a new sub-ceiling of 800 land-based MIRVed ICBMs, with ALCM-armed B-52s included within that limit. At the time, the Soviet Union had plans to build 900 such missiles, while the United States had 550. The new sub-ceiling would thus prevent Moscow from building 100 of its planned MIRVed ICBMs while allowing Washington to add 250 ALCM-armed B-52s.[48] In short, there would now be two sub-ceilings: one strictly for land-based MIRVed ICBMs and another for all other MIRVed missiles (including cruise missile–carrying bombers).

The administration developed two additional proposals. One was that if a single ICBM with a warhead was MIRVed, then all ICBMs of that type would be counted in the MIRV sub-ceiling. The second followed along similar lines: if any missile silo was used to launch a MIRVed missile, then all silos of that type would be counted as MIRV launchers. This latter motion on launchers was related to 120 Soviet silos, each armed with an older SS-11 missile, near the towns of Derazhnya and Permovaisk. Prior to SALT I, the Soviets had begun construction of 30 new silos at each site to house the SS-19 and started remodeling the older SS-11 launchers. Consequently, both sets of silos looked exactly the same. This made it impossible for American satellites to tell which missile was which, meaning that there was no way to know exactly how many MIRVed weapons there might be at the two locations. While the Soviets claimed that only the 60 new silos should be included in the limits on MIRVed launchers, the United States insisted that because of the inability to tell one missile from the other, all 180 should be covered by the MIRVed launchers limit.[49] There was, of course, no guarantee that the Soviets would accept any of these proposals. Moreover, Washington still wanted to include the Backfire in any agreement, which Moscow would surely reject.

Nor was there any guarantee that a quick resolution of the dispute over SALT would mean Senate ratification. By August Jackson had become upset with what he regarded as too many concessions by the United States and an unwillingness by the Soviet Union to make compromises of its own. If the White House stood firm, he wrote, then "[t]he Soviets will come to us." His anger grew stronger in September. Not only did he dislike the administration's willingness to continue abiding by SALT I's provisions after they expired, but he charged the White House with having "abandoned" the proposals it made in March. He attacked as well the 2,500-kilometer limit on ALCMs as a major concession without any corresponding give by the Soviets on their ICBMs and SLBMs.[50]

A final complaint of the Washington senator's was the lack of White House consultation with Congress. This was, in fact, a matter that repeatedly created friction between the executive and legislative branches. Thrilled to have a president from the same party, the speaker of the House, Thomas "Tip" O'Neill of Massachusetts, expected a close working relationship with Carter. Standing six feet three and weighing over 250 pounds, with a head of white hair that he brushed back, a bulbous nose, long ears, a deep voice, and a gift for telling a good story, O'Neill had leanings more liberal than those of Carter. Even so, the Massachusetts lawmaker understood the importance of political give-and-take and was prepared to make compromises in the name of party loyalty. To his chagrin, he found the new president did not share his convictions. "[W]hen I tried to explain [to Carter] how important it was for the president to work closely with Congress," recalled O'Neill, "he didn't seem to understand" and even threatened "to go over the heads of the representatives by appealing directly to the voters" to get what he wanted. Other lawmakers found similar treatment. For instance, John Stennis (D-Mississippi), the influential chairman of the Senate Armed Services Committee, recalled being invited to the White House only once during Carter's tenure.[51]

Even White House insiders noted the president's failure to grasp the world of Beltway politics. Bert Lance, a longtime friend of the president's and, for a time, Carter's director of the Office of Management and Budget, commented that because he saw himself as a trustee of the people, Carter assumed "that as long as he did what he thought was right and that he reached that decision based on what was in the best interest of the people . . . then those other things would fall into line." Vance added that since Carter viewed himself as an outsider who believed he owed nothing to Congress, and because the president presumed lawmakers did not have the interests of the American people at heart—the trustee mentality—he had "almost a contempt for Congress which members of Congress felt and which made it difficult to carry through difficult political issues where you needed the Congress's help if you were ever going to get your program put into effect." Not only did Capitol Hill dislike being ignored, but the lack of consultation made it hard for its members to know where Carter's priorities were. This became especially troublesome when policies interfered with one another, such as human rights and arms control.[52]

It soon became clear that there would be no quick resolution to the unsolved issues involved in SALT. In September, Carter and Vance, in discussions with Gromyko, made some headway. The Soviet foreign minister refused to accept the U.S. proposal of including ALCM-carrying heavy bombers in the MIRVed ICBM sub-ceiling, instead calling for its inclusion in the higher MIRVed sub-ceiling of 1,320 (which would prevent the United States from building 250 ALCM heavy bombers to stay within the 1,320 limit). In return, Gromyko offered to accept 820 (rather than 800) for the cap on MIRVed ICBMs. Vance and Carter responded by suggesting a limit of 1,200 rather than 1,320 for the higher MIRV sub-ceiling (which would include ICBMs and SLBMs), with the additional 120 slots set aside for ALCM-carrying bombers; if the United States built more than 120 such bombers, it would have to destroy a MIRVed ICBM to stay within the 1,200 cap. This Moscow accepted. Gromkyo acquiesced to counting all of the launchers at Derazhnya and Pervomaisk as MIRVed in return for a higher overall ceiling of 2250 launchers, which Carter found a fair suggestion.[53] In short, on the contentious issues of caps on overall launchers, MIRVed launchers, MIRVed ICBMs, ALCM-carrying bombers, and Derazhnya and Pervomaisk, the countries had found common ground.

Yet hurdles remained. Gromyko had refused to provide production information on the Backfire and continued to insist that it would not have an intercontinental capability. Nor could Washington and Moscow agree on what constituted a "new" ICBM. Was, for example, an advanced version of an existing missile a "new" missile? Meanwhile, neoconservatives such as Jackson were irritated by what they saw as an increasingly weak SALT accord and the White House's decision to curb its criticism of the Soviets' human rights violations. Then, in October, the Carter administration added a new issue: the banning of telemetry encryption.[54]

During test flights, rockets send back data that allow individuals on the ground to monitor their performance. Much of the information about U.S. missiles was common knowledge and could be found in media reports or books on weaponry. This was not the case with the more secretive Soviet Union. To keep its missiles' capabilities secret, Moscow oftentimes encrypted (encoded) the telemetry its rockets sent back.

The use of encryption disturbed the head of the Central Intelligence Agency, Stansfield Turner. He charged that if Washington could not assess the performance of Soviet rockets, then Moscow might be able to circumvent SALT's provisions. Turner, wrote Robert Gates, a CIA official at the time who later became the agency's director, "had the administration over a barrel. Unless [he] could assure the Senate that U.S. intelligence could adequately monitor Soviet compliance with a SALT treaty, it had no chance of being ratified."[55] Even without the complication caused by encryption, it is unlikely much progress would have taken place. When Gromyko came to Washington in May 1978, he, Carter, and Vance could not agree on such matters as the Backfire or what constituted a "new" missile. Still, encryption made the chances of success all the more distant.

Furthermore, had Gromyko returned home in May 1978 with a signed SALT accord, its ratification would have been even more in doubt than it had been in 1977. Carter's foreign policy decisions, such as those on human rights and the B-1, had upset members of the upper house. Domestically, the president had angered African-Americans, women, labor, and their representatives in the Senate because of his decision to emphasize combating inflation as opposed to unemployment. Finally, a number of senators pointed to the Soviets' continued arms buildup and Moscow's support for communist movements and nations around the world. Add to all of this complaints over the lack of executive consultation, and SALT's chances in mid-1978 did not look good.

CTB, MBFR, the Indian Ocean, and CAT

Nor were discussions going well on another arms control matter, a comprehensive test ban (CTB) treaty. To Carter, banning all nuclear testing would limit the proliferation of atomic weapons. Hence, within a week of his inauguration, he wrote Brezhnev and asked that the two superpowers sign such an understanding. Six months later, talks got underway and, for a time, seemed on the road to success. In an important concession, the Soviets offered to suspend all peaceful nuclear testing and expressed their willingness to accept two American proposals: the first would allow each nation to place seismic devices on the other's territory to check for nuclear tests, while the second would permit on-site inspections if either country insisted on it.[56]

Opposition within the United States, however, moved the administration to reconsider its position. The Joint Chiefs of Staff (JCS), the Department of Defense, members of Congress, and employees at the Los Alamos and Livermore laboratories held that the U.S. CTB proposal would threaten American security by indefinitely halting all testing and that the provisions for verification were not foolproof. With these considerations in mind, in May the White House called for an agreement with a three-year life span. It was the beginning of a retreat that ultimately killed the CTB and heightened Soviet skepticism about America's commitment to arms control.[57]

The backtracking on the part of the administration on the CTB once again reflected a lack of coherent planning on the part of the Oval Office. It was one thing to seek a ban on nuclear testing. It was another to get all those with a stake to support it. The president might have had some success had he delegated authority to a person or a group of people who endorsed the CTB proposal. Instead, his advisers divided over the issue, with Vance supporting it and Brzezinski opposed. The lack of unity within the White House made it easier for the CTB's detractors to weaken it. Granted,

completion of the CTB talks prior to the signing of SALT would have in-
cited a hornet's nest once a treaty came up for ratification. In that respect,
it made sense to complete SALT before proceeding with the CTB.[58] But the
failure to consider all of the complexities involved in a CTB, combined
with the divisions within the executive branch itself, all but doomed the
test ban talks from the start.

The Mutual Balanced Force Reduction (MBFR) negotiations also looked
stillborn. Begun in the early 1970s, the purpose of MBFR was to reduce the
size of the conventional forces of the North Atlantic Treaty Organization
and the Warsaw Pact in Europe. The talks had stalled in 1976 but resumed
in June 1978 when the Soviets accepted the West's demand that both sides
limit themselves to 900,000 personnel: 700,000 ground troops and
200,000 air force personnel. At issue was how many troops both sides
would have to cut to reach that limit. The West believed the numbers submitted by the Warsaw Pact were too low, and the talks deadlocked again.[59]

Discussions to demilitarize the Indian Ocean were not going much better. Until the late 1960s, the United States gave little attention to that part
of the world, assigning responsibility for its protection from the communists to Great Britain. But London's decision to withdraw its military presence from Southeast Asia in the mid-1960s and the deployment of Soviet
warships to the Indian Ocean drew Washington's anxious attention. Much
of the world's oil traveled through that ocean from the Middle East, and
the United States did not want to see a growth of Soviet influence there.[60]

Yet by the early 1970s both superpowers had reason to adopt some kind
of arms control agreement for the Indian Ocean. Many Americans pointed
to the expense involved in an arms race with the Soviets in that body of
water; just the cost of constructing facilities on the British-controlled
island of Diego Garcia had raised complaints in Congress. For the Soviets,
an arms control regime would, as in the case of SALT, enhance their reputation as a nation of peace and restrict the American military buildup in
South Asia.[61]

Carter, seeking to improve relations with the Soviets, decided that it
was not enough simply to limit the number of weapons in the Indian
Ocean; it was necessary to seek its demilitarization. With that in mind,
Vance, Brzezinski, and Brown, at a March meeting of the Special Coordinating Committee, suggested that the secretary of state present the idea
during his visit to Moscow later that month. That Vance did. The Soviets
found the suggestion worthy of consideration.[62]

Meanwhile, the various bureaus and departments in the U.S. government wrangled over how to achieve demilitarization. There was a general consensus in favor of a limitation of weapons in the Indian Ocean
as a foundation for a disarmament pact. Even the Navy and JCS, which
appeared likely to frown at the idea of removing military forces from the

Indian Ocean, went along, probably because they ascertained that the ultimate result of the talks, if they succeeded, would be arms limitation, not complete demilitarization.[63]

The negotiations began in June in Moscow but soon bogged down. The Soviets wanted to bar the United States from placing long-range bombers capable of carrying nuclear weapons or submarines with long-range nuclear missiles in the region, while Washington sought to prevent Moscow from basing aircraft on the ocean's boundary. They could not come to terms on the geographic limits of any demilitarization agreement, and they questioned how to verify the provisions of an accord, if reached. Soviet help in transferring Cuban troops to the Horn of Africa in November 1977, along with a corresponding hardening of U.S. Soviet policy, killed further progress for the remainder of the administration's term.[64]

The conventional arms transfer (CAT) discussions looked more encouraging. Since the middle of the 1970s, the U.S. public and members of Congress had expressed anxiety about American sales of conventional weapons, which had been growing for some time. The concern was that the proliferation of sophisticated conventional armaments not only made wars elsewhere more likely but smeared America's reputation abroad. Carter wanted to get rid of the United States' image "as a 'merchant of death.'" Realizing the Soviet Union also had augmented its exports of conventional weapons, and cognizant that other nations—such as America's West European allies—also sold arms to Third World countries, the incoming president wanted them to join his initiative to curb such sales.[65]

Although there is no proof that high-level officials in Moscow had given much thought to restricting arms transfers, they had several reasons to cooperate. As with SALT and the CTB, it would improve the Soviets' image in the West, which the Kremlin could use in trying to draw support from U.S. allies for American policies of which it did approve. Furthermore, a treaty on conventional arms sales could reduce tensions elsewhere in the world that might otherwise drag the superpowers into a confrontation with one another. Finally, such an agreement would make it harder for anticommunist leaders or movements in the Third World to stop the spread of communism.[66]

It was during a visit to Western Europe in January 1977 that Vice President Mondale first raised the idea of CAT with allied officials. He found skepticism from the allies who, before agreeing to curtail their arms sales, wanted to see proof that both the United States and Soviet Union would do so. The administration therefore approached the Kremlin. The first round of talks, held in the U.S. capital at the end of the year, were encouraging. In May 1978, a second round began in Helsinki, Finland. More progress took place there, opening the door to a third round, planned for July, again in Helsinki.[67]

It was in preparation for that third phase that divisions within the Carter administration once again appeared. Brzezinski, the Arms Control and Disarmament Agency (ACDA), the JCS, and the Defense Department maintained that a conventional arms accord first required the United States and Soviet Union to reach an understanding on what types of weapons or weapons systems were more advanced than others. Indeed, they said, it was important to take into account the sophistication of weaponry in one part of the world versus another; what constituted an "advanced" weapons system in, say, Kenya, might not be so in Thailand. Once having achieved agreement with the Soviets on definitions of arms, ACDA, the JCS, and Defense wanted to focus on the least controversial topics, using the resolution of those issues to set the foundation for addressing the more difficult matters.[68]

Vance and the Americans' lead negotiator, Leslie Gelb, disliked their colleagues' recommendations. What mattered most, they insisted, was to look at arms sales to regions of the world without trying to develop some common definition of system types. Furthermore, to start small as ACDA, Defense, and the JCS favored could cause the talks to go on indefinitely. The White House decided in favor of State. Meanwhile, the Soviets accepted much of the U.S. position, thereby opening the door to hope that they could reach an agreement on conventional arms sales.[69]

The Neutron Bomb Controversy

If America's allies wondered about Washington's commitment to curb conventional arms sales, they, as well as Congress, questioned the president's decision to forego production and deployment of the neutron bomb. Also known as the enriched radiation weapon (ERW), this was a nuclear device deliverable by artillery or missile. Unlike conventional atomic munitions, the neutron bomb produced a massive blast of radiation that killed only people without causing damage to cities. The United States had examined the use of ERWs since the late 1950s, but it was not until 1976 that Congress passed and President Ford signed legislation calling for the weapon's funding and development.[70]

It was one thing to approve funding, another to provide it. In June 1977, Walter Pincus, a reporter for the *Washington Post,* published a story attacking the ERW on moral grounds. If it were used, its victims would suffer horribly, with "convulsions, intermittent stupor and lack of muscle coordination. Death is certain in a few hours to several days." Pincus's article turned U.S. voters against the weapon and prompted a debate in Congress, especially in the Senate, over appropriating money for the bomb. During consideration in mid-1977 of a bill to provide funding for the Energy Research and Development Administration (ERDA)—which would oversee the development of the ERW—Senator Mark Hatfield (R-Oregon), a strong proponent of human rights and a leading opponent of the bomb, offered an amendment barring any appropriations. Yet the ERW had its backers, among them Senators Jackson and Sam Nunn (D-Georgia).[71]

Carter found himself in a catch-22. If he refused to approve the new weapon, he would anger the U.S. military, which wanted it, as well as members of Congress. And to cancel the ERW on the heels of his decision on the B-1 bomber would compel his critics to charge him with weakness vis-à-vis the Soviets. But if he proceeded with the ERW's production and deployment, he would upset a number of lawmakers and many Americans who considered the weapon immoral and a violation of the president's promotion of human rights. It also would contradict Carter's call for disarmament.[72] It was for these reasons that in July the president announced he would wait to make a decision.

But Carter gave the clear impression he was leaning in favor of the bomb. In July, he had written to Senator Stennis who, like Jackson, was a conservative Democrat and a strong supporter of defense spending. Carter told the Mississippi lawmaker that while he had yet to make a decision on the bomb, he wanted the Senate to vote against the Hatfield amendment and appropriate money for the ERDA. Stennis certainly received the impression that Carter ultimately would endorse the ERW's production, if not its deployment, and offered a rider that would delay funding pending a presidential determination. The Senate adopted this language and passed the measure later that month. In September, the House endorsed a similar appropriations bill.[73]

Making matters more complicated was West Germany. The ERW would be deployed in that country, yet many West Germans did not want it. Chancellor Helmut Schmidt actually favored deployment, but he had no intention publicly to take a position. In part, it was personal. Of Carter's height, with neatly combed hair that he parted on his left side, a rectangular face, and an intensity reflected in his eyes, the West German leader from early on had come to dislike Carter. Desirous to defend détente, and determined that the United States give greater consideration to West Germany's interests, he shared the feeling of other European officials that the U.S. president's human rights initiative was "preachy," unnecessarily provocative to the Soviets, and a threat to cordial East-West ties. Quiet diplomacy, believed Schmidt, had succeeded in bringing 70,000 Germans out of communist-controlled Eastern Europe; "renewed tensions could halt this flow and cause other East-West problems." It was also political. Knowing how many West Germans felt about the ERW, Schmidt had no intention of putting his neck on the line until his American counterpart had firmly decided what to do.[74]

Carter's top foreign policy advisers favored production and deployment of the ERW. Both Brown and Brzezinski saw it as providing a deterrent to the Soviets; Vance, though personally opposed to it, concurred on strategic grounds with his colleagues. All shared the view as well that America's NATO allies, particularly West Germany, should share in any decision on deployment rather than leaving it all on the shoulders of the United States. Having received the same indication as Stennis that Carter would endorse the ERW, Brzezinski, Brown, Mondale, and Vance all decided to proceed with discussions with America's allies. In this case, the president's advisers were at fault for not informing him of their intentions. It appears they feared that letting him know might prompt him to cancel the weapon.[75] But with Carter sending a double message—publicly determined to await a decision while seemingly personally supportive of production and possibly deployment—they should have waited for instructions from him.

In April 1978, to the surprise of Brown, Brzezinski, Vance, and other ERW defenders, Carter announced he would forego the bomb's production or deployment. He later stated that he was infuriated after learning during a trip to Georgia about his advisers' discussions with America's allies and the lack of a commitment from those allies to "deploy or accept it." Carter's decision brought criticism from at home and abroad, especially after word leaked that his advisers had wanted him to produce and deploy the weapon. Nunn commented that it made America look weak in the face of the Soviet threat. Senator Howard Baker (R-Tennessee) called it "another in a long line of national defense mistakes" by Carter. "First we give away the B-1 bomber and now we are going to give away the neutron bomb." Schmidt accused the president of forsaking his nation and of "disengag[ing] from Europe."[76]

Schmidt's self-righteous language hid the fact that he had never publicly expressed his feelings about the weapon or that he privately endorsed it. Yet the White House also deserved criticism. Carter had not only sent a double message, but his advisers had acted without instructions. U.S.–West European tensions, already on the rise because of Carter's human rights initiative, grew because of the ERW.

Nuclear Nonproliferation

Atomic weaponry was directly linked to a final part of Carter's arms control efforts, that of nuclear nonproliferation. The U.S. government had taken little interest in the spread of nuclear technology until the 1970s. It was true that Washington had signed the Nuclear Nonproliferation Treaty (NPT) in 1968 and ratified it in 1970. But it was not until after India's nuclear test in 1974 that U.S. officials made nuclear nonproliferation a priority.[77]

Carter brought attention to the issue during the 1976 campaign. He had a personal connection to the topic, having been sent in 1952 to Canada to investigate what had happened at an experimental nuclear reactor that had suffered a meltdown and released radioactive material into the air. "The experience," commented a Carter friend, Peter Bourne, "made a deep impression on [him]." The president also saw a connection between nonproliferation on the one hand and arms control and human rights on the other. Following his inauguration, Carter announced his intention to keep other nations from developing a nuclear capacity or enhancing their existing capabilities. He realized, he told an audience at Notre Dame University in May 1977, that his stance might create "friction" with other countries, but in his opinion, there was the issue of the greater good.[78]

Nonetheless, as in the case of human rights, the president never seemed able to come to grips with implementing the nuclear nonproliferation initiative. Indeed, as in the case of human rights, he found he could not compartmentalize policies; rather, he had to compromise one initiative in the name of another. Such became apparent in U.S. nonproliferation policy toward South Asia.

Historically, the two most powerful nations of South Asia, Pakistan and India, had a tense relationship. Between 1947, when these two countries gained independence from Great Britain, and 1971, they had fought three wars, the first two over the disputed region of Kashmir and the third because of the effort of East Pakistan—later Bangladesh—to seek independence from Pakistan.

Aggravating those tensions was India's acquisition of nuclear weaponry. New Delhi had begun research into nuclear power almost immediately after World War II. But India realized it needed outside help to develop its atomic energy program and therefore turned to the United States. The result was a thirty-year agreement signed in 1963 by which the United States built and supplied nuclear fuel to two reactors at the west Indian town of Tarapur. New Delhi, though, refused to sign the NPT, charging that it violated the nation's sovereignty. Six years after the promulgation of the NPT, India used the information it had acquired from its nuclear power program to successfully detonate an atomic bomb.[79]

The acquisition of nuclear weaponry by its long-time enemy alarmed Pakistan. Pakistan's own nuclear energy program dated back to 1965, when it signed an accord with Canada to build and supply uranium to a heavy water reactor, the Karachi Nuclear Power Plant (KANUPP).[80] Following India's nuclear test, Pakistan sought to obtain its own atomic weapon. Unlike New Delhi, however, Islamabad had no way to reprocess the uranium. Uranium for a nuclear power plant is delivered in fuel rods. The fuel is eventually used up, leaving behind waste. Some of it can be recycled, or reprocessed, while the rest, which is highly radioactive, must be properly disposed of so that it cannot harm the environment. One of the products of reprocessing is plutonium, which can be used in a weapon. As KANUPP did not have the ability to turn its uranium into plutonium, Pakistan had to find a way to reprocess the waste from that plant.

In 1976, Prime Minister Zulfikar Ali Bhutto signed a contract with France to construct a reprocessing plant in Pakistan. This arrangement startled both Canada and the United States, neither of which wanted to see another nuclear-armed nation on the Asian subcontinent. Ottawa immediately halted all fuel shipments to KANUPP, while Washington offered Bhutto 100 A-7 warplanes if he would give up his plan to acquire the reprocessing plant. When Bhutto failed to give a positive response, the United States turned its efforts to convincing France to forego the project.[81]

Thus, upon assuming office, President Carter found himself having to contend with two nations in South Asia that had a history of warfare, one of which had acquired nuclear weapons and another that was attempting to do so. For personal, political, and strategic reasons, he leaned in favor of India. Personally, he had an interest in India, as his mother had served there for several years as a member of the Peace Corps. Politically, he supported the return of democracy to India, marked by the election in March 1977 of Morarji Desai after a two-year state of emergency imposed by the previous prime minister, Indira Gandhi. The opposite was the case in Pakistan, where protests against Bhutto took place following accusations that he had rigged his victory in elections held that March. Four months later, the Pakistani military staged a coup, overthrowing Bhutto, installing General Muhammad Zia-ul-Haq as the country's new leader, and imposing martial law. Repeated promises by the new regime to hold elections consistently went unfulfilled. Strategically, Carter determined that close relations with India were more vital to the protection of U.S. interests in the region than ties with Pakistan.[82]

This hard line toward Pakistan became clear in September 1977, when the administration, citing human rights violations and Islamabad's desire to acquire nuclear power, withdrew the offer of A-7s and then suspended all economic aid. While the latter amounted to only $50 million, the symbolic impact, particularly on top of the decision not to proceed with the A-7 sale, infuriated the Pakistani government. Meanwhile, Washington continued to urge Paris not to proceed with the sale of the reprocessing plant. That pressure, in conjunction with France's concern that Pakistan intended to use the nuclear technology to develop an atomic weapon, prompted Paris in 1978 to suspend indefinitely its contract with Islamabad.[83]

India did not find such treatment. In fact, Carter fought congressional efforts to limit nuclear assistance to India. In March 1978 Capitol Hill took action against those nations that already had a nuclear power program, passing overwhelmingly the Nuclear Non-Proliferation Act (NNPA). This law required the United States within eighteen months to stop providing nuclear aid to any nation that refused to agree to have its atomic facilities meet a list of safeguards established by the International Atomic Energy Agency (IAEA). The president called the law overly restrictive, but he still signed it. First, vetoing the legislation would have contradicted his own avowed desire to stop the proliferation of nuclear weapons and would have been overridden anyway. Second, the bill gave the president an eighteen-month window, during which he could provide India with nuclear material and, hopefully, convince Desai to accept IAEA safeguards. Finally, even after that eighteen months was up, the law gave the president some leeway. The U.S. Nuclear Regulatory Commission (NRC) had to review any licenses to ship nuclear fuel to another nation; it would then issue a nonbinding recommendation to the president as to whether he should sign off on it. Simply put, the White House did not have to accept the NRC's advice. Yet there was one final step, which was to get congressional approval. If the president refused to accept the NRC's recommendation, Capitol Hill could stop the shipment, but only if a majority of both houses voted to do so. Thus, if Carter threw out the NRC's advice and could convince either the House or Senate to back his decision, the United States could ship the fuel.

The first test of this legislation took place in April 1978. At the time Carter assumed office, India had applied for approximately 7.6 tons of nuclear fuel for the Tarapur plant. The NRC evenly split, with two votes for and two against, over whether to endorse the shipment. Carter had promised to ship the fuel if Desai affirmed he would not develop more nuclear weapons and aligned India's nuclear policy with that of the United States; the Indian prime minister acceded to both requests. Failure now to provide the fuel, argued Carter, would make Desai less willing to abide by this agreement and kill any hope of getting New Delhi to acquiesce to IAEA safeguards. The president thus signed off on the license. Some members of Congress, among them Representative Christopher Dodd (D-Connecticut), Richard Ottinger (D-New York), and Clarence Long (D-Maryland), attempted, but failed, to override the president's decision. Still, it left a sour taste in the mouths of many observers, who saw the president once again inconsistently applying and contradicting what he said was a core policy of his administration. "Of all of the delights of the Carter administration," commented the *Wall Street Journal* following Carter's approval of the Tarapur license, "none tops the continuing burlesque of its policy to constrain the proliferation of nuclear weapons."[84]

★　　To his credit, President Carter's decision to tackle head-on the topics of human rights, arms control, and nuclear nonproliferation brought him in line with growing concerns in the United States and abroad about the dangers posed to humankind by repressive regimes and the arms race. On the issue of human rights, Carter went even further than his predecessors. While previous presidents had sought to curb the arms race, none had made human rights a central component of their foreign policies.[85]

It was Carter's execution of his foreign policy that by mid-1978 made it appear to be in disarray. The shift from absolutism to pragmatism, a lack of direction from the Oval Office, and bureaucratic infighting made for an erratic human rights initiative, one that brought criticism from both neoconservatives and new internationalists alike. The inconsistent application of human rights drew fire upon SALT, and complaints about that treaty's provisions and the paucity of executive consultation made its ratification increasingly remote. Confusion regarding the president's intentions had a deleterious impact upon the ERW. Bureaucratic infighting had left the CTB in doubt, the Indian Ocean talks had bogged down, and the president had raised questions over his preparedness to make exceptions to the policy of nuclear nonproliferation. Only the CAT discussions looked promising. For a president who wanted "95 percent of something," it looked as though he would get far less than that.

Maybe most important, the president never provided the American public an overarching vision that would give his foreign policy meaning. The ingredients were there. Carter, for instance, could have argued that despite inconsistencies and even contradictions, his human rights, arms control, and nuclear nonproliferation initiatives were part of a broader vision of a peaceful, democratic world that would protect America's political and security interests abroad. But the president's determination to solve problems individually rather than attempt to place them within the context of a broader national mission made that impossible. All that the public was left with, then, were inconsistent and contradictory policies. Brzezinski himself later admitted that the White House failed to explain clearly to Americans "what we were doing and where we were heading."[86]

With so many of his individual initiatives a muddle and his larger vision incoherent, Americans, not surprisingly, lost faith in Carter's handling of the nation's foreign policy. His approval rating fell from 48 percent in the middle of 1977 to 22 percent a year later. By July 1978, only 34 percent of Americans approved of his handling of U.S.–Soviet relations, versus 43 percent opposed.[87] Unless the president could achieve more success on his individual initiatives and provide the public an overarching vision in which those initiatives played a part, those numbers were likely to fall further, and his reelection would become more and more unlikely.

NEGOTIATING PEACE...

Three

★   "All during the day we were anticipating massive violence in Panama if the treaties were defeated," President Jimmy Carter wrote in his diary on April 18, 1978. "When the vote started at 6:00, we were fairly sure that we would have all three of the doubtful senators with us, and that's the way the vote came out—exactly the same as it was on the first treaty." He added later, "I was exhausted, exhilarated, and thankful. We had finally passed this hurdle, one of the most onerous political ordeals of my life."[1]

    The ratification of the Panama Canal treaties in 1978 marked a major success for the Carter administration; the signing of the Camp David Accords later in the year added another feather to the president's cap. Yet these were just two of numerous initiatives designed to end regional or intrastate conflicts abroad, an endeavor that drew the administration's attention to places throughout the world, including not just Latin America and the Middle East, but also Europe and Africa. It became more than the administration could handle. In the process, policy initiatives interfered with one another, divisions within the administration as a result of Carter's managerial style once again became apparent, and the American people remained unsure what the larger purpose of these initiatives was.

The Cyprus Dispute

    One of the international conflicts that drew the president's attention was the Greco-Turkish dispute over the island of Cyprus. Greece argued that it had had communities on Cyprus for thousands of years, whereas Turkey pointed to the Ottoman conquest of the island in the 1570s. During World War I, the British took control of Cyprus and administered it until 1960, when the island gained its independence. However, Greek Cypriots since at least the late 1800s had desired unification with Greece, and this movement gained steam after 1960. Turks on the island grew restless, leading to armed clashes between themselves and the Greeks. In 1974, right-wing Greeks, supported by the repressive military-led government in Athens, overthrew the Greek Cypriot president, Archbishop Makarios III, and installed a new leader. Turkey, seeing this as an effort by Greece to acquire the island, and charging that it had to protect the Cypriot Turks, invaded. The war ended later that year, with Turkey controlling about 40 percent of the island. In 1975, the United Nations began negotiations to establish a single government for Cyprus, but differences between the Turks and Greeks over its composition thwarted any agreement before the 1976 U.S. presidential election.

What made matters even more complex was the impact of the Greco-Turkish war upon the North Atlantic Treaty Organization (NATO) and U.S. relations with Greece and Turkey. Both President Richard Nixon and National Security Adviser Henry Kissinger had supported the Greek military regime. When Turkey attacked Cyprus, however, the junta resigned, and a civilian government assumed power, led by Constantine Karamanlis. Karamanlis, angered by U.S. backing for the junta, and believing America to be behind Turkey's attack on Cyprus, promptly withdrew Greece from NATO.[2]

Simultaneously, the U.S. Congress took action against Turkey. In violation of U.S. law, the Turks had used American-supplied weapons during their invasion of Cyprus. Angry lawmakers instituted an embargo on military aid to Ankara. The Turkish government retaliated in 1975 by closing over two dozen U.S. military bases in Turkey.[3]

About a month before the 1976 U.S. election, Cyrus Vance had brought Carter's attention to the Cyprus dispute and convinced the presidential nominee, if he won the election, to take steps to solve it. Finding a solution acceptable to Greece and Turkey would prevent the possibility of another regional war, thereby saving human lives improve U.S. ties with both nations; hopefully draw Greece back into NATO and restore America's base rights in Turkey; and, ultimately, strengthen the policy of containment. The month after his inauguration, Carter sent Clark Clifford, whose distinguished Washington career dated back to his days as an adviser to Harry Truman, to Greece and Turkey to assess the situation. Clifford found Karamanlis concerned about his country's tensions with Turkey. In Ankara, Prime Minister Suleiman Demiral insisted that there was no connection between U.S.–Turkish relations and the Cyprus dispute. But he promised to ask the Turkish Cypriot leader, Rauf Denktaş, to show flexibility if Clifford could get Cypriot President Makarios—who had returned to his post following Karamanlis's assumption of power—to show some flexibility of his own. Traveling to Cyprus next, Clifford determined that Makarios was prepared to accept "a federal division of Cyprus." Denktaş, for his part, focused "on the grievances of the Turkish community in Cyprus." Returning home, Clifford reported that there was reason for hope for a settlement.[4]

During the next several months, there was little progress. In the Turkish elections, held in June 1977, Bülent Ecevit's Republican People's Party gained seats, but his inability to form a coalition government allowed Demeril to remain in power. Still, it was clear that Demeril's political strength had waned, and the nation's continuing economic problems further weakened his position. Two months later, Makarios passed away. While Paul Henze, a National Security Council (NSC) specialist on intelligence coordination, believed that this would open the door to a more moderate official who would accept a compromise with the Turks, there was little the United States could do until new elections determined Makarios's successor.[5]

Matters grew more difficult starting in November. That month, Karamanlis's party, New Democracy, did not do as well in parliamentary elections as had been anticipated. Meanwhile, the left-wing Panhellenic Socialist Movement, led by Andreas Papandreou, gained seats. Henze commented that Karamanlis had purposely called for the election "to strengthen his own position to deal with the tough foreign policy issues that have to be faced," including Cyprus. Karamanlis *"emerges weaker now than he was before"* [emphasis in original]. The longer it took to settle the dispute over Cyprus and to get Greece to rejoin NATO, the less likely either would take place. Then, the following month, a dozen high-level members of Demirel's party defected, prompting the Turkish prime minister to resign. Ecevit became prime minister.[6]

Vance and NSC Adviser Zbigniew Brzezinski oftentimes did not see eye-to-eye, but in this case, they joined forces and called for repeal of the embargo on Turkey. Secretary of Defense Harold Brown seconded them. All argued that the continuation of the embargo would impede close U.S.–Turkish relations, with the result of both making a settlement on Cyprus less likely and endangering America's regional interests. The president seconded their call for the embargo's repeal.[7]

Carter's request, which apparently was made without prior consultation with lawmakers, angered numerous Democrats, including virtually the entire party leadership. Senators Thomas Eagleton of Missouri, Paul Sarbanes of Maryland, and Daniel Patrick Moynihan of New York, and Representative Benjamin Rosenthal of New York, all issued statements of dissent, charging him with violating his arms control and human rights policies. Realizing the intensity of the opposition he faced, Carter urged the Turks to demonstrate positive movement on Cyprus. Meeting with a visiting Ecevit on May 31, the president asked for some give on Ankara's part, insisting that it would resonate well in Congress and make it easier for him to get lawmakers to end the embargo. Ecevit promised to do what he could, but he placed the failure of progress on Cyprus at the feet of Karamanlis and Makarios's successor, Spyros Kyprianou. Nor did a meeting later that same day with Karamanlis offer any more reason for hope. The

Greek prime minister urged Carter not to lift the embargo and said that Turkey's proposals to resolve the Cyprus dispute—which he insisted would permanently divide the island—were not acceptable to Kyprianou. If Ecevit really wanted an agreement, said the Greek Cypriot leader, he would not only make a better offer but force Denktaş to accept it: "I do not control Kyprianou but Ecevit controls Denktaş."[8]

Thus, by the middle of 1978, there was little reason for hope that the Cyprus dispute could be resolved. Neither side showed any willingness to budge. Furthermore, the president again had raised the hackles of members of his own party in Congress. And he had once more drawn charges of compromising and inconsistently applying key components of his own foreign policy, in this case, arms control and human rights.

Southern Africa

Another impasse, and one that would also hurt Carter on Capitol Hill, was the president's response to the situation in southern Africa, where white minority-led governments maintained control over populations that were predominantly black, and where there were serious concerns about regional stability. One of the countries in question was Rhodesia (now Zimbabwe). Until 1964, Rhodesia had been part of the British-led Federation of Rhodesia and Nyasaland, which also incorporated today's countries of Zambia, Zimbabwe, and Malawi. That year, London dissolved the federation, giving Malawi and Northern Rhodesia (today's Zambia) independence. But the British government refused to grant Southern Rhodesia, renamed Rhodesia, its freedom until the government in Salisbury allowed universal suffrage.

Ian Smith, the colony's premier, responded angrily. Born in 1919 in Rhodesia, Smith had served during World War II in the Royal Rhodesian Air Force. After the war, he won election to the colony's general assembly. He eventually became minister of the treasury under Winston Field, the leader of the Rhodesian Front (RF), who assumed the prime ministership in 1962. Two years later, the RF, charging Field with not doing enough to secure Rhodesia's independence, replaced him with Smith.

Smith was strongly opposed to permitting black majority rule in Rhodesia. As far as he was concerned, his colony's political system was not racist; rather, he argued, as blacks became more educated and wealthy, they would eventually assume control of Rhodesia. Yet he also made clear that he would not accept majority rule as a prerequisite to independence. In fact, as he later wrote, the effort by blacks to gain political control was nothing short of a communist conspiracy designed to destroy Rhodesia.[9]

With the backing of Rhodesia's whites, who shared Smith's unwillingness to accept majority rule, Smith declared Rhodesia's independence in 1965.

Black nationalists in Rhodesia countered by forming two groups, each seeking to establish black majority rule, and that together became known as the Patriotic Front (PF): the Zimbabwe African National Union (ZANU), led by Robert Mugabe, and Joshua Nkomo's Zimbabwe African People's Union (ZAPU). ZANU, which received arms from China and Romania, and ZAPU, which obtained weapons from the Soviet Union, engaged in a guerrilla campaign to overthrow Smith. While numbering only about 700 in March 1976, their forces grew to over 5,500 by the end of 1977 and more than 11,000 by early 1979.[10] The British put pressure of their own on Smith, imposing economic sanctions on his government. The United Nations followed suit in 1968, passing a resolution that called for comprehensive sanctions against Salisbury.

As the international community attempted to force concessions from Smith, U.S. policy toward his government wavered. At first the Nixon administration supported the sanctions. In 1971, however, the president signed the Byrd Amendment. Sponsored by Senator Harry Byrd (D-Virginia), this legislation lifted a U.S. embargo on imports of Rhodesian chrome. In so doing, Washington implicitly endorsed the Smith government, making the Rhodesian leader less prepared to accept majority rule. But then, in 1976, President Gerald Ford shifted policy again. Armed insurrections in the Portuguese colonies of Mozambique and Angola had led to independence for both in 1975; communists took power in each of the new countries. Worry that the rebellion in Rhodesia would bring about the collapse of the Smith government prompted Henry Kissinger, now secretary of state, to propose, with South African backing, a plan that would bring about majority rule in Rhodesia within two years; otherwise, he feared, communists might take control there as well. The black nationalist organizations in Rhodesia rejected the proposal, insisting instead on having authority turned over to them more quickly.[11]

That Kissinger would invite South African participation, and even more so that Pretoria would agree to take part, seems odd. South Africa, like Rhodesia, had a white minority government. That nation's system of apartheid, which severely restricted the rights of black South Africans, had made South Africa an international pariah. Furthermore, as in Rhodesia, the government faced internal opposition from black organizations, most notably the African National Congress and the Pan Africanist Congress (PAC). Although Washington after World War II found in Pretoria an ally in the effort to contain the spread of communism, the postwar civil rights movement in America, and the Sharpeville massacre of 1960 in South Africa—when South African police fired on and killed nearly one hundred PAC-organized demonstrators—moved the White House to join in the condemnation of apartheid.

South Africa also had come under international criticism for its occupation of Namibia. Formerly known as South-West Africa, this territory had been placed under a South African mandate following World War I. The independence movements that swept across Africa after World War II increased pressure on Pretoria to give South-West Africa its freedom, but the South African government balked. An infuriated United Nations revoked Pretoria's mandate. In the 1960s a guerrilla group, the South-West Africa People's Organization (SWAPO), operating out of bases in Zambia and later communist-controlled Angola, launched attacks on South African forces in Namibia. The United Nations, supported by the United States, passed numerous resolutions urging South Africa to remove its military presence from Namibia and arrange a settlement that would permit Namibia's independence. Peace in Namibia, though, required negotiations with SWAPO, something South Africa rejected because of SWAPO's close relationship with the Angolan government and its receipt of arms from the Soviet Union.[12]

It was in part because of the pressure to end apartheid and to leave Namibia that South African Prime Minister John Vorster became convinced to join in the effort to get Smith to adopt majority rule. Pretoria anticipated that in so doing, it would reduce criticism of apartheid and its occupation of Namibia, if not improve its standing in the eyes of the world. But Vorster had additional reasons for supporting Kissinger's plan for Rhodesia. Like the secretary of state, the South African leader feared that the instability in Rhodesia could lead communism to take hold there, thus placing an enemy state on South Africa's northern border. Also, Kissinger had offered to allow South Africa to resolve its own racial problems if it pressured Smith and moved toward Namibian independence; in short, the secretary of state was willing to permit apartheid's continuation in return for positive movement on Rhodesia and Namibia.[13] But Vorster's endorsement of Kissinger's proposal could not hide his refusal to end apartheid, and his use of repression against anti-apartheid protestors in South Africa, such as the police shooting of protestors at Soweto in 1976, only served to fuel international admonishment of his government.

After assuming office, President Carter devoted more attention to U.S. relations with black Africa than any of his predecessors, and did so for several reasons. One was his belief that white minority rule violated the human rights of black Africans. On that basis alone, he had no intention of accepting Kissinger's plan for Rhodesia, which would absolve South Africa's apartheid system. A second was his concern for regional stability. Thirdly, he wanted to cater to African-American voters. By the 1960s, a grassroots movement had developed in the United States among African-Americans in opposition to apartheid, marked by the activities of such groups as the Congress on Racial Equality, the American Committee on Africa, the Black Leadership Conference on Southern Africa, and the Black Forum on Foreign Policy. Partly because Carter himself repeatedly denounced apartheid, many African-Americans had supported his candidacy in 1976. Finally, Carter judged that condemning apartheid would please Nigeria and the so-called Front Line states of Angola, Botswana, Mozambique, Tanzania, and Zambia. All of these countries also had doubts about America's preparedness to support majority rule in southern Africa, doubts reinforced by the Byrd Amendment. Nigeria additionally was a vital supplier of oil, thus giving the Carter administration even more reason to call for an end to white-led governments in Africa.[14]

Carter's top foreign policy advisers shared his determination to end white rule in Rhodesia and South Africa and to achieve Namibian independence. It was over the means to achieve these goals that they differed. Brzezinski held that any settlement had to take into account the Soviet threat, which he saw as key to the region's troubles. Not only was the Kremlin actively supporting Nkomo in Rhodesia, but it had helped ferry thousands of Cuban troops to Angola by early 1976. The NSC adviser felt that in applying pressure on Rhodesia or South Africa, the White House had to bear in mind their concerns that any settlement not permit an expansion of Moscow's influence in the region.[15]

Yet Brzezinski himself admitted that in the early months of the administration his role when it came to U.S. policy toward southern Africa "was of secondary importance." Rather, the State Department assumed the lead. Here, Vance found favor for his policy of deemphasizing the Soviet threat from several appointees, including Assistant Secretary for African Affairs Richard Moose and Ambassador to the United Nations Andrew Young. A career foreign service officer, Moose had worked for the National Security Council during the presidencies of Lyndon Johnson and Richard Nixon. Young, whose post came with full cabinet status, was a key member of the 1960s civil rights movement, a former member of the Trilateral Commission, and the first African-American to hold so high a post in the U.S. government. His appointment, thought Carter, would not only cater to African-American voters in the United States but send a strong signal to blacks in Africa of his commitment to their interests. While these officials in State shared Brzezinski's concern that instability in the region could benefit the communists, they regarded indigenous factors, such as apartheid, and not Soviet machinations, as central to the region's troubles.[16] Once blacks in Rhodesia and South Africa received majority rule, and once Namibia obtained independence, groups like SWAPO, ZANU, and ZAPU would no longer have reason to seek communist support. The United States might even be able to draw Marxist Front Line nations like Angola and Mozambique toward the West.

Carter shared the sentiment in State. He too wanted any U.S. initiative to be part of a larger international effort. In January 1977, to bring America's Rhodesian policy in line with that of the United Nations, the president called for repeal of the Byrd Amendment. That same month, Young suggested that the members of the UN Security Council cooperate on resolving the Namibian problem; thus was created the Contact Group, made up of the United States, Canada, Britain, France, and West Germany. Headed by Young's deputy, Donald McHenry, the Group's purpose was to arrange a Namibian settlement acceptable to all sides. Then, in February, Carter sent Young on a multination African tour, where the UN ambassador not only received encouragement for the revocation of the Byrd Amendment but suggestions for the best way to resolve the conflict in Rhodesia. Young's trip served to encourage African officials of the administration's seriousness and to send a strong message to Pretoria and Salisbury that the White House wanted to see positive change in the southern part of the continent.[17] The following month, Congress, over Byrd's objections, repealed his amendment.

Around the same time as the Byrd Amendment's revocation, Britain's foreign secretary, David Owen, arrived in Washington, where he and Vance offered to sponsor a conference that would bring together all of the parties in conflict in Rhodesia and negotiate a settlement. But Vance wanted the United States to act as a junior partner in this endeavor. Brzezinski opposed that idea, favoring a "more independent" role. Neither Vance nor Carter, though, wanted Washington to assume responsibility for solving Rhodesia's problems.[18]

Finding a settlement acceptable to all sides was no easy task. Although a desire to throw Smith out of power united ZANU and ZAPU, each of them wanted to assume control when blacks gained majority rule. Following their meeting, Owen and Young established the Anglo-American consultative group, headed by John Graham of the Foreign Office and U.S. Ambassador to Zambia Stephen Low. In July Graham and Low presented a settlement proposal to the PF and Smith. Mugabe immediately rejected it, arguing that it left unclear whether ZANU or ZAPU's army would assume authority during the transition to black rule. Carter himself complicated matters in August when, to the anger of Low and America's Africa experts, he said he favored a proposal suggested to him by Tanzanian President Julius Nyerere and supported by the PF, which, following Smith's removal from power, would dismantle the Rhodesian leader's military and replace it with one run by the PF; in return, Nyerere would endorse the Anglo-American settlement and promise to try to get the other Front Line states to follow suit. Low knew that Smith would never accept a program that would require his dismissal and the destruction of his military. Yet both he and Graham realized that with Carter and one of the leaders of the Front Line states desirous to establish a new Rhodesian military, it was important to incorporate this suggestion into any settlement proposal.[19]

Following further discussion, the consultative group decided to make "only a vague reference" to the subject of Rhodesia's military. Owen and Young then traveled to Africa to explain the proposal's specifics to the Front Line states and South Africa. While the Front Line leaders liked the plan, Vorster did not. The South African head of state from the start had distrusted the Carter administration. He particularly did not appreciate its position on human rights. In May, a visiting Vice President Walter Mondale had insisted that the South African prime minister give all South Africans the right to vote (which, of course, would open the door to majority rule), grant Namibia its independence, and continue working with the United States to arrange a peace settlement in Rhodesia. While willing to help on Rhodesia, Vorster balked at the other demands. A comment by Young that the presence of Cuban troops in Angola was a stabilizing force engendered further reproach from Pretoria.[20]

The Carter administration found itself stuck, largely because it had again unsuccessfully sought to compartmentalize policy. For opponents of apartheid, the best way of forcing Pretoria's hand was to convince other countries to use economic sanctions, including divestment of business interests. Yet the Vorster government had shown no willingness to give in to such pressure; indeed, divestment might make South Africa all the less willing to cooperate on majority rule at home, Namibian independence, or Rhodesia. "We have economic sanctions under review," commented Thomas Thornton, an NSC specialist on South Asian and UN affairs, "but are somewhat inhibited in bringing pressure to bear while we are soliciting their help in solving Rhodesia and Namibia." Another problem was that the Vorster government could retaliate in ways harmful to U.S. interests. South Africa was the home of much of the noncommunist world's known reserves of vanadium, chrome, manganese, and gold; if Pretoria struck back at U.S. sanctions by curbing shipments of those materials to Washington—which in fact Minister of Mines Fanie Botha threatened to do if the White House did not back off—then the United States might find itself at the mercy of the Soviet Union, which had large supplies of those minerals. As Assistant Secretary of the Treasury C. Fred Bergsten commented, "[T]he U.S. is more vulnerable to South African economic sanctions than South Africa is to U.S. action."[21]

Consequently, the Carter administration decided to give priority to its Rhodesian and Namibian initiatives and deemphasize its concerns over South African violations of human rights; once its concerns in Rhodesia and Namibia were out of the way, the White House could return to the matter of tearing down apartheid. As early as March 1977, the president "rejected any immediate punitive measures against South Africa," preferring their use only if Pretoria "failed to make significant progress toward 'power sharing' with the black majority." Rather than urge divestment, administration officials, including Carter and Young, argued that the best way to bring about change in South Africa was to promote foreign *investment,* which would increase job opportunities for blacks and convince those businesses in South Africa to give their black workers more freedoms. That Young, who was so active in the U.S. civil rights movement, would support such a program appears bizarre. But he noted that banks in Georgia had proven vital to abolishing segregation in the 1960s; U.S. investment in South Africa, he maintained, would have a similar impact.[22]

If the Carter administration hoped that it could continue to expect Vorster's cooperation in Rhodesia, it was wrong. When Owen and Young arrived in Pretoria on August 29, Vorster told them that Smith would never accept the Anglo-American proposed settlement and refused to use his influence over his Rhodesian counterpart.[23]

Nonetheless, Owen on September 1 announced the Anglo-American peace proposal, which included transferring power from Smith to an interim, British-led government; a new constitution that provided for universal suffrage; "free and impartial elections"; and the establishment of a new army "based primarily on the liberation forces." Unfortunately, getting Smith to accept this program came into question, as a day earlier, the Rhodesian leader's party overwhelmingly won that country's parliamentary elections. Although Smith indicated his willingness to talk, it was clear that he felt his position was secure, making a resolution to the crisis in Rhodesia more doubtful. Furthermore, the White House knew that Smith had been holding negotiations with two black leaders in Rhodesia, Bishop Abel Muzorewa and Ndibaningi Sithole, hoping to convince them to join him in an internal settlement that would not include Nkomo or Mugabe.[24]

The same month as Owen's announcement, Vorster ordered a crackdown on black protesters. One of them, Stephen Biko, a black resistance leader, was beaten to death by South African police. Biko's murder prompted over four dozen African nations in October to call upon the UN Security Council to impose sanctions on South Africa, including banning foreign investment. Washington, still in need of Pretoria's cooperation on Rhodesia and Namibia, vetoed the sanctions. It did endorse a measure passed early the following month to impose an arms embargo on South Africa, the first time the international organization had voted to enact such a measure against one of its members. Yet the embargo was little more than symbolic, as most countries, including the United States, had already unilaterally cut weapons transfers to Pretoria. When the UN General Assembly voted overwhelmingly in December in favor of embargoing oil shipments to South Africa, the United States was one of ten nations to abstain. Carter also rejected congressional pressure to raise tariffs on imports of South African chrome. The failure of the administration to take a harder line with Pretoria did not please apartheid's critics in the United States, such as the Congressional Black Caucus and university students, who wanted stiffer sanctions imposed on South Africa.[25]

In February 1978, as the consultative group searched for a formula acceptable to all of the parties in Rhodesia, Smith announced that he had signed an agreement with Muzorewa and Sithole for an internal Rhodesian settlement that would guarantee black majority rule in the nation's parliament and a black prime minister but would leave whites in control of virtually all other governmental institutions, including the police and armed forces. The Salisbury Plan, as it became known, found opposition from Graham, Low, Vance, and Young, who regarded it as an attempt to retain white control in Rhodesia that both the PF and most nations outside of Rhodesia would reject. Low and Young further held that Smith's settlement could move the PF to turn even more to the Soviet Union for help. The plan, though, had its supporters. A number of members of the U.S. Congress, including Byrd, urged the White House to accept the settlement. Brzezinski also gave it his endorsement. The consultative group, he said, had failed and, through its failure, had done nothing to stop the spread of Soviet influence in Africa. The Salisbury Plan, though, would allow "moderate Africans [to] take over from Smith," thereby providing an opportunity to ward off communist designs on Rhodesia.[26]

Rather than choosing sides, Carter took a middle road: while stating that the settlement was "inadequate," he refused to condemn it; he also ordered Young to abstain on a resolution rejecting the Salisbury Plan. His stance pleased no one. Liberal lawmakers and African-Americans considered Carter's response an implicit endorsement of the internal settlement; conservatives argued that the president should have followed up by lifting the sanctions on Rhodesia; and Mugabe, Nkomo, and the Front Line states questioned whether the president was sincere in his support of a settlement that appealed to all parties in Rhodesia.[27]

Carter's refusal to endorse or reject the Salisbury Plan was not just a case of paper-clipping the policies of Vance and Brzezinski. Personally, he was not adverse to Smith's proposed settlement. A couple of months earlier, Vance had expressed his concern about the state of the talks on Namibia. It was vital to get all the parties involved to reach an agreement, he warned, "before South Africa implements irreversible steps leading to an 'internal settlement.'" Carter wrote back, "'Internal' solutions are better than nothing."[28]

As for Namibia, it looked like no solution was soon in coming. The administration realized that any agreement for Namibian independence had to please not just South Africa and SWAPO but also the Front Line states, which had good relations with SWAPO and could influence the Namibian guerrillas. In April 1978, the Contact Group proposed to the Security

Council a plan by which the UN would oversee the withdrawal of South African troops, followed by elections for a new, independent Namibian government in December. But in September, Vorster, who had decided to resign as prime minister and seek the nation's presidency, announced that he would not accept the proposal.[29]

By the middle of 1978, the administration's south African policy had turned into a mess. Finding it could not simultaneously attack South Africa for human rights violations and achieve forward movement on other matters, the White House compromised its human rights initiative and resisted calls for economic sanctions. Instead, it supported continued foreign investment while encouraging—but not insisting—Pretoria give black workers more rights. This policy failed to move the Vorster government to give way on apartheid or Namibian independence, or to pressure Smith. In Rhodesia, the president had called for a settlement that would bring about majority rule, yet refused to condemn the Salisbury Plan, despite the fact that it was clearly designed to keep whites in power. Consequently, he had angered not just members of Congress on both sides of the aisle, but opponents of white minority rule abroad.

South Korea

If Carter's unwillingness to reject Smith's internal settlement bothered Capitol Hill, his decision to withdraw U.S. forces from South Korea caused even greater consternation. Since the end of the Korean War, The United States had maintained a military presence on the Korean peninsula to protect South Korea from another North Korean attack. In 1969, however, President Nixon announced that the United States could no longer financially or politically afford to devote so much of its resources to containing communism and asked America's allies to assume more responsibility for their own defense. The next year, Vice President Spiro Agnew publicized an administration plan to withdraw all American soldiers from South Korea within five years. But continued tensions on the Korean peninsula convinced Nixon and later Ford not to proceed with that plan.[30]

Jimmy Carter revived discussion of a U.S. withdrawal, making it one of his proposals during the 1976 campaign. Not only was it expensive to maintain that force on the Korean peninsula, which in 1977 included 41,000 combat troops, but Carter disliked the repressive nature of the government of President Park Chung-hee.[31] Removing American forces from the peninsula would thus provide the additional benefit of distancing the White House from Park.

Shortly after his inauguration, the president announced his intention to proceed with the removal of U.S. troops. The reaction from both South Korea and Japan was sharp. Neither had received advance notice of

Carter's plan. Furthermore, to Seoul, the removal of American troops might invite another North Korean attack. To Tokyo, it could create regional instability and threaten Japan's security.[32] Japan, which in 1952 had signed a defense treaty with the United States, had reason to wonder whether Carter would abide by that commitment.

In an attempt to calm Japan's nerves, Vice President Mondale on February 1 traveled to Tokyo to meet with Prime Minister Takeo Fukuda. Repeating statements made by the president during the campaign, Mondale commented that the South Korean military, with the help of U.S. air support, could defend South Korea and pointed to the human rights situation in that nation. Fukuda addressed Japan's concerns about the state of affairs on the Korean peninsula and his own nation's security. He attempted but failed to convince Mondale to ask Carter to change his mind.[33]

South Korea was less obdurate, but it had no intention of giving Carter all he wanted. On February 14, the U.S. president wrote to Park, assuring him that the United States remained committed to South Korea's security and—despite his own policy on conventional arms transfers—that he would ask Congress for $275 million in military aid for Seoul so that it could purchase weapons to defend itself. He warned, though, that continued human rights abuses in South Korea could make it difficult to convince Congress to approve the assistance package. Park, who realized, however much he did not like it, that the United States intended to withdraw its military presence on the ground, requested that it take place in a way that would avoid giving the North the impression it could safely launch an attack. He refused, though, to give ground on human rights. The communist threat to South Korea, he wrote, necessitated that he take firm steps to protect his nation. "[T]he overwhelming majority of the Korean people realize that the reservation of some of their rights is unavoidable in order to ensure the security, stability and the very survival of the nation." None of those arrested had had their rights violated; all were being tried "by an independent judiciary in open and fair courts."[34]

But it was at home that Carter faced the strongest resistance. Behind the scenes, U.S. intelligence officials pointed to the North's military superiority over the South, while the Joint Chiefs of Staff (JCS) emphasized the importance of the American military presence as a deterrent to North Korean aggression and a buttress to Japanese security. Moreover, just as Fukuda had complained about the lack of consultation, so did members of Congress, among them fellow Democrats such as Senators John Glenn of Ohio, Gary Hart of Indiana, and Henry Jackson of Washington.[35]

The White House, however, was unbending. At a Policy Review Committee (PRC) meeting on April 21, the attendees, who included Vance, Brown, Brzezinski, and Central Intelligence Agency Director Stansfield Turner, commented that while the North held a military advantage over the South, Washington could continue deterring Pyongyang as long as it withdrew U.S. troops "slowly," provided "substantial assistance to the Republic of Korea in augmenting its firepower and overcoming other deficiencies in its defenses," and offered "air, naval, and logistic support for the foreseeable future." The issue was how fast to proceed. State wanted to remove all troops in three stages over a five-year period; the NSC supported withdrawing "two brigades by 1980" and then waiting to decide what to do about the third; Defense preferred the withdrawal of one brigade, to take place in 1978, holding off until 1982 to pull out the others; and the Arms Control and Disarmament Agency (ACDA), which was most strongly opposed to the withdrawal plan, wanted to remove only 700 troops, "with subsequent withdrawals contingent on reduction of tension."[36]

Despite this divergence of opinion, later that month Carter announced his determination to get all U.S. troops off the peninsula within five years. Brown, Brzezinski, and even Vance urged him to allow for some flexibility in the event of "unforeseen changes in the political/military situation, and to preserve diplomatic leverage vis-à-vis Pyongyang and/or Seoul." Carter rebuffed them. Any suggestion that the United States might not remove its ground forces, he maintained, could move Park to increase tensions on the peninsula to stop further withdrawals.[37]

To make Park understand that a U.S. departure was inevitable, the president sent Brown and Philip Habib to Seoul in May. The two emissaries explained that one brigade (6,000 troops) would be removed by the end of 1978, followed by a second (9,000 soldiers) in 1980. The last contingent would leave "within the four-five year period decided by [the] president." They added that the administration was considering a variety of "compensatory measures" to strengthen South Korea's military. The problem was that while Carter had no intention of linking human rights to any U.S. military aid to South Korea, Congress might, and therefore Park had to reduce his repression.[38]

In July, the U.S. government put the finishing touches on its compensation package. It included $275 million in new military aid from fiscal year 1978 through 1981, leaving behind an additional $800 million in military equipment, the continuance of joint military exercises, and the strengthening of the American air presence in the region. However, implementation of these measures had to occur before any withdrawals could take place. This meant that if Congress decided to balk on compensation, troop reductions would have to wait.[39]

In fact, it looked like that might just happen. In May, a top U.S. military officer, General John K. Singlaub, added his voice to those of lawmakers like Glenn and Jackson. He told the *Washington Post* that if enacted, the withdrawal program would open the door to a war on the peninsula. The president, stung by this criticism, had Singlaub relieved of command

and ordered him back to the States.[40] Still, that a high-ranking military official would make such a statement certainly gave Congress all the more reason for pause.

Compounding matters was the "Koreagate" scandal. At its center was the South Korean Central Intelligence Agency (KCIA), which, through the offices of a South Korean businessman, Park Tong-sun, sent bribes to U.S. lawmakers in the hopes of influencing American policy toward Seoul. In 1975, the Ford administration quietly began an investigation of Park's activities. The following year, the *Washington Post* broke the story. President Park promptly announced that he had no part in the affair, hoping that in so doing, he could protect himself and avoid any damage to U.S.–South Korean relations.[41]

Lawmakers had no intention of letting either Park off so easily and, in early 1977, commenced their own probe. Although the Carter administration, abiding by the president's campaign promise for open and honest government, turned over documents relevant to the investigation, the affair raised anew questions about Washington's relationship with the leadership in Seoul. That fact, combined with the need to get Capitol Hill to endorse the proposed compensation package, disturbed Brzezinski. He told Carter in July that there was clearly a lack of support among lawmakers for the withdrawal plan, and to get the compensation package approved, "the Administration will have to mount a very major effort involving the expenditure of significant political capital without any certainty that such an effort can succeed on the Hill." He concluded that congressional support for keeping the troops in Korea, along with Koreagate, "may warrant some adjustment of our withdrawal policy."[42]

That very possibility bothered the president, particularly after the Justice Department handed down thirty-six indictments against Park Tong-sun, including bribery and fraud. The problem was that he had already returned to South Korea. Both Carter and Attorney General Griffin Bell asked President Park to extradite his namesake to the United States, but the South Korean leader balked. Park's intransigence prompted both Senator Glenn and Representative Les Aspin (D-Wisconsin) to caution that they were prepared to link Park Tong-sun's return to the United States to the compensation package then under consideration. In Seoul, U.S. Ambassador Richard Sneider warned President Park that refusal to send Tong-sun to Washington would make it appear that he was hiding something, thereby complicating matters.[43]

The House of Representatives hinted at just how bad things could become when, in November, it killed several attempts to cut U.S. aid to Seoul but demanded that the Park government cooperate with the Koreagate probe. President Park realized the trouble that further stalling could cause. He consented to sending Tong-sun to the United States to testify in court in return for the businessman's immunity from prosecution. Assistant Attorney General Benjamin Civiletti considered this "a good agreement" but warned that everything hinged on the response of lawmakers.[44]

Congress had no desire to let South Korea off so easily. It demanded that Tong-sun testify before its Committee on Standards of Official Conduct. The speaker of the House, Tip O'Neill (D-Massachusetts), and Representative John Rhodes (R-Arizona) went a step further. They submitted a resolution that called for not just Tong-sun but also South Korea's former ambassador to the United States, Kim Dong-jo, to appear before them. Michel Oksenberg, an NSC expert on East Asia, informed Brzezinski that because of his close ties to President Park, the South Korean leader likely would not permit Kim to testify; the U.S. government would take a similar stance "if the tables were reversed." The problem was that if O'Neill persisted in his demand, the compensation package might die.[45]

As the White House fretted over whether it should attempt to get Kim to Capitol Hill, Park Tong-sun appeared in Seoul before members of the Committee on Standards of Official Conduct. Granted immunity, he admitted the KCIA had ordered him to try to influence U.S. officials and provided details on payments to members of Congress that totaled some $750,000 between 1970 and 1975. He also implicated Kim Dong-jo, thus adding to the desire of lawmakers that he too appear before them.[46]

Indeed, matters grew more disconcerting for the administration in the following weeks. During an interview on the television show *Meet the Press,* the special counsel to the Standards of Official Conduct committee, Leon Jaworski, insisted that Kim testify before Congress. "[W]e face a serious possibility of stalemate with Jaworski over access to Kim Dong-jo," Oksenberg's colleague, Michael Armacost, wrote to Brzezinski on February 10. "If Jaworski attempts to use the equipment transfer package as leverage to get his way, we may find our troop withdrawal policy unraveling." He felt that the best thing for the administration to do was to postpone for a year the first withdrawals of U.S. troops. The White House could still complete the removal of American forces within the proposed four-to-five-year time period. But by holding off the first withdrawals, lawmakers could focus their attention solely on Koreagate, thereby preventing them from linking the scandal to the withdrawal compensation package.[47]

With the equipment transfer legislation in trouble, Brzezinski advised the president to alter the withdrawal schedule somewhat. Rather than remove an entire brigade by the end of 1978, he suggested only one battalion (about 700 soldiers); the rest of the brigade would be removed within the following "six months in order to provide Congress additional time to act on the equipment transfer bill." Carter accepted the recommendation.[48] But he clearly had every intention of removing all American ground forces by 1982.

The president's decision, however, did not resolve the matter of Kim's testimony. On June 22, the House voted to withhold all U.S. economic aid to Seoul, totaling $56 million. While this had little impact upon the Park government, it was another indication of the growing frustration in Congress and a dangerous sign that continued stalemate over Koreagate could have an impact upon U.S. military aid to South Korea—in this case, the compensation package.[49]

The decision to withdraw from South Korea also created friction with the Japanese and not just because Tokyo opposed the U.S. plan. Having taken the position that America's allies had to do more to defend themselves, and now prepared to reduce its presence on the Korean peninsula, the United States wanted Japan to assume a larger regional role. This would require Tokyo to increase its own defense spending. At issue was how hard to press the Fukuda government. Brown favored pushing Tokyo hard, but both Armacost and U.S. Ambassador to Japan Mike Mansfield resisted. "Japan ranks ninth in the world in military expenditures," commented Mansfield, and also helped cover the cost of "upkeep of U.S. military forces in Japan." Fukuda, for his part, told Carter in March 1977 that "Japan is making its best effort . . . to strengthen qualitatively its military capabilities."[50] Yet by the middle of 1978, the two nations had not reached a settlement on Japan's military spending.

The Panama Canal Treaties

If the plan to withdraw U.S. troops from South Korea and discussions with Japan over its military appropriations were not going well, the same could not be said with regard to one of the administration's most significant achievements: the signing of two treaties that turned the Panama Canal over to Panama. In 1903, the United States had signed a treaty with the Panamanian government, giving it control over the canal and the adjacent land. Over time, though, Panamanians had come to regard U.S. possession of the waterway and the surrounding Canal Zone as an affront to their nation's sovereignty. Following serious riots in 1964, the two nations began talks designed to transfer the Canal Zone to Panama. These negotiations culminated in an eight-point statement of principles signed in 1974 by Secretary of State Kissinger and Panamanian Foreign Minister Juan Track, which called for turning the waterway over to Panama on a specific (though undetermined) date and giving Panama a greater share of the revenue generated from the canal than it had received in the past.

The Ford administration appointed Ellsworth Bunker, whose long experience in diplomacy had included negotiations with North Vietnamese officials during the Vietnam War, as head of the U.S. delegation that would attempt to put together a treaty. Bunker, however, found his flexibility limited by domestic U.S. politics. This became especially apparent during the 1976 race for the Republican nomination. Former California Governor Ronald Reagan, who proved a formidable challenger to Ford, denounced the incumbent president's willingness to turn the canal over to Panama. "When it comes to the canal," Reagan declared, "we bought it, we paid for it, it's ours."[51]

In the 1976 campaign, Carter said that while he would permit continued negotiations, he would not give up control of the canal. But after assuming office, he had a change of heart. First, the new president sought to give more emphasis to North-South issues and had himself a long-standing interest in Latin America. Furthermore, he believed that the United States historically had adopted a paternalistic attitude toward its southern neighbors, which bred resentment in the hemisphere toward Washington. Carter thought that returning the canal to Panama was not just morally right but—and despite his focus on the hemisphere when it came to human rights—would improve U.S.–Latin American relations. Additionally, if the United States did not soon turn the canal over to Panama, then Panamanians might do as Egypt had done in 1956 to the Suez Canal, which was to block it. Or they might damage it in one way or another. Finally, success on the issue would show Carter's ability and that of his administration to handle difficult issues, thereby providing a test run for another agreement that was also likely to generate debate, the Strategic Arms Limitations Treaty (SALT) between the United States and the Soviet Union. It was partly this last reason for turning the canal over to Panama that made the president want to reach an agreement on the waterway in 1977, before SALT came up for ratification. It was also because Carter concluded that his "political strength [would be] greatest" during his first year in office.[52]

Unlike with so many other issues, there was no discord between Vance and Brzezinski regarding the canal. "We saw the canal's strategic significance as having diminished while its potential as a source of conflict with the Panamanians had increased," wrote the NSC adviser. Vance could attest to this personally, having served as President Lyndon Johnson's representative to Panama, where he worked to defuse the 1964 canal crisis. From that moment, he realized that Panamanians considered U.S. control of "the canal and zone as an affront to their national dignity and sovereignty."[53]

Not surprisingly, Panama's leader, General Omar Torrijos, also wanted a treaty. It would bring an end to a festering irritant in U.S.–Panamanian relations. He also faced growing resistance to his leadership, caused primarily by worsening economic troubles. Getting control of the canal and, consequently, expanded revenue from the tolls paid by ships using it, could help him address those economic ills.[54]

Panama became the first Latin American subject considered by the White House during Carter's term. In late January, the PRC recommended that the administration inform Torrijos of its willingness to proceed with a new treaty.[55] Carter decided to retain Bunker as the chief negotiator but assigned Sol Linowitz, a long-time proponent of turning the canal over to Panama and another Trilateral Commission member, as co-negotiator. The plan, proposed by the U.S. delegation and accepted by their Panamanian counterparts, was to sign two treaties. One, a canal treaty, would establish the process of turning the waterway over to Panama at the end of 1999. The second, a neutrality treaty, would focus on keeping the canal both open and neutral once Panama assumed control over it.

The negotiations, which began in the middle of the following month, quickly ran into trouble when the White House, at the insistence of Defense Secretary Brown and the JCS, called for the right to maintain bases in Panama, which the United States could use to keep the canal open after 1999. Torrijos rejected what he regarded as essentially a blank check for Washington to intervene in Panama. For nearly three months, the talks remained deadlocked. Not until May did they make progress again, after the JCS decided that it did not need bases in Panama to protect the canal. As finally written, the neutrality treaty gave the United States the right to protect the waterway, but only against external threats; Panama would assume responsibility for defending it against internal dangers.[56]

The second treaty also proved problematic. The U.S. and Panamanian governments agreed to establish a Panama Canal Commission (PCC) made up of five Americans and four Panamanians, which would oversee the gradual turnover of the canal to Panama until Panama fully assumed control over it. Where the two countries were at loggerheads was on the issue of monetary compensation. In June, Panama's chief negotiator, Rómulo Escobar Bethancourt, demanded an indemnity of $1 billion to compensate Panama for U.S. use of the canal following the "unjust" 1903 treaty. In addition, Panama wanted $300 million annually and $50 million in military aid. Carter called this "a ridiculous request," and Linowitz made clear to his Panamanian counterparts that the Senate would never approve such an amount. Carter and U.S. Ambassador to Panama William Jorden convinced the Panamanians that Panama would do very well financially with the increased revenue from the canal. Panama thus received a $10 million annuity as well as $10 million, adjusted for inflation, provided to the members of the PCC to cover public services (such as police, firefighters, and trash collectors).[57] On September 7, at a ceremony attended by leaders from numerous Latin American nations, Carter and Torrijos signed the two agreements.

About three weeks later, the Senate began deliberations on the pacts. Not since the post–World War I Treaty of Versailles did the upper house engage in a debate as long as that over the canal treaties. Opponents were well organized and included over a dozen organizations, among them the American Conservative Union, Citizens for the Republic, Veterans of Foreign Wars, the American Legion, and the Young Republicans. Using a combination of direct-mail and telephone campaigns, along with protests that they knew would draw media attention, the treaties' adversaries charged that Torrijos was a communist sympathizer for having previously visited Cuba and a dictator who violated the human rights of his people, and that turning the canal over to Panama would endanger U.S. security and economic interests. U.S. public opinion strengthened the opposition. Some senators received as many as 4,000 letters opposed to the treaties. Polls found a majority of Americans determined to hold on to the canal. Supporters, who were much more poorly organized, denied all of these charges, adding that ratification of the agreements would improve U.S.–Latin American relations.[58]

The administration began an intense campaign to get the treaties ratified. The president received endorsements from the JCS, the National Council of Churches, and numerous corporations. He met with or called those senators who had yet to decide what position to take—sometimes contacting them more than once. Mondale, Brown, and the JCS did lobbying of their own, as did First Lady Rosalynn Carter, who contacted the wives of at least two senators known to oppose the agreements in the hopes that they could change their husbands' minds. Both administration officials and their allies gave speeches around the country. And maybe most important, the White House obtained the countenance of influential conservatives, including William Buckley, Kissinger, and Ford, thereby placing a damper on neoconservative opposition.[59]

In February 1978, a poll for the first time found more Americans (45%) in favor of ratification than opposed (42%). Still, this did not guarantee Senate approval. Lawmakers in the upper house questioned whether the neutrality treaty permitted the United States to protect the canal from a domestic Panamanian threat. Escobar said it did not, but Linowitz knew Americans would not stand for that interpretation. To overcome the lack of clarity in the neutrality treaty, in October 1977 the White House had invited Torrijos to Washington, where the Panamanian leader and Carter approved a "statement of understanding" that granted the United States authorization to defend the canal but not the right to intervene in Panama's internal affairs. This met the concerns of a number of senators, among them the influential minority leader, Howard Baker (R-Tennessee).[60] Together with Majority Leader Robert Byrd of West Virginia, Baker rounded up enough support to approve the neutrality treaty 68 to 32, a mere one vote more than required for ratification.

Attention now turned to the second treaty. Senator Dennis DeConcini, a conservative Democrat from Arizona, created a furor when he proposed an amendment that would give the United States the right to act unilaterally if the canal's operations were endangered. This motion threatened to undermine the statement of understanding, if not the entire treaty process, as Panama would never accept such a provision. Robert Byrd saw to it to recast DeConcini's amendment as simply a statement of reservation and warned his Arizona colleague, "I will not accept any changes." DeConcini, who was in his first term, knew it was not smart to cross paths with the influential West Virginian and backed down.[61] The second treaty then passed, by the same vote as the first.

Passage of the treaties represented a major success for Carter. He had convinced the American public to support ratification. Through intense lobbying, and with the vital assistance of Baker and Majority Leader Byrd, the Senate had given its endorsement. A festering problem in U.S.–Latin American relations had been resolved.

Yet there was a price to be paid for this success. That the treaties had passed by the slimmest of margins showed that a large number of Americans resisted transferring the waterway to Panama. Indeed, a number of senators who had voted for the treaties lost their seats in 1978, making others reluctant to adopt positions that could end their political careers as well. That fear helped explain in part Senate reluctance to approve SALT in 1979. For the time being, however, the White House could bask in its achievement. And more good news was to come, this time the Middle East.

The Camp David Accords

Ever since its creation after World War II, the nation of Israel had found itself at odds with its Arab neighbors. It had fought and won wars against them in 1948 and 1956. Then, in the 1967 Six-Day War, it defeated Egypt, Jordan, and Syria, capturing the Sinai Peninsula from Cairo; the West Bank and Jerusalem from Amman; and the Golan Heights from Damascus. The war also forced about 300,000 Palestinians to flee their homes, leaving over 700,000, most of them in the West Bank, without a homeland. Six years later, the Israeli military successfully fended off a combined Egyptian-Syrian assault. The United Nations reacted to the 1967 and 1973 conflicts with resolutions 242 and 338, respectively. The former called upon Israel to withdraw from the territory it had captured—though it did not say how far back the Israelis had to pull their forces—and for all the nations in the Six-Day War to respect each other's boundaries. The latter urged the implementation of Resolution 242 and requested that Israel and its Arab neighbors start negotiations that would bring about a lasting Middle East peace. A conference had begun that same year in Geneva to achieve a comprehensive regional settlement, but it had failed to get far.

During the 1976 campaign, Carter had taken a middle, if not contradictory, stance toward the Arab-Israeli conflict. He urged Israel to return most of the land it had captured in 1967 and proposed the establishment of a Palestinian state in the West Bank. But to please domestic Jewish opinion, he stated as well his support for Israel's desire to have "defensible borders," which observers assumed referred to Jerusalem's interest in keeping those same lands. Furthermore, he refused to recognize the Palestinian Liberation Organization (PLO), a body formed in 1964 that used acts of terrorism as part of a stated campaign to destroy Israel.[62]

As was the case with Panama, however, Carter shifted gears upon taking office. He now decided it was vital to reach an agreement to end the conflict in the Middle East. A devout Christian, he had a strong interest in the region. He believed that bringing an end to the crisis there could bring him political points at home. The Middle East was a vital supplier of oil, and continued instability in the region posed a threat to America's economic well-being. He also regarded finding a solution to the Palestinian refugees as in accordance with his own support for human rights.[63]

Carter's advisers further shaped his thinking. Vance's experience in the Cyprus and Vietnam negotiations encouraged the president's belief that the Palestinian issue required resolution. Brzezinski, like other trilateralists, held that a Middle East settlement could bring stability to a very important area of the globe. He and William Quandt, who was now the NSC's Middle East expert, had drafted a Brookings Institution report in 1975 that called for a comprehensive agreement, including Palestinian representation at any regional discussions and a Palestinian state. Other members of the administration, such as Vice President Mondale and domestic adviser Stuart Eizenstat, were less supportive of a policy that could anger Israel and American Jews, who represented one of the Democratic party's strongest constituencies. But Carter leaned toward his secretary of state and NSC adviser.[64]

If there was to be a comprehensive settlement, it had to be made fast. As with Panama, the president had the most political capital in his first year in office, which could easily decrease as his term wore on. Yet obtaining a settlement was easier said than done. Between March and June, Carter held talks with Israeli Prime Minister Yitzhak Rabin, Egyptian President Anwar Sadat, Prince Fahd of Saudi Arabia, Jordan's King Hussein, and Syrian President Hafiz al-Assad. Sadat indicated his desire for a return of the Sinai and for some form of Palestinian autonomy. He also asked the United States to get more actively involved in the peace process, maintaining that it was the only way to guarantee peace. The other Arab leaders wanted Israel to give on the occupied territories and the Palestinians.

Rabin, though, opposed any talks that might require PLO or other Palestinian representation, refused to fully withdraw the Israeli presence from the West Bank or Golan Heights, and rejected a Palestinian state on the West Bank.[65]

Israeli opinion grew more hard-line because of statements Carter made. During a March town meeting in Clinton, Massachusetts, the president expressed his interest in a Palestinian homeland. He also repeatedly commented that the Palestinian issue had to receive priority at the Geneva conference.[66] Rabin and his advisers concluded Carter was trying to impose his will upon them and feared that the president's comments could play into the hands of Menachem Begin, the head of the hard-line Likud Party.

Carter's utterances aroused resentment at home as well. The White House received one thousand letters per week from Jews and Israel's non-Jewish defenders, charging it with not supporting Israel enough. Further rankling American Jews was Carter's decision to bar the sale of two dozen Israeli Kfir fighters to Ecuador, which Ford had approved. Because the planes had U.S.-built engines, Carter had the right to block the transaction. His decision fit in with his effort to limit the transfer of conventional weaponry, which was all the more important in light of ongoing tensions between Ecuador and Peru. But to Latin Americans, it was one more example of Carter picking on them. To Israelis, it was one more instance of an anti-Israeli U.S. policy.[67]

Quandt commented years later that if Carter was to make headway in the Middle East peace process, he needed "an Israeli partner willing to accept the concept of 'territory for peace' with each of its neighbors." Such might have been possible had the Labor Party remained in power. "But Carter was not sufficiently political in his thinking to consider how his statements and actions might affect the Israeli domestic political scene." While the Rabin government was already facing problems because of charges of corruption among some of its members,[68] the U.S. president did not help.

Indeed, in May, the unwanted happened when the Likud Party won the parliamentary election and appointed Begin prime minister. Born in Poland in 1913, the new Israeli leader had lost most of his family in the Holocaust. In 1941, he traveled to British Palestine, where he acted as an interpreter. After his release from military duty, he became head of the Irgun, a militant Jewish organization that engaged in terrorist activities as part of an effort to drive Britain out of Palestine.

Relatively short, with a round head, a large nose, and, by the time of his election, a receding hairline, Begin had a sharp analytical mind and was a voracious reader who would look over every detail involved in the issue with which he was dealing. A strong supporter of the teachings of Vladimir Zee Jabotinsky, who had taught that Israel had the right to the lands it had controlled in ancient times, Begin intended to use his intellect and attention to detail to maintain control of Judea and Samaria, the terms he and his supporters used to refer to the West Bank.[69]

Two months after his election, Begin arrived in the United States. Despite expectations that the two leaders would end up quarreling, Carter found his counterpart to be intelligent and gracious. The president promised not to impose a settlement on Israel; Begin indicated his willingness not only to resume the Geneva talks but to permit discussion of all issues there. Yet this show of flexibility hid serious differences. Begin and Carter clashed over whether Resolutions 242 and 338 required Israel to withdraw from "all" the occupied territories—Carter said they did—or just "some"— as Begin maintained. Furthermore, the Israeli prime minister adamantly opposed discussions with the PLO or even a mixed Arab-Palestinian delegation at Geneva, and he would not give up the West Bank. Complicating matters even more was the PLO's demand for a "national homeland for the Palestinian people" as the price for its joining the peace process.[70]

The White House found itself in a bind. At the time, ratification of the Panama Canal treaties was still in doubt, the president's proposal for a comprehensive program to curb America's use of energy had less than resonating support, and the White House was being criticized for a scandal involving the head of the Office of Management and Budget, and a friend of the president's, Bert Lance.[71] The administration needed some kind of foreign policy success to offset these troubles.

Thus, in October, the White House did something that even Vance and Brzezinski admitted was a mistake. During the 1976 campaign, both the secretary of state and NSC adviser had asserted that any Mideast settlement required at least indirect Soviet support; otherwise, Moscow might attempt to undermine an agreement by riling radical Arab opinion. Moreover, the president himself believed that the Soviets and Americans saw eye-to-eye on resolving international problems. It was for these reasons that Vance first raised the idea in May 1977 with Foreign Minister Andrei Gromyko of a joint U.S.–Soviet statement that would call for a comprehensive Middle East peace settlement. A joint statement might serve the additional purpose of forcing Israel to make concessions to the Palestinians, thus increasing the chances of a comprehensive settlement. For the Soviets, a joint statement would further underscore America's acceptance of superpower parity and enhance Moscow's prestige.[72]

In October, the White House and Kremlin together issued a communiqué calling for a new Geneva Conference. It talked of "the legitimate rights of the Palestinian people," which the PLO had used to justify its fight against Israel, but said nothing about Resolution 242, which had recognized Israel's right to exist. As was the case with the Korean withdrawal plan, the administration at no point had run by Congress its plan for the communiqué to judge how lawmakers or wider domestic opinion might respond. While the PLO and much of Arab opinion supported it, a furious Begin accused the United States of trying to force Israel to accept a peace settlement, and American Jews and their allies demonstrated outside the White House. Some 150 lawmakers expressed their anger, among them senators from both sides of the aisle: Baker, Moynihan, Jackson, Robert Dole (R-Kansas), and Jacob Javits (R-New York). "This is a step in the wrong direction," commented Jackson, while Dole referred to it as an "abdication of Mideast leadership by President Carter." Realizing the anger the communiqué had generated in the United States, Israeli Foreign Minister Moshe Dayan threatened to turn to American public opinion if the administration did not rethink its strategy.[73]

Carter engaged in damage control, making clear that the United States supported Israel's security and that Israel had the right to secure borders. Simultaneously, he contacted Sadat, asking for the Egyptian president's help to revive the Geneva process. Sadat had all along been skeptical of the conference, judging that it would accomplish nothing. Since July, and with Washington's knowledge, he also had been holding secret talks with Begin,[74] during which he suggested that he and his Israeli counterpart meet. Begin liked the idea and invited Sadat to Jerusalem. Sadat immediately accepted, hoping that he might be able to break the stalemate in the current talks.

That the leader of one of Israel's enemies would come to visit became a major news story. Yet it reflected a man who was anything but an ideologue. Sadat shared Begin's receding hairline, but aside from that, the two leaders were quite different. Oval-faced, mustached, and a few inches taller than Begin, with a bright smile, Sadat was outgoing and gregarious, while the Israeli prime minister was introverted and aloof. Sadat did not share Begin's interest in detail; he preferred to leave the specifics up to his advisers. Whereas Begin tended to make decisions following discussions with his aides, Sadat had a history of acting without consulting those around him. Finally, the Egyptian president was more willing than the Israeli prime minister to compromise his philosophical beliefs if it would help him achieve his political goals.[75]

Although Sadat came to Israel to throngs of people, his junket incurred the wrath of Arab opinion. Saudi Prince Fahd, for example, was furious, insisting that the only way to settle the Palestinian problem was if Arabs stuck together. Even Sadat's own foreign minister, Ismail Fahmy, resigned in protest. Additionally, the visit did not move Begin much. The prime minister offered to withdraw Israel's presence from the Sinai Peninsula, but he refused to grant Palestinian autonomy in the West Bank and Gaza. King Hussein and the Saudis stated that they would not partake in any talks until Israel complied with the UN's demand that it leave the occupied territories. Syria also showed no willingness to budge. "The United States," Syrian Ambassador to the United States Sabah Kabbani told Brzezinski, "could not be both mediator and ally in Israel." Israel had to "give something" if Syria was to reconsider its stance. However, there was nothing, continued Kabbani, to show that Jerusalem was prepared to make the concessions Damascus wanted.[76]

Nor was the Kremlin happy. To Moscow, Sadat's trip to Jerusalem was part of a larger American plot to push the Soviet Union out of the Middle East. The United States, Soviet General Secretary Leonid Brezhnev charged, was in violation of the American-Soviet communiqué, which called for the superpowers to work together to reconvene the Geneva conference and achieve a comprehensive Mideast peace settlement. Carter denied that he had any intention of undermining the Geneva process, but the Soviets believed he was acting duplicitously.[77]

The Kremlin had what it saw as further evidence of American two-timing when Carter asked Begin and Sadat to come to Washington. To the U.S. president, direct American involvement offered the best chance of reaching a comprehensive settlement. Sadat arrived first, on February 3, departing five days later; Begin came the following month. When the Israeli leader arrived, Carter was prepared to fight. The U.S. president opposed an attack by the PLO on an Israeli bus earlier in the month that left three dozen people dead. But he declared that Israel's response, an invasion of southern Lebanon, from which the PLO conducted operations, went overboard. He also insisted that Jerusalem had to comply with the UN resolutions by withdrawing from all of the occupied territories. He proposed that after five years, the Palestinians could decide whether to join with Israel or Jordan or continue under an interim government. Begin balked at all of these suggestions. Carter, irate, refused to walk Begin to his waiting limousine when the talks ended and then told lawmakers that it was the Israeli prime minister who was preventing an agreement.[78]

The president then once again angered American Jews when he offered to sell 60 F-15 fighter jets to Saudi Arabia. This was part of a $4.8 billion deal that included the sale of 50 F-5Es to Egypt and, to please U.S. Jewish leaders, 15 F-15s and 75 F-16s to Israel. The purpose was to demonstrate American support for Israel while showing Egypt and other Arab states what moderation could bring them. Moreover, the administration regarded Saudi support as vital for U.S. Middle East policy and American foreign policy at large. As Vance put it, Saudi Arabia was "of immense importance in promoting a course of moderation in the Middle East . . . and more broadly, in world affairs, as in petroleum and financial policy." Jewish leaders protested the sale, asserting that it would endanger Israel by giving the Saudis advanced aircraft. Carter's trustee mentality kicked in again. Commented friend and adviser Peter Bourne, the president saw the

Jewish lobby, and indeed all lobbying groups, "as threatening to distract him from what he believed was the right thing for the country as a whole." To get the support of pro-Israeli senators, the administration offered another twenty F-15s for Israel and promised not to give the Saudis equipment that could increase the offensive capabilities of their aircraft, such as external fuel tanks. And to force the issue, the White House declared that this was a package deal that Congress would have to approve or reject in its entirety. After intense debate, the Senate killed a resolution that would have prevented the transaction, marking the most serious defeat ever for the Jewish lobby.[79]

Despite Israeli anger, Begin appeared to want an Egyptian-Israeli peace agreement, for it could help guarantee Israel's security. Both Sadat and Carter sought a settlement as well. Earlier Rosalynn Carter had suggested inviting the two Mideast leaders to the presidential retreat at Camp David, and the U.S. president now asked her what she thought of doing just that. "Are you willing to be the scapegoat?" she asked. "What else is new?" he replied. When he wondered out loud what might happen if he made no headway, she told him, "you can guarantee that you won't fail if you don't try anything. You can also guarantee that you won't succeed."[80] It was all the president needed to hear.

Camp David, a half-hour ride by helicopter from the White House, is a 143-acre facility surrounded by woods. Those who visit can stay in one of several nicely adorned cabins and enjoy hiking, biking, swimming, bowling, fishing, or watching movies. The president engaged in intense preparation for the upcoming summit, reading numerous briefing books about the members of the Israeli and Egyptian delegations and policy issues. The first lady got the talks off to a good start by recognizing the religious devotion of the three leaders and suggesting that they open the conference with a joint statement in which they would request the world pray for a successful meeting. Carter, Begin, and Sadat seconded the idea. All also understood that such a joint declaration would have significant political overtones.[81]

Interestingly, the discussions at Camp David created another dispute between Vance and Brzezinski. Quandt recalled that Brzezinski wanted to bug the cabins of the Egyptian and Israeli delegations. Vance disliked the idea, and the president sided with his secretary of state. "But I can tell you that the Egyptians and the Israelis thought we were doing it," commented Quandt, and throughout the negotiations "they had all of their private conversations outdoors."[82]

The talks themselves proved much more difficult than the initial sign of unity suggested. At their first meeting on Tuesday, September 5, Sadat presented an Egyptian plan that called for Israeli withdrawal from the occupied territories, the right of the Palestinians to return to their original homes, and Palestinian autonomy. Two days later, an uncompromising

Begin rejected the proposal. Nor would the prime minister accept Carter's suggestion that he suspend further construction of Israeli settlements in the West Bank and Gaza strip or for a Palestinian autonomous region tied to Jordan. He even refused to give up the Sinai settlements, which Egypt insisted upon. The discussions between the Israelis and Egyptians became so acerbic that they stopped meeting in the same room. Carter and his advisers were forced to act as intermediaries, meeting separately with the Egyptian and Israeli delegations.[83]

Of the two groups, Carter found the Egyptians easier to deal with. "I would draft a proposal I considered reasonable," he later wrote, "take it to Sadat for quick approval or slight modification, and then spend hours or days working on the same point with the Israeli delegation." With the latter, he sometimes had to turn to "a good dictionary and thesaurus" to determine the exact meaning of words, such as "self-rule," "refugee," and the like. "The Egyptians were never involved in these kinds of discussions with me. On any controversial issue, I never consulted Sadat's aides, but always went directly to their leader."[84]

On September 8, the president presented to Begin a U.S. proposal for a settlement, which included Israeli compliance with Resolution 242, "with minor adjustments." The U.S. document called for Palestinian self-determination as well. Begin turned it down, minus a provision that allowed Israeli forces to remain in the West Bank after the five-year transition to Palestinian autonomy. Carter was furious with the Israeli leader, telling his wife that Begin was a "psycho."[85]

The president now decided to separate Sinai from the West Bank–Gaza issue, with himself leading discussions on the former and Vance overseeing those on the latter. The Israelis, and particularly Begin, proved unwilling to give on either Israel's settlements in the Sinai or on Palestinian autonomy. Therefore, on Friday the 15th, Carter informed the two delegations that the conference would end Sunday with or without an agreement. Furthermore, he would report to Congress what happened at Camp David. It was obvious that he would blame the Israelis for any failure. Almost immediately afterward, Carter learned that Sadat had packed his bags and was preparing to leave. The president urged him to stay, declaring that the Egyptian president's departure would severely damage U.S.–Egyptian relations, lead Sadat to be charged for the conference's failure, politically harm the Carter administration, and kill Sadat's effort to bring about peace. As a carrot, Carter offered that the Egyptian president make any Egyptian-Israeli agreement dependent upon the approval of the Egyptian and Israeli legislatures. Sadat promised to remain. Not so with his foreign minister, Muhammad Kamil, who was irate when he learned of the suggestion of legislative approval. Sadat, Kamil wrote later, even proclaimed he would "sign anything proposed by President Carter without reading it." Believing his boss had gone too far, and furious at Sadat's consistent failure to consult him, Kamil offered his resignation, which the Egyptian leader promptly accepted.[86]

Meanwhile, Begin found himself under growing pressure to tear down the Sinai settlements. Not only did Dayan favor doing so, but so did Ariel Sharon, his minister of agriculture, and Defense Minister Ezer Weizman. The prime minister therefore announced on Saturday to a pleased Carter that he would allow Israel's parliament, the Knesset, to decide whether Israel would withdraw from the Sinai. He further accepted wording that made reference to the "legitimate rights of the Palestinian people" (though he opposed any language that might allude to an independent Palestinian state). He promised that Israel would not establish new settlements during the Palestinian autonomy talks. Finally, Sadat, Begin, and Carter decided simply to state their positions on Jerusalem without determining its status.[87]

The resulting accords, signed on September 17, called for Israel to withdraw from the Sinai, including all of its settlements and military bases, in return for Egyptian recognition of Israel and the establishment of normal Egyptian-Israeli relations. Furthermore, a committee made up of Egypt, Jordan, and Israel would oversee the transition of Palestinian autonomy over a five-year period. At the end of that transition period, Egypt, Israel, Jordan, and the Palestinians would determine the final status of the West Bank and Gaza.[88]

The Camp David Accords represented a major accomplishment for the Carter administration. The president had established a foundation for peace between two long-standing enemies, Egypt and Israel, and had opened the door to a Palestinian settlement. Although Carter himself did not say so, it is highly likely that he hoped that once Israel and Egypt proved they could get along, the door would be opened to a more comprehensive settlement in the future.[89]

The Egyptian and Israeli leaders, the U.S. public, and the American media all hailed what the president had achieved. The *New York Times's* Hedrick Smith called the accords "a spectacular success for the personal diplomacy of President Carter," while the *Wall Street Journal* commented that Carter had "broken the deadlock that has gripped Israeli-Egyptian negotiations since the collapse of President Sadat's dramatic November initiative." Members of Congress introduced resolutions in both houses proposing that Carter receive the Nobel Peace Prize. Approval of the president's job performance hit 51 percent, 13 points higher than a few months earlier.[90]

The problem, as some analysts pointed out at the time, was that the accords failed to resolve some key issues. They did not address Israel's settlements in the occupied territories. While the accords gave a "self-governing authority" the power to oversee "full autonomy" for the Palestinians, it left it up to the signatories to determine what powers that authority would have. While "free" elections were to be held to name that authority in the West Bank and Gaza, they would take place under Israel's occupation government; nothing in the accords provided for independent oversight of the elections. Lastly, the agreements declared that Jerusalem's status had to be determined by future talks. "The indications are certainly that the Arab reading and the Israeli reading of such lines are quite different," wrote the *New York Times*'s William E. Farrell. Not surprisingly, the Palestinians rejected the accords, as they provided them no guarantees of autonomy or their ability to return home.[91] In short, the president had made significant progress toward achieving peace between Israel and Egypt, but there remained serious, if not impossible, hurdles to overcome before a comprehensive settlement had any chance of fruition.

Additionally, the United States violated once again its conventional arms sale policy. As part of the Camp David Accords, Washington promised Egypt $1.5 billion in military aid, which Cairo used to buy three dozen F-4 fighter jets, hundreds of missiles, and numerous other weapons. Meanwhile, Carter offered Israel $3 billion in weaponry and help to build two airfields to replace those Israel would have to give up once it left the Sinai Peninsula. The president no doubt reasoned that this aid would give him leverage over Egypt and Israel and please the domestic Jewish lobby.[92] But as events soon demonstrated, it did not give him the influence for which he had hoped.

★   Carter could end the summer of 1978 with a sense of accomplishment. He had registered two major coups in his effort to promote peace abroad. Ratification of the Panama treaties resolved what had long been a serious problem in Washington's relationship with Latin America. Equally, if not more important, Carter had brought peace to two long-time enemies with the signing of the Camp David Accords.

Yet these successes could not hide some serious shortcomings in the administration's foreign policy. Camp David and the Panama Canal were only two of numerous initiatives aimed at resolving crises in Europe, Latin America, Africa, and the Middle East. To try to restore calm to those trouble spots while simultaneously promoting human rights, ratifying a SALT agreement, curbing conventional arms sales, demilitarizing the Indian Ocean, stopping nuclear testing, and ending the proliferation of nuclear technology was simply more than any administration could handle, particularly one led by a president who failed to prioritize initiatives, who believed it possible to compartmentalize them, and who did not provide a sense of mission for the nation. And this list did not include the president's numerous domestic initiatives, including welfare and tax reform, passage of a comprehensive energy program, a reduction in the inflation rate, and ratification of the Equal Rights Amendment for women. The White House ended up having to compromise its policy on arms sales in the effort to end the dispute over Cyprus and curtail its denunciation of South African apartheid to obtain Pretoria's help in Rhodesia and Namibia; and it found both its human rights and arms control policies directly affected as it tried to withdraw the U.S. military presence from South Korea and settle the Israeli-Egyptian conflict.

The president's foreign policy also continued to cause consternation at home. Vance and Brzezinski kept having their disagreements, most notably with regard to Rhodesia; the president's decision to paper-clip their opposing viewpoints in his response to the Salisbury Plan pleased no one. Carter's apparent—and privately admitted—favoritism for Egypt angered American Jews and Israel's lobby in Congress. Lawmakers still complained that Carter did not consult with them. It was true that the president had worked with Capitol Hill to get the Panama Canal treaties passed, thereby demonstrating what he could accomplish if he tried; that he failed to do so on many other occasions, particularly at a time when Congress was trying to make its influence felt in the aftermath of the Vietnam War and Watergate, was a serious error on his part. While Carter could not see into the future, ratification of the Panama Canal treaties would come back to haunt him later. Clearer at the time was that the Camp David Accords, while a significant achievement, left numerous issues unresolved. With so many of the administration's other initiatives by the middle of 1978 either dead in the water or floundering, it was all the more reason to doubt the likelihood of a successful foreign policy.

President Carter overseeing the swearing in of Andrew Young as U.S. ambassador to the United Nations. Young would become a controversial figure during the president's term in office. Courtesy Jimmy Carter Library.

National Security Adviser Zbigniew Brzezinski (on the left) conferring with Secretary of State Cyrus Vance. These two top foreign policy advisers waged a battle, which Brzezinski eventually won, to influence the direction of the Carter administration's foreign policy. Courtesy Jimmy Carter Library.

President and Mrs. Carter having their weekly lunch in the Oval Office. The first lady was one of the president's chief advisers and tended to take a harder line than he on diplomatic matters. Courtesy Jimmy Carter Library.

President Carter holding a briefing with his top advisers on U.S. China policy, August 1977. Counterclockwise from the left: National Security Adviser Zbigniew Brzezinski, Secretary of State Cyrus Vance, President Carter, Secretary of Defense Harold Brown, and Vice President Walter Mondale. Courtesy Jimmy Carter Library.

President Carter and Omar Torrijos (on the far right) sign the Panama Canal treaties with Organization of American States Secretary General Alejandro Orfila looking on, September 1977. The signing and ratification of those treaties was a major success for the Carter administration. Courtesy Jimmy Carter Library.

President Carter meeting with Muhammad Reza Pahlavi, the shah of Iran, in November 1977. The White House managed its Iran policy poorly. Courtesy Jimmy Carter Library.

President Carter meeting with Soviet Ambassador to the United States Anatoly Dobrynin and Secretary of State Cyrus Vance. Dobrynin later mused that both his government and the Carter administration handled their bilateral relationship poorly. Courtesy Jimmy Carter Library.

Senators Sam Nunn of Georgia (with glasses on) and Henry Jackson of Washington meeting with President Carter. Jackson and Nunn were two of the most vocal critics of the president's arms control initiatives. Courtesy Jimmy Carter Library.

President Carter meeting with National Security Adviser Zbigniew Brezinski (in foreground) and Director of Central Intelligence Stansfield Turner (holding closed folder). There is a debate about whether Brzezinski was responsible for Turner's lack of access to the Oval Office. Courtesy Jimmy Carter Library.

(above) Egyptian President Anwar Sadat (on the left), Carter, and Israeli Prime Minister Menachem Begin, with Secretary of State Cyrus Vance looking on, following the signing of the Camp David Accords between Egypt and Israel. The Camp David agreements marked one of the greatest successes of the Carter administration. Courtesy Jimmy Carter Library.

(opposite page/ top) Soviet Foreign Minister Andrei Gromyko and Secretary of State Cyrus Vance during discussions on the Strategic Arms Limitations Treaty, September 1978. Courtesy Jimmy Carter Library.

(opposite page/ bottom) From left to right: German Chancellor Helmut Schmidt, British Prime Minister James Callaghan, Carter, and French President Giscard d'Estaing during their summit at Guadeloupe in January 1979. Anglo-American relations during Carter's term in office were considerably better than U.S. ties with West Germany and France. Courtesy Jimmy Carter Library.

President Carter and Chinese Premier Deng Xiaoping signing the agreement normalizing Sino-American relations. Courtesy Jimmy Carter Library.

...*and* PROSPERITY

Four

★ "Damn it, enforce the existing law," complained one U.S. steel-worker. Commented Fred Darden, vice president of the Independent Radionic Workers of America, following news that Zenith corporation was laying off 5,600 employees and moving much of its operations to other countries, "We're trying to tell American workers that today it's Zenith, but tomorrow it could be your job." In October 1977 a group of angry laborers carried signs complaining that the president was not doing enough to help them. "Carter Doesn't Care Because Overseas Works for Peanuts," read one of their placards.[1]

Criticisms such as these reflected the precariousness of America's economic well-being at the time Jimmy Carter became president. High levels of unemployment and inflation, dependence on imported oil, and a burgeoning deficit all required attention. The White House believed that it could solve the nation's problems through fiscal conservatism, energy conservation, and closer cooperation with West Germany and Japan. By the middle of 1978, though, a solution to global economic weaknesses appeared far off. America's trading partners did not want to do all that Washington wanted them to, protectionist sentiment grew in the United States, and Carter found his ideas for restoring the nation's economic health at odds with a more liberal-minded Congress.

The country's economic well-being tied in with another matter, the law of the sea. Access to manganese nodules on the ocean bed pitted U.S. corporations against foreign governments, all of which saw an opportunity for making large sums of money. Consequently, the White House had to straddle a fence between its desire to please domestic constituents and the need to take into account the welfare and interests of the developing world, with which Carter wanted better relations.

The Locomotive Strategy

The United States that had emerged from World War II was a true economic powerhouse, unchallenged by any other nation. It had a strong dollar and an enormous industrial base, and countries ravaged by the war needed its products. The results were yearly trade surpluses and low rates of inflation and unemployment.

By the early 1970s, however, the country faced several interrelated challenges that had severely affected its economic well-being. The first was growing competition on the world market. For much of the postwar period, the United States had supplied the plurality of exports to the capitalist world. But as the economies of West Germany and Japan in particular recovered from World War II, U.S. businesses found that dominance curtailed. For instance, in 1955, 32 percent of all goods imported by the world's major capitalist countries came from the United States; by 1970, that number had been cut to 18 percent. The decline was even more telling when looking at specific items. Whereas the United States produced 42 percent of the world's iron ore in 1950, it had fallen to 10 percent in 1975. During those same years, American production of oil as a percentage of global production declined from 40 percent to a mere 14 percent.[2]

But those goods produced by the West Germans and Japanese traveled not just to capitalist countries other than the United States. They also went into the U.S. market. Japanese televisions provide a good example and one that would become a sore point in Washington's relations with Tokyo during the Carter years. Because of effective marketing, the number of Japanese TVs sold in the United States increased almost 150 percent between 1975 and 1976, reaching 2.5 million units, or 40 percent, of the U.S. market, in the latter of those years. The reduction in American exports and greater competition within the domestic market forced U.S. corporations, like Zenith, to curtail production and cut jobs. Unemployment went up, reaching nearly 8 percent in 1976.[3]

The decrease in American exports and growth in imports from West Germany and Japan played their part in causing a U.S. deficit. Throughout the twentieth century, the United States had had a trade surplus, but in 1971, it recorded its first shortfall. That deficit, though, was not just the result of imports from Asia and Europe. U.S. spending to pay for the war in Vietnam had outpaced revenue. Then there was the matter of oil. Americans' demand for fuel had meant greater dependence on imported petroleum. In the 1950s, American oil companies produced all the oil used by U.S. consumers. By 1960, however, the United States bought just over 15 percent of its petroleum from other countries; by 1976, that number had increased to 50 percent. Partly as a result, the deficit hit $5.9 billion in 1976.[4]

Tied to the deficit was inflation. Spending on the Vietnam War drove up prices, as did oil. Just how susceptible the United States was to petroleum-driven inflation was demonstrated during the embargo instituted by the Organization of Petroleum Exporting Countries (OPEC) in 1973. Ostensibly designed to punish the United States for its support of Israel, the year-long embargo was also aimed at America's Western allies. OPEC's action drove up oil prices 400 percent, to $8 a barrel. By 1976, the cost of petroleum had gone up even more, reaching $12 a barrel. It was the higher cost for petroleum that had the greatest impact upon inflation in the United States, which stood at 6 percent in 1976.[5]

A final matter was the declining value of the dollar. Concerned that the end of World War II could open the door to a depression similar to that which hit the world after World War I, over forty nations, at the behest of the United States, met at Bretton Woods, New Hampshire, in 1944. There they agreed to set up two organizations, the International Bank for Reconstruction and Development (which today is one of the institutions that make up the World Bank) and the International Monetary Fund (IMF), to provide funding for reconstruction in Europe and the Third World. As the United States provided at least half of the capital for both institutions, it had enormous influence in them. U.S. officials also convinced the attendees at Bretton Woods to tie the value of the dollar to gold, with all currencies convertible to dollars or gold. For Washington, this made sense, as it possessed about 75 percent of the globe's gold.

By the late 1960s, the Bretton Woods system had run into serious trouble. The increase of both the U.S. deficit and inflation drove down the value of the dollar. Jittery foreign and domestic holders of dollars therefore exchanged those dollars for gold, causing a run on America's gold reserves. In 1971, President Richard Nixon, determined to keep the country's reserves from being drained, uncoupled the dollar from gold. Now, the dollar would "float," with its value determined by the market.

Once it began to float, the dollar depreciated in value. This had the impact of making American goods more affordable and imports more expensive. Not surprisingly, the devaluation of the dollar did not please America's trading partners, including the West Germans and Japanese. But a cheaper dollar did not guarantee America's economic well-being. Because their products were now more expensive than similar items made in America, U.S. trading partners faced the possibility of having trouble selling their goods abroad. This, of course, could leave those countries with no choice but to curtail production, which would mean cutting the wages of their workers or laying them off outright. The fewer people with jobs, the fewer who could afford to purchase imports, such as those coming in from the United States, thereby hurting America's business sector.

Then there was oil. Petroleum was (and is) sold in dollars. A depreciated dollar meant cheaper oil. While that pleased Americans, who wanted to pay less for gas, it did not make OPEC happy. It was entirely possible that the oil cartel might respond by cutting petroleum production; the resulting increase in gas prices in the United States could have a deleterious impact upon the nation's economy.[6]

In sum, Carter came into office facing a number of domestic and international economic problems, including inflation, unemployment, a deficit, a devalued dollar, angry American trading partners, and the prospect of another oil shock. The administration's solution was what became known as the "locomotive strategy." Influenced by the Trilateral Commission, and developed at the Brookings Institution by American, Japanese, and European economists, this approach held that the world had become increasingly interdependent since World War II. As the United States, Japan, and West Germany dominated international trade, it was essential for them to expand their economies. In so doing, they would be able to import more goods from not just each other, but from other industrialized nations (such as France and Great Britain) and the developing world. Production in each of those nations would climb, reducing unemployment; inflation in each would decrease and the value of their currencies would increase; greater access to one another's markets would reduce national deficits; while oil prices would likely go up as the dollar appreciated, it would reduce the possibility of OPEC cutting production; and an increase in gas prices would force Americans to conserve energy if not look for alternative energy sources, thus making the United States less susceptible to future oil shocks.[7]

The locomotive strategy had widespread support in the West. The Organization for Economic Cooperation and Development, which represented two dozen European and North American nations, as well as Japan, gave it their endorsement. Members of the European Community (EC) did as well, particularly Great Britain, which faced high rates of both unemployment and inflation.[8]

Economic Stimulus and Energy Use

To implement the locomotive strategy, the Carter administration proposed a package of initiatives to stimulate the U.S. economy. It included $900 million in cuts in corporate taxes, a small increase in spending on public works programs to provide jobs, and a $50 rebate for all taxpayers. The White House opposed a larger tax cut or rebate, or greater appropriations for public works. A fiscal conservative, Carter believed such measures would increase inflation—the reduction of which he had made his number one economic concern—and unnecessarily increase the U.S. deficit, which experts concluded would hit $25 billion by the end of 1977.[9]

Simultaneously, the administration sent Vice President Walter Mondale to West Germany and Japan to convince them to take steps to spur their economic growth. Largely because of the 1973 OPEC oil embargo, Bonn's rate of growth had slowed from an average of 8 percent in the 1950s to a mere 2 percent after 1973. Even so, Mondale found West German Chancellor Helmut Schmidt reluctant to cooperate. Schmidt, who had a degree in economics and had served as finance minister under his predecessor, Willy Brandt, understood the White House's concern. But he strongly resisted any program that could spur inflation. That subject, inflation, was a sensitive one for the West German government. After World War I, the German economy had been the victim of skyrocketing prices, which devalued the Deutschemark to the point that in 1923 one dollar bought 4 billion marks. A loaf of bread alone in the early 1920s cost two million marks. Schmidt asserted that funding an expansive economic stimulus program would again drive up his country's inflation rate, which in the mid-1970s was running at about 4 percent. He also had serious doubts about the effectiveness of Carter's stimulus program, judging that it would likely increase American prices.[10]

The Japanese proved more amenable to the administration's proposals. Unlike Bonn, Tokyo historically had accepted the idea of using government programs to promote business. It was for this reason that Prime Minister Takeo Fukuda explained his preparedness to enact economic programs similar to that of the United States to achieve a 6.7 percent rate of economic growth for the following fiscal year. Mondale also raised the issue of Japan's export of both televisions and steel. Just as the American TV industry was facing difficulties by the time Carter took office, so was its steel industry. Japan had newer and more efficient steel plants, allowing it to produce just as much steel as the United States; moreover, Japanese steelworkers were more productive than their American counterparts, permitting Tokyo to sell steel in the United States at low cost. Mondale warned that failure to do something about Japan's television and steel exports would breed protectionism in the United States. Fukuda blamed the problem on Americans' desire for TVs at a time "of reduced inventories among U.S. color TV manufacturers. This had caused a sudden upsurge in Japanese exports." He promised, however, that Tokyo was attempting "to control this" and that he would look into the matter of steel exports.[11]

In the hopes of getting all three Western powers in line, in February Carter wrote to his West German and Japanese counterparts in support of a proposal made by a number of industrialized nations to have a meeting in London to discuss, among other things, economic issues. Both Schmidt and Fukuda agreed, though whether they would make any progress remained in question. For instance, in March, Carter himself raised with Fukuda the imbalance of trade between the United States and Japan, pointing specifically to televisions, and urged Tokyo voluntarily to take steps "to alleviate the problem." Again, the prime minister gave no indication of his inclination to do that. In the past Japan had registered trade deficits with the United States, he said, and "therefore . . . one should not attach too great importance to the figures in any one year." He was confident that Japanese television sales would decline during 1977, while his planned expansion of the Japanese economy would improve sales of American imports, thereby cutting down the U.S. deficit.[12]

Fukuda soon changed his mind on televisions. In September 1976, attributing Japan's aggressive marketing of TVs in the United States to the loss of American jobs, the Committee to Preserve American Color Television Sets (COMPACT), which represented U.S. television industry owners and workers, sent a petition to the International Trade Commission (ITC) requesting a curtailment of Japanese TV imports. A week before the Japanese prime minister held his talk with Carter, the ITC ruled in COMPACT's favor, suggesting that the United States gradually raise tariffs against Japanese TVs. Concerned that the U.S. president might end up doing just that, Tokyo announced in April their preparedness to restrict TV exports to America.[13]

With Tokyo willing to cooperate, the Carter administration asked Robert Strauss to undertake discussions with the Fukuda government. The former treasurer of the National Democratic Party, Strauss had developed a reputation even before Carter's election of being a successful troubleshooter. Through Strauss, Carter had come to know moneyed interests in the party; in return for his assistance during the campaign, the new president appointed Strauss to the post of special trade representative. Strauss proposed limiting television imports to 1.2 million units, 800,000 fewer than that favored by the Japanese. Both sides, though, understood that continued dispute over this subject threatened bilateral U.S.–Japanese relations. Consequently, they compromised in May, with Washington agreeing to 1.75 million TVs.[14] Yet this represented the resolution of only one issue among many affecting U.S.–Japanese economic relations.

One of those other issues that had a direct impact on the entire locomotive strategy was Carter's economic stimulus program. Liberals had already attacked the president's proposals for not doing enough to curb unemployment, which they saw as more important than reducing inflation. Then, in April, Carter decided to forego the $50 tax rebate, concluding that recent signs of an economic recovery made the refund unnecessary. Officials on Capitol Hill, who, albeit reluctantly, had supported the rebate, were taken aback. "It was a little less than fair to those of us who supported it against our better judgment and worked hard to get it passed," commented the chairman of the House Ways and Means Committee, Al Ullman.[15] The president's decision also raised questions in the minds of Schmidt and Fukuda as to how committed he was to economic stimuli.

Then there was America's use of energy. Carter determined that the nation was ready for a comprehensive program to conserve energy. During the winter of 1976–1977, numerous businesses and schools had had to close because of a lack of natural gas. Shortly after assuming office, Carter ordered his energy adviser, James Schlesinger, to put together a comprehensive program that would curb the use of fossil fuels while encouraging the development of alternative energy sources. Schlesinger and a small group of aides put together the program without giving lawmakers or even administration officials who would play a role in implementing the program, such as Treasury Secretary Michael Blumenthal or Council of Economic Advisers Chairman Charles Schultze, a chance to give it a detailed going-over before its presentation to the public in April.[16]

Without such vetting, it is not surprising that the program ran into trouble from almost the beginning. Its over 110 provisions included taxes on "gas-guzzling" cars, domestic oil production, and gasoline if Americans used an excessive amount of it; a crude oil equalization (COET) or wellhead tax that would increase the price of domestically produced petroleum to world levels; and federal regulation of natural gas shipped within a state. Included as well were a number of incentives, among them tax credits, to encourage energy conservation.[17] The program was sure to raise the hackles of numerous interest groups, including the automobile and oil industries, and their representatives in Congress.

Nuclear Nonproliferation

Energy also brought U.S. attention once again to the matter of nuclear nonproliferation. While in the cases of Pakistan and India the propagation of atomic technology was tied closely to the issue of arms control, for West Germany and Japan, it was more directly linked to their economic well-being. In 1975 Bonn had signed the largest commercial agreement in its history, the sale of a nuclear power plant to Brazil, worth some $5 billion. For a slowing German economy, the transaction meant much-needed revenue, if not jobs. For Brazil, which imported about 80 percent of its oil, the plant offered an alternative source of energy.[18]

Carter resisted the sale of the plant. Brazil had not signed the Nuclear Nonproliferation Treaty (NPT), and both he and members of Congress contended that Brasilia might use the German-supplied technology to build a nuclear weapon. Therefore, shortly after taking office, the president asked Schmidt to shelve the transaction and consider alternatives. An angry German leader replied that because the sale was for peaceful purposes, it did not violate the NPT. When Carter sent his wife to Latin America in 1977, one of her stops was Brazil, where she asked President Ernesto Geisel to forego the plant. Geisel spurned her request.[19]

The matter of nonproliferation caused even greater troubles for Japan. At the time Carter took office, Japan was in the process of constructing a nuclear reprocessing plant at Tokai Mura, located northeast of Tokyo. Japan, which relied heavily on imported oil and coal for energy, regarded this facility as a way to cut energy costs by offering an alternative source of power. Because the reprocessing of nuclear fuel produced weapons-grade plutonium, the Carter administration had Mondale express Washington's concerns during his February visit to Tokyo. Fukuda, while sympathetic, refused to budge. The Japanese, he said, understood the danger of nuclear weapons, having had atomic bombs dropped on Hiroshima and Nagasaki during World War II. Furthermore, Japan shared America's desire to prevent the proliferation of nuclear technology. Taking the same position as Schmidt, Fukuda argued that there was a difference between atomic information used for peaceful purposes and that used for making weapons. As Japan planned to use Tokai Mura strictly for power, the plant did not violate the NPT.[20]

Yet it was more than just U.S. pressure that perturbed the Japanese. Tokyo wanted to begin tests at Tokai Mura that summer before starting full-scale operations, but because Japan had no domestic source of uranium, it turned to the United States; as U.S. policy stated that Tokyo could not reprocess uranium without Washington's approval, the White House had the right to deny the fuel needed for the plant and prevent the facility from functioning. Additionally, the Fukuda government contended that the Carter administration had altered earlier U.S. policy. Ryukichi Imai, sent by the Japanese prime minister in March to discuss the Tokai Mura plant with administration officials, commented that Tokyo "had developed its nuclear program, including the Tokai facility, following U.S. guidance and stimulus." The shift in U.S. policy, Imai said, "will cause distrust and suspicion" within Japan toward the United States. Finally, there were political issues for Fukuda. The plant's cost, some $200 million, had embarrassed the prime minister's government, and Fukuda's Liberal Democratic Party had suffered a setback in elections held the previous December. There were other nations, like France, that already had reprocessing plants in operation, the prime minister explained to Carter shortly after Imai's visit. "[I]f those now in use were allowed to continue operation, and the United States were to tell Japan that it could not initiate the tests . . . scheduled to begin this summer," he warned, "this would create difficulties for the Japanese Government in the Diet and with the people."[21]

The United States now found itself, as Michael Armacost, the senior Asia specialist on the National Security Council, put it, "*in a genuine bind.*" He wrote his boss, Zbigniew Brzezinski, that giving the Japanese the go-ahead to start tests "would undercut our efforts to encourage the Europeans to follow suit." But if the White House stood firm in its current position without any give by nations such as West Germany, it "would confirm a suspicion held by some Japanese that we are not only prepared to tolerate discriminatory arrangements *between nuclear weapons states and non-weapons states, but among non-weapons countries (e.g. Germany and Japan) as well*" [emphasis in original].[22]

There were also political considerations within the United States. The president sought to apply his nonproliferation policy not only internationally, but domestically. In April 1977, over the objections of interested members of Congress, he had vetoed appropriations for reactors near the Clinch River in Tennessee and at Barnwell, in South Carolina, because they reprocessed fuel. To allow Tokai to start tests would increase pressure on the White House to allow those domestic facilities to do the same. If the administration refused, it would be accused of hypocrisy both abroad and at home and anger a Congress already unhappy with the administration's inconsistent application of its foreign policy, its determination to focus on curbing inflation rather than unemployment, and its general lack of consultation. But, Brzezinski warned Carter, "if we were pushed to open Barnwell, we could find our entire international plutonium policy unraveling."[23]

Carter had once again rushed into a decision without permitting time for consideration of the intricacies involved. To insist that other nations not sell nuclear technology or to restrict their own atomic power programs threatened to jeopardize U.S. relations with key allies (and in this case, two allies vital to the locomotive strategy), to arouse anew charges of inconsistently applying its policy of nuclear nonproliferation should the White House allow them to proceed with their atomic plans, and to create additional difficulties with a Congress frustrated with the Oval Office.

Disagreements with Japan and West Germany over trade and nuclear policy, combined with Schmidt's distaste for Carter's human rights initiative, moved many observers to believe that when the London Economic Summit convened in June, the attendees would have trouble getting along. There were tensions. British Prime Minister James Callaghan recalled the West German chancellor "coming to London in a smouldering mood, exacerbated by Carter's method in handling discussions," such as with regard to the Brazilian nuclear plant. As it turned out, though, things went rather well. Carter had vigorously prepared for the conference and impressed his colleagues with his knowledge of the issues and willingness to listen to his allies. For instance, he admitted that he had not been sensitive to West Germany's desire to see the Brazilian transaction through.[24] Later that year, Schmidt promised to suspend such arrangements in the future.

Still, the leaders at London accomplished little. Had the meeting taken place earlier in 1977, when West Germany and Japan were in the process of launching that year's economic programs, they and the United States might have set precise goals for economic growth. But with the year nearly halfway over, Bonn and Tokyo had no desire to do that. Rather, they simply repeated their hope of achieving their goals: a 5 percent growth for West Germany and the aforementioned 6.7 percent for Japan.[25]

Nor did Carter and Fukuda reach a final settlement on Tokai Mura, agreeing simply to continue bilateral discussions, which recommenced in the middle of June. By that time, it was obvious to administration officials that the dispute over the plant had become a serious matter. The Japanese government wanted to adhere to its plan of starting tests in the summer; failure to meet that deadline would hurt an already politically vulnerable Fukuda even more. The problem for the White House was finding a compromise that would allow for tests to begin at Tokai while permitting the Carter administration to hold to its nuclear nonproliferation pledge. Carter himself intervened, telling his ambassador to Japan, Mike Mansfield, to inform Fukuda, "I will personally expedite the compromise decision." He added, "Give me options without delay."[26]

By the end of July, the administration had put together three options. The first was to have Tokai use some U.S.-provided fuel to conduct experimental tests under International Atomic Energy Agency (IAEA) safeguards. The second called for the plant to begin reprocessing fuel as planned, during which Japan would agree to conduct coprocessing experiments. Through coprocessing, Tokai would not be able to separate plutonium, meaning that it could not produce weapons-grade nuclear material. That, however, would also require Japan to make modifications to the plant. The final option would prevent Tokai from starting operations until it had been modified so that it could "perform only experimental work on coprocessing." After considering the options, the president in August declared that he favored the second.[27]

Successes and Unanswered Questions

August and September brought the president several pieces of good news that had direct relevance to the locomotive strategy. First, through intense lobbying by the White House and help from Speaker Tip O'Neill (D-Massachusetts), the House of Representatives passed Carter's energy program minus, significantly, the standby gas tax. Then, in September Japan and the United States reached an agreement on Tokai Mura, by which Washington for two years would supply fuel to Japan; during this period, Tokyo would conduct research into coprocessing. In return, the Japanese pledged not to construct the facility it had planned to attach to Tokai that would permit for the conversion of plutonium.[28]

Nevertheless, the locomotive strategy was not out of the woods. U.S.–Japanese trade issues remained a sore point. Japanese steel exports played a part in the collapse of the U.S. steel industry in the summer and fall of 1977, during which fourteen mills closed their doors, others slowed production, and 20,000 workers lost their jobs. In September, United States Steel Corporation charged Japan with "dumping" steel on the U.S. market. Carter promised that to protect America's steel industry, he would, if necessary, raise tariffs. Not wanting to create new waves in U.S.–Japanese relations so soon after resolution of Tokai Mura, Fukuda quickly restricted steel exports. However, Tokyo still maintained a significant share of America's steel market, while U.S. companies found it difficult to gain more access to that of Japan. An administration projection that it would face a $27 billion deficit for 1977, $18 billion higher than in 1976, made the curtailment of imports and the expansion of exports all the more imperative.[29]

Worse, the president's energy program ran into serious trouble in the Senate. Democrat Russell Long, the powerful chairman of the Finance Committee, succeeded in killing the wellhead tax, charging that it would hurt his home state of Louisiana, the economy of which relied heavily on oil and gas. Furthermore, senators rejected federal regulation of natural gas, voting instead in favor of deregulation of natural gas prices. It was now up to a House–Senate conference committee to work through the differences between the bills they had passed, which proved painstakingly slow.[30]

Carter later admitted that "in retrospect it would have helped had I had more meetings with the members of the Senate."[31] Whether additional consultations with lawmakers would have made a difference in passing his energy program is not clear. But it was another of many examples of the president's failing to brief members of Congress, with the result of leaving lawmakers feeling bitter and the president frustrated.

The difficulty of getting the locomotive strategy on track moved the White House to enact new measures. To combat the depreciation of the dollar, the Federal Reserve Board (FRB) increased its holdings of German marks, thereby allowing it to purchase more dollars from abroad if necessary and keep the value of the U.S. currency up. Simultaneously, the FRB raised interest rates by 0.5 percent to reduce borrowing. These policies succeeded in stabilizing the dollar through the middle of 1978.[32]

Meanwhile, Washington intensified the pressure on Japan and West Germany. Because of both Tokyo's failure to meet its economic growth targets and the U.S. trade deficit, in late 1977 the president established an interagency group to develop suggestions for the Fukuda government. The goal was to push Japan into a "monthly current account deficit" by the end of the 1978 fiscal year and a "significant deficit" for 1979. This would require Japan to do such things as boost imports by abolishing quotas, lower tariffs, and establish "import financing volume targets"; reduce exports; give foreign banks greater access to the Japanese market; and increase growth targets for 1978.[33]

These suggestions created a stir among administration officials. Mansfield called the U.S. trade deficit with Tokyo "unacceptable." But in light of other difficulties, both past and present—such as the dispute over nuclear nonproliferation and Carter's proposal to remove U.S. troops from South Korea—it was important to make sure the White House did not put too much pressure on Tokyo. To do so could upset a relationship between two countries that had a lot of common interests, such as containing the spread of communism. Mansfield went on to say that the "Japanese, frustrating though they sometimes can be, are probably [the] most cooperative and supportive ally we have." Armacost agreed that the two nations' policies converged in many respects but felt that Mansfield "obscure[d] other important considerations," including Tokyo's failure to address its trade surplus. To Armacost, there was little chance that Fukuda would take action on that issue "without the determined application of strong external pressure." While that might cause problems in bilateral relations, those difficulties were "manageable."[34]

Indeed, "this is a good time to move forward," Armacost continued. "The trade statistics and balance of payments figures leaves [sic] Japan vulnerable to criticism from nearly everyone, and they hate to be isolated." Moreover, the White House "took their interests into account in resolving the Tokai issue, and Fukuda recognizes some obligation to reciprocate." Since the Japanese prime minister did not face elections in the near future, he could enact policies that he might otherwise be loathe to support. Brzezinski shared this assessment of taking a tough line, as did most of his administration colleagues. They thus developed a plan that called for Mansfield to "make a strong presentation to Fukuda," after which Strauss's office would "propose a package of short-term and medium-term measures to inject greater balance in Japan's trade with the U.S."[35]

In mid-November, an interagency group left for Tokyo and apparently had an impact. The following month, Fukuda announced a series of proposals to reduce Japan's trade surplus, including restricting tariffs on a variety of goods and increasing import quotas on others and seeking a 7 percent growth rate for 1978. This program met with approval in Washington. But, warned Mansfield, the United States should not demand more of the prime minister, lest it wanted to threaten "the basic relationship that is so important to both sides."[36]

Nor did Fukuda's promises bring an end to serious questions surrounding the entire locomotive strategy. Just prior to the London Summit, Congress had passed much of Carter's economic stimulus package—minus the tax rebate—which helped the United States achieve a 5.5 percent rate in economic growth, 0.3 percent below its stated goal. Japan and West Germany, though, failed to reach their targets: Bonn achieved only 2.6 percent in growth. Tokyo, for its part, fell over a full point short of its goal of 6.7 percent. These differences in economic growth played their part in a U.S. unemployment rate that stood around 7 percent and, combined with continually growing demand for imported oil—$47 billion in 1978 versus $28 billion in 1977—served to increase the deficit, which hit records of $26.7 billion in 1977 and $28.5 billion the following year. Added to these problems was a nagging inflation rate of about 6 percent, which fed a continued decline in the value of the dollar. Although Blumenthal and Schultze did not believe there was reason to panic, "[w]e would be in serious trouble . . . if there should occur a massive capital flight from the dollar and a sharp depreciation of its value in foreign exchange markets." That would "create major disturbances in money, capital and commodity markets that could threaten the stability of the domestic and international financial systems, detract from U.S. ability to exercise leadership in world affairs, exacerbate inflationary pressures in the United States by increasing import prices, increase protectionist pressures and lead OPEC to raise oil prices."[37]

In January 1978, Strauss traveled to Tokyo where, following two days of negotiations, he formalized an economic agreement with the Japanese. According to a joint communiqué, Japan would seek to meet the targets announced by Fukuda the previous month. Meanwhile, the United States would work to curb inflation, take actions of its own to improve its balance of payments, and institute an energy policy. Strauss was pleased with the outcome, especially with regard to Japan's preparedness to open its market to U.S. imports. Still, it was vital to make sure Tokyo upheld its end of the bargain.[38]

With the Japanese now on board, American attention turned to West Germany. In December 1977, Schmidt, concerned about the devaluation of the dollar, suggested holding the next international economic summit in Bonn in July. Carter liked the idea, and Henry Owen, an ally of Brzezinski's whom Carter named as an ambassador-at-large, saw an opportunity for advantage. "The chief leverage we have," he told Mondale in February 1978, "is to threaten implicitly not to hold a mid-July Summit in Bonn, as Schmidt plans, unless German growth improves." Owen himself drew such linkage in a discussion with Count Lambsdorff, Bonn's economic minister, explaining that Japan's "growth target is now 7 percent and U.S. growth projects for 1978 are fairly good," leaving "Germany [as] the main uncertainty." Blumenthal made that connection more explicit later that month when he told German officials that the United States would not go to Bonn unless the Schmidt government announced some kind of specific program for economic growth.[39]

Prime Minister Callaghan took the opportunity to act as middleman between Washington and Bonn. Born in 1912, Callaghan had served as an intelligence officer in the Royal Navy during World War II. A member of the Labour Party, he had worked as chancellor of the exchequer and then foreign secretary for Prime Minister Harold Wilson. When Wilson unexpectedly resigned in 1976, Labour chose Callaghan to succeed him.

Callaghan had not known Carter but sought early on to develop a close working relationship with the new president. Not only did Britain and the United States historically have close ties, but Callaghan believed that their common naval background, as well as a common religious background—Callaghan was also of Baptist upbringing—would set the foundation for a solid friendship. At the same time, the prime minister was close to Schmidt. Thus, he hoped to act as an intermediary between the new U.S. administration and America's continental European allies. For instance, shortly after the London summit, he had written to Carter, urging the U.S. president to "find common ground" with Schmidt on matters relating to both détente and nuclear nonproliferation. In a short response, Carter had promised to "do his best to alleviate Schmidt's concerns" (though ultimately the relationship between the U.S. president and West German chancellor never improved).[40]

Callaghan also worked to bring the West German and American governments together on economic matters and, acting as middleman, helped Bonn and Washington work out a package of measures acceptable to both sides. The United States promised to bring down inflation and to curb oil imports. Specifically mentioned as a way to reduce energy usage was the COET, despite Long's strong resistance to that measure. The president followed up by announcing in April that he would limit raises for federal workers and urged both industry and labor voluntarily to restrict increases in prices and wages. Additionally, he continued to press Congress to get his energy program (COET included) passed. Schmidt, for his part, set a goal of 3.5 percent growth for 1978 and promised to enact stimulus measures if it appeared it would not be attainable otherwise. However, the chancellor kept his part of the package quiet for fear that announcing it at the wrong time would generate a backlash from the Bundesback—Germany's central bank—and the German public at large, both of which worried that economic stimuli could generate inflation. A pleased Carter wrote his West German counterpart that "we are now on firm ground in fixing the date definitely for July 16."[41]

To the Bonn Summit

Although the Bonn Summit was now set, Vance, Blumental, Brzezinski, and Owen sent a warning to Carter that the meeting would fail if the big three economic powers did not meet their goals. For the United States, this meant curbing inflation and energy use. If Washington and Bonn "deliver, the others are likely to fall in line." They urged Carter to "[e]xpress confidence" that Congress would take action on his energy program, including the COET. Should lawmakers not pass the COET "by a certain date"—they suggested December 31, 1978—then Carter, after consulting congressional leaders, would act to increase the price of domestically produced oil "to the world level by 1980." They cautioned, "If we cannot promise action on energy and the Germans and others then hold back on growth, our balance of payments prospects will deteriorate and there is likely to be a resurgence of heavy pressure on the dollar." Furthermore, Germany would almost certainly raise tariffs to help its producers compete against U.S. imports.[42]

Schmidt shared this uncertainty about America's ability to stop the dollar's depreciation. It was for that reason that he proposed Europe's monetary integration. Members of the European Community conducted the majority of their trade with each other. Furthermore, they permitted freer trade than the United States did with foreign countries. Consequently, the nations that made up the EC were more susceptible to monetary fluctuations and currency depreciation than America. In 1977, European Commission President Roy Jenkins proposed the establishment of what became known as the European Monetary System (EMS), which would integrate the currencies of the EC. As a member of the EC whose nation had suffered economically from the dollar's depreciation, Schmidt took up the idea.[43]

In April 1978, Schmidt, in cooperation with French President Giscard d'Estaing, issued a proposal for integrating Europe's currencies. Just before Bonn, the EMS received the backing of the European Council. Furthermore, Schmidt made U.S. acceptance of the EMS a prerequisite for stimulating his economy. This the United States agreed to. "We will be happy to cooperate with the European Community in studying aspects of the proposed arrangements," a briefing paper for the Bonn Summit noted.[44]

A month before Bonn, Carter held a meeting with congressional leaders on his energy program. It was not for consultation but notification. If Capitol Hill did not pass his energy program, he warned, he would levy a fee of $5 to $6 per barrel of oil to force Americans to conserve fuel. An angry Senator Robert Dole (R-Kansas) submitted an amendment that would prohibit Carter from imposing any such increase. The president thus turned to Senate Majority Leader Robert Byrd (D-West Virginia), asking him to go to Europe and reassure America's allies that Washington would take positive steps on energy. Byrd returned a few days before the Bonn Summit believing he had met European concerns, even going so far as to tell Schmidt and other European officials "that an energy bill would be on [Carter's] desk before [Congress's] adjournment."[45] As it turned out, the upper house failed to take any action prior to the president's departure.

Carter thus went to Bonn without an energy package. Even so, he promised to allow the price of U.S. oil to rise to world levels by the end of 1980. Prior to the summit, Tokyo unveiled a program to import $1 billion in goods to reduce its trade surplus. Schmidt, meanwhile, waited until the summit's second day before publicly announcing his stimulus package. The timing was perfect. By the middle of 1978, union workers, who supported the chancellor's Social Democratic Party, as well as leftists within the party wanted to see economic expansion. There was little concern that such a program would cause inflation, as the dollar's depreciation had allowed the mark to gain value. Moreover, West Germany had a high unemployment rate, and an economic stimulus program could create jobs. Consequently, Schmidt's announcement received widespread approbation. Italy, France, and Great Britain promised their own stimulus programs.[46]

The Bonn Summit was in one respect a success. It "was the first and only time" during Carter's term "that participants managed to agree on a coordinated package of measures." Still, much remained unresolved. The attendees took no action on the dollar or protectionism, Carter's energy program had yet to pass, and inflation continued to trouble the United States. And the attendees only agreed to consider the EMS rather than endorse it. (Ultimately, the EMS provided a foundation for the development of the currency used today throughout much of Europe, the Euro.)[47]

The Problem of Mexico

Carter did not ignore nations outside those involved in the locomotive strategy. Among the most important was Mexico because of its extensive commercial ties to the United States and its oil reserves. Relations between the two countries had deteriorated, both because of a feeling by the Mexican government that Washington had ignored it and because of the large number of Mexican immigrants entering the United States illegally. Desirous to shift the focus of America's diplomacy to North-South relations and to improve U.S.–Mexican ties, Carter invited as his first state visitor the Mexican president, José López Portillo, who came to the White House in February 1977.

Yet relations between the two countries never became as close as Carter wanted. Immigration proved one sticking point. The president's labor secretary, Ray Marshall, and unions such as the AFL-CIO sought to restrict immigration, particularly Mexican immigration, in an attempt to open more jobs for Americans and reduce the unemployment rate, which in 1977 was more than 7 percent. Agricultural firms in the Southwest fought back, asserting that there was a lack of domestic workers willing to work for them. Carter split the middle. In August 1977, he proposed granting amnesty to those aliens who had been in the United States for at least seven years while simultaneously strengthening enforcement of immigration laws and adding more border officers. His suggestion created a storm of controversy. Opponents in Congress charged the president with legalizing illegal activity and encouraging immigration, while his aides became concerned that tightening immigration laws would upset Hispanic-American voters. By the time Carter left office, the subject of illegal immigration had not been resolved.[48]

But what hurt bilateral relations the most was energy. Following the discovery of new oil reserves in Mexico, López Portillo proposed building a gas pipeline to the United States and entered into negotiations to sell the gas to several U.S. gas companies. The White House warned the Mexican government that the price at which it wanted to sell the gas to the American firms was too high and that it first had to finalize any agreement with the administration before proceeding with the negotiations with those companies. For reasons that are unclear—speculation ranges from López Portillo's not understanding the issue to gas companies assuring him that the U.S. government would accept any contract between them and Mexico—the Mexican president did not listen. In August 1977, his government signed a deal with the American firms. López Portillo never forgave Carter when the president refused to approve the contract. It would require months of further negotiations before the two countries finally reached a settlement on energy.[49]

The Law of the Sea

As the Carter administration attempted to find some kind of formula acceptable to it and Mexico, it devoted attention to another international economic matter: the law of the sea (LOS). Of particular concern to the White House was deep seabed mining. What had brought this topic to the forefront of world interest was manganese nodules, which contained nickel, copper, magnesium, and cobalt, and which scientists since the 1870s had known existed on the ocean floor. When the nodules were first discovered, the technology did not exist to access them. But this changed as the twentieth century progressed. In 1965, John Mero, a mining engineer, published *The Mineral Resources of the Sea,* in which he pointed out not only that the technology was available to mine underwater minerals and ores, but that it would be relatively cheap to do so. Numerous companies in developed countries like the United States, Great Britain, and Japan, which had the requisite know-how, saw the opportunity for enormous profits.[50]

In 1967, Malta brought the matter before the United Nations. Its ambassador, Arvid Pardo, warned that without some kind of international law regulating access to the nodules, "a competitive scramble for sovereign rights over the land underlying the world's seas and oceans [would begin], surpassing in magnitude and in its implication last century's colonial scramble for territory in Asia and Africa." Tensions would build, not only between those nations that were more developed and had the mining technology and those that did not, but among the developed countries themselves, which could cause "at the very least a dramatic escalation of the arms race," if not war.[51]

Complicating matters were declarations by a large number of developing nations extending their jurisdictional claims beyond coastal waters. Some asserted sovereignty over water twelve miles from their shores, others as far as two hundred miles. By 1973, when the United Nations began its third Conference on the Law of the Sea (UNCLOS III), "some 4,500,000 square nautical miles of ocean had been subjected to unilateral claims, five times the area so claimed in 1945."[52] Even if the UN accepted the two-hundred-mile jurisdiction, it would still leave unclear who controlled or had the right to regulate the seas beyond two hundred miles.

The first two UNCLOS meetings, held in 1958 and 1960, had failed to make significant progress.[53] About 148 countries, along with officials from the UN and various organizations, attended UNCLOS III. Its first five sessions, the last of which concluded in September 1976, had made little headway on any of the outstanding issues. Thus, when the sixth session opened in 1977, the question was whether Carter could achieve success where previous attempts had failed.

The new president sought to improve North-South relations, and for that reason he wanted to take into account the desire of developing nations to have some right of access to the nodules. At the same time, he could not ignore the longing of U.S. companies to have some guarantee of mining rights on the deep seabed. To try to find a solution acceptable to all sides, a week after the inauguration the president called for the establishment of the Interagency Group for Law of the Sea to determine the U.S. negotiating position at UNCLOS. Its chair was Elliot Richardson, a liberal Republican who had experience in law of the sea issues.[54]

Carter's appointment of Richardson again caused friction with Congress. Lawmakers like to have people appointed from their states or at least to have the president consult with them on such appointments. Senator John Glenn (D-Ohio) angrily commented that those persons Carter selected from Ohio "were not active Democrats and that he found out about the appointments only from the press." The Richardson appointment caused similar consternation. Richardson was from Massachusetts, the home state of House Speaker O'Neill, yet the president failed to inform O'Neill of his choice for the law of the sea post in advance.[55]

The president instructed Richardson to seek a settlement that would protect American interests, including assuring miners access to deep seabed minerals. Although he gave the U.S. delegation leeway in reaching such an agreement, actually achieving it would not prove easy. Of the issues considered by UNCLOS, the most important was deep-sea mining. In 1964, a group of 77 developing nations (which by 1980 numbered over

100) joined together into what became known as the Group of 77 (G-77). It sought to redress what its members charged was the dependence of the developing world upon the globe's industrialized nations, which gave the latter economic advantages over the former. That concern prompted the G-77 to support the 1973 OPEC oil embargo, which its members felt could open the door to a new, more equitable economic order. That same concern made its members reluctant to give up their extensive oceanic claims, for they could include vast resources of mineral ores. The Group was prepared to compromise, but only insofar as permitting the establishment of an international "authority" that could regulate access to the deep seabed, thereby providing a more level playing field for all nations. Moreover, that authority could decide which nations and private groups or persons could join it.[56]

While the United States accepted in principle the idea of such an authority, it disagreed with the G-77 over how it would function. Further complicating matters were U.S. mining companies and members of Congress who had little patience to wait for UNCLOS to achieve a settlement that might never take place and little willingness to accept an agreement, if reached, that might not be beneficial to their interests. (Said Northcutt Ely, a representative for U.S. Steel Corporation, to Richardson prior to the latter's departure for the 1977 UNCLOS session, "I hope you fail.") Therefore, Capitol Hill pressured the White House to declare its position should lawmakers seek to pass a bill giving U.S. mining firms guaranteed access to the seabed. Carter, upon Brzezinski's recommendation, decided that the White House "should *not support any* legislation at this time because of the disruption this would cause in the LOS negotiations" [emphasis in original]. However, administration officials would publicly comment on the proposed measure, for "it will indicate to other countries that the U.S. is prepared to unilaterally move ahead with deep-seabed mining if agreement is not reached on a treaty." That, in turn, would "give us some leverage over the progress of the negotiations." Indeed, the White House warned that it would not stop lawmakers' effort to get the legislation passed.[57]

Richardson had some uneasiness with this proposed strategy. By the middle of June, a bill on deep-seabed mining was about to be submitted to the full House of Representatives for discussion. The question, Richardson wrote his deputy, George Aldrich, was whether the mining industry would see that legislation as so beneficial that it would pressure the Senate to reject any UNCLOS treaty on deep-sea mining, even if that treaty was in line with the law passed by Congress. In such an event, "the U.S. would be seriously embarrassed. Negative consequences vis-à-vis both G-77 countries and European allies with commercial seabed interests of their own, would follow." Aldrich shared Richardson's trepidation. But in his mind, he and his superior had to support the legislation for several reasons. The first was leverage. Passage of a seabed mining bill would show the developing world America's intention to "exploit the minerals from the seabed." Failure to back such legislation would reduce "the necessary negotiating leverage to produce a satisfactory treaty." Furthermore, in the future the United States would have to have access to the manganese nodules. Finally, to support the bill would give the companies developing deep mining technology a feeling that their efforts were worth it. "If I am correct in that analysis, then we have no choice but to run the risk of American commercial opposition to a successful treaty, if and when we are able to obtain one."[58]

If the Carter administration believed public statements regarding the pending legislation would give it leverage, there was no indication it had an impact. Whereas developed nations such as the United States argued that all countries, as well as licensed private companies, had the right to mine the seabed, the Group of 77 held firm to placing the exploitation of manganese nodules in the hands of an international authority. While the U.S. government did not outright reject the establishment of such a multinational body, it wanted that organization to work under specific conditions. Still, this was not nearly as much progress as Richardson had desired. When the sixth session came to an end in July, he called much of its work "[s]everally and collectively unacceptable."[59]

★   On virtually every aspect of his proposals to strengthen the American and international economies, President Carter by the middle of 1978 found himself in trouble. In certain respects, his difficulties were beyond his control. While Carter had achieved some level of compromise with West Germany and Japan on economic stimuli packages and nuclear nonproliferation, he could not force those countries, essential to the success of the locomotive strategy, to do all that he wished them to do. He also could not make the G-77 give as much as the United States favored on matters respecting the law of the sea.

But the president was partly responsible for the conundrum in which he found himself. His unwillingness to consult with Congress, and even with interested members of his own administration, prior to submission of his energy program jeopardized its passage. His determination to give priority to combating inflation rather than unemployment did not please liberal members of his party; he made matters worse when he rescinded his proposed tax rebate after lawmakers had spent a substantial amount of political capital to support it. He had once again failed to take into account all of the ins and outs of his nuclear nonproliferation initiative. While he did successfully reach accords with West Germany on the sale of atomic technology and with Japan on Tokai Mura, it was at the cost of once again opening himself up to charges of inconsistency. If the president continued to implement policy without consulting with Congress or taking into account the complexities involved in policy making, then his plans to shore up both the national and international economies surely would fail.

HARDENING

Five

★   In a major foreign policy speech he gave at Wake Forest University in March 1978, President Jimmy Carter warned about the "ominous inclination on the part of the Soviet Union to use its military power" abroad, giving special notice to the Kremlin's activities "in Africa." In light of the Soviets' military buildup, the United States and its allies had to respond in kind. "We will not allow any other nation to gain military superiority over us." And, while desirous to cooperate with the Kremlin on such issues as arms control, he warned that if Moscow "fail[ed] to demonstrate restraint in missile programs and other force levels or in the projection of Soviet proxy forces into other lands and continents," cooperation would become impossible.[1]

Carter's comments at Wake Forest were significant. First, they represented the beginning of a revival of Cold War anti-Sovietism and a rejection of new internationalism. The president had shared Secretary of State Cyrus Vance's conviction that Moscow saw eye-to-eye with America's desire to collaborate on reducing international tensions. His language now began to sound more like that of Zbigniew Brzezinski, the head of the National Security Council (NSC), who had long contended that U.S.–Soviet relations were marked by competition, not cooperation.

This revolt against new internationalism was not limited to the executive branch. By the end of 1978, 40 percent of Americans felt the Soviet Union was stronger than the United States, versus 14 percent who believed otherwise. This compared with 31 and 18 percent, respectively, in June of that year and 27 and 21 percent, respectively, in December 1976. Patrick Caddell, the administration's pollster, wrote in May 1978, "Since foreign policy/defense concerns have been secondary matters in recent years, nothing in our structured quantitative research prepared us for the below surface anxiety and concern over these issues that the open end interviews revealed." He advised the president that "the public was moving in a more conservative direction."[2]

This changed attitude made itself felt in the midterm election. Democrats had succeeded in maintaining control of both houses of Congress, but those lawmakers supportive of downplaying the centrality of U.S.–Soviet relations and giving more attention to human rights or North-South ties found themselves under assault. Of the twenty senators who had signed the Panama Canal treaties and who were up for reelection in 1978, thirteen either did not run or were defeated. Republicans failed to renominate Clifford Case (R-New Jersey), a seventeen-term member of the House, who had been a leading proponent of new internationalism; a moderate member of the GOP, Massachusetts's Edward Brooke, lost his bid for another term. Among Democrats, those who failed to win reelection included Representatives Helen Meyner of New Jersey, California's Yvonne Burke, and Pennsylvania's Joshua Eilberg, and Senators William Hathaway of Maine, Richard Clark of Iowa, and Colorado's Floyd Haskell. But maybe the most important lawmaker who went down in defeat was Robert Fraser (D-Minnesota), a key figure in making human rights a central component of U.S. foreign policy in the early and mid-1970s. Meanwhile, conservative Republicans, among them Senators Jesse Helms of North Carolina, Idaho's James McClure, and South Carolina's Strom Thurmond, held onto their seats. Joining their ranks were such freshmen as Alan Simpson of Wyoming and New Hampshire's Gordon Humphrey.[3]

Second, the gradual revival of anti-Sovietism had an impact on U.S. policy not just in Africa but elsewhere. The White House normalized relations with China and rejected normalization with Vietnam and Cuba. Simultaneously, the president adopted a tougher line with the Kremlin at the conventional arms transfer talks, with the end result that those discussions broke down.

Finally, that Carter would talk about both cooperation and competition demonstrated a problem that had created and would continue to pose problems for his administration at home and abroad: the paper-clipping of policy. Carter had begun to use the language of Brzezinski in reference to U.S.–Soviet relations, but he continued to incorporate that of Vance. Consequently, observers were confused about whether the shift toward anti-Sovietism was only temporary or something more permanent.

Africa and the Growth of Brzezinski's Influence

From very early on, Brzezinski had sought to convince the president to assume a harder line toward the Soviet Union than the chief executive had favored. The NSC adviser wanted to link arms control talks with the Soviets to Moscow's activities in other parts of the world and to use improved relations with China as a lever against the Soviet Union. Vance, who opposed linkage and feared normalization with China could disrupt the Strategic Arms Limitations Treaty (SALT) discussions, had succeeded in convincing the president not to move in Brzezinski's direction.

Matters in Africa changed Carter's mind. Of particular concern was the Horn of Africa. Sticking out several hundred miles into the Arabian Sea, today it consists of the nations of Somalia, Ethiopia, Eritrea, and Sudan. An arid, desolate, and impoverished part of the world, the Horn is strategically located on the edge of the oil-rich Middle East and along the shipping route through the Suez Canal and the Red Sea.

It was its location that made the Horn of interest not just to the United States but the Soviet Union. It appears as well that the anticolonial movement that had swept through Africa after World War II drew Moscow's attention to the Horn. Europeans who had once controlled much of the African continent had been giving their colonies freedom. In some cases, such as Angola, Mozambique, Kenya, and Algeria, this transition involved varying levels of violence; in others, including Somalia and Tanzania, it took place more peacefully. The Kremlin calculated that the removal of colonial rule would open these newly independent countries up to communism.[4]

Thus, when an opportunity to spread their influence into the Horn presented itself in Somalia, the Soviets could not resist. There, the commander of the Somali army, General Muhammad Siad Barre, overthrew in 1969 the government of Prime Minister Muhammad Ibrahim Igaal. Moscow had provided training and weaponry for the Somali army since the early 1960s, and it was through his contacts with Soviet officers that Siad Barre had become enthusiastic about communism. Upon assuming power, he established a communist government in the capital, Mogadishu. He also drew his nation closer to the Soviet Union, which culminated in 1974 in a treaty of friendship with the Kremlin. Under the agreement, Moscow would supply Mogadishu with military aid in return for access to the Somali port of Berbera. During the next three years, the Kremlin provided some $300 million in military assistance to Somalia, helped the Somalis build an army of 30,000 troops, and gave Mogadishu numerous tanks and aircraft.[5]

That same year brought what appeared to be good news for the Kremlin in Somalia's neighbor, Ethiopia, when a military junta, known as the Provisional Administrative Council (PMAC) or Derg, overthrew the government of Emperor Haile Selassie. By 1977 one of the Derg's top leaders, Major Mengistu Haile Mariam, had succeeded in eliminating his rivals and emerged as his country's leader. Like Siad Barre, the Derg and Mengistu had been inspired by socialism. And they, like the Somali leader, sought closer relations with the Soviet Union.

On the surface, it would seem the Kremlin would grab at this opportunity to have Ethiopia join Somalia as a communist ally. In 1972, Egyptian President Anwar Sadat had expelled Soviet advisers and aircraft from his nation because of what he regarded as a lack of support on Moscow's part. Five years later, Sudan followed suit.[6] Ethiopia and Somalia, it would appear, could make up for these losses.

But the Soviets had reason for caution. For one, Somalia, following its achievement of independence in 1960, had adopted an irredentist policy and laid claim to portions of neighboring Kenya and Djibouti and the Ethiopian-controlled region of the Ogaden. The Kremlin realized that if it seemed overly enthusiastic in promoting ties with Ethiopia, it could make the Somalis suspicious of its intentions. Additionally, it could not ignore a report it received from Fidel Castro, who in 1977 traveled to the Horn and met with the Somali and Ethiopian leaders. The Cuban president had nothing but praise for Mengistu and disdain for Siad Barre, whom Castro portrayed as being less a socialist tied to the international communist cause and more a nationalist interested in Somalia's well-being, be it socialist or capitalist. Mengistu fed his Cuban counterpart's suspicions by depicting himself as more wedded to socialism than Siad Barre. Moreover, knowing well of the tense relationship between the Soviet Union and China, he assured Castro that he had curbed Ethiopia's once-close ties with Beijing.[7]

Siad Barre's decision in July 1977 to invade the Ogaden all but confirmed Castro's suspicions. Why the Somali leader chose that particular moment is not clear, but he justified his conduct on the grounds of assisting a supposed Western Somalia Liberation Movement. It is known that he judged he stood a good chance of success. Since the early 1960s, Ethiopian military forces had been kept busy trying to put down a rebellion in Eritrea. Eritrea had been an Italian colony from the late 1800s until World War II, when the British liberated it. After the war, the United Nations voted to make Eritrea an autonomous region of Ethiopia despite Eritrean demands for independence. In 1962, however, Emperor Selassie abolished Eritrea's autonomous status and placed it under the control of his government. His decision sparked the Eritrean uprising, which continued into the 1990s. With the Ethiopians busy in Eritrea, Siad Barre had every reason to believe he could easily take the Ogaden.

The Soviets found themselves in a tricky situation, as they now had two client states in conflict. Of the two, they leaned in favor of Ethiopia. First, repeated efforts by the Kremlin to convince Siad Barre to stop his aggression in the Ogaden had failed to elicit a positive response. Second, the Soviets now likely shared Castro's reports about the Somali leader's commitment to socialism. Finally, Ethiopia was more strategically important than Somalia. Both bordered the Gulf of Aden, but Ethiopia's southeastern corner lay right where the Gulf and the Red Sea—which led to the vital Suez Canal—met. Thus, in May 1977 the Soviets signed an arms agreement with Ethiopia. In November, Somalia retaliated by unilaterally breaking its friendship treaty with Moscow. Almost immediately afterward, the Kremlin transported a large sum of military aid to Addis Ababa as well as 12,000 Cuban combat troops and 1,500 Soviet advisers; these forces launched a counterattack starting in early 1978 that began to push the Somalis out of the Ogaden.[8]

The issue for the Carter administration was how to respond to these developments in the Horn. For much of the Cold War, the United States, seeing Ethiopia as the key to the Horn, had provided that nation with hundreds of millions of dollars in military aid. But Selassie's failure to implement reforms in the face of growing opposition to his rule convinced Washington to reevaluate its relationship with Addis Ababa. Following Mengistu's emergence as the PMAC's leader, the Carter administration cut all U.S. aid, citing human rights violations. Mengistu struck back in April 1977 by closing American installations in Ethiopia, with the exception of the embassy and the office of the Agency for International Development. Trying to draw an angry Mengistu away from the Soviet Union, therefore, would not be easy. Simultaneously, the White House knew it would probably receive requests for help from Somalia. If the administration refused, then it might lose any opportunity for influence in the Horn. But if it gave Mogadishu too much assistance, then it might anger Ethiopia and other African nations that distrusted Siad Barre and give the Soviets and Cubans justification for their military presence.[9] On top of these considerations, there were questions for the White House about whether it should put pressure on the Soviets—if so, what measures to use and whether that pressure should include linking the situation in the Horn to other matters in U.S.–Soviet relations.

Both Vance and Brzezinski wanted to see a reduction of Soviet influence in the Horn. How to achieve that goal—and whether they should couple Moscow's activities in the region to U.S.–Soviet ties writ large—divided them. To the secretary of state the crisis in the Horn was a local one in which, unfortunately, the Soviets and Cubans in late 1977 had involved themselves. To try to curtail Soviet and Cuban interference in the region, he called for giving limited aid to both Mengistu and Siad Barre, making sure than none of that assistance could be used to wage war. He did not support the idea of linking Soviet activities in the region to other issues, such as the ongoing SALT negotiations. The NSC adviser demurred. The crisis in the Horn was another example of Soviet expansionism, which had to be stopped, even if it meant tying Moscow's venture to SALT as well as possibly the Indian Ocean demilitarization talks.[10] He also demonstrated a preparedness to provide military aid to Mogadishu.

During 1977 and into 1978, Vance, supported by Defense Secretary Harold Brown, prevailed. In early 1977, the Somalis requested both U.S. weapons and political support. The White House agreed to explore the possibility of providing economic aid to Siad Barre's government but opposed the idea of any military aid for the time being. As the attendees at an April Policy Review Committee (PRC) meeting noted, it was possible that Siad Barre was "trying to play both us and the Soviets at the same time," and to provide such weapons would anger not just Ethiopia but Kenya and Djibouti. Simultaneously, the PRC proposed shipping non-lethal military aid (trucks and jeeps) already in the pipeline to Ethiopia but withholding shipments of more deadly matériel, including jets and ammunition, even if Addis Ababa had already paid for it. Finally, the committee suggested extending economic aid to Kenya and strengthening existing ties with Sudan.[11]

This policy of maintaining a calculated distance from Somalia and Ethiopia continued through the summer. In June and July the Siad Barre government expressed a desire for arms. Carter refused to supply U.S. weapons but offered "in principle" to ask America's allies to provide defensive equipment to Somalia.[12]

Siad Barre's decision to invade the Ogaden may have been driven in part by Carter's offer of help; the Somali leader possibly assumed that Washington would exchange weapons for closer relations with his government. If that was indeed his supposition, it was wrong. Rather, the Somali attack forced the United States to back away from Somalia even further. Washington informed Mogadishu that it could not proceed with its offer to ask its friends to help Somalia unless Siad Barre removed his forces from the Ogaden. This did not stop the Somalis from continuing efforts to convince the White House to change its mind. For instance, after abrogating its treaty with the Soviets in November, the Somali government, apparently believing this move would please the Carter administration, made another request for arms. It was again rebuffed. Yet the White House did not want to lose all opportunities for contacts with the two Horn nations, and so it agreed to proceed "with two small aid projects in Ethiopia to show our concern for its people" and to consider providing "some medical aid" to both countries.[13]

Additionally, and despite its promise to curb military sales to other nations, the Carter administration sold millions of dollars of weapons to surrounding countries, including nearly $170 million in F-5 fighters and C-130 cargo planes to Sudan. While the White House justified this as necessary to contain the threat posed by Cuban and Soviet troops in the Horn, it was another example of inconsistency in policy.[14]

Up to this point, Vance's judgment that the Horn crisis was a local affair had convinced the United States to maintain contacts with both Ethiopia and Somalia. As the secretary later wrote, he and other State Department officials concluded that eventually "the Ethiopians would oust the Soviets from their country as had happened in Egypt and the Sudan." The arrival of Soviet and Cuban troops starting in November 1977 did not alter that conclusion. Rather, it was a case of Moscow trying to exploit a situation of immediate advantage to it. Eventually, through cautious negotiations and calculated aid to both the Siad Barre and Mengistu governments, it would be possible to bring the war over the Ogaden to a halt and, in the longer term, Soviet influence in the region would decline.[15]

Brzezinski continued to demur. It was important to take a tougher line, he insisted, lest the White House lose more political points at home. "I feel that we are confronting a growing domestic problem involving public perception of the general character of [our] policy," which was "seen as 'soft,'" the NSC adviser wrote to Carter. "Our critics . . . will ask for some examples of 'toughness,' and exploit against us such things as . . . the current Cuban activity in Africa."[16]

Carter showed a willingness to listen more closely to Brzezinski. Shortly after the Cuban-Soviet intervention in the region, the president gave his NSC adviser the go-ahead to give press briefings on the situation, thereby allowing Brzezinski to publicize his views. Meanwhile, in January 1978, Carter informed U.S. allies in the region that the United States wanted a negotiated end to the dispute in the Horn. But he then opened the door to linkage: "We have again reminded the Soviets that if they persist in their intemperate actions in the Horn we will be forced to reduce efforts to work with them in other areas."[17]

This was a perfect example of the president paper-clipping policies. A negotiated settlement of the Horn crisis assumed some form of Soviet involvement and that Moscow would act in good faith. That was Vance speaking. But to charge the Soviets with not acting in good faith and to link their actions with other subjects in U.S.–Soviet relations was all Brzezinski.

In the same message, Carter wrote that the administration had informed Mengistu that it would "support negotiations on Eritrea to keep it federated with Ethiopia."[18] With the help of countries such as Syria and Iraq, Eritrea had by 1977 acquired enough weaponry that it was prepared to kick Ethiopia's troops out. But the arrival of Soviet and Cuban forces allowed Mengistu to launch a counteroffensive that forced the Eritreans to retreat.

It is possible that Carter's willingness to support Ethiopian-Eritrean negotiations was the result of an idea generated by Paul Henze, the NSC's specialist on intelligence coordination. Henze had strongly resisted the State Department's call for negotiations on the Ogaden, arguing that it would get nowhere. What made more sense, he contended, was to focus on finding a settlement to the dispute between Eritrea and Ethiopia. Not only would a resolution that maintained Eritrea's federation with Ethiopia gain the favor of the Mengistu government, but Soviet resistance to such talks would turn world opinion against Moscow.[19]

Although Henze balked at negotiations on the Ogaden, there was intense pressure upon the United States from its European allies to open talks on that very matter. Unlike Brzezinski, most of America's friends in Europe did not see the Somali–Ethiopian conflict as a threat to world peace; rather, like Vance, they viewed it as a local matter unrelated to East-West relations writ large. Even James Callaghan, Britain's prime minister and a good friend of Carter's, in a comment clearly aimed at the NSC adviser, criticized the "Columbuses who have lately discovered Africa."[20]

To Henze's frustration, State proposed five-power talks including the United States, Britain, France, Italy, and West Germany on the Ogaden; he grew even more annoyed when those discussions resulted in an accord to seek a negotiated settlement on the Ogaden that made no mention of Eritrea. "State seems lusting to draw the Soviets into discussion of the Horn," he argued. Instead of focusing on negotiations on the Ogaden that he charged would get nowhere, Henze urged the White House to emphasize Eritrea. Doing so would put both the Kremlin and Cuba on the defensive, "and we ourselves can come down comfortably on the side of human rights, peace and Ethiopia's territorial integrity by doing so. We have nothing to lose by trying." In fact, in an amazing suggestion, Henze offered giving Ethiopia the country of Djibouti in return for giving Somalia the Ogaden.[21] (There is no evidence that suggestion got anywhere beyond the paper on which it was written.)

Brzezinski also rejected State's motion and proposed sending a carrier task force to the region. Although the Soviets had informed Washington that Ethiopia would not invade Somalia, Brzezinski reasoned that the presence of American warships would demonstrate to U.S. public opinion how seriously the White House took the situation, rally Americans behind SALT, preserve Washington's credibility abroad, and "make the Cubans think twice about participating in [an] invasion of Somalia." This suggestion aroused the strong resistance of Vance, Brown, and the Joint Chiefs of Staff. Vance asserted that Brzezinski's proposal would undermine any hope of a political settlement by seeming to lean in Somalia's favor. Furthermore, both he and Brown insisted that if the United States sent warships to the area and, in the event of an invasion of Somalia, did not use them, then America's credibility would be blemished.[22]

Carter rejected the idea of sending warships to the region. But he demonstrated his continued shift to a harder line on March 2 when he told a group of reporters that Soviet interference in the Horn "would make it more difficult to ratify a SALT agreement or a comprehensive test ban agreement if concluded." As far as he was concerned, "the two are linked because of actions by the Soviets. We don't initiate the linkage."[23] This, of course, was not the first time the president had suggested linking the Horn to other topics in U.S.–Soviet relations. But it was the first time he had made it public.

The president's statement left observers at home and abroad confused. Moreover, the same day Carter made his comment, Vance told the Senate

Foreign Relations Committee, "There is no linkage between the SALT negotiations and the situation in Ethiopia." The U.S. media immediately
picked up on the discrepancy. So did Moscow. Soviet Ambassador to the
United States Anatoly Dobrynin informed long-time diplomat and Carter
administration roving ambassador Averell Harriman that the Kremlin was
not sure "what the President's position really was."24

Both Harriman and Henze realized the administration had gotten itself
into a mess. On March 8, Harriman met with Carter only to find Brzezinski there as well. "I couldn't be quite as blunt as I wanted to be," he
mused. He told Carter that it was important to make as few public statements on the Horn as possible to avoid shaking up U.S.–Soviet relations.
Brzezinski did not buy it, pointing to the dangers posed by the Cuban and
Soviet presence in the region. While not minimizing the danger, Harriman
repeated that it was vital to keep a lid on public commentary. Turning to the
Vance-Brzezinski split, he noted that "the press was full of attempts to show a
difference between the two points of view." Henze shared this concern. American statements on the Horn had left U.S. allies confused "about what principles we stand for, whom we really favor, what pressures and what kinds of
force (if any) we are willing to use." Most serious, he wrote, the incongruity in
U.S. policy "adds to the impression, at a time when he least needs it, that the
President is leading an amateurish, inept Administration that neither knows
what it wants nor how to go about getting it."25

If Harriman and Henze agreed that the administration's message was
confused, they at least partly disagreed over who was responsible. To Harriman, it was Brzezinski, who in his view threatened a peaceful settlement
in the Horn and U.S.–Soviet relations more generally. To Henze, it was the
failure of White House officials, including Brzezinski, to focus on his proposal on Eritrea. Implicitly, though, Harriman and Henze concurred that
the president was ultimately at fault. Rather than presenting a single,
clear, consistent message, Carter had combined the ideas of his secretary
of state and national security adviser, with the result of leaving observers
at home and abroad bewildered. As Henze explained, "The countries of
the Horn, of the rest of Africa and the Middle East, the world at large and,
last but not least, the U.S. public all seem confused about some aspects of
U.S. policy toward the Horn." The White House had to articulate its "policy more comprehensively than we have done." Someone high up in the
administration had to explain that the United States, unlike the Soviet
Union, had "not interfered in the internal affairs of any countries in the
area"; that it had not provided large amounts of weaponry to any of the
Horn nations or encouraged them to act aggressively; and that it had
"never intervened militarily in the region."26

The Soviets also criticized the administration. The same day Harriman
met with Carter, Siad Barre, whose forces had taken a beating at the hands

of the Ethiopians and their Cuban allies—Somalia had lost almost 8,000 men, about three-quarters of its tanks, and half its air force—announced his intention to withdraw from the Ogaden, the process of which was largely completed within a week. The Ethiopians did not take advantage of the situation and cross into Somalia. Yet none of this meant the end of the continued presence of Soviet and Cuban troops in Ethiopia. Dobrynin expressed to Vance his country's willingness to reduce its presence in Ethiopia, but continued U.S. criticism made that difficult, as it would appear Moscow was withdrawing "under pressure."[27]

The president, though, kept up the pressure in his Wake Forest speech, which he presented a day after Dobrynin's talk with the secretary of state. Brezhnev responded to Carter's comments by pointing to "forces" within the U.S. government that wanted to create "an atmosphere of fear and hostility." While those "forces" had not fully succeeded in their efforts, he continued, they had done enough to make the administration look indecisive and inconsistent. Drawing upon linkage himself, he warned that continued American assaults on Soviet policy in Africa would endanger SALT.[28]

The administration, at least through the remainder of 1978 and into 1979, maintained its policy of not providing arms to Somalia. Although Siad Barre had pulled his troops out of the Ogaden in March, intelligence that he was aiding rebels in the region, knowledge that he had angered numerous African nations, and news of human rights violations in Somalia convinced the Carter administration to limit its help to economic and humanitarian assistance. The White House, however, continued to put heat on the Kremlin. For instance, in May, Carter berated visiting Foreign Minister Andrei Gromyko, declaring that he "could not believe that the Cubans could put 40 or 50 or 60 thousand men into Africa without the Soviet Union's tacit approval or encouragement." Gromyko rebuffed the president, pointing to the Kremlin's efforts to get Siad Barre to leave the Ogaden and contending that Ethiopia had asked for both Soviet and Cuban assistance. Carter rejected Gromyko's claims on Soviet activities in Ethiopia, charging that Ethiopia's forces were being "directed by a Soviet general," an allegation Gromyko denied.[29]

It was not just the Horn that began to weigh on Carter. He also worried about the situation in the southern part of the continent. One of the nations that drew his attention was Angola. Relations between Cuba and Angola dated back to 1965, when Angola was still a Portuguese colony. Portugal's refusal to grant Angola independence had opened the door to the formation of several revolutionary groups: the Popular Movement for the Liberation of Angola (MPLA), led by Agostino Neto; the National Liberation Front of Angola (FNLA), commanded by Holden Roberto; and Jonas Savimbi's National Union for Total Independence of Angola (UNITA). Of these groups, the MPLA had ties to communism. It was that ideological link that produced a meeting between Che Guevara, a former member of the Castro regime who had left Cuba in 1965 to foment communist revolutions elsewhere in the world, and MPLA officials. Following the collapse of Portuguese rule in 1974, the relationship between Havana and the MPLA grew even tighter. The United States, aware of the MPLA's communist leanings, expanded already-existing aid to the FNLA and UNITA. There is no evidence that the MPLA or Cuba knew of the U.S. assistance, but they were aware that the pro-American president of Zaire, Mobutu Sese Seko, had sent troops into northern Angola to support the FNLA.[30]

By the middle of 1975, Angola was in the midst of a civil war. Concerned about the MPLA, in August Cuba established a military mission to advise its communist allies; weapons also arrived from Havana for the MPLA's use. By early November, Cuba's assistance and the MPLA's own determination had helped that group achieve several victories, to the point that it looked like Neto was about to become the country's new leader.[31]

The MPLA's successes disturbed South Africa. Pretoria controlled Namibia, which bordered Angola to the south, and where South African forces were busy battling the rebel South-West Africa People's Organization (SWAPO). Concerned that a Neto victory in Angola could threaten its hold on Namibia, South Africa provided weapons and advisers to UNITA and the FNLA; when that failed to stem the MPLA tide, South Africa invaded Angola. The MPLA immediately asked Cuba for help. Determined to assist fellow communists, and frightened that if they did nothing Neto might turn to the Chinese, the Soviets in October 1975 began an airlift that would eventually bring 12,000 Cuban troops to Angola by the following January. Neto and his Cuban allies then succeeded in routing the South Africans. Pretoria, having suffered severely, and aware of a decision by the U.S. Congress in December 1975 to stop covert funding for Angola, pulled its forces back to the Namibian-Angolan border.[32]

Upon taking office, Carter and Vance judged that the best way to bring about stability in southwestern Africa was to achieve Namibian independence under the auspices of the United Nations. This would serve several purposes. It would mean an end to South African involvement in that territory and to the wider conflict there. Furthermore, the withdrawal of South African forces and the stabilization of matters in Namibia would undermine Cuba's excuse for having military forces in Angola.[33]

This was all easier said than done. Angola was the home for another organization, the Congo National Liberation Front (FNLC). Formed in 1968, its original purpose was to seek independence for the Katanga, a mineral-rich region of Zaire. As part of that effort, it sought to overthrow Zairean President Mobutu. Several failed attempts, however, had forced the FNLC into exile in Angola. There the organization fought alongside the MPLA, which also opposed Mobutu because of his support for the FNLA, and gained new recruits.[34]

In March 1977, 1,500 members of the FNLC invaded the Katanga from the Angolan region of Shaba and began driving toward the important town of Kolwezi. Mobutu's forces, frought with a lack of discipline, were unable to stop the attack. Scared by an offensive that he charged was the work of the MPLA and the Soviet Union, the Zairean leader asked for international help.[35]

Carter, seconded by Vance, refused to be drawn into the conflict. Not only was there a lack of Soviet or Cuban involvement, but U.S. intervention could anger African nations whose support for the negotiations in Rhodesia and Namibia was critical. This is not to say the administration did nothing. The loss of Kolwezi would give the FNLC control over much of the world's cobalt and copper and jeopardize regional U.S. investments. Therefore, Washington extended moral support to a decision by France, Egypt, Sudan, and Uganda to send troops to the area. This coalition succeeded in stopping the FNLC advance and forced the rebels to flee back to Angola.[36]

The FNLC, however, had not given up. In May 1978, it invaded again, this time with a better-armed and larger force. Kolwezi fell quickly. Again, the State Department took the position that there was no evidence of Soviet or Cuban involvement, but this time Carter, backed by Brzezinski, decided otherwise. The administration, commented the NSC adviser, had "evidence [which] sustains the proposition—more than that, sustains the conclusion that the Cuban Government and in some measure the Soviet Government bear the responsibility for this transgression." With the help of U.S. aircraft, France and Belgium deployed some 2,000 troops. The FNLC quickly retreated into Zambia, and soldiers from several African countries, including Gabon and Togo, arrived to police the region. Not long thereafter, Neto and Mobutu reached a settlement whereby they would not support insurgents invading their nation from the other, and the region quieted down.[37]

The administration's response to the second invasion of Katanga was very different from the first. The first time, the White House did not provide material support to stop the FNLC attack on the Katanga; the second time, it did. The first time, the White House said nothing about Cuban or Soviet backing for the FNLC; the second time, it did. No longer did Washington deem the situation in southwest Africa as an African affair but instead placed it in the context of the larger East-West conflict. "We believe that Cuba had known of the Katangan plans to invade," Carter contended, "and obviously did nothing to restrain them from crossing the border."[38]

Yet while berating the Soviets, Carter still held out hope for cooperation. "We want to increase our collaboration with the Soviet Union," and to see human rights upheld in Africa, he told an audience at the U.S. Naval Academy in July. "The persistent and increasing military involvement of the Soviet Union and Cuba in Africa could deny this hopeful vision." But then he added, "The Soviet Union can choose either confrontation or cooperation. The United States is adequately prepared to meet either choice." This double message, which represented another example of Carter paper-clipping the language of Vance and Brzezinski, confused observers at home and abroad. The *Washington Post*'s headline the following day was "Two Different Speeches," while the *Washington Star* asked, "Did Carter Leave Them All Baffled with Annapolis Speech?" The answer to that question was yes. Donald McHenry, who succeeded Andrew Young as ambassador to the United Nations, commented that the speech "read as if one person wrote the first part and a second person wrote the second part." Dobrynin informed the Kremlin that "Soviet-American relations during the Carter Administration have been characterized by instability, major swings."[39] The question was in what direction U.S. policy toward the Soviet Union would ultimately swing and how far.

One indication of the answer to that question was the breakdown of the comprehensive test ban (CTB) and conventional arms transfer (CAT) negotiations. The former had made little progress, as the president faced opposition from Congress, the Pentagon, and the Energy Department to any proposal that might indefinitely suspend nuclear testing. By 1979, the CTB negotiations were dead. On CAT, the Carter administration had accepted State's position, which would include discussion of superpower arms sales to all nations. But in the changed environment of mid-1978, the president joined Brzezinski and Brown in stating that he would not agree to talk about U.S. arms sales to strategically important allies such as Saudi Arabia, South Korea, or Iran. Added to this list of countries that were off limits was China; indeed, Carter went so far as to order the U.S. delegation to the negotiations to walk out if the Soviets raised America's East Asia policy.[40] That the White House would adopt State's position, only to change its mind and embrace that of the NSC and Defense, no doubt further confounded the Kremlin.

Normalization of Relations with China

The refusal of the United States to discuss China at the CAT negotiations was directly related to another indication of the changed state of U.S.–Soviet affairs after mid-1978: the White House's decision to normalize relations with China. After over twenty years of civil war, the Chinese communists, led by Mao Zedong, in 1949 succeeded in kicking out of power that country's noncommunist government. The United States retaliated by providing aid to the noncommunist leadership—which had fled to the nearby island of Taiwan—and imposing a trade embargo on Beijing. In 1955, the United States took its relationship with Taiwan a step further by signing a defense treaty with the noncommunist government. Beijing resented the U.S.–Taiwan alliance, regarding Taiwan as a part of China, and it believed it had the right to "liberate" that island, by force if necessary.

Not surprisingly, the Chinese communists turned to the Soviet Union for help and signed an alliance with Moscow in 1950. But by the end of that decade, the Sino–Soviet relationship had begun to falter. Following the death of Josef Stalin in 1953, the Soviet Union adopted a policy of "peaceful coexistence," arguing that while communism would eventually defeat capitalism, it would do so peacefully; Mao rejected the Soviets' new stance, charging that it violated communist doctrine, which called for violent revolutions against capitalist nations. The two former allies began to exchange increasingly belligerent polemics and, in 1969, engaged in an armed border skirmish.

Following the doctrine of "the enemy of my enemy is my friend," Mao began to see the United States as an ally against his new, more serious Soviet threat. President Richard Nixon and his national security adviser, Henry Kissinger, also wanted better relations with China, seeing it as a way to counter Soviet influence and, in the process, divide and weaken the communist world. This effort to improve Sino–American relations bore fruit with Nixon's trip to China in 1972, making him the first president, former or sitting, to visit that country since the communists seized power.

The Sino–American rapprochement of 1972, though, did not automatically lead to the normalization of relations between the two nations. The sticking point was Taiwan. For years, the United States had viewed the government in Taipei as the legitimate Chinese government. Nixon reversed that policy, arguing that the government in Beijing represented China and that Taiwan was a part of China. But cognizant of widespread U.S. public and congressional support for Taiwan, he refused to cut ties to Taipei. This the People's Republic refused to accept. In the "Shanghai Communique," which Nixon and the Chinese signed during his visit, the communists set forth three conditions the United States would have to meet to achieve normalization of relations, all of which related to Taiwan: Washington would have to terminate its official relations with Taipei, abrogate the U.S.–Taiwan defense treaty, and pull all U.S. troops off the island. Although Nixon had hoped to meet these requirements following his reelection in 1972, the Watergate scandal brought down his administration. His successor, Gerald Ford, refused to move forward toward normalization, concluding that it would anger Americans, most of whom backed Taiwan, and disrupt the SALT process.[41]

After his election, Carter determined to normalize Sino–American ties, but that was easier said than done. Both the president and his advisers realized that normalization would require meeting the conditions of the Shanghai Communique. Chinese Ambassador Huang Zhen made as much clear on February 8, 1977, when he met with the new American head of state. The U.S. president had concerns about accepting those demands. He wanted China to resolve its differences with Taiwan peacefully, despite China's repeated statements that it reserved the right to use force. Moreover, cutting ties to Taiwan, the president stated, "poses a very difficult problem for the U.S." To take that step, Carter later wrote, would anger members of Congress, whose support he needed for ratification of the Panama Canal treaties he hoped to sign.[42]

The issue, therefore, became how fast to push toward normalization. This question led to another dispute between Brzezinski and Vance. Since at least 1972, when he published his book *The Fragile Blossom,* Brzezinski had called for improving relations with China. To do so, he maintained, offered a number of advantages. It would frighten the Soviets, who would then have to keep military forces along the Sino–Soviet border, thus reducing the threat the Kremlin posed to the North Atlantic Treaty Organization. It could give the United States a bargaining chip, which it could use to get Soviet concessions at the SALT talks. Finally, it would allow the United States to make up for its withdrawal from Vietnam and offset Soviet machinations in Southeast Asia.[43] Vance challenged Brzezinski's assessment. While the secretary of state favored normalization, to take that step now would upset the Soviets, thereby destroying any chance of signing SALT.

Carter leaned in favor of Vance. He decided to test the waters but had no intention of rapidly normalizing relations. Proof of this concerned the point at which the president asked his foreign policy advisers to conduct a detailed study of Sino–American relations. During his first month in office, the president submitted presidential review memoranda (PRMs), asking for policy reviews of SALT, the Panama Canal, arms transfers, nuclear proliferation, the law of the sea, Cyprus, and at least a dozen other subjects. However, he did not submit a PRM (PRM-24) on China until early April. It was still another two months before administration officials sent their response to that review request. They concluded that if Washington did not formalize its relationship with Beijing, the People's Republic would lose faith in the United States and, though unlikely, might even seek to restore its relationship with the Soviet Union. An exchange of ambassadors, however, might frighten Moscow, encouraging it to become more willing to make concessions to Washington on other matters.[44]

The next issue was the conditions under which the United States would agree to normalize relations. PRM-24 concluded that the People's Republic could not politically risk backtracking on the demands it had made under the Shanghai Communique. But in meeting those conditions, the authors felt that Washington could ask Beijing to yield on other subjects, such as permitting the United States to continue to sell arms to Taiwan or promising to liberate Taiwan only by peaceful means. Finally, rather than abrogating the 1955 defense treaty with Taipei immediately, as demanded by Beijing, Washington could ask for a year's notice, as required by that defense agreement.[45]

A final matter was arms sales. Both Brzezinski and Secretary of Defense Brown wanted to relax the embargo so as to permit the United States to transfer technology to Beijing and to have Washington endorse European military transactions with China. For them, this improvement in Sino–American military cooperation would put pressure on the Soviets to make concessions to the United States. Vance objected, as did the majority of the drafters of PRM-24. They held that providing such technology would infuriate the Soviets and endanger SALT.[46]

PRM-24 ultimately leaned in favor of Vance's position. It called for moving toward normalization but warned against measures that might prove counterproductive vis-à-vis Moscow, most notably arms sales. The president signed off on all of these conclusions reached by his foreign policy advisers.[47]

The question for the White House was how accommodating Beijing would be. To find out, Carter sent Vance in August to the Chinese capital. The president had stated that he had no intention to "ass-kiss" the Chinese as he believed Nixon had done. For that reason, as well as his desire to see how much the People's Republic might bend, Carter asked the secretary of state to present to China's leaders "a maximum position" on Taiwan. Specifically, he told Vance to discuss with Chinese officials the matters of the peaceful liberation of Taiwan and the sale of U.S. defensive arms to the government in Taipei.[48]

When Vance arrived in August, he confronted a government different from that which had existed at the time of Nixon's visit. Mao had died in September 1976, and the period afterward saw a struggle between the new premier, Hua Guofeng, and Deng Xiaoping to succeed him. Deng had had much of his power stripped from him in early 1976, but with Mao's death, he had gradually reasserted himself. In Deng's view, China had to modernize as quickly as possible. Beijing had proposed to increase dramatically its production of steel, iron, coal, natural gas, and hydroelectricity by 1985, but it lacked both the capital and know-how to do so much in so little time. The West had both the money and the expertise the People's Republic needed. With the help of nations such as the United States, China could begin the process of modernization, which would serve two purposes. First, it would strengthen the hold of the Chinese Communist Party (CCP). Starting in the mid-1960s, Mao had called upon the Chinese people to rid their country of those Chinese who had veered away from his view of what a "true" communist was. The resulting Cultural Revolution, which lasted until Mao's death, fractured both the communist party and the country as a whole and shook its economy. Through modernization, the nation's economic health would be restored and, with that, the faith of the people in the CCP. Second, modernization would strengthen China militarily, allowing it to handle the growing Soviet threat. Many of Deng's colleagues in the party shared his vision and, a month before Vance arrived in China, appointed Deng as vice premier. Consequently, Deng was given control over the People's Republic's foreign policy.[49]

Per his instructions, Vance acknowledged that while Taiwan was "a part of China," there was pro-Taipei sentiment in Washington, which the Carter administration could not ignore. It was for this reason that the United States would want to continue having economic and scientific relations with Taiwan and informal diplomatic ties. Meanwhile, the White House would withdraw all remaining military forces on Taiwan. Lastly, Washington intended to make a statement favoring the peaceful resolution of the Taiwan dispute; if China could issue a similar declaration, it would have a positive impact upon U.S. public and congressional opinion and make it easier for Carter to complete the normalization process.[50]

Vance anticipated the Chinese would reject the U.S. proposals, but he did not expect how vehement that rejection would be. Foreign Minister Huang Hua declared that the United States had paid only "lip-service" to Beijing's three demands and referred to the liberation of Taiwan as an internal matter. Deng seconded his foreign minister. He further called informal U.S.–Taiwan relations unacceptable, as it would amount to "an Embassy that does not have a sign on its door."[51]

Despite the Chinese rejection of the administration's proposals, Brzezinski still believed early normalization was possible. Deng had not rejected peaceful reunification with Taiwan. Nor had he explicitly stated that Beijing would oppose a U.S. statement favoring a peaceful resolution of the Taiwan dispute. It also appears that the Chinese were aware of PRM-24, as the NSC adviser noted as well that Deng had said nothing about Washington's desire to provide Taipei with defensive weaponry.[52]

Carter, though, seconded by Vance, decided to put normalization on hold. Both the president and secretary of state viewed other issues as more important to the administration. The Panama Canal treaties, which were signed in September, were up for Senate ratification; to agree to normalization of relations with China would anger Taiwan's supporters in Congress and endanger the Panama agreements. The SALT talks were still in limbo. And the president had to devote time to other parts of his foreign and domestic agendas, including the Middle East peace talks and passage of his comprehensive energy program. There was not time, Carter later wrote, to give adequate attention to China. "Besides, it was not the right moment to tackle another highly controversial issue."[53]

Though Vance held the upper hand with regard to normalization, Brzezinski refused to give in. Through Michel Oksenberg, one of his East Asian specialists, Brzezinski let the CCP leadership know of his desire to travel to China. The Chinese, cognizant that the NSC adviser was a stronger proponent of early normalization than Vance, issued him in

November a formal invitation to visit. At the same time, Brzezinski persistently pressed Carter to let him travel to Beijing, gaining the support of both Mondale and Brown. The vice president, recalled Brzezinski, "sensed the Administration needed a foreign policy success." The defense secretary thought that it now was all the more essential to develop a closer strategic relationship with China; in light of Vance's hesitancy at normalization, he held that State should not have responsibility for the trip. Vance fought his colleagues, charging that it would leave unclear who the country's foreign policy spokesperson was and that more time was needed to consult members of Congress.[54] For the time being, the president stood by his secretary of state.

But in March 1978, the president changed his mind, siding with Brzezinski and approving his proposal that he travel to China. Soviet activities in Africa, and particularly in the Horn, had moved the president toward a worldview more in line with that of his NSC adviser. Indeed, Carter now concluded, the United States could use normalization as a lever to pressure the Soviets on other matters, including the Horn and SALT, and possibly draw support for SALT from lawmakers who had doubts about that treaty. Moreover, with the Panama Canal agreements completed and, in the fall of 1978, ratified, he could normalize ties with China without having to worry about the impact of that step upon his plans for the canal.[55] Finally, Japan had recently established full relations with Beijing. If Washington waited too long, Tokyo's normalized ties with China would give it an advantage over the United States in the area of trade.

Vance remained skeptical. Even though the Senate had approved the Panama Canal treaties, normalization could easily disrupt SALT. Yet with Carter desirous to normalize Sino–American relations, the secretary of state wanted it done quickly so that Congress would not find itself considering that issue at the same time SALT came up for ratification.[56]

In May, Vance put together a memorandum that became the basis for the instructions Carter sent Brzezinski later that month. The NSC adviser was to explain that the United States had "made up its mind" to seek normalization based upon the conditions of the Shanghai Communique. However, in return, the Chinese would have to accept five U.S. conditions, which the administration had developed since Vance's trip. Having been shaken by the CCP's response to the secretary of state's presentation the year before, the first two U.S. stipulations offered concessions to Beijing. First, rather than ask China to announce it would settle the Taiwan issue peacefully, the United States would make a unilateral statement calling for a peaceful settlement of that matter and insist that the People's Republic not contest that proclamation. Second, instead of requesting the right to maintain an informal diplomatic presence in Taipei, Washington would have an unofficial body represent it. On top of these two conditions, the United States wanted the right to continue selling Taiwan defensive weaponry, to abrogate its defense treaty with Taiwan within a year rather than immediately, and to maintain all other agreements with Taipei.[57]

When Brzezinski met with Hua Guofeng and then Deng during his visit, he did not raise all of these issues, calculating it was best to put some of them off until the negotiations had made headway. He made clear that the president wanted to normalize relations based upon the Shanghai Communique. He also asked the Chinese to understand the support in the United States for Taiwan, making it necessary for Washington to express its desire for a peaceful resolution of that matter and, after normalization, to uphold its commitment to defend Taipei's security. Brzezinski took note that neither Chinese official appeared opposed to continued U.S. arms sales to Taiwan or a unilateral American statement on settling the Taiwan issue peacefully.[58]

The NSC adviser made sure as well to appeal to China's anti-Soviet policy. He brought with him a delegation that included Deputy Secretary of Defense Morton Abramowitz, who briefed Chinese officials on Soviet military strength, and the well-known political scientist Samuel Huntington, who discussed Washington's relations with Moscow. As further proof that he was a friend of the People's Republic, the NSC adviser joked during a visit to the Great Wall, "Last one to the top gets to fight the Russians in Ethiopia." Such comments led the Chinese to refer to him as the "polar bear tamer," "polar bear" being a reference to the Soviet Union.[59]

If Brzezinski and Carter gathered that the former's trip to China would convince the Soviets to make concessions on SALT, they were wrong. This is not to say that the NSC adviser's junket hindered the SALT process. Dobrynin later commented that the main reason for the lack of progress on an arms control agreement was not Brzezinski's trip but Carter's attacks on Soviet and Cuban activities in Africa and on Moscow's violations of human rights, as well as continuing disagreements in the SALT talks themselves, such as over the Backfire bomber. That Gromyko did not raise the China issue in conversations he had with Carter and Vance in late May further attests to the lack of impact Brzezinski's trip had. Still, it would be wrong to say that the NSC adviser's visit to Beijing had no effect on U.S.–Soviet relations. Coming on the heels of Egyptian President Anwar Sadat's trip to Israel—which the Kremlin viewed as not in accord with the October 1977 U.S.–Soviet joint statement on the Middle East—and recent clashes on the Sino–Soviet border, Moscow surmised that the Carter administration hoped to use the NSC adviser's junket to China to put further pressure on it. What the Soviets did not know was how far Washington might go in using the "China card."[60]

During the next six months, discussions took place in both China and the United States, with Leonard Woodcock representing the administration in Beijing and Brzezinski and Assistant Secretary for East Asian and

Pacific Affairs Richard Holbrooke overseeing discussions with Chinese officials in the United States. These negotiations were held in the utmost secrecy with only a limited number of people in the know; otherwise, there
might be a leak that would generate an uproar among the U.S. public and
Congress. The president and his advisers hoped to complete normalization prior to the signing of SALT, as they realized they could not handle
congressional debates over both matters at the same time. Lastly, there
was an understanding that normalization should be announced as soon as
possible after the upcoming midterm election.[61]

Woodcock would play a key role in these talks. He was, according to
State Department Director for Chinese Affairs Charles W. Freeman, "a man
of strong will and excellent, seasoned judgment, and personable." His staff
respected him, for he did not "pretend to expertise on China"; in fact, he
neither spoke Chinese nor had studied Chinese history but he "was an excellent judge of character and a fine negotiator." To Woodcock, a formula
to achieve normalization was possible. On the one hand, while there were
tensions between China and Taiwan, they were not serious. On the other,
the United States could not force the People's Republic to give up its right
to forcibly liberate Taiwan, just as China could not make Washington give
up on Taipei. This left only one option, which was for the United States to
issue a unilateral statement that it have the right to defend Taiwan if
threatened. Indeed, looking at the recent discussions between U.S. and
Chinese officials, Woodcock found no evidence that either side would reject such a proposal.[62] Carter concurred.

Woodcock, Brzezinski, and Holbrooke decided to work through the easier topics and then move to the tougher ones. At first it appeared there
would be no problem achieving normalization. When Holbrooke in September told liaison officer Han Hsu that the United States wanted the
right to sell weapons to Taiwan, Han declared Washington was "not in
conformity with the spirit of the Shanghai Communique." But he also
commented that China would "watch how the U.S. will act in the days to
come." Oksenberg commented that Han's response was "carefully crafted"
and "ambiguous," suggesting that the Chinese had neither the intention
to cut off discussions on normalization nor to reject outright the sale of
weaponry to Taiwan. In a meeting later that month with Chai Zemin,
Carter repeated America's desire to sell arms to Taiwan. Furthermore, Washington intended to make a unilateral statement calling for a peaceful resolution of the Taiwan dispute and to maintain the defense treaty with Taipei for
a year following normalization. To try to soothe the Chinese, the White
House invited Deng or Hua Guofeng to visit Washington. SALT was nearly
completed, U.S. officials explained, and the resolution of that matter would
automatically be followed by a Carter-Brezhnev summit. If the Chinese would
accept these American conditions, then "they could have their summit before

the Russians." Chai did not rule out the United States's selling defensive weapons to Taiwan, and he promised that Beijing would not contradict a U.S. statement on the peaceful resolution of the Taiwan dispute.[63]

Nicholas Platt, an East Asian specialist on the NSC, found other encouraging signs. Beijing now talked about "unification" with Taiwan rather than its "liberation" and had commented that "unification" was something that would happen at some unknown point in the future. Adding to all of this Chai's comments, it was clear to Platt that the People's Republic wanted both normalization and a reduction of the political difficulties the administration would face when that took place.[64]

Platt's observations were correct. Beijing had become very apprehensive about the increasingly close relationship between the Soviet Union and China's neighbor to the south, Vietnam. China and Vietnam historically had a tense relationship, with Beijing viewing Vietnam as within the People's Republic's sphere of influence. During the Vietnam War, both China and the Soviet Union had provided North Vietnam with economic and military aid, but following the end of that war and North Vietnam's successful conquest of the South in 1975, those old animosities reappeared. Hanoi therefore turned ever more to Moscow for support, which Beijing regarded as Soviet meddling in a part of the world China saw as strategically important. All the more reason, therefore, for the People's Republic to tighten its ties with the United States. Moreover, Deng, who favored the rapid normalization of relations, had by late 1978 largely assumed power from Hua Guofeng and obtained more latitude to accept Washington's conditions.[65]

December 15 proved to be the key day. That morning Chai and Brzezinski disagreed over whether the United States would have the right to sell defensive arms to Taiwan, with Chai warning that the sale of such weapons could make the peaceful reunification of Taiwan difficult. Caught off guard, as the CCP leadership earlier had shown no serious opposition to arms sales to Taipei, the White House instructed Woodcock to contact Deng. An angry Chinese leader declared himself opposed to such arms sales, as they not only represented to him a continuation of the U.S.–Taiwan defense treaty but, echoing Chai, would make it impossible to achieve peaceful reunification of China. At the same time, the Chinese premier had no desire to allow this issue to undermine normalization. Thus, he asked that during the year prior to abrogation of the U.S.–Taiwan defense treaty Washington "not make any new commitments to sell weapons to Taiwan." This the White House promised. Deng followed by accepting the U.S. invitation for a visit following normalization.[66]

Later that day, the two nations issued a joint communiqué, in which they announced their intention to normalize their relations on January 1 of the following year. The United States would terminate the U.S.–Taiwan defense treaty and maintain relations with Taipei through an unofficial entity. Finally, Washington hoped for a peaceful resolution of the Taiwan dispute and planned to sell defensive arms to Taiwan after a one-year suspension. The Chinese, for their part, expressed their opposition to the arms sales and called the liberation of Taiwan an "internal affair."[67]

The issuing of that communiqué came as a surprise to Vance. Just before its release, he had left for the Middle East to try to break through on the final topics in the conflict between Israel and Egypt, assuming that the announcement on normalization would occur after he had a chance to meet with Soviet Foreign Minister Gromyko later that month. His hope was that he could wrap up the remaining issues related to SALT prior to January 1. With that arms control agreement all but completed, the administration could announce normalization and then submit SALT to the Senate for ratification; the secretary of state's anticipation was that the normalization announcement would reduce opposition in the upper house to SALT. But all of this assumed SALT would be signed first. Brzezinski, without any input from State, convinced the president to push up that announcement to December 15, reasoning that further delay increased the chances of a leak.[68]

The Impact of Normalization

Vance later claimed the December 15 announcement dashed his desire to complete SALT at the end of 1978. In fact, it did not have that much of an impact. Even before December, the SALT talks were not going well. In July 1978, in the hopes of achieving a breakthrough, Vance made a new proposal to Gromyko, which he said had to be accepted as a whole. First, while both sides could test-flight a new intercontinental ballistic missile (ICBM), neither could deploy such a weapon until 1985. The one exception would be with regard to submarine-launched ballistic missiles (SLBMs), thus allowing the United States to develop its new Trident II and the Soviets their Typhoon. Both had multiple independently targetable reentry vehicles (MIRVs) on them, allowing each missile to hit more than one location. Second, any existing ICBM and SLBM that had the number of warheads on it increased would be regarded as a new missile rather than simply an altered existing type. Hence, if the Soviets added more warheads to an existing missile, such as an SS-17 or SS-19, it would be considered the one new missile permitted by SALT, and Moscow in that case would not be permitted to build its Typhoon. Finally, the United States would not accept including air-launched cruise missiles in the subceiling that limited both sides to 1,320 MIRVed launchers. Gromyko, to Vance's frustration, rejected the U.S. package. When the Soviet foreign minister made a counterproposal in September that included limits on the range of cruise missiles and the number of cruise missiles that heavy bombers could carry, and which imposed no restrictions on SLBMs, Vance dismissed it. Nor did the Soviets accept continued American demands to include the Backfire bomber in SALT.[69]

Complicating progress was how fast the two superpowers would have to destroy the requisite number of weapons to reach the 2,250 ceiling on launchers. The Soviets, who would have to eliminate 150 of their launchers to achieve the ceiling, wanted flexibility on how fast to do it. The American negotiators, though, insisted upon a more certain deadline, which they set at June 1981.[70]

Most important, however, was the failure of the two sides to see eye-to-eye on telemetry encryption. Not only did the United States want to be able to monitor Soviet tests, but Washington, as a result of a revolution in Iran, had been forced to close facilities in the northern part of that country that it had used to gather intelligence on the Kremlin's activities. It thus became all the more important to have some kind of ability to verify Soviet compliance with SALT if the administration had any hope of seeing the treaty ratified. Dobrynin later pointed out that it was the dispute over telemetry encryption, and not the announcement on normalization, that prevented the signing of SALT by the end of 1978. Both Assistant Secretary of State for Political and Military Affairs Leslie Gelb and Robert Gates, a member of the CIA and later head of the agency, concurred.[71]

While a shock to them, most Americans, including members of Congress, favored normalization. What upset lawmakers were the lack of consultation and the requirement to cut relations with Taiwan. In late 1977, Carter had received warnings from Capitol Hill that if he did not consult with Congress on Sino–American relations, it could cause a "divisive debate" regarding U.S. China policy. Indeed, in 1978, the Senate unanimously approved a resolution insisting upon consultation prior to changing the U.S.–Taiwan defense treaty. Thus, when Carter suddenly announced his intention to normalize ties with China and alter the status of U.S.–Taiwanese relations, Jesse Helms commented that the administration was about "to sell Taiwan down the river." Democrats such as Senators Ted Kennedy of Massachusetts and Ohio's John Glenn shared Helms's concern. Members of Congress thus proposed legislation that would provide a firmer U.S. guarantee of Taiwan's security.[72]

Carter and his advisers knew such a law would destroy normalization. They also knew that Congress had no intention of backing down. Therefore, the White House asked lawmakers to endorse a bill that provided the executive branch with some flexibility. After further discussion, Capitol Hill approved legislation that gave the president the leeway he sought. The Taiwan Relations Act, as it was named, declared that the United States would view as of "grave concern" any effort to resolve the Taiwan issue by nonpeaceful means and that Washington should provide

Taipei with defensive military equipment. The first part of the bill simply was a statement of principle; as for military aid, Congress could not require the executive branch to provide weaponry to Taiwan. In short, the legislation gave Carter the very flexibility he wanted. The Chinese leadership, while not pleased with the act, understood what the law required of the White House and thus did not allow it to undermine normalization.[73]

Also shocked and dismayed was Taiwan. The Taiwanese government and people felt betrayed by the United States and made their feelings all too clear when Undersecretary of State Warren Christopher arrived about two weeks after the normalization announcement to explain to Taiwan's leadership America's new policy. As his car took himself and U.S. Ambassador Leonard Unger from Taipei's airport to their hotel, they were met by an angry mob that threw eggs, tomatoes, cans, and rocks at the vehicle, breaking every window and Unger's glasses, and leaving both U.S. officials with cuts from flying glass. Then, as the Taiwanese police stood by doing nothing, some in the crowd jumped on the car, while others shook it and still others reached through the windows, attempting to drag the two Americans out. It took nearly an hour for the car and its frightened occupants to escape the mob. Although Christopher continued with his mission, he did so only after insisting upon, and receiving, armed protection from the Taiwanese government.[74]

On March 1, the United States and China opened their respective embassies in each other's capitals. With normalization now complete, Washington and Beijing could turn their attention to economic and military issues. Two topics of particular concern were those of claims and assets. After taking control of China in 1949, the communist leadership had seized U.S. investments there; Washington had retaliated by freezing the assets of the People's Republic in America. Settling these matters would protect both sides from lawsuits and allow them to establish closer trade relations. However, it was not until May 1979 that Beijing and Washington finally came to terms, with the Chinese offering to pay $80.5 million and the United States announcing it would unblock China's assets that October.[75]

With claims and assets out of the way, the United States and the People's Republic could turn their attention to trade. Of particular interest to the Carter administration was granting most-favored nation (MFN) status to China; the White House maintained that normalizing Sino–American trade would not only benefit U.S. commercial interests but reduce the American trade deficit. The State Department, not wanting to offend the Soviet Union, urged the White House to offer MFN status to Moscow as well. At issue here, though, was the Jackson-Vanik Amendment, which required communist nations to permit free emigration in return for MFN status. The Soviet Union had refused to meet that demand. During his visit to Washington in January, Carter had raised the emigration issue with Deng, who replied, "If you want me to release ten million Chinese to come to the United States, I'd be glad to do so." Deng's retort pleased Carter, who decided to exempt the People's Republic from Jackson-Vanik. And with the deterioration in U.S.–Soviet relations, the president had all the more reason to grant MFN to Beijing but not Moscow. However, it was not until January 1980 that the Senate followed suit, and only after the administration, at the behest of lawmakers from textile-producing states, imposed import quotas on Chinese textiles. The granting of MFN status to Beijing allowed Sino–American trade to double between 1979 and 1980, to about $5 billion.[76]

The United States demonstrated less preparedness to cooperate militarily. Brzezinski had brought Abramowitz with him during his May 1978 visit, and, around the same time, the administration indicated its willingness to support Western European arms sales to the People's Republic. In May of the following year, Carter told Chai of his interest in developing closer strategic relations. But military ties between the two countries remained largely stagnant. Citing the Taiwan Relations Act, Chai rejected a proposal by Brzezinski to have U.S. warships visit Chinese ports. Furthermore, the CCP wanted to see whether normalization and Beijing's decision in the spring of 1979 to allow its alliance with Moscow to expire would make the Soviets more willing to negotiate about improving Sino–Soviet relations.[77] Not until late 1979 did the United States and China begin to strengthen their military ties.

Normalization Put Off—Vietnam

While the decision to normalize relations with China might not have had a significant impact upon SALT or Sino–American military cooperation, the same could not be said for its effect upon U.S. policy toward Vietnam. Starting in 1965, U.S. combat troops had fought in South Vietnam to prevent its fall to communist-led rebels in the South and attacks by communist North Vietnam. But the growing unpopularity of the war had moved Washington to seek a negotiated settlement that would permit it to withdraw. These talks culminated in the 1973 Paris Peace Agreement. Under its provisions, Washington had to remove all U.S. troops from South Vietnam within two months of a ceasefire and offer economic aid to North Vietnam to help it rebuild from the war; meanwhile, Hanoi promised to return all American prisoners of war, to help locate U.S. troops missing in action (MIA), and to respect South Vietnam's self-determination. Neither side fully abided by the agreement. In 1975, North Vietnam invaded and conquered South Vietnam; Congress retaliated by passing legislation barring the U.S. government from providing economic aid to now-unified communist Vietnam.

Between the Paris Peace Agreement and its conquest of the South, North Vietnam had shown little interest in normalizing relations with the United States. Almost immediately after unifying the nation, however, Hanoi changed its mind, under the condition that the U.S. government abide by its pledge to provide economic aid. President Ford, pointing to the communists' violation of the Paris accords, refused.

Upon taking office, Carter, Vance, and Holbrooke all indicated a willingness to normalize relations with Vietnam. They held that doing so would moderate Hanoi's attitude toward its noncommunist neighbors and keep Vietnam from turning to the Soviet Union or China for assistance. Accordingly, less than two weeks after the inauguration—in other words, months before the White House reviewed its China policy—the president asked for a review of U.S. policy toward Vietnam, including the possibility of normalizing relations with that nation. However, before providing any aid, Carter and Vance wanted Vietnam to account for all American MIAs; such a step, they posited, would please congressional opinion, allowing the administration more freedom to normalize ties with Hanoi.[78]

Talk of normalizing relations with Vietnam did not please the NSC's coordinator for Asia, Michael Armacost. "[F]rom the vantage point of Asia, the first impressions of the Carter Administration are not terribly reassuring," he wrote Brzezinski in February 1977. The White House seemed to care more about its relations with the Kremlin than with Beijing, planned to withdraw U.S. military forces from South Korea, and seemed to be reassessing its "base requirements in the Philippines." A major move toward normalization with Vietnam, he reasoned, would lead U.S. allies in Asia to see a "reversal of our priorities." If the president was determined to proceed with his plans for Vietnam, he urged taking things slowly and giving serious consideration to how America's regional friends might view U.S. normalization with Hanoi.[79]

Yet normalization increasingly appeared unlikely. In May, Holbrooke began talks with his Vietnamese counterpart, Phan Hien. Phan insisted that his nation would not account for any MIAs until the United States promised aid to his nation. This Holbrooke refused to do. But he also did not want to see the talks break down. He urged Carter to tell members of Congress that a lack of flexibility on aid could prevent "Vietnamese movement on the MIA question."[80]

By late November, the failure to break the deadlock at Paris moved Vance to suggest that the United States take steps short of normalization without lifting the embargo on aid, such as opening up an interests section —a U.S. diplomatic presence, but not one that connoted formal relations as would an embassy—in Hanoi. Brzezinski vehemently resisted; Carter overruled him. The NSC adviser, therefore, offered that Holbrooke say nothing about an interests section "if the Vietnamese abuse the United States in their initial presentation." This Carter approved.[81]

In the spring of 1978, the Vietnamese shifted their position, largely because of events related to Cambodia. Cambodia and Vietnam had long distrusted one another, and the two disputed the location of their border. Desirous to prevent a Cambodian–Vietnamese war, the Chinese urged restraint, but the Vietnamese believed that Beijing's request was part of its historical quest to dominate the region. Concerned about China's designs, Vietnam turned to the Soviet Union. Angered, the People's Republic gave more and more military aid to Phnom Penh, while Cambodian and Vietnamese troops skirmished and refugees flooded into Vietnam. The Vietnamese leadership concluded that to stop China, Cambodia, and the flow of refugees, it had to overthrow the Cambodian government.

The Vietnamese understood not only that an attack on Cambodia would likely mean war with China but that the United States was moving toward closer relations with the People's Republic. Intent on dividing Washington and Beijing—which might restrain the Chinese—Hanoi expressed its preparedness in May 1978 (the same month Brzezinski visited China) to normalize relations with the United States without insisting on economic aid as a prerequisite. The change in the Vietnamese position again divided State and the NSC. Holbrooke realized that U.S. policy toward China and Vietnam's tensions with Cambodia would complicate matters, but if the administration could normalize relations with Hanoi, it would be "a significant foreign policy achievement." Oksenberg was much less sanguine, calling the obstacles to normalizing relations with Vietnam far greater than Holbrooke made them out to be.[82]

Brzezinski seconded his Asia expert. To him, Vietnam's relationship with the Soviet Union was the main issue, and normalizing ties with Hanoi would upset what he saw as a more important initiative, that of normalization with the Soviets' enemy, communist China. When Christopher informed Carter that the Vietnamese had formally given up their demand for aid and wanted to move rapidly toward normalization, Brzezinski convinced the president to defer any decision to avoiding "prejudic[ing] our efforts with the Chinese."[83]

Brzezinski later commented that had he not opposed normalizing relations with Vietnam, the administration would have moved forward on it.[84] There is some truth to this. The White House by the middle of 1978 had decided to take a harder line toward the Soviet Union, which included formal ties with China; to have normalized relations with Vietnam, a Soviet ally, would have jeopardized the White House's desire for closer ties with Beijing.

But Brzezinski's comment also was evidence of self-ingratiation. While the NSC adviser had had an impact, there were other issues that pushed the administration away from recognizing Vietnam. One was pressure from important lawmakers, such as Senator Henry Jackson (D-Washington), who also wanted to improve ties with China and warned the president that formalizing relations with Vietnam threatened that goal.[85] Another was the Vietnamese "boat people"—Vietnamese nationals who had been fleeing their nation since 1975 and whose plight had drawn the attention of people all over the world. To recognize Vietnam would seem to suggest that good relations with Hanoi were more important than the fate of those trying to escape that government. Finally, there was Vietnam's decision to invade Cambodia in December 1978, which infuriated America's Southeast Asian friends, such as Thailand and Indonesia. The White House had no intention of making those allies angry by seeking closer relations with Hanoi.

Normalization Put Off—Cuba

The toughened U.S. policy toward the Soviet Union and its allies also had an impact upon discussion of normalizing ties with Cuba. U.S.–Cuban relations had soured following Fidel Castro's successful overthrow in 1959 of the leader of that nation, Fulgencio Batista. An avowed communist, Castro had taken steps that infuriated American officials, including making anti–U.S. statements, expropriating American property, and cozying up to the Soviet Union. Washington struck back by cutting diplomatic relations with Castro's government, imposing a trade embargo on Cuba, and attempting (but failing) to remove Castro from power.

Upon taking office, Carter demonstrated a willingness to improve, and even formalize, relations with Cuba. Both he and Vance announced Washington's preparedness to begin negotiations with Havana "without preconditions." Normalization, though, would require Castro to take certain steps, such as ending the violation of the rights of his people and withdrawing his country's military forces from Angola.[86]

Senator George McGovern (D-South Dakota) shared the idea of improving economic relations with Cuba, reasoning that Castro would realize the importance trade with America would have for his country. To maintain that commerce, Havana would likely moderate its position on issues of importance to Washington, such as on U.S. property it had expropriated. Furthermore, normalization would "open up Cuban society" in directions favorable to the United States. While McGovern did not favor completely abolishing the embargo, he believed that lifting restrictions on the trade of food and medicine made sense.[87]

McGovern's proposal caught Vance's eye. He told the president a few days later that he endorsed a partial lifting of the embargo, with two caveats. One, the Cubans had to reciprocate. Vance noted that Assistant Secretary for Inter-American Affairs Terence Todman was about to leave for Cuba and would tell the Cubans that the United States was willing to consider removing the embargo on food and medicine if Cuba showed

reciprocity on matters such as releasing U.S. prisoners in Cuba and allowing Cubans in the United States to visit loved ones. Two, he did not want
to lift the embargo on sugar, which was Cuba's primary export. To remove
trade restrictions on that product "would be to give away most of our bargaining position." Interestingly, and despite his more anti-Soviet senti-
ments, Brzezinski shared Vance's willingness to consider a partial lifting of
the embargo (minus sugar). This is no doubt at least partly explained by a
comment Carter wrote on Vance's memo: "Don't forget Cuban troops all
over Africa."[88] The NSC adviser could thus be assured that the president
would link normalization and the elimination of the embargo to a withdrawal of Cuba's military presence in Angola (and, later, the Horn).

Todman arrived in Cuba in April. While there, he and Cuban officials
signed agreements establishing their maritime boundary on fishing rights.
They also promised to open interest sections in each other's countries.[89]

This would be as far as the negotiations got. Cuba's presence in Africa
stopped further progress toward normalization. At a PRC meeting on August 3, State, Commerce, and Treasury advanced partially lifting the embargo on trade, assuming that Cuba would respond by restraining its activities in Africa. The NSC, Defense, and JCS, though, wanted Cuba to
curtail what it was doing in Africa before giving consideration to a relax-
ation of the embargo. Asked to choose between the two sides, Carter selected the latter.[90]

Castro refused to budge. The Cuban leader told Senator Frank Church (D-
Idaho), who had traveled to Cuba the same month as the PRC meeting, that
Cuban troops were in Angola to stop a South African invasion of that country; it had nothing to do with the United States and was not an issue on
which he would negotiate. With the arrival of Cuban forces in the Horn of
Africa later that year, further U.S. discussion of normalization came to a
halt. When Vance in January 1979 proposed continuing efforts to improve
relations with Cuba, Carter told him to maintain the "status quo."[91]

★   Thus, starting in early 1978, America's foreign policy began to
change. Differing definitions of détente were at the heart of it. To the Soviet Union, détente meant it had equal status as the United States but did
not require it to give up supporting communist movements and governments around the world. To the United States, it meant the Kremlin, as an
equal, had the responsibility of protecting the status quo and maintaining
global stability.[92] When Moscow violated America's interpretation of détente, the Carter administration began to give up its earlier emphasis on
redirecting U.S. diplomacy toward North-South matters. A return to concentrating on relations between East and West and the containment of
Soviet-inspired communism commenced.

This gradual restoration of a foreign policy similar to that of earlier Cold War administrations had widespread ramifications. The United States adopted a tougher position at the CAT negotiations, leading to their breakdown. President Carter rejected Secretary of State Vance's hope to defer normalization of ties with communist China until after SALT's ratification, preferring instead to follow Brzezinski's call for early normalization. Moreover, to please Beijing and send a message to the Soviet Union and its allies, the United States abandoned any consideration of improving relations with Vietnam or Cuba.

But Carter had not completely given up his belief that cooperation with the Soviet Union was possible and that Washington and Moscow could successfully consummate a SALT agreement. The result was the paper-clipping of policy. The president used both tough and tender rhetoric in his Wake Forest and Naval Academy speeches and specifically with regard to the Horn of Africa. He had done the same when it came to policy toward Rhodesia, where the United States had some concern that continued instability could open the door to the communists. The end result in all of these cases was confusion, both at home and abroad.

The PROBLEMS *of*

PEACE *and* PROSPERITY

Six

★   It was Valentine's Day, 1979. The U.S. ambassador to Iran, William Sullivan, had just finished having a conversation with his press attaché, Barry Rosen, when, Sullivan recalled, "a murderous barrage of automatic-weapon fire opened up on the embassy from all sides. . . . Window panes shattered, lead flew everywhere, and we had no recourse but to dive for the deck and slither across the floor to the safest spot we could find." Iranian militants, supported by snipers on nearby rooftops, had begun an attack on the embassy.[1]

As the militants broke in, Sullivan, knowing that the marines guarding the facility were outnumbered, ordered them not to return fire so as to avoid unnecessary bloodshed. Meanwhile, he and most of his staff sought safety in the communications vault on the embassy's second floor. Luckily, and to Sullivan's relief, another group of Iranians arrived, fired on the militants, and got them to lay down their weapons. After about an hour, a very frightening situation was over.[2] Or so it seemed.

That attack on the U.S. embassy in Iran was a portent of things to come for relations between the two countries. Moreover, the crisis in Iran became added to a list of ongoing or new efforts by the Jimmy Carter administration to promote peace and prosperity worldwide. Here the White House had only limited success. Attempts to bring peace to Cyprus failed, the plan to withdraw U.S. troops from South Korea was shelved, a Chinese invasion of Vietnam jeopardized the Strategic Arms Limitations Treaty (SALT) and normalization of relations with Beijing, and little progress was made on international economic issues. Meanwhile, the administration seemed unable to come to grips with not just the crisis in Iran but one in Nicaragua. The White House did regain access to military bases in Turkey and consummated an Egyptian–Israeli peace treaty in 1979. The former success, though, came only at the expense of angering fellow Democrats, while the latter required the administration once again to compromise its own principles with regard to Middle East peace.

Cyprus Unresolved

By the middle of 1978, the effort to resolve the dispute between Turkey and Greece over Cyprus was not going well. Part of the problem was Turkey's financial situation, which made it hard to keep Ankara focused on Cyprus. Carter, though, remained committed to the assumption that lifting the U.S. arms embargo on Turkey would generate forward movement on Cyprus. In mid-July, Undersecretary of State Warren Christopher wrote that the administration had to do several things to convince Congress to lift the embargo. First, the White House had to point to the "political and symbolic significance" of such a move, such as the positive impact it would have on U.S.–Turkish relations. Second, it had to demonstrate that an improvement of military ties between Washington and Ankara—no doubt he included a hope that Turkey would reopen U.S. military bases it had closed when the United States imposed the embargo—would be beneficial to the policy of containment. Finally, it had to convince lawmakers that lifting the embargo would not "upset the Greek-Turkish military balance."[3]

In September, Congress lifted the embargo, with the catch that the White House had to report every two months on progress toward solving the Cyprus dispute. Turkey followed up by reopening the U.S. bases. But there was clearly dismay, particularly among Democrats, to ending the military sanctions. In the Senate, for instance, 32 Democrats voted against repeal versus 30 in favor. It was only through large-scale support from Republicans that the embargo's abolishment took place.[4]

The following month the president had hope that a resolution on Cyprus might be at hand, when he learned that Turkish Cypriot leader Rauf Denktaş had agreed to meet with his Greek counterpart, Spyros Kyprianou, and resume negotiations. As before, Denktaş wanted any settlement to be "bizonal" in nature, by which the smaller Turkish population on the island would receive equality with the Greeks or autonomy. "Our task now," commented Christopher, "is to develop a framework statement which both parties can accept as a basis for resuming negotiations." Carter wrote in the margin, "Let's push this *hard*" [emphasis in original].[5]

The administration accordingly spent the next month preparing a multipart plan designed to achieve a final resolution, which it presented in late November. It included (1) turning Cyprus into a two-zone "federal state," with one zone controlled by the Greeks and the other by the Turks;

(2) a federal constitution that would guarantee the rights of all Cypriots; (3) a federal government that included "a two-house legislature, with the upper house evenly divided between Turks and Greeks and the lower house based upon population"; (4) the establishment of regional governments; and (5) the withdrawal of all non-Cypriot military forces, which would require both Greece and Turkey to remove troops from the island. Yet this proposal did not get far. "Traditionally, what is positive to the Greeks is negative to the Turks and vice-versa," commented the *New York Times*. Both sides found provisions in the plan they did not like and blamed the other for preventing a solution. For example, in January 1979, Christopher met with Turkish Prime Minister Bülent Ecevit, who accused the Greek Cypriots of purposely stalling. The undersecretary informed the Turkish leader that his country had to stop "blam[ing] all their problems on Greek-Cypriot tactical considerations."[6]

By the summer of 1979, the administration had all but given up on trying to bring about a resolution to the Cyprus crisis. "Neither Greek nor Turkish Cypriots have been sufficiently unhappy with the status quo on the island to make significant concessions to generate movement toward permanent settlement," National Security Adviser Zbigniew Brzezinski wrote Carter around May. "It is difficult to see how any move the United States could make, whether the initiative came from the legislative or executive branches, could help now."[7] And there matters stood for the remainder of Carter's term.

The Egyptian–Israeli Peace Process

Greco–Turkish distrust was not the only reason for the failure to bring a resolution to the dispute over Cyprus. Another was that the White House found its attention drawn to what it considered more important issues. One of those was the Egyptian–Israeli peace process. The lack of clarity of the Camp David Accords became a problem when Israeli and Egyptian officials arrived in Washington in October 1978 to begin talks on their bilateral peace agreement. Under pressure from other Arab nations, Egyptian President Anwar Sadat continued to press the Israelis on Palestinian autonomy in the West Bank and Gaza; he linked that issue to his willingness to exchange ambassadors with Israel and complete the bilateral peace process. The Israelis, however, showed no preparedness to give.[8]

Carter believed that Sadat "did not give a damn about the West Bank" and was more interested in autonomy in Gaza. If that was the case, then, he concluded, an Egyptian–Israeli peace agreement was possible. Therefore, in February, Carter, Secretary of State Cyrus Vance, and Brzezinski held talks with the Israeli and Egyptian foreign ministers, Moshe Dayan and Mustafa Khalil, respectively. Carter made clear to them the importance of reaching an agreement quickly. Next, he invited both Sadat and Israeli Prime Minister Menachem Begin to meet with him in Washington; Sadat refused, saying that Khalil had full authority to speak for Egypt. Though reluctant to come to the U.S. capital without Sadat present, Begin changed his mind upon prodding from the U.S. president. After further discussion, it appeared a resolution might be possible.[9]

By March, the issues separating the Israelis and Egyptians had been reduced to just a few. Among them was Begin's desire for access to petroleum: with the Iranian revolution and the turning over of oil wells in the Sinai to Egypt, Israel had no guaranteed supply of fuel. For Egypt, it was Palestinian autonomy. Sadat, as Carter had anticipated, proclaimed that he would sign no agreement that did not provide some possibility of Palestinian autonomy in at least Gaza. To try to finish the peace process, Carter, as in the Camp David negotiations, put his reputation on the line and flew to the Middle East in March. Discussions in Jerusalem and Cairo bore fruit. Egypt adopted Israeli wording on Palestinian autonomy, which called for setting a twelve-month "goal" to resolve that matter. Furthermore, the Israelis and Americans worked out an arrangement by which the United States would give Israel oil if Egyptian supplies from the Sinai did not meet Jerusalem's requirements. Finally, Jerusalem accepted Cairo's demand that it withdraw its military forces from the western Sinai within nine months; Egypt promised to exchange ambassadors within a month of the completion of that withdrawal. At the end of March, the two countries inked the peace treaty. At the end of January 1980, Israel completed its withdrawal from the Sinai, and the two nations exchanged ambassadors the next month.[10]

Carter commented shortly after his return to the United States, "The Israelis are without a doubt the most difficult people I have ever dealt with." Even so, he could claim another diplomatic success, having convinced Israel to join Egypt in signing a peace agreement and exchanging ambassadors. But this was only achieved by skirting the key issues of Israel's withdrawal from the occupied territories and Palestinian autonomy. The treaty said nothing about what would happen if the Israelis did not meet the "goal" of Palestinian autonomy within twelve months, and there was no language requiring Israel to comply with UN resolution 242. The response of Arab countries ranged from silence to hostility. Egypt's membership in the Arab League was suspended, as was economic aid from Arab nations. Sadat found himself further isolated in the Middle East.[11]

It is not surprising in retrospect that the autonomy talks ran into trouble, as Israel refused to grant such rights to the Palestinians. Carter, though, could not give the matter the kind of personal attention as in the past. In the summer of 1979, news broke that his ambassador to the United Nations, Andrew Young, had met with a representative of the Palestinian Representation Organization. The unauthorized meeting outraged Israel and American Jewish opinion and temporarily stalled the Middle East negotiations. Carter's decision to force Young's resignation infuriated African-Americans and required the White House to concentrate on damage control. The president's decision to appoint another African-American, Young's deputy Donald McHenry, to the ambassadorship helped cool the furor. But even as the White House got past Young's removal from office, it had to contend with other matters, including the economy, a report that Carter aide Hamilton Jordan had used cocaine, the quest to see SALT ratified, and the approach of the 1980 election campaign.[12]

Revolution in Iran

And there was another Mideast crisis about which the White House had to worry, in Iran. The precursors to what became the Islamic revolution in Iran date as far back as World War II. Because of their dislike for their Soviet neighbor to the north and the British, who controlled portions of the Middle East, many Iranians openly supported Germany during the war. Determined to prevent Iran and its valuable petroleum reserves from falling into Nazi hands, Soviet and British troops occupied the country. Moscow and London also saw to it to force out Iran's ruler (shah), Reza Muhammad Pahlavi, and replace him with his son, Muhammad Reza. Once the war ended, both the British and Soviets withdrew their troops, but London, through its Anglo-Iranian Oil Company, retained control over Iran's petroleum. This infuriated Iranian nationalists, including many members of the Iranian Parliament, or Majlis, which in 1951 appointed Muhammad Mossadegh as the new prime minister.

The shah proved unable to control his new, highly popular prime minister. Mossadegh nationalized the Anglo-Iranian Oil Company, placing its holdings under the control of his government. Britain countered by boycotting Iranian oil imports. That Iran's prime minister would take over the interests of a noncommunist ally convinced the administration of U.S. President Dwight Eisenhower that Mossadegh was at the very least a communist dupe. Determined to keep communism from taking hold in Iran, Eisenhower turned to the Central Intelligence Agency (CIA) to get rid of the problematic Iranian leader. Mossadegh got wind of plots to overthrow him and ordered the arrest of troublemakers. Pahlavi, aware of the CIA's intentions, assumed that he too might become a target of Mossadegh's and fled to Italy. Meanwhile, the CIA went into action, literally paying people to take to the streets, where they destroyed pro-Mossadegh newspapers and attacked members of Iran's communist Tudeh Party. Not desirous himself to become a victim of what appeared to be a widespread revolt against his government, Mossadegh resigned and was placed under house arrest (where he remained until his death in 1967). A much-relieved shah returned home.

From that point, the United States became a major player in Iran. While the shah's government now controlled the nation's oil reserves, a group of foreign oil companies—including American firms, which received a 40 percent interest in Iranian crude—oversaw the management and refining of the petroleum. Using these ties to the West and the money he made from oil sales, the shah implemented a large-scale modernization program. Militarily, Pahlavi received hundreds of millions of dollars in aid from Washington, including aircraft; by 1974 Iran purchased more military wares from the United States than any other nation. The CIA also established monitoring stations in northern Iran to track Soviet activities. Economically, Western experts helped the Iranian monarch replace the traditional markets, or bazaars, with modern supermarkets and department stores.[13] Politically and socially, the shah promoted Iran's secularization, permitting Western-style movies, music, and dress to become more prevalent and allowing women more rights. Additionally, to help him monitor (and eliminate) those who opposed his policies, the CIA worked with the shah to establish a secret police, the National Security and Information Organization, better known as SAVAK.

The paucity of unrest in Iran by the early 1970s suggested that Pahlavi had a firm hold on his country. But looks were deceiving. The modernization program failed to meet expectations. It drew peasants from the countryside to the cities, causing crop production to fall and forcing the nation to purchase food abroad. Peasants competed with middle-class Iranians for jobs and housing, both of which were too few in number. Corruption among members of the upper class, fed by the inflow of oil revenue; a 30 percent inflation rate by 1977, driven up by heavy military spending; the shah's repression; and the lack of democratic institutions to give the lower and middle classes a greater voice in government only fed the frustration among those groups.[14] Meanwhile, the Westernization and secularization of Iranian society drew the ire of Iranian fundamentalists. Many of these opponents of the regime, secular or not, rallied around an Islamic cleric, the Ayatollah Ruhollah Khomeini. Born around the turn of the century—it is unclear if his year of birth was 1900 or 1902—he had begun to study the Qu'ran at age six. He continued his education through his older brother, who was himself an ayatollah, and then from Ayatollah Abdul Karim Haeri-ye Yazdi, one of Iran's most influential clerics.

Khomeini had come to detest Reza Muhammad Pahlavi, whom he felt had strayed from proper Islamic ways, and the younger shah's secular policies only fueled that rage. After Khomeini began to speak out in the early 1960s and demanded the shah's ouster, SAVAK had him arrested and exiled to Iraq. For the next fifteen years, he would, from abroad, continue calling for resistance to the Iranian monarch.

Some scholars have argued that Carter's election forced the shah to begin liberalizing his regime to meet the new president's demand that all countries respect the rights of their people.[15] It was true that the shah's lack of knowledge about Carter and the new president's human rights initiative had an impact. Yet there was more to it than that. Some of Pahlavi's advisers had convinced him that his policies, most notably his use of repression and failure to open the political process, had only served to strengthen his opponents. The shah also faced criticism from Western European nations for his violation of human rights. Thus, to meet his internal and external critics, the shah instituted a variety of initiatives starting in mid-1976, including releasing political prisoners, curbing press censorship, and encouraging more Iranians to join the Rastakhiz Party, which the shah had created in 1975.[16]

In addition, and despite his rhetoric, Carter approached Iran cautiously. While declaring in his inaugural address that his human rights policy would be "absolute," the administration announced within weeks that it had to make exceptions for countries vital to U.S. economic or geopolitical interests. Iran was one of them. "Iran was seen as the major force for stability in the oil-rich Persian Gulf," Vance later wrote. "Its military strength ensured Western access to gulf oil and served as a barrier to Soviet expansion. Its influence in the Organization of Petroleum Exporting Countries made it important to the American economy." Brzezinski shared this sentiment.[17] Thus, when Vance traveled to Tehran in May 1977, he quietly pressed the shah to curb human rights violations but avoided any rhetoric or threats that might disturb relations between the two countries.

If anything, the White House continued past policies. During his May stopover in the Iranian capital, Vance invited the shah to visit the White House and promised that Carter would proceed with an agreement signed between President Gerald Ford and the shah by which the United States would sell Iran 160 F-16 fighter jets. He added that the administration also supported the Iranian leader's desire to acquire airborne warning and controls (AWACS) aircraft. Pahlavi insisted these highly sophisticated planes, which could survey a two-hundred-mile radius of airspace, were vital to the protection of his nation. Proponents of the sale in America noted the AWACS transaction would bring down the cost per plane to the point that Congress would likely approve funding so the U.S. military could buy them as well.[18]

In fact, it was on Capitol Hill where the sale of the AWACS faced its strongest opposition. The White House wanted to furnish seven of the aircraft to Iran. Democratic Senators Frank Church of Idaho, South Dakota's George McGovern, John Culver of Iowa, and Ted Kennedy of Massachusetts, and Representatives Donald Fraser of Minnesota, California's Leo Ryan, and Massachusetts's Gerry Studds and Michael Harrington, among others, lined up against the administration. These new internationalists accused Carter of violating his own policy of curbing conventional arms sales abroad. They further cited a report of the General Accounting Office that declared the aircraft too sophisticated for Iran's military to handle, thus increasing the possibility that they might fall into the Kremlin's hands. In the face of such resistance, in the summer of 1977 Carter withdrew the request, but only temporarily. Intense lobbying during Congress's recess by the White House, aerospace companies, and Jews, who were pleased by Iran's support for Israel, convinced Capitol Hill to vote in favor when it reconvened later that year. To further cement lawmakers' approval, Carter had especially sensitive technology removed from the aircraft and promised not to sell Tehran any more advanced weaponry until Washington had assurances that Iran's military could use it without American assistance.[19]

Carter realized that the sale of the AWACS violated his arms control initiative. Even so, he wrote to the shah in late May, "I wish to give you my personal assurances that this policy will not disturb the close security relationship which has developed between our two countries over more than a quarter of a century." As it turned out, the Carter administration during 1977 and 1978 provided more military assistance to Iran than Presidents Richard Nixon or Ford. During Carter's term in office, approximately one-third of all U.S. foreign military sales went to Iran, including not just the AWACS, but F-4, F-5, F-14, and F-15 fighter jets, and more than nine hundred military helicopters.[20]

In November 1977, Pahlavi and his wife came to the United States. While the American and Iranian leaders and their spouses took part in ceremonies on the White House lawn, pro- and anti-shah demonstrators clashed in the nearby streets. Police had to use tear gas to disperse the crowds. Some of the gas wafted to the White House, forcing the Pahlavis and Carters to pull out handkerchiefs and dab the tears that ran down their cheeks. Afterward, the president privately raised the human rights issue with his Iranian counterpart. Carter appeared to accept Pahlavi's comment that the latter was doing all he could to meet the opposition's demands. Following the shah's departure, Carter commented he found Pahlavi "a likeable man" who was "calm and self assured . . . and surprisingly modest in demeanor."[21]

Shortly after the November visit, Carter asked his wife where she would like to spend New Year's. The first lady said in Tehran with the Pahlavis. Thus, in December, the first couple traveled to the Iranian capital. While there, the U.S. president toasted the shah, calling Iran "an island of stability in one of the more troubled areas of the world" and referring to the shah as the leader with whom he had the greatest "sense of personal gratitude and personal friendship."[22]

Iran was anything but stable. The shah's liberalization policy had allowed his opponents finally to speak out with less fear of retribution than before. In February and again in May 1977, the shah permitted the publication of letters castigating his government.[23] Carter's actions and words disheartened those who had hoped the president would force the Iranian monarch to end his repression and cede some or all of his authority to the people. The shah's determination to remain in power, and America's unwillingness to give up on its long-time ally, convinced more and more of Pahlavi's opponents that only more radical, violent methods could bring about success for their cause.

The smoldering flames in Iran exploded in January 1978, when a state-run newspaper denounced Khomeini. By this time, the ayatollah had become a hero to many in Iran, who by 1970 had started calling him "imam." While the meaning of that word varies, many Shi'ite Muslims—and Iran is a predominantly Shi'ite country—define it as an Islamic religious leader who is appointed directly by God. It was the first time in over 400 years that Iranians had referred to a living person as imam. Outraged at the treatment of the person they saw as handpicked by God to lead them, Muslims in the holy city of Qum, the cleric's former hometown, launched protests. The shah's security forces responded with force, killing about 25 people. Rather than stopping the protests, the crackdown caused them to spread, to Tabriz in February and Tehran by May. The shah, who by all accounts was much less decisive than his father, was not sure what to do and ended up employing both sticks and carrots. Government forces arrested and killed protesters, SAVAK kidnaped others, and bombs damaged opposition offices. But fearful of both the internal and international repercussions of a massive crackdown, the monarch offered concessions to his opponents, firing the head of SAVAK in July and, to make the clergy happy, banned pornographic movies.[24]

These moves had little effect. In August, 377 people died when arson destroyed the Rex Theater in the city of Abadan. A search for the culprit turned up empty-handed, but Iranians blamed SAVAK. When a group of Iranians demonstrated in Tehran, the shah's security forces fired on the crowd, killing anywhere from 700 to 2,000 people. This only served to inflame Iranian opinion all the more, with the shah's countrypersons calling upon the army to help overthrow, if not kill, him. Pahlavi, unsure what to do, imposed martial law while simultaneously opening talks with moderates in the opposition.[25]

Throughout, Carter held firm to aiding the shah. In March, and over the objections of the Bureau of Human Rights, the White House approved the sale of tear gas to Iran. Incredibly, and despite his own nuclear nonproliferation program, the president even reached an oral agreement with the shah to provide Iran with atomic power plants, assured that Tehran would abide by international safeguards and not provide such technology to other countries.[26]

The fact was that Carter had no idea just how precarious the shah's situation was. Partly this was the fault of the diplomatic corps. Only 10 percent of American diplomats fluently spoke the Iranian language, Farsi, which made it hard to gather information. Sullivan was not among the Farsi speakers. Tall, thin, silver-haired, and oftentimes referred to as "egocentric," the ambassador had experience in southern and eastern Asia as well as Europe. He had not wanted the Iran post when Carter offered it to him; knowing he was near the end of his career, he had wanted a "dream job," which to him would be ambassador to Mexico. Nor had he served in the Middle East. Yet he took the assignment and soon began sending home optimistic reports. While the protests were a cause for concern, he wrote, the shah would persevere.[27]

The Central Intelligence Agency did not help matters. Here, blame can be laid at the feet of the CIA's director, Stansfield Turner. Born in Illinois in 1923, Turner had attended college for two years in Massachusetts and then transferred to the Naval Academy, from which he graduated the same year as Carter. He served for over three decades in the navy, rising up the ranks. In 1970, he was appointed rear admiral. Two years later, he was both promoted to vice admiral and named the president of the U.S. Naval War College in Rhode Island. In 1975, he received the rank of full admiral and was placed in command of the forces of the North Atlantic Treaty Organization (NATO) in southern Europe. He found his new post boring, though, and was happy to accept Carter's nomination as director of central intelligence (DCI). The Senate quickly confirmed the nominee.

At first glance, it would appear that Turner would play a significant role in the administration's policy making. The president had admired Turner since their days at Annapolis, and he believed that his nominee could restore the CIA's reputation, which had been scarred by the Church committee reports. Indeed, at Turner's request, the president gave him the job of coordinating the whole intelligence community, including such groups as the National Security Agency and the State Department's foreign intelligence division. "Some day," Carter reportedly said, "Turner might make a Secretary of State in the mold of George Marshall."[28]

Turner, however, ran into a myriad of difficulties. Because he had not risen up the ranks of the CIA, he was regarded within the agency as an interloper who did not deserve the post. More damaging, he placed his faith on technology rather than humans to gather intelligence. He relieved dozens of agents from duty, some with detailed knowledge of Iran. As a result, the agency shared Sullivan's assessment of the situation in Iran. "The regime has a better than even chance of surviving the present difficulties," the CIA reported on September 1, 1978, "and the Shah will probably be able to maintain his position through the early 1980s." Turner later admitted he erred in not only relieving so many CIA officers but for not demanding "a thorough review of where the shah stood."[29]

Yet even if Turner had had extensive and accurate information, there is the question whether he would have gotten Carter's ear. Although Carter respected Turner, the two of them had not known each other well in Annapolis. Furthermore, Carter found his DCI's briefings boring. At first, Turner gave the president a briefing at least once each week on topics chosen by the DCI. But they gradually became more and more infrequent. Most scholars blame Brzezinski, contending that the NSC adviser limited the CIA director's access to the Oval Office. Robert Gates, who worked for the agency during the Carter years, demurred, recalling that "Zbig suggested to Carter on several occasions that Turner be invited" to the weekly briefing. However, Gates continued, "Carter turned him down—on one occasion firmly telling him to drop the subject."[30]

A final contributing factor to the administration's ignorance was the lack of attention devoted by top U.S. officials to Iran. SALT, the Rhodesian civil war, the Horn of Africa, U.S. bases in the Philippines, monetary policy, and the Camp David negotiations took up much of Vance's and Brzezinski's time. In addition to these matters, the president had to concern himself with a variety of domestic initiatives, including welfare and tax reform, national health insurance, hospital cost containment, and high levels of inflation and unemployment. Hence, when Carter received word from Vance and Brzezinski in September that the shah wanted a show of support, the president, rather than stopping and thinking about the possible ramifications, called Pahlavi and gave it. The shah subsequently made Carter's statement public, further angering an Iranian public that saw the president and shah in bed together.[31]

All the while, the signs in Iran grew increasingly ominous. Martial law had curbed the demonstrations, but it had failed to stop them. Then, in October, Iranian oil workers went on strike. By the end of the month, wrote Vance, the work stoppage had "reached severe proportions," with the loss of oil revenue costing Iran "about $60 million per day, or approximately 95 percent of its foreign exchange earnings." Deciding that his prime minister, Jafar Sharif-Emami, had proven unable to bring an end to the protests, the shah decided in November to replace him with a military regime led by General Gholamreza Azhari. The shah succeeded in convincing the oil workers to return to their jobs by threatening to fire them if they did not, and he had opposition leaders arrested. He convinced Iraq to deport Khomeini somewhere further from Iran, believing that it would weaken the opposition. Simultaneously, in a nationally aired address, he repeated his promise of free elections and apologized for the "past mistakes, unlawful actions, oppression and corruption" within his government.[32]

To the shah's adversaries, it was the same story they had heard before: unfulfilled promises made by a leader determined to remain in power. The protests continued. Getting Khomeini out of Iraq made no difference. The cleric settled in a town near Paris, where he made thousands of cassette tapes of his speeches, which his followers smuggled into Iran. Nor could Azhari do much to stop the demonstrations. An increasingly confused shah considered a military crackdown out of the question, as he did not want to bring international condemnation upon his government. Nor was there any guarantee that the Iranian army, of which 40 to 50 percent were conscripts, would agree to the use of force. Indeed, for all the shah and Azhari knew, many of those draftees might actually turn against the government if ordered to fire on demonstrators, which could cause a civil war. Thus, while the new government threatened to arrest those violating martial law, Pahlavi refused to permit the army to shoot at protesters.[33]

It was just before Pahlavi appointed Azhari that Carter learned how serious the shah's situation was. Sullivan reported that the monarch's days "might be numbered." Treasury Secretary Michael Blumenthal was to leave on an earlier-planned trip to the Middle East to discuss oil prices, and Carter gave him the additional job of finding out how accurate Sullivan's report was. It was not Blumenthal's first trip to the region. He had stopped off in Iran on a similar mission the year before and found Pahlavi in firm control of the nation.[34]

What the treasury secretary discovered this time caught him off guard. Rather than strong and decisive, Pahlavi appeared depressed and confused. "This man is a ghost," the treasury secretary commented as he left his meeting with the Iranian monarch. Upon his return, Blumenthal convinced Carter to find someone who was not part of the administration to lead an independent investigation of the shah's situation. The treasury suggested George Ball, President Lyndon Johnson's undersecretary of state; Carter accepted the recommendation. Following his inquiry, Ball concluded that Pahlavi's government could not survive and recommended that the United States convene an Iranian "Council of Notables" made up of people from all the major groups in Iran (except the Tudeh Party), which would oversee the formation of a new government. While the shah would retain his title and his role as commander in chief, the council would make all decisions. Undersecretary of State Christopher, sitting in for Vance—who was then in the Middle East—found Ball's report convincing, but Brzezinski rejected it, advising instead that the shah institute a military crackdown on the opposition.[35]

The disagreement between Christopher and Brzezinski typified a larger quarrel between NSC and State over Iran policy. Up through the fall of 1978, Sullivan had reported that the shah could survive if he instituted reforms, but the recent events in Iran left him feeling much more pessimistic about Pahlavi's future. Even with the military government, there was little likelihood that the shah could remain in power. Consequently, he wrote shortly after Azhari's appointment, "we need to think the unthinkable at this time in order to give our thoughts some precision should the unthinkable contingency arise." Both Christopher and Henry Precht, State's Iran desk officer, seconded the ambassador. Pahlavi's position, wrote the undersecretary, was "precarious." For Precht, the shah had "only a marginal chance of surviving as a constitutional monarch." The United States needed "to move now with definite steps towards a post-Shah future in Iran."[36] Sullivan recommended that the United States send an official to Paris to meet with Khomeini. Vance considered this a reasonable request and named Theodore Eliot, inspector general of the foreign service. Carter, though, vetoed the Eliot mission.

It was Brzezinski who had convinced Carter not to endorse Eliot's appointment. The NSC did not share State's pessimism regarding the shah's chances of survival and asserted that a hard-nosed response by the military would quell the dissent. "I am reasonably optimistic that the immediate crisis will be surmounted," Brzezinski told Chinese Ambassador Chai Zemin. Largely ignoring the domestic origins of the opposition movement, he blamed the protests on "rightist reactionaries and Soviet radicals." It was the latter group that especially worried him, as he suggested that failure to support the shah could allow the Soviet Union to gain influence in Iran. He blamed State's reports on ignorance and personal animosities, alleging, for instance, that Precht "was motivated by doctrinal dislike of the Shah and simply wanted him out of power altogether." David Aaron, Brzezinski's deputy, shared his boss's contention that a tough approach would succeed.[37]

But the most outspoken critic of State was Gary Sick, the NSC's Iran specialist. He talked of a "gradual choking off of any useful communication" with Precht. However, he focused most of his vituperation upon Sullivan. He considered inane the ambassador's proposal to prepare for the "unthinkable." "It is very unlikely that any U.S. president would ever have associated himself with a plan that called for the United States to dismiss peremptorily the entire top military leadership of a foreign nation and then delegate responsibility for selecting replacements from a group of revolutionary leaders." He also accurately charged the U.S. ambassador with giving rosy reports of the situation in Iran, only to suggest now that the shah might have to depart. To Sick, Sullivan's change of heart only bred confusion within the shah's government as to whether it could continue to expect U.S. backing.[38]

Carter rejected the idea of a military crackdown, contending it would cause unnecessary bloodshed. Aside from that, he agreed with the NSC and, at the suggestion of Acting Secretary of Defense Charles Duncan—

Secretary Brown was in Europe for a NATO meeting—sent to Tehran General Robert Huyser. Huyser, the deputy commander of the U.S. military in Europe, in 1978 had helped reorganize Iran's military. In the process, he gained the trust of the shah and came to know many of the leaders of Iran's armed forces. His job was to convince the Iranian military to stay in Iran if the shah left. But Huyser ran into a myriad of problems. Iran's military leaders feared they would be killed if the shah left and they stayed behind. He found his work contradicted by that of Sullivan, who, angered with the cancellation of the Eliot mission, charged the U.S. president with making a "gross and perhaps irretrievable mistake by failing to send [an] emissary . . . to see Khomeini." Finally, there was a lack of leadership from the White House. Carter later commented that he should have fired Sullivan for insubordination; rather, he allowed Sullivan to remain in his post until February 1979, when the ambassador resigned in protest of U.S. Iran policy. This left both the shah and the Iranian military confused: Who spoke for the United States, Huyser or Sullivan, and would Washington give it support if it assumed power in a post-shah Iran? The U.S. government never made it clear. "We personally prefer that the Shah maintain a major role in the government," Carter told reporters, "but that's a decision for the Iranian people to make."[39] Thus, with Sullivan and Huyser at odds, and Carter waffling, the shah's uncertainty grew, while Iran's armed forces had no reason to expect U.S. support if it took action of its own.

Whether a more decisive stand by the administration would have made a difference is questionable. Even had the White House clearly stated its willingness to support a military-led government, the shah had throughout shown no preparedness to use widespread force against his people. Had he given an order to his generals to crack down on the protests, the Iranian armed forces might still have stood aside. To ask conscripts to fire upon their own people risked not only massive desertions but civil conflict. A divided Iran might play into the hands of the Soviet Union, which Iran's generals saw as a greater threat than Khomeini.[40] Still, there is no question that the Carter administration's indecisiveness left Iran's military confused as to whether it would receive U.S. backing if it did attempt to seize power.

The lack of leadership from the Oval Office had another impact: it prevented the administration from making contingency plans for the shah's fall. Carter and the NSC strongly resisted suggestions from advisers such as Ball, Sullivan, and Precht to give consideration to relations with a post-shah government. A differently organized bureaucracy would have made it easier for the administration to confront this crisis or at least have facilitated "analyzing the nature of the successor regime."[41]

Not certain if he had U.S. support, and realizing he faced widespread resistance in Iran, at the end of December the shah appointed Shahpour

Bakhtiar, a member of the opposition National Front and a Pahlavi critic, as the new prime minister. Bakhtiar only accepted the post on the grounds that the shah leave the nation, dissolve SAVAK, and release all political prisoners. Pahlavi acquiesced. On January 16, he departed, declaring he needed some rest but intending to return to Iran as a constitutional monarch. News of his departure prompted tens of thousands of Iranians to take to the streets in celebration. On February 1, Khomeini returned to throngs of followers so large that he could not get to the city by car and had to travel via helicopter.[42]

Khomeini now faced the prospect of consolidating his power in a country with pro-shah military officers who might try to overthrow him. That concern soon dissipated, as the armed forces decided to stay neutral rather than risk civil war. Knowing that he had neither the support of the military nor Khomeini, Bakhtiar resigned. Mehdi Bazargan became the leader of a new Provisional Government (PG). But as Bazargan was one of Khomeini's advisers, the locus of power fell into the hands of the imam and the fundamentalist-dominated Revolutionary Council.[43]

Having not prepared itself for the shah's fall, the Carter administration had no certainty as to what it could expect from the new Iranian government. "Reports on Khomeini's foreign policy views and contacts give little insight into his specific plans," the CIA reported in January. "[W]e can have confidence only in generalizations about the Ayatollah's foreign policy attitudes." Nor could State provide much insight. Even scholars with expertise on Iran were divided over what type of nation a Khomeini-led Iran might become.[44] Uncertain what would happen next, the administration adopted a policy of wait-and-see.

The first signs were mixed. On the one hand, both Huyser and the American embassy in Iran became the target of anti-American propaganda, causing the general to request, and Carter to agree, for him to return to the United States in early 1979. Then came the Valentine's Day attack. On the other hand, the assault on the embassy in mid-February had been brought to an end by the new Iranian government. Khomeini still faced opposition from various groups, including secular leftists, and did not want to make Washington so angry that it might help them. Therefore, he had sent to the American compound a group of militants led by PG member Ibrahim Yazdi, who brought an end to the hostage-taking and then apologized for the incident. The quick resolution of the Valentine's Day affair left Precht hopeful that the Carter administration might be able to work with "moderates" in the new Iranian government and establish closer relations between it and the United States.[45]

The White House had all the more reason to seek a working relationship with the Khomeini regime, as it knew it would face criticism from the shah's allies that it had "lost" Iran. It was also this concern that made

Carter determined to successfully complete the Camp David peace process. Yet with a crisis in Iran to add to his list of concerns, Carter assigned Robert Strauss, who had previously acted as his special trade negotiator, to reach a Palestinian settlement. The choice did not please Vance, who, having been in battle with Brzezinski over the past two years, now saw himself as having to contend as well with Strauss; the secretary of state threatened to resign, only convinced after a long talk with Mondale, Strauss, and Jordan to stay on. As it turned out, Strauss, who had no experience with Middle East diplomacy, ended up conflicting with Vance over who had authority in overseeing the Mideast peace process. Furthermore, Strauss found Begin and Sadat at odds: Begin would not accept the type of Palestinian autonomy Sadat favored, while Sadat, under pressure from advisers who charged him with having given up too much at Camp David, wanted the United States to play a bigger role in promoting an autonomy settlement.[46]

Afghanistan and North Yemen

If the troubles in the Middle East were not enough, the White House had to concern itself with another new crisis, this time in Iran's neighbor, Afghanistan. In 1973, Sardar Muhammad Daoud Khan, the former prime minister, overthrew the nation's royal family, which had been accused of corruption and criticized for its failure to resolve Afghanistan's economic troubles, and seized control of the government. But Daoud's failure to bring economic stability, his purging of leftists from his government, the deterioration of his relationship with the Soviet Union, and his refusal to accept dissent to his rule prompted the communist People's Democratic Party of Afghanistan (PDPA) to stage a coup in late April 1978. Daoud was killed, and PDPA leader Nur Muhammad Taraki became the nation's leader.

Afghanistan's turn to communism gave rise to another Vance-Brzezinski disagreement. Prior to the coup, the United States had provided economic aid to Kabul. Citing a lack of evidence of Soviet complicity in the recent events in Afghanistan, Vance called for a continuation of that assistance to limit Soviet influence over the new government. Brzezinski, though, saw Moscow's handiwork in the change of leadership and argued for cutting ties with Kabul and instituting covert operations to undermine the Kremlin's plans for Afghanistan. For the time being, Carter backed Vance and sent a new ambassador, Adolph Dubs, to Kabul.[47]

Taraki, however, turned to the Soviet Union for help to build up his country's economic infrastructure. His government also passed secular legislation that included the right to vote for women and a ban on forced marriage, and it instituted a program of land reform. These initiatives angered many traditional Muslims in the country who, by the middle of the year, had begun a violent revolt against the leadership. The regime countered with such measures as executing or forcibly exiling its opponents, but it failed to put down the uprising.

In February 1979, during one of these spurts of violence, Dubs was abducted by Islamic radicals and killed. As far as the United States was concerned, the Soviet Union was somehow involved in the murder, either having taken part in the planning or having purposely avoided steps that might have prevented Dubs's death. While Undersecretary of State for Political Affairs David Newsom proposed limiting the American response to not appointing a replacement for Dubs, Brzezinski, with Mondale's support, and over the objections of a more cautious-minded DCI Turner, convinced Carter in April 1979 to secretly offer assistance to Taraki's opponents. In July, the order went out to the CIA to provide a half million dollars in nonlethal military aid, via Pakistan, to the Afghan rebels. The Saudis, desirous to aid Muslim brethren and make life difficult for the Soviets, offered financial assistance of their own.[48] It was the beginning of what would under the Ronald Reagan administration become a major commitment to the Afghan insurgency.

The United States also increased its commitment to North Yemen. Achieving independence from Britain in 1968, South Yemen had turned to communism. It became known as the People's Democratic Republic of Yemen (PDRY) and tightened its relationship with the Soviet Union and Cuba. North Yemen, better known as the Yemen Arab Republic (YAR), formed six years earlier, also had ties to Moscow. Although the two Yemens had plans for unification, disagreements between them placed those plans on hold.

By the mid-1970s, the United States, alongside Saudi Arabia, had developed closer relations with the YAR, providing assistance to modernize the North's army. Then, in July 1978, the president of the YAR was killed, reportedly at the hands of PDRY agents. In February of the following year, North Yemeni President Ali Abdullah Saleh told the U.S. ambassador to his country that South Yemen, with Soviet support, had launched an attack on the YAR. Brzezinski argued that losing North Yemen on top of Ethiopia and Iran would endanger the shipment of goods, including oil, from the Middle East to the Suez Canal, place Saudi Arabia in jeopardy, and make the United States look weak in the Middle East. He convinced the president in March 1979 to send the aircraft carrier *Constellation* to the area, AWACS aircraft to Saudi Arabia, and $390 million in weaponry to North Yemen.[49]

This assistance to the YAR was important for several reasons. For one, there was no solid evidence that South Yemen had launched a major assault; even the staff of the U.S. embassy in North Yemen was not sure of the validity of Saleh's claim. Second, that Carter, in violation of his own arms control initiative, would provide nearly $400 million in weaponry despite the lack of solid evidence of a PDRY attack demonstrated how much anti-Sovietism had come to dominate his administration's foreign policy. Finally, the assistance to the YAR did little to turn it away from the Soviet Union. In fact, a few months later, the North Yemeni government signed an arms agreement with Moscow that was far larger than that it had reached with Washington.[50]

The Sino–Vietnamese War

Combined, commented Brzezinski, the troubles in the Near East and Afghanistan had created an "arc of crisis," which offered not only to destabilize the entire region but to open the door to greater Soviet influence. "The resulting political chaos could well be filled by elements hostile to our values and sympathetic to our adversaries," he warned.[51]

But the crises that risked affecting America's interests actually went beyond the region in question. Southeast Asia was a case in point. There, relations between the People's Republic of China and Vietnam had grown steadily worse. Beijing did not appreciate Hanoi's decision to tighten its ties with Moscow. Charges by the Chinese that Vietnamese troops had entered territory claimed by the People's Republic fueled Beijing's anger. Then, in the fall of 1978, Vietnam fomented a refugee crisis by forcing tens of thousands of ethnic Chinese from Vietnam, many of whom set sail on crude boats, hoping to escape to Malaysia or other countries in Southeast Asia.[52] The Chinese joined numerous nations, among them the United States, in condemning Vietnam.

Then came what, for China, was the final straw. In 1975, with Vietnamese support, the communist Khmer Rouge, led by Pol Pot, overthrew the Cambodian government of Lon Nol. Pol Pot then began a brutal policy of repression that killed at least 1 million Cambodians, or about 25 percent of his nation's population. The Khmer Rouge–Vietnamese alliance, however, began to fall apart as Pol Pot distanced himself from Hanoi and turned more to Beijing. Cambodian troops also staged incursions into territory claimed by both Cambodia and Vietnam. Following talks with their Soviet ally, in November 1978 the Vietnamese launched an invasion of Cambodia, forcing Pol Pot and the Khmer rouge into the western part of the country and installing Hang Samrin as the country's new leader.

It would seem on the surface that, despite his own unwillingness to normalize relations with Vietnam, Carter would welcome the developments in Cambodia. The president had referred to Pol Pot as the "worst violator of human rights in the world today." The new Cambodian government was, by comparison, far less violent. But sharing Brzezinski's determination to befriend China and contain the Soviet Union and its allies, the president set aside his predilections and instead backed Chinese military shipments that went through Thailand to Pol Pot and the Khmer Rouge. And, if Pol Pot did return to power, then, Carter hoped, he would prove less repressive. The president's violation of his own human rights policy did not go unnoticed. Carter had to condemn, not assist, Pol Pot, argued Democratic Representative Norman Dicks of Washington, whose actions "rivaled 'those perpetrated in Nazi Germany during World War II, and which make human rights violations in Chile, Uganda, and the Soviet Union pale by comparison.'"[53] Arguably, the White House had also violated its policy on conventional arms transfers. While the weapons did not come from the United States, Washington aided their shipment.

The Chinese, meanwhile, decided that it was not enough simply to provide weapons to their Khmer ally. To Beijing, Hanoi's invasion of Cambodia was an attempt by Vietnam to expand its—and, by extension, Soviet—power in a part of the world that China regarded as within its sphere of influence. At the end of January 1979, Chinese Premier Deng Xiaoping arrived in the United States to celebrate the normalization of Sino–American relations. During his visit, he informed Carter and the president's advisers of Beijing's decision to launch an invasion of northern Vietnam and teach it "an appropriate limited lesson." Rather than insist that China not launch the attack, Carter only asked the People's Republic to restrain itself. Commented CIA agent and later DCI Gates, "This had to have been the best signal Deng could have hoped for," for Carter had made no suggestion that an invasion of Vietnam would inhibit the normalization process.[54]

There is no way to know whether, by putting more pressure on China, the Carter administration could have dissuaded the People's Republic from attacking Vietnam. Beijing obviously considered Hanoi's activities in Cambodia as a serious threat to China's interests and might have attacked even if the United States had issued public denunciations of its new ally. What is clear is that the president had placed two key components of his foreign policy in danger by asking only for Chinese restraint. One was normalization of relations with China. The president himself had commented to Deng that a Chinese attack on Vietnam would likely draw Hanoi international sympathy, and it might even convince an American public that normalization with an aggressor like the People's Republic was not in U.S. interests. The other was SALT. Morton Abramowitz, the deputy assistant secretary of defense, warned both Carter and Mondale on February 1 that a Chinese attack on Vietnam would surely push Hanoi more into Moscow's arms and could convince the Vietnamese government to give the Soviets the right to establish a permanent naval presence in Vietnam. Such an event might push U.S. opinion against SALT's ratification.[55] But in an atmosphere where Carter had drawn closer to Brzezinski's view of the world, the president was willing to take those risks.

By February 16, the Chinese had amassed aircraft and about 170,000 soldiers along their border with Vietnam. The following day, they attacked. To maintain its flexibility and avoid any damage to the normalization or SALT processes, the White House denied any advance knowledge of the invasion and called upon both China and Vietnam to end hostilities. The Soviets did not buy it. They refused to discuss any compromises that might bring the SALT talks to a successful end until the People's Republic withdrew its troops. They also accused the administration of duplicitous behavior and hinted that they might use force against the Chinese. Although Moscow never made any provocative moves against the People's Republic—at least in part because the wording of its treaty with Vietnam did not commit it to military action—had it done so, Beijing would have had ample warning: during the crisis, Brzezinski held daily meetings with Ambassador Chai during which he gave the emissary U.S. intelligence on Soviet military deployments.[56]

On March 5, the Chinese began their withdrawal from Vietnam, which they completed on March 16. It appears that Beijing considered its capture of the northern Vietnamese provincial capital of Lang Son as providing the final stamp on its "lesson," and, therefore, it could pull out having felt it had achieved success. With the war over, the administration could now breathe easier. Despite the risks it had taken, the White House successfully avoided a storm it could have easily gotten itself into. It had fended off efforts by lawmakers, some of whom saw the attack upon Vietnam as proof that China could not be trusted, to reaffirm America's determination to defend Taiwan.[57] Instead, the president got the milder Taiwan Relations Act. Nor had the Chinese assault killed SALT. But it had delayed the process, to the detriment of those negotiations.

"Holding in Abeyance" the Withdrawal of Troops

There was worse news regarding the White House's intention to withdraw troops from South Korea. That plan already had been held up in part by congressional opposition, but even more so by the Koreagate scandal. Lawmakers had become incensed by the refusal of South Korean President Park Chung-hee to send his former ambassador in Washington, Kim Dong-jo, to Congress to provide testimony about the scandal; in turn, Capitol Hill threatened not to pass a compensation package that would provide military equipment to South Korea after U.S. troops left. In the summer of 1978, the new U.S. ambassador to South Korea, William Gleysteen, and South Korean Foreign Minister Park Tong-jin reached an agreement by which they would send questions to Dong-jo in return for assurances by the government in Seoul that he would submit "concrete factual information regarding his financial transactions with Members of

Congress." Kim did so by early September, asserting that he had offered money only to one person, former Representative Jerome Waldie (D-California). Although the House Ethics Committee charged Kim with supplying answers that were both false and incomplete, Speaker Tip O'Neill held that Kim's answers were truthful; the Senate Select Committee on Ethics shared O'Neill's conclusions. Commented Platt in early October, "Koreagate is [d]ying."[58]

But if the administration believed it now possible to proceed with the withdrawal of American forces, that became highly unlikely when, in January 1979, the *Army Times* published a report leaked to it on North Korea's military capabilities. The report concluded that the North's army had 40 divisions rather than the original estimate of 29, and 2,600 tanks instead of 2,000. Immediately, the administration came under intense pressure from lawmakers to forego the withdrawal plan. A bipartisan group from the Armed Services Committee who had stopped off in South Korea on the way home from a visit to China privately told Gleysteen—who himself disliked Carter's plan—that the president should call off any troop reductions and made their complaints public upon their return to Washington. For instance, Senator Sam Nunn (D-Georgia) said that proceeding with troop withdrawals would "reduce deterrence" and "increase the possibility" of another Korean war. The White House was put on the defensive. "Ever since the Congress became aware of our upgraded intelligence estimates of the North Korean order of battle," Brzezinski informed Carter that same month, "pressure has been building for a review of our policy of withdrawing U.S. combat forces form the Republic of Korea." He continued that he, Vance, and Secretary of Defense Harold Brown "agreed that the revised estimates . . . warrant a thorough review . . . of the withdrawal policy."[59]

Placed on the defensive, Carter announced that the United States was "holding in abeyance any further reductions," pending a reevaluation of North Korea's capabilities. This did not mean he had totally given up the idea. In fact, during Carter's visit to Seoul in June 1979, President Park urged him to keep troops in South Korea, pointing out not only that it would take time for the South to build up its military, but that the North's armed forces might be able to maintain their superiority over those of the South. Carter replied that he could not promise he would keep U.S. forces in the South, yet also expressed frustration that the continued disparity of forces on the peninsula might mean American troops would have to remain indefinitely. It soon became clear to the president that he had no choice but to accept the continued presence of U.S. military forces. In July, and to the pleasure of both the South Koreans and the Japanese, he reiterated his February decision to keep American troops on the peninsula pending the review of forces there.[60] By the time the administration's term came to an end, U.S. troops had not been removed.

Revolution in Nicaragua

The administration also mishandled a crisis in Nicaragua. With American support, Anastasio Somoza García, the head of the Nicaraguan National Guard, had seized power in that country in 1936. For more than forty years, the Somoza family retained control of Nicaragua: Anastasio's son, Luis, assumed power in 1956 when his father was assassinated, and then, upon his death in 1967, authority transferred to Luis's brother, Anastasio Debayle.

Because of their anticommunist stance, the Somozas were granted large amounts of economic and military aid by the United States, which over-looked their corruption and repressiveness. Most notable was an earth-quake that hit the capital, Managua, in 1972. Countries from around the world sent millions of dollars in aid to help the country rebuild, only to have Somoza skim off much of it for his own use. Meanwhile, the Nicaraguan people suffered. The top 5 percent of Nicaraguans made 30 percent of all the nation's income, while the bottom 50 percent took in only 15 percent. In the countryside, the wealthiest 5 percent of Nicaraguans owned 85 percent of the land, while almost 40 percent were landless. So-moza himself came to control one-third of the nation's useable land, its airlines, television and radio stations, and banks, an empire worth almost $1 billion.[61]

Such conditions motivated Somoza's opponents to rally against him. The most radical opposition force was the Sandinista National Libera-tion Front (FSLN), better known simply as the Sandinistas. Founded in 1961 and named in honor of the early twentieth-century Nicaraguan revolutionary Augusto Sandino, it engaged in guerrilla warfare against the government.

As it had done with the Gerald Ford administration with regard to hu-man rights, it was Congress that forced the Carter White House to address U.S. policy toward Nicaragua. In the spring of 1977, Representative Ed Koch (D-New York), a new internationalist and "Watergate baby," pro-posed removing from a foreign assistance bill military aid for Managua. The demand split the State Department. The Bureau of Human Rights, cit-ing Somoza's repression, supported the Koch proposal. Terence Todman, the head of the Bureau of Inter-American Affairs, railed against it, citing the need to protect Central America from "hostile forces and bases."[62]

As he had done elsewhere, Carter paper-clipped policy. Believing that economic and military aid offered levers to move other countries to re-spect the rights of their citizens, the White House sought to get Congress to appropriate the money. The administration also took into account So-moza's allies on Capitol Hill, among them Democratic Representatives John Murphy of New York, a friend of Somoza's since childhood, and, more importantly, Texas's Charles Wilson. A conservative Democrat and influential member of the Foreign Operations Subcommittee of the House Appropriations Committee, Wilson could have a significant impact upon U.S. foreign policy. With Wilson's help, in June the House appropriated funding for the military assistance to Nicaragua. But to please more liberal-minded lawmakers like Koch, as well as to encourage Somoza to enact positive change, the Carter administration refused to release the money. While this carrot-and-stick policy was aimed at trying to get Somoza to reform his regime, it gave the appearance of a confused administration to those outside of Nicaragua; to Somoza's opponents, it demonstrated the reluctance of the United States to get rid of the Nicaraguan leader. Indeed, when Somoza suffered a heart attack in July while showering at the home of his mistress, the administration sent a U.S. Air Force ambulance aircraft to take him to Miami for treatment. For the FSLN, it was further proof that the White House had no intention of giving up on its long-time Nicaraguan ally.[63]

The fact was that the Carter administration saw little reason to push Somoza out of power, as the Sandinistas seemed too weak to offer much of a threat to him. This was one reason why, during the remainder of 1977, the White House largely ignored what was happening in Nicaragua. Additionally, the administration shared Todman's conviction that the United States not embarrass Somoza and use quiet, behind-the-scenes diplomacy to get him to enact reforms. Finally, Carter, Brzezinski, Vance, and even Christopher, whom Vance had largely assigned to oversee Latin American issues, had other matters to which to attend, such as the Middle East peace talks, the Panama Canal treaty negotiations, and SALT.[64]

The January 1978 murder of Pedro Joaquín Chamorro, a well-respected newspaper editor and critic of the Somoza government, forced the White House's hand. The assassination set off protests throughout Nicaragua that continued for months, with the demonstrators blaming the Somoza government for Chamorro's death. The White House, at Christopher's recommendation, sought to distance itself from Somoza without abandoning him. That, however, did not sit well with Wilson. In 1977, the administration had suspended all new economic aid to Nicaragua, including two Agency for International Development (AID) loans, because of the repression there. In the spring of 1978, the Texas lawmaker threatened to kill a foreign aid bill if the White House did not release the two loans. Desirous to avoid angering Wilson, the White House, at Christopher's suggestion, released the loans.[65]

Carter made matters worse in June. After the Nicaraguan dictator offered to cooperate with the Inter-American Commission on Human Rights (IACHR) and to give amnesty to his political opponents, the president decided to send him a letter to encourage the continuation of such moves. In this case, Vance, HA, the Inter-American Bureau, and even Brzezinski thought that it was a bad idea to send the message, for it was likely Somoza would publicize it. But Carter ordered it delivered. The president should have listened to his advisers. Somoza later wrote that the "letter, if publicly known, could assist me greatly in warding off my enemies. I was not interested in a collector's item, and without being able to use the letter, that's what it was." With that reasoning, the Nicaraguan leader made it public.[66]

News of the president's sign of approbation had an impact both in the United States and in Nicaragua. At home, the White House came under attack for inconsistency. How could it deny aid to Nicaragua for violating human rights, only to provide it despite any lack of real change there?[67] And how could Carter praise Somoza when he had only made offers to the IACHR and his political opponents?

Elsewhere in Latin America, the letter made Somoza's enemies all the more determined to push him out of power. Venezuelan President Carlos Andrés Pérez, a friend of Chamorro's and an advocate of Carter's human rights policy, had become disheartened by the U.S. president's apparent unwillingness to abandon the Nicaraguan dictator and became furious with news of Carter's message. Pérez determined to get rid of Somoza, which, by early 1979, meant secretly providing assistance to the Sandinistas.[68]

In Nicaragua, the note gave Somoza all the proof he needed to deflect demands that he give up the presidency, while it annoyed the Nicaraguan dictator's opponents, who had hoped the United States would edge him out. Moderate elements who wanted Somoza gone formed the Broad Opposition Front (FAO) in the summer of 1978 and sought both domestic and international help for their cause. In August, the FAO launched a general strike to overthrow the government. That same month, Sandinista commandos seized control of the National Palace, where the Nicaraguan Congress was then in session, and took 1,500 people hostage, among them one of Somoza's cousins. They only left after Somoza, fearful his relative might be killed, met their demands, including money, the release of several Sandinista prisoners from jail, and safe passage out of the nation for the commandos themselves. Not only did the Sandinista raid make Somoza look weak and prompt spontaneous acts of insurrection throughout Nicaragua, but it drew attention away from the FAO and to the FSLN. Then, as the fighting in Nicaragua continued, the FAO suffered a serious blow when, in September, the Sandinistas convinced one of its most influential leaders, Alfonso Robelo, to join them.[69]

The government struck back hard at its opponents. National Guard forces shelled and bombed cities to destroy opposition forces, killing numerous civilians. Women were raped; health care facilities, schools, and Red Cross centers were destroyed; and boys and men between the ages of 13 and 30, regarded as possible enemies, were rounded up and jailed or executed. Rather than crush the Sandinistas, these hard-handed tactics only served to push more of the population into their hands and, in the process, weaken the moderate FAO.[70]

The growing strength of the Sandinistas, and the increasing impotence of both the Somoza government and the FAO, posed a serious problem for the Carter administration. U.S. Ambassador Mauricio Solaun suggested that Somoza offer to resign in 1980 rather than serve out his term until May 1981. Viron Vaky, who had replaced Todman in April 1978 following Todman's reassignment as ambassador to Spain, was less willing to give. The United States, he reasoned, had to get Somoza to give up power and replace him with a moderate government led by the FAO. But such a move would have to take place quickly, he continued; otherwise, the FAO, already weakened by Robelo's departure, might fall apart, leaving no moderate alternative to the Sandinistas. Once again, though, the administration was wracked by division. The NSC's Brzezinski and Robert Pastor and the State's Christopher and Anthony Lake rejected Vaky's proposal. They thought it abandoned the policy of nonintervention—even though that policy was nonexistent—and risked bringing to power a government too feeble to protect the nation against the Sandinistas. The president seconded the majority of his advisers. He had all the more reason for caution, for in September, about 70 lawmakers, including Murphy, Wilson, and House Majority Leader James Wright urged him to support the Somoza government. Carter did not want to risk endangering other initiatives by pushing Somoza out.[71]

With the situation in Nicaragua getting worse, the Carter administration latched onto a Costa Rican proposal to have several Central American nations mediate an end to the fighting. Somoza quickly nixed the idea. Deciding it had no choice if it was to keep Nicaragua out of Sandinista hands, the White House concluded it needed to assume a leading role in any negotiations and sent William Jorden, the former ambassador to Panama, to Nicaragua to convince Somoza to come on board.[72]

At first, it looked like a negotiated settlement was possible. Somoza now accepted the U.S. proposal (though only because he believed he could use it to remain in power). Wanting to make negotiations a multilateral effort, the White House obtained the endorsement of the Organization of American States (OAS), which named a team made up of the United States, Guatemala, and the Dominican Republic. William Bowdler, the American representative and head of the team, even got the FAO's approval. Bowdler had been instructed to preserve the National Guard. Although Representative Tom Harkin (D-Iowa) charged that maintaining the Guard demonstrated "absolutely no commitment to the Nicaraguan people's right of self-determination," Bowdler persuaded the FAO to accept the Guard's perpetuation, though only after the Front got him to accept the "reorganization" of the Guard to get rid of those officers most tied to the violations of human rights.[73]

Hopes for a negotiated settlement were soon dashed. For one, the Sandinistas denounced the negotiations, seeing them as simply a way to retain Somoza's control of Nicaragua. For another, Somoza showed no indication he would resign. Vaky insisted that the United States turn up the heat on Somoza, but Brzezinski, on Pastor's advice, convinced Carter not to do that. The United States, Pastor had asserted, should not continue America's past policy of overthrowing governments. Moreover, the U.S. midterm elections were coming up, Pastor had written, and putting pressure on Somoza could be used against the administration by its opponents. Rather, after the election, the president, with the support of Pastor and Brzezinski, and over the objections of Vance, Christopher, Vaky, and Bowdler, proposed a national plebiscite to determine whether Somoza would remain in power. Realizing he would not succeed in changing the president's mind, Bowdler suggested having an International Authority oversee the vote and convinced the FAO to second the supervised plebiscite. But in January 1979 when Somoza rejected the proposal, an angry Bowdler left Nicaragua, while the FAO declared the talks over.[74]

Despite these ominous signs, the administration still remained cautious about coming down too hard on Somoza. In early 1979, Wilson again threatened to undermine a foreign aid bill if the White House, in retaliation for Somoza's stubbornness, cut off $12 million in economic aid the Texan claimed the administration had promised to give the Nicaraguan leader. Administration officials, including Henry Owen, the NSC's special representative for economic summits, and Brzezinski, warned Carter against challenging the influential lawmaker. The president, therefore, only eliminated $150,000 in military training for the Guard. Years later, one State Department official angrily criticized Carter's unwillingness to go further, charging him with "vacillati[on]" and the White House with "tip toeing around when it should have been far more forceful in pursuing policy."[75]

By this time, the loss of Robelo and its own willingness to back proposals that Somoza repeatedly rejected had severely weakened the FAO. One-third of the fifteen groups that had originally joined it had left by January 1979. In the meantime, the Sandinistas continued to gain strength. They received assistance from Cuba, Venezuela, and Costa Rica, all of which wanted to see Somoza overthrown. While the United States had information of this aid for the FSLN, it largely ignored it, as legislation relevant to completing the turnover of the Panama Canal to Panama was coming up for a vote; the White House did not want to suffer the embarrassment of losing that vote by acknowledging the outside help the FSLN was receiving. Moreover, the administration had other issues about which to worry, most notably the revolution in Iran and the SALT talks, and problems at home, such as a gas shortage that hit the nation in the spring of 1979.[76]

And it faced a new problem in Latin America, the overthrow of the government of Grenada by the Marxist People's Revolutionary Party, also known as the New Jewel Movement (NJM). New Jewel had formed in 1973 to challenge the repressive leadership of Eric Gairy. Gairy had ruled the island since 1951, when Great Britain granted the islanders universal suffrage. In March 1979, while Gairy was out of the country, the NJM staged a coup, installing Maurice Bishop as the nation's new prime minister.[77]

Since Britain still had influence in Grenada, the United States had London take the lead in handling matters there. Cognizant that they might find themselves in trouble, Bishop and the NJM assured foreign, including American, officials that they wanted good relations with Washington. The U.S. ambassador, Frank Ortiz, suggested that Washington attempt to establish friendly ties with Bishop's government, as it could prevent the NJM from turning too much to Cuba for support. The White House agreed, recognizing the Bishop government on March 22, but with the admonition that it respect the constitutional rights of Grenadians.[78]

Bishop did just the opposite. Three days later, the new prime minister suspended the constitution and announced he would retain his emergency powers. On the orders of the White House, Ortiz warned Bishop not "to develop closer links to Cuba." Declared the angered Grenadian leader, "No country has the right to tell us what to do or how to run the country, or who to be friendly with." He then announced that Grenada had established formal diplomatic ties with Havana. While perturbed, the White House still believed it could draw Bishop away from Cuba. On the suggestion of some of his advisers, Carter provided aid to other nations in the region, in the hopes that in return they would encourage Grenada to moderate its attitude.[79]

With its focus in the Caribbean and Central America drawn to Grenada, it was not until June, when it became clear that Somoza's regime was on its last legs, that the White House re-involved itself in Nicaragua. While there was general congruity in opinion that Somoza had to resign quickly and make room for new leadership, there was a split among administration officials over what that new leadership should be. Vaky advanced that a Sandinista takeover of Nicaragua was inevitable and the United States had to resign itself to that fact. The FSLN's members not only "were not committed Marxists," but their need for U.S. economic aid for Nicaragua would temper whatever radical beliefs they had.[80]

Brzezinski did not buy it. He held that the Sandinistas were a real threat, and there was no way to moderate their behavior. Moreover, to acquiesce to an FSLN victory so soon after the fall of the shah of Iran would prompt charges that Carter had "lost" not just Iran but Nicaragua to the forces of radicalism; in turn, passing SALT would become all the more difficult. He proposed a "Government of National Reconciliation" that

would have both the support of the National Guard and the power to negotiate with the Sandinistas to end the war. Furthermore, to guarantee a
peaceful transition of power, he suggested an "inter-American peacekeeping force" be sent to Nicaragua. Although Vaky and others in State explained that neither the FSLN nor OAS would accept the idea, Carter, himself worried about the impact of Somoza's downfall upon SALT, bought
into it. On June 21, Vance, against his better judgment, brought the
peacekeeping force proposal before the OAS and accused the FSLN of seeking Cuban help. The OAS refused to accept the charge of Cuban-Sandinista
collaboration. And, as State had warned, neither the FSLN nor OAS, both
of which wanted nothing short of Somoza and his hated National Guard
out of power, adopted the White House proposal.[81]

Had the United States demanded Somoza leave office in the fall or early
winter of 1978, when the FAO had some semblance of strength, a centrist
government might have been able to assume power. Now, it was too late,
and Washington had no choice but to reconcile itself to a Sandinista government. In fact, events in Washington and Nicaragua actually made that
easier for the administration. At home, Congress on June 20 nixed several
amendments designed to kill the Panama Canal legislation under consideration; this meant that the White House no longer had to worry about Murphy
or Wilson or how they might affect that legislation. That same day, members
of the National Guard executed ABC journalist Bill Stewart. Americans were
infuriated and all the less willing to save the Guard. "The response by the
public," Pastor recollected, "was unlike anything I had seen since I had been
in the White House. . . . One consequence of the tragedy was that it quieted
the thunder from the right in the United States."[82]

On June 27, Lawrence Pezzullo, the U.S. ambassador to Uruguay, met
with Somoza after having been asked to replace Solaun, who had left his
post earlier that spring. Pezzullo's jobs were to seek Somoza's departure, to
maintain the integrity of the National Guard, and to see the establishment of a transitional government made up of conservative and moderate
opposition groups, in which the FSLN would play at most a limited role.[83]
All but the first proved unattainable. Most Nicaraguans rejected any idea
of keeping the Guard, while the White House was fooling itself to assume
that Nicaraguans would accept a government that did not include the
highly popular FSLN. On July 17, Somoza fled the nation for the United
States; two days later, the Sandinistas took over the government. The issue
for Washington now was how to handle this unwanted turn of events,
which the White House should have seen coming months earlier.

Conservatives charged the Carter administration with "losing"
Nicaragua. The only way the United States, though, could have saved the
Somoza government was through a military intervention, which even the
president's critics opposed.[84] Where Carter did err was in a contradictory
policy that combined nonintervention with intervention and support for

human rights with support for a repressive government. When it became clear that Somoza was not going to survive, the White House attempted to find a moderate alternative, when in fact the best opportunity for such an alternative had passed.

The Locomotive and the Law of the Sea

The news on the economic front was not much better. The president could point to a successful meeting in February 1979 with Mexican President José López Portillo, at which they reached an accord regarding the importation of Mexican gas into the United States, thus bringing an end to an issue that had clouded relations between the two countries. On the larger issue of the locomotive strategy, though, the news was less promising. Carter had hoped that Tokyo could reach its 7 percent goal for growth. Yet in September 1978, Prime Minister Takeo Fukuda informed Carter that Japan's economy was expanding slower than normal. Furthermore, Americans remained agitated by the imbalance of U.S.–Japanese trade. U.S. Ambassador to Tokyo Mike Mansfield placed the blame on American companies raising the price of goods they sold domestically, which allowed Japan to improve its sales in the United States.[85] But for most Americans, Tokyo's trade practices were at fault.

As proof Americans could point to an agreement reached between Mansfield and the Fukuda government in December 1978, by which Japan would increase its importation of U.S. citrus products. Japanese dock workers joined angry Japanese citrus farmers by oftentimes refusing to unload the American imports. If they did and the fruits reached a store, they might have already spoiled. Spoiled or fresh, they were marked with an American flag. Then there was the price of the fruit: a "small package" of imported tangerines cost as much as $60. Thus, the Japanese ended up avoiding the American fruit, be it because of its quality, the fact that it was not domestically produced, or its price.[86]

There was some progress in April of the following year, when talks with Tokyo resulted in a Japanese agreement to appreciate the yen, voluntarily restrict exports to the United States, reduce tariffs on some industrial items (such as computers), and increase imports of manufactured goods. Still, wrote Nicholas Platt, difficulties remained. The United States wanted Japan to open up its markets further. Meanwhile, the Fukuda government wanted concessions from the United States, including keeping its markets open to Japanese products, strengthening the dollar, controlling inflation, and "leav[ing] them alone on economic issues."[87]

Carter had no intention of leaving the Japanese alone. During discussions with Prime Minister Masayoshi Ohira in early May, the president drew attention to Japan's need to reduce its trade surplus. The prime minister stated that he had taken steps to expand domestic demand and increase imports and cited signs of progress. Yet he told Carter that the United States could help itself by controlling inflation and stabilizing the dollar.[88]

The following month, the Tokyo economic summit took place. Carter called it possibly "the most important Summit conference ever held." The United States committed itself to limiting its oil imports to the 1977 level of 8.5 million barrels a day, while the European Community would hold its to 1978 levels during that same period. Japan would adopt a limit of 5.4 million barrels (the 1979 level) during 1980 and then be allowed to increase its daily use to 6.3 to 6.9 million barrels. In return for permitting it to import more oil, the Japanese promised a 5.7 percent growth rate in 1980 to meet U.S. calls that it encourage more imports.[89]

That Japan was allowed to increase its use of petroleum, and that the United States set for itself limits that were actually larger than the year before, showed that the international community had yet to find a resolution regarding petroleum imports, which had been an area of contention between them at previous summits. In an attempt to control Americans' use of oil, in April Carter had announced his intention to start removing all controls on oil on June 1, 1979. He also pushed for passage of his windfall profits tax. When Congress failed to show any willingness to pass the tax, the president went ahead and instituted decontrol.[90]

The measures the president adopted at Tokyo and at home had little impact. The oil workers' strike in Iran had caused the price of petroleum to go up. Then, to make matters even worse, the Organization of Petroleum Exporting Countries, which met at the same time as the nations at Tokyo, decided to increase oil prices. Petroleum rose to as much as $21 a barrel, 50 percent higher than it had been six months earlier. Gas prices in the United States doubled. A lack of fuel supplies compelled some stations to shut down; those with gas saw long lines of cars, with drivers literally waiting hours to fill up. By late June, about 70 percent of all gas stations in the country were closed. In Levittown, Pennsylvania, frustration over the lack of gasoline led to a two-day riot in July. Stuart Eizenstat told the president, "All of this is occurring at a particularly inopportune time. Inflation is higher than ever. A recession is clearly facing us."[91]

Nor were things going well at the law of the sea negotiations. At the time the sixth session of UNCLOS III concluded in July 1978, there was serious concern in the White House that Congress might take unilateral action on deep-seabed mining that could undermine the UN's work. But it soon became a nonissue, at least for the time being. Although the House passed a bill acceptable to the administration, the Senate did not have a chance to act on it before Congress adjourned.[92]

Elliot Richardson had resisted using the threat of congressional legislation to promote movement at the law of the sea talks, but he ultimately relented, as opposing it offered more costs than benefits. In August 1979 the press got word of this policy. Even so, the special negotiator maintained his position of fighting actual passage of such legislation prior to completion of any law of the sea treaty. He argued that to pass the bill prior to a treaty would rile the Group of 77 and undermine any possibility of an agreement acceptable to the United States. Vance, Brzezinski, and some lawmakers backed him. Yet achieving a treaty seemed far off. As the second part of the eighth session ended in New York in August 1979, the attendees had reached agreement that a nation's territorial sea could extend a maximum of twelve miles. Still unresolved were other issues, such as a system to determine under what conditions a country could exploit the deep seabed beyond that twelve-mile limit.[93] By the time Carter left office, the United States and the other members of UNCLOS had failed to come to a final settlement on the law of the sea.

★ The Carter administration could point to some success in its attempts between the middle of 1978 and mid-1979 to promote peace and prosperity. It had restored U.S. access to military facilities in Turkey, had brought about normalized relations between Egypt and Israel, and had taken part in a successful economic summit at Tokyo. But these accomplishments came at a price. The president opened himself up to criticism for violating his human rights and conventional arms control policies in ending the Turkish arms embargo. He had to compromise his own desire for a comprehensive Mideast peace settlement to get the Egyptian-Israeli peace treaty. And the agreements reached at Tokyo did little to resolve outstanding issues concerning trade and the use of oil.

If anything, the scorecard looked gloomy. The main purpose of bringing Greece and Turkey to the negotiating table, that of ending the dispute over Cyprus, proved stillborn. The White House suffered a major embarrassment when it had to give up its proposed plan to withdraw U.S. troops from South Korea. The Chinese invasion of Vietnam drew criticism from those who were upset by Carter's decision to end America's treaty commitments to Taiwan, endangered Sino–American normalization, and delayed completion of the SALT process. The law of the sea negotiations appeared deadlocked. Maybe most important, revolutions in Iran, Nicaragua, Grenada, and Afghanistan had brought to power governments that were not only anti-American but, in some cases, pro-Soviet.

Admittedly, there was little the Carter administration could do in some instances. It could not force Greece, Turkey, and their Cypriot compatriots to see eye-to-eye; China from invading Vietnam; the Group of 77 from making demands that they felt were beneficial to their interests; or Afghanistan from turning to the Soviets for support. Nor, short of outright military intervention, could it save the shah or Somoza, or end Bishop's control of Grenada.

Yet it would be wrong to argue that the White House was entirely the victim of forces beyond its control. Carter's decision to undertake so many different initiatives and his managerial style of decision making made it difficult, if not impossible, for the administration to devote the necessary attention to each of these issues, and divisions between the NSC and State only compounded matters. Consequently, the White House put its credibility on the line by assuming that it could get Turkey and Greece to come to terms or that it could convince Congress to accept the withdrawal of U.S. troops from South Korea. It supported Pol Pot and the Khmer Rouge, despite Carter's own admission of their brutality. It mishandled the revolutions in Iran and Nicaragua, giving moral or material aid to those governments despite both their repression and clear signs of unrest, and then, after it was already too late, attempting to find centrist alternatives to Islamic fundamentalism and leftist radicalism. Lastly, it believed that it could use offers of assistance to moderate the attitude of governments that had very little reason to trust the United States.

It was not surprising, therefore, that by the middle of 1979, observers had all the more reason to see the Carter administration as hypocritical and even outright inept. In late May, a Gallup poll found Carter with only a 37 percent approval rating. While this was primarily the result of the state of the economy, only 45 percent of respondents to a *New York Times*–CBS survey a couple of months earlier had approved of his handling of the nation's foreign policy; by June, it was down to 36 percent.[94]

Consequently, Carter's political future seemed in doubt. Ronald Reagan, the former governor of California and the likely Republican candidate for the presidency, lambasted Carter for his turning over the Panama Canal to Panama, his handling of the crisis in the Horn of Africa, and his human rights policy, which Reagan charged hurt U.S. ties with anticommunist allies like Argentina. Even Democrats had started to defect, urging Senator Edward Kennedy of Massachusetts to challenge Carter for the party's nomination. Tall, handsome, with a bright smile and a head full of curly dark hair, Kennedy came from a family with a long and controversial political history. Kennedy himself had started his service in the Senate in 1962, when he was elected to the seat held by his brother John, who had decided to run for the party's nomination. A member of the party's liberal wing, Kennedy had complaints about Carter's foreign policy, such as what he saw as a weak human rights initiative. But much of his anger was aimed at Carter's domestic programs, particularly the president's refusal to champion the senator's proposal for a national health insurance program. Although Reagan, of course, had not yet secured his party's nomination, and although Kennedy had yet to declare whether he would run, polls taken in the middle of 1979 showed Carter trailing them both.[95] Without some kind of major foreign or domestic political success, Carter's chance for reelection, indeed, for renomination, looked bleak.

"DETENTE IS DEAD"

Seven

★   No one expected it would last. Chief of Staff Hamilton Jordan felt it would be over within a day. Ted Koppel, a reporter for ABC News, reluctantly left a family outing to cover a story that he believed "had no legs."[1] Little did Koppel know that the Iran hostage crisis, which began in November 1979, would make his a household name. Little did Jordan know that the crisis would become one of the most serious political issues for President Jimmy Carter and his administration.

Indeed, the hostage crisis was one of several matters that offset two successes for the White House in the last half in 1979. The first, in which the White House played a direct role, was the signing in June of the Strategic Arms Limitations Treaty (SALT II). The second, which President Carter had sought to achieve but which the British finally consummated, was an agreement at the end of the year that brought majority black rule to Rhodesia. Yet in addition to the never-ending hostage crisis, the White House had to contend with strong opposition in both the United States and Europe to SALT's provisions, as well as reports of both a Soviet brigade in Cuba and Sandinista efforts to spread their revolution beyond Nicaragua. Then, at the end of the year, the Kremlin invaded Afghanistan, placing the future of SALT and détente itself in serious doubt.

Success? The Signing of SALT II

By early 1979, both the United States and the Soviet Union wanted to complete the SALT process as soon as possible. "Beyond the extraordinary substantive stakes involved," Secretary of State Cyrus Vance wrote Carter, "failure to conclude and gain approval of a SALT II Agreement would be seen as a major setback here and abroad. The negative effect on Soviet thinking about our relations could be profound and long lasting." "All true," the president wrote in the margin. The White House might have moved toward an increasingly anti-Soviet tone, but the president clearly had not given up hope on completing SALT. The result was a mixed message in his speeches at Wake Forest and the U.S. Naval Academy in 1978. Carter repeated himself in February 1979 at Georgia Tech. The United States, he told the audience, could "not let the pressures of inevitable competition overwhelm possibilities for cooperation." Yet it also could not "let cooperation blind us to the realities of competition."[2] The Soviets, for their part, wanted to retain as much of détente as possible, and SALT would bring sanity to an arms race that might otherwise get out of control.

This determination to get through the final areas of disagreement convinced both sides to make concessions between the end of 1978 and the spring of 1979. Rather than demanding that the Soviets reduce the number of launchers to 2,250 by June 1981, Washington gave them until the end of that year. In return for getting the Kremlin to stop demanding that the United States ban all air-launched cruise missiles (ALCMs) with a range of more than 2,500 kilometers, the White House accepted Moscow's insistence to prohibit through the end of 1981 any sea- and land-based cruise missiles with a range of over 600 kilometers. Meanwhile, the Soviets agreed to limit the number of warheads on their SS-17 and SS-19 missiles. With regard to what constituted a "new missile," the Carter administration gave Moscow the leeway that it had demanded. Rather than insisting that any change to an existing weapon would make it a new one, the White House stated that it would allow for a change of plus or minus 5 percent of launch weight (how much the missile normally weighed when fueled and armed) and throw weight (how much explosive power a weapon had). It also accepted an alteration of greater than 5 percent if it was caused by the removal of "warheads and a corresponding amount of fuel." The Pentagon favored that last proposal as well, for it would assist the military's work on America's missile program. The Soviets sanctioned a U.S. proposal to ban only that telemetry encryption that inhibited verification of compliance with SALT rather than all encryption. Finally, Moscow promised not to give the Backfire an intercontinental capability and to restrict its production to thirty each year.[3]

What is most interesting is that these provisions were much closer to Vladivostok than to the deep cuts proposal the Carter administration had offered in its first year. In retrospect, one must wonder whether the White House could have achieved SALT in 1977 rather than 1979 had it used Vladivostok as the starting point rather than seek deep cuts right off the bat. Soviet Ambassador to the United States Anatoly Dobrynin later suggested as much. "With such a package we could have had an early summit, reopened the high-level direct dialogue and cleared the air. That might also have opened the possibility of another and earlier SALT agreement than the one we finally did get at the 1979 summit in Vienna."[4] Of course, even with an arms control pact signed in 1977, the president still would have had to overcome opposition in the Senate from people like Henry Jackson (D-Washington). But even into 1978, there was widespread support for SALT. Mobilizing that sentiment through a public relations campaign, coupled with proper consultation with lawmakers, could have helped Carter's cause, as had been the case with the Panama Canal treaties. Though unlikely, the president might even have gotten Jackson on board by promising that his Vladivostok-based treaty would set the stage for another settlement based on deep cuts. Instead, the president did not get SALT signed until 1979.

The Soviets had repeatedly made clear that a U.S.–Soviet summit was impossible until all the topics surrounding SALT had been resolved. Those matters finally settled, Carter traveled to Vienna, Austria, where he met with Soviet Secretary General Leonid Brezhnev. Brezhnev clearly was not in good health. He suffered from arteriosclerosis and overuse of tranquilizers. According to Dobrynin, Brezhnev's health had declined to the point that he relied heavily upon prepared papers. Several different versions were ready for use, depending upon the reply he was to give. This did not go unnoticed by the Americans at the meeting. Leslie Gelb, the director of the State Department's Bureau of Politico-Miliary Affairs, recalled that the Soviet leader looked "ill and waxen . . . [and] operated almost exclusively from a text in front of him which he read, and if there was anything raised beyond the text, he would turn to Soviet Foreign Minister [Andrei] Gromyko, who would conduct the conversation with Mr. Carter or Mr. Vance, and Mr. Brezhnev would stare ahead, maybe comprehending, maybe not." National Security Adviser Zbigniew Brzezinski had a similar recollection. "Brezhnev struck me as a genuinely pitiful figure," he wrote, "struggling valiantly to represent the Soviet Union as best he could in spite of grave physical infirmity."[5]

At Vienna, Carter, Brezhnev, and their advisers addressed more than just SALT. Discussions on the Mutual Balanced Force Reduction got nowhere. The two also held talks on the Soviet presence in Africa, which proved just as fruitless.[6] Thus, while by no means small, the only accomplishment to come out of Vienna was the signing of SALT. The accord had one overall ceiling and three sub-ceilings. The overall ceiling on launchers would be reduced from 2,400 to 2,250 by the end of 1981. Within that ceiling was a sub-ceiling of 1,320 for MIRVed ICBMs, SLBMs, and ALCM-armed bombers. Within that sub-ceiling was another that limited both superpowers to 1,200 MIRVed ICBM and SLBM launchers. Finally, of those 1,200 launchers, a maximum of 820 could be MIRVed ICBMs. Aside from the ceilings and sub-ceilings, each country could develop one new ICBM, and new SLBMs were limited to fourteen warheads. Any existing missile could not have more warheads on it than it had at the time SALT was signed. Bombers could not carry more than twenty ALCMs. As noted above, the Soviet Union would not give the Backfire an intercontinental capability and would limit production of that aircraft to thirty a year. Through the end of 1981, both countries would not deploy ground- or sea-launched cruise missiles with a range of more than six hundred kilometers. Lastly, SALT banned encryption that inhibited verification. To further verify compliance, any launcher that had been known to fire a particular type of missile would always be counted as a launcher for that missile; this would avoid the problem posed by the Soviet launchers at Derazhnya and Permovaisk. And any missile that had been tested with more than one warhead would always be considered a MIRVed weapon. The president returned home, hopeful that the Senate would ratify the agreement.

SALT Assailed at Home . . .

The upper house began its deliberations on SALT the next month. In the changed atmosphere at home, getting it ratified would be an uphill battle. The Soviets' military buildup during the 1970s and the Kremlin's activities in Africa had increased distrust of Moscow as well as a desire that the United States bolster its own military. By 1978, over half of Americans felt their nation's strength and influence had fallen behind that of the Soviet Union; by June of that year, 53 percent wanted a tougher Kremlin policy, while only 30 percent called for curtailing tensions. By the end of 1978, 32 percent of Americans wanted increased expenditures on defense, twice the number who favored spending reductions. Support for SALT, meanwhile, had fallen from over 70 percent in early 1978 to 42 percent in November of that year, and then to 30 percent in September of 1979, nine points lower than opposition to the treaty.[7]

Leading the charge against SALT was the Committee on the Present Danger (CPD). Even before the Vienna summit, the CPD had spent $750,000 to kill the treaty. Its members testified before the Senate and spoke on numerous radio and television shows, charging the SALT process with having failed to stop Soviet adventurism abroad or its military buildup. SALT did not permit on-site verification to assure Moscow's compliance, and the loss of America's intelligence posts in northern Iran would make verification all the more difficult. Vance later charged the CPD with having "a great deal to do with undermining SALT."[8]

The CPD was not alone. It was part of a larger organization, the Coalition for Peace through Strength. Formed in 1978, its membership included nearly 200 lawmakers by the time SALT came up for ratification. The Coalition, as well as a separate group, the American Security Council, published reports, produced films, and mailed letters to convince Americans to pressure their senators against SALT. The pact's proponents, including Americans for SALT and the Disarmament Working Group, were more poorly organized and spent far less money than the CPD or the Coalition for Peace. Letters arriving in the Senate ran decisively against SALT's ratification.[9]

The White House fought back with its own public relations campaign, similar in intensity to the one it had used to get the Panama Canal treaties ratified. SALT would improve U.S.–Soviet relations and curb the arms race, the administration argued. As for verification, the White House confessed that it could not absolutely guarantee Moscow would follow to the word each provision of the accords. But any cheating that affected the strategic balance would be so large as to be easily detected by American technological assets. Even without the Iranian intelligence posts, the White House assured the country, it could use satellites, radar systems, and communication intercepts to adequately guarantee that Moscow adhered to the pact.[10]

The effort of the administration to bolster the pro-SALT lobbying groups proved ineffective. This was reflected not just in public opinion polls. In the Senate, there was widespread concurrence with the CPD's concerns about the treaty. Senator Jesse Helms (R-North Carolina) denounced the idea of "adequate verification." During testimony on the treaties, Helms asked Secretary of Defense Harold Brown whether Brown's wife "would be happy if he came home and announced to her that he had been 'adequately faithful.'" New Hampshire's Gordon Humphrey, one of several Republican freshmen opposed to SALT, insisted that the United States retain "military superiority over those Russian bastards."[11]

A number of Democrats had their own concerns about SALT. Senator Jackson, who by the end of 1977 had turned against the administration's arms control efforts, announced that the White House had made too many concessions to the Soviets. Others, among them Wisconsin's William Proxmire and South Dakota's George McGovern, opposed the pact on the grounds that it did not do enough to limit the superpowers' nuclear stockpiles.[12]

Even lawmakers who might have supported SALT had reason for pause. The Senate's vote in favor of the Panama Canal treaties cost a number of members of the upper house their seats in 1978; there was reluctance to make a similar mistake. One of the colleagues of the new Senate majority leader, Howard Baker (R-Tennessee), commented that Baker was "'tired' of paying a political price for 'doing the right thing.'" The Tennessean was willing to sign on to SALT, but only if Carter accepted changes, including a provision that the Soviets destroy all of their large SS-9 and SS-18 missiles.[13]

In an attempt to convince senators to change their minds, Carter, shortly after he signed SALT, announced the formation of a Rapid Deployment Force (RDF), which would be stationed such that it could respond to crises outside the North Atlantic Treaty Organization's (NATO) jurisdiction, with particular focus on the Middle East and northeastern Africa. The RDF, first proposed by Brzezinski in 1977, would have a force of 100,000 men.[14] It would provide the United States with the ability to respond quickly to crises in the Middle East and northern Africa and defend American interests in the region.

In another concession, Carter announced his preparedness to deploy the MX missile system. It was a compromise he did not like making. "It was a nauseating prospect to confront, with the gross waste of money going into nuclear weapons of all kinds," he wrote in his diary in June. CIA Director Stansfield Turner and America's military leadership also opposed the new system, insisting that the Soviets "could easily counter the MX deployment . . . by fitting their existing missiles with more warheads." But Brzezinski convinced the president that without approval of the MX, there was little chance of SALT getting through Congress.[15]

Carter's efforts to please the opposition had little effect. He refused to accept Baker's conditions on the SS-9 and SS-18. The superpowers had engaged in over two years of discussions to get SALT signed, and he had no intention of making a demand of the Soviets that they would reject.[16] The RDF might be nice in dealing with small, regional threats abroad, but not against a Soviet nuclear strike on the United States.

The MX also aroused consternation. After a period of debate, the administration decided the best way to deploy each of its proposed 200 MX missiles was in a "racetrack system," by which each missile could be moved to one of 23 shelters. This meant the Kremlin would have to hit a total of 4,600 shelters to guarantee destruction of the entire MX arsenal. Since the Soviets would want to use at least two warheads per shelter to guarantee the destruction of each one, they would have to use at least 9,200 warheads to destroy just the MXs. Under SALT, though, Moscow would be limited to 7,000–8,000 warheads. Thus, argued the White House, the Soviet Union would never have the ability to destroy America's MX arsenal, let alone the entire U.S. nuclear stockpile. As noted, both Turner and America's military leadership did not buy that argument. Meanwhile, that the MX would be based in Utah and Nevada brought disapproval from both voters in those states and their representatives in the upper house: Republicans Orrin Hatch, Jake Garn, and Paul Laxalt, and Democrat Howard Cannon. Proxmire and McGovern decried the MX on the grounds that it was too much of a concession to those in the Senate who opposed SALT. Others questioned whether the racetrack system, which might cost as much as $100 billion, was worth it and whether it would even function properly. Senator Ted Stevens (R-Alaska) mused that "we cannot accept any basing mode so expensive it will soon be abandoned, so complex and untested that it will never work, so prone to delay that it will come into service years after it is needed."[17]

By August, the Senate's focus had shifted from SALT's provisions to the U.S. military budget. Key here was Democratic Senator Sam Nunn of Georgia, highly regarded in Congress as an arms control expert. Flanked by Jackson and John Tower (R-Texas), as well as the highly respected former secretary of state Henry Kissinger, Nunn insisted that the White House increase its defense budget for the next fiscal year by 5 percent and make that commitment public. The Georgian's demand put the White House in a tight spot. "I can envision winning SALT without Jackson and possibly even without Baker," conceded one administration official, "but without Nunn, we're dead."[18]

Complicating matters for the White House was the announcement in September 1979 by Senator Frank Church (D-Idaho) of the "discovery" of a brigade of Soviet combat troops in Cuba. The events leading up to Church's statement traced back to the Cuban missile crisis of 1962. News then that the Soviet Union had put offensive nuclear missiles in Cuba had brought the superpowers to the brink of war; the emergency only ended after Moscow withdrew the missiles and promised never to put offensive weapons again on the island. However, it had left several thousand troops in Cuba. The administration of John F. Kennedy had asked the Kremlin to remove those soldiers. It received no response and dropped the subject.[19]

In the summer of 1978, the United States learned that the Soviets had put MIG-23 aircraft in Cuba. This plane was more advanced than what was at that point the most sophisticated aircraft in the Cuban air force, the MIG-21. Furthermore, it could carry nuclear weapons. For a brief period, the United States questioned whether the Soviets had violated the 1962 agreement but, based upon intelligence information, determined that the MIG-23s were there solely for defensive reasons.[20]

Yet the arrival of the new MIGs convinced Brzezinski to order more continual aerial surveillance of Cuba. In June, the National Security Agency (NSA) concluded, based upon existing intelligence, that there was a Soviet brigade in Cuba. This information was leaked to several lawmakers, among them Senator Richard Stone (D-Florida). Stone, who had raised hackles in his district for voting in favor of the Panama Canal treaties, was in a bid for reelection in 1980. In the hopes of covering himself, he went public with what he knew. However, he received little attention, likely because the White House promptly denied that the Soviet presence in Cuba had significantly changed since 1962.[21]

Then, in August, communication intercepts and new photographs showed that the brigade, which numbered 2,000–3,000 men, was engaged in training exercises. The administration now labeled it a "combat brigade"—which implied it was offensive in nature—even though its actual purpose was unclear. Moreover, as there was no evidence that this force was new and in violation of the 1962 agreement, the White House allowed the CIA to publish the findings later that month in its daily publication, the *National Intelligence Daily*. Two days later, using the data disclosed in the *Daily*, the magazine *Aviation Week* made the news public.[22]

But what turned out to be far more damaging was Vance's decision to have Undersecretary of State for Political Affairs David Newsom contact eight members of Congress and tell them about the brigade. One of those lawmakers was Church. The Idaho senator, who had once advocated improving U.S.–Cuban ties, and who too had voted for the Panama Canal treaties, found himself in 1979 under attack from the American Conservative Action Coalition and his chances of surviving the 1980 campaign in doubt. In an attempt to save himself, he charged the White House with having allowed Soviet troops in Cuba. His attack, which Carter called "absolutely irresponsible," put the administration on the defensive and brought to the fore once again the Vance-Brzezinski dispute. Robert Pastor, the NSC's Latin American expert, was on his honeymoon, which he had to cut short to deal with this latest imbroglio. He recalled that Vance "wanted to play down the brigade issue," while Brzezinski wanted to highlight it as evidence of the "increasing threat of Soviet-Cuban military collaboration." Vance had the support of Vice President Walter Mondale and White House counselor Lloyd Cutler, while Press Secretary Jody Powell, Chief of Staff Jordan, and First Lady Rosalynn Carter backed Brzezinski. Rather than choose one side or the other, the administration again tried to split the difference. Vance told reporters that while the Soviet military presence had existed in Cuba for years, the White House would "not be satisfied with the maintenance of the status quo."[23]

As had occurred in the case of the Horn of Africa, the administration's vacillation and inconsistency in responding to the Cuban crisis caused confusion abroad and at home. "We did not understand why [the brigade] became an issue all of a sudden in 1979," recalled Dobrynin. Soviet officials were not sure if Church was simply trying to get reelected, if SALT's opponents were attempting to prevent its ratification, or if the United States was seeking to alter the 1962 understanding. The Kremlin stated that the brigade's duty was to train Cuban troops. However, to try to make things easier for Carter, Moscow indicated that it had no intention of giving it a combat role. Meanwhile, senior White House adviser Hedley Donovan and counsel Lloyd Cutler convinced Carter to have a group of sixteen senior diplomats, among them former Franklin Roosevelt adviser Averell Harriman; former Truman adviser Clark Clifford; Dean Rusk, Lyndon Johnson's secretary of state; and Kissinger, to assess the situation. Known as the Citizens Advisory Committee on Cuba—and more informally called the "Wise Men"—they judged that the brigade had been in Cuba since the 1960s, did not pose a danger to American security, and the White House had managed the whole affair poorly. "No incident in which

I was involved during the Carter administration," Clifford later penned, "was handled more ineptly than the case of the Soviet brigade in Cuba."[24]

The conclusions of the Wise Men did little to bring the crisis to an end. Both Tower and Church insisted that SALT's ratification was impossible as long as the brigade remained in Cuba. In an attempt to get past the current difficulty, on October 1 Carter announced that the brigade represented "a political challenge to the United States" and that he intended both to increase aerial surveillance of Cuba and to strengthen U.S. military forces in the Caribbean. Then, to refocus the Senate's attention on SALT, he added that "the greatest danger to American security is not the two or three thousand troops in Cuba [but] the breakdown of a common effort to preserve the peace and the ultimate threat of nuclear war."[25]

Carter's comment finally brought an end to the brigade crisis, but it did nothing to appease SALT's opponents. It was not until the end of October that the Democrats were able to get the Senate to return its attention to SALT by asking Carter to tell Congress of his plans for defense spending over the next five years. Even so, the damage had been done. In November, the Foreign Relations Committee approved SALT by only a nine-to-six vote. This was less than the two-thirds Carter would need to get Senate approval and suggested that SALT's future did not look good. That the Senate Armed Services Committee followed suit by voting against the treaty 10-0, with seven abstentions, only added to the likelihood that it would not receive the upper house's endorsement.[26]

. . . and Abroad

America's European allies had their own complaints about SALT. The British supported East-West cooperation and arms control, but SALT addressed only intercontinental weapons, which, by definition, had a range of greater than 5,500 kilometers; it did not eliminate the threat posed by the Backfire bomber or restrict long-range theater nuclear forces (LRTNF), which referred to missiles that could travel 3,000 to 5,000 kilometers and which, while unable to strike the United States, could hit any location in Western Europe.[27]

One such weapon was the SS-20. This advanced missile, which the Soviets had begun to deploy in Eastern Europe in 1976 to replace their older SS-4s and SS-5s, carried three warheads. It had a range of 5,000 kilometers, surpassing the 2,000- and 4,000-kilometer ranges of the SS-4 and SS-5, respectively, and could hit any NATO country in about fifteen minutes.[28]

The British and French had their own nuclear weapon programs, which gave them some semblance of protection against the new Soviet missile. West Germany was another story. Though it had the ability to develop its own nuclear weapons, since World War II it had adhered to a policy of not

doing so. Its decision to sign the Nuclear Nonproliferation Treaty reinforced Bonn's unwillingness to develop its own atomic deterrent. Chancellor Helmut Schmidt thus had serious concerns about his country's ability
to fend off the danger posed by the SS-20. He remembered Carter not
sharing his sentiment. "This is none of your business," the president reportedly told him. "America is the great strategic nuclear power and will
maintain an overall balance. So why should you worry about the SS-20?"[29]
This obviously was not the response Schmidt wanted to hear and intensified the poor relationship between the two leaders.

Carter soon changed his mind about facing up to the Soviets' LRTNF.
His decision to forego production and deployment of the neutron bomb
in 1978 not only raised questions in Europe about his competence but
about the willingness of the United States to defend its allies against the
threat posed by the SS-20. Accordingly, when Carter, Schmidt, French
President Valéry Giscard d'Estaing, and British Prime Minister James
Callaghan met at Guadeloupe in January 1979—the French-controlled island was chosen because its would give the participants privacy, away
from the prying eyes of the news media—the president indicated his willingness to put American LRTNF in Europe to counter the SS-20s. Schmidt
offered to permit the deployment of these weapons on West German soil,
but only if other continental European countries did as well. West Germany "already had a bigger concentration of nuclear weapons (American
ones of relatively short range) on its soil than any other nation," and the
chancellor did not want to add to that reputation without some cooperation from his NATO allies. Schmidt further insisted that any deployment
be coupled with renewed efforts to limit the number of weapons the superpowers had in Europe, which might not only reduce the risk of war but
give a shaky détente new vigor. By the end of March, NATO had decided
to deploy 200 to 600 ground-launched cruise (GLCM) and Pershing II missiles and had also accepted Schmidt's proposal for negotiations.[30]

Following further talks, in July the White House fixed the number of
LRTNF to deploy at 572: 108 Pershing IIs and 464 GLCMs. Putting two different types of missiles in Europe would make it harder for Moscow to
know whether one or both would be used in response to Soviet aggression, thereby adding to the West's deterrence capability. And the Pershing
II would give the Kremlin all the more reason for pause, for it could travel
1,800 kilometers, well over twice the range of the Pershing I, and hit
Moscow itself inside of ten minutes. Italy and later Great Britain announced they would accept some of the GLCMs, meeting Schmidt's desire
that West Germany not be the only NATO country to have them. Brezhnev angrily denounced the plan. While the SS-20s were not pointed at the
United States, he said, Washington would have even more missiles of its
own within striking range of the Soviet Union. In an attempt to stop the

West, in October Moscow offered to reduce the number of medium-range missiles—which could travel 1,000 to 3,000 kilometers—it had facing Europe and to withdraw 20,000 soldiers and 1,000 tanks from East Germany if NATO did not proceed with the Pershing and GLCM deployments. But since it said nothing about the 140 SS-20s it had deployed by the middle of 1979—in addition to its approximately 450 SS-4s and SS-5s—the West showed no interest. In mid-December, NATO decided to proceed with the deployment of the 572 missiles starting in 1983 but kept alive the idea of negotiations.[31]

The failure to reach an agreement between NATO and the Warsaw Pact over LRTNF said much about SALT's shortcomings. While SALT looked unlikely to receive the endorsement of the Senate, its failure to address weapons other than those with intercontinental capability meant that the arms race continued. SALT might, in this respect, be compared to the Egyptian–Israeli peace treaty. It represented a step forward—in this case, a step toward curbing the arms race—but left some major, if not vital, issues unaddressed.

Partial Success in Southern Africa

As the White House fought for ratification of SALT and attempted to strengthen NATO's nuclear force, it continued to seek majority rule in Rhodesia and the withdrawal of South Africa's military presence in Namibia. The administration ultimately could point to success in Rhodesia, though it was due less to the work of the United States and more to British efforts. Namibia proved a different story.

Following his internal settlement, also known as the Salisbury Plan, in early 1978, Rhodesian Prime Minister Ian Smith had engaged in a two-track policy of refusing to negotiate with the black Patriotic Front (PF) while simultaneously trying to promote the internal settlement as a road to black majority rule. Carter had not endorsed the Salisbury Plan, but he had not rejected it either. His judgment had upset both those lawmakers who believed the internal settlement justified a removal of U.S. sanctions on Rhodesia and those who felt that it simply represented a way of continuing white control.

In July, the Senate fought back an effort by Helms and S. I. Hayakawa (R-California), two of the most vocal champions of the Salisbury Plan, to remove the sanctions on Rhodesia. Instead, the upper house adopted a compromise proposal made by Clifford Case (D-New Jersey) and Jacob Javits (R-New York) that would lift the sanctions by the end of the year if Carter concluded that the Smith government had shown a willingness to hold a conference among all the parties vying for influence in Rhodesia, and if all of those groups subsequently had the opportunity to partake in national elections.[32]

There was no evidence that Smith was prepared to embrace either proposal. In October 1978, the Rhodesian leader accepted an invitation to visit the United States offered to him by over two dozen U.S. senators, including Helms and Hayawaka; these lawmakers wanted to rally American public opinion behind the internal settlement. Assistant Secretary for African Affairs Richard Moose and TransAfrica, a U.S. organization representing dozens of influential African-Americans in and out of Congress, urged the White House to reject the visa applications of Smith and his entourage. But Vance concluded that doing so "would give Hayakawa and his allies new leverage to terminate sanctions." He thus approved the visit. While in the United States, Smith offered to meet with the PF at an all-parties conference. However, attacks by his military forces launched on a refugee camp in Zambia and on rebel Zimbabwe African National Union bases in Mozambique killed any chance that rebel leaders Joshua Nkomo and Robert Mugabe would attend. By the end of the year, the Anglo-American effort was all but dead.[33]

In April, the Rhodesian elections took place. Over 60 percent of blacks voted, electing Bishop Adel Muzorewa as the nation's first black prime minister. Under Case-Javits, the president had to determine whether the elections were in fact fair and open to all voters. Supporters of the sanctions, led by Representative Stephen Solarz (D-New York), and including the Congressional Black Caucus, launched a lobbying effort to keep them in place. Opponents did little lobbying of their own. Margaret Thatcher, the Conservative Party candidate who had recently won the British prime ministership, had been an outspoken critic of Foreign Secretary David Owen's Rhodesia policy; those who wanted to see the sanctions lifted assumed that the new British leader would endorse the internal settlement. But Thatcher had determined that any arrangement in Rhodesia had to guarantee peace. After talking with her foreign secretary, Peter Carrington, she chose not to recognize the Salisbury Plan. In June, facing calls from lawmakers and prominent African-Americans—including Corretta Scott King and Jesse Jackson—charging that the elections did not give blacks in Rhodesia a fair opportunity to express their opinion, and concerned about the impact a decision to revoke the sanctions would have upon America's standing in much of Africa, Carter decided to maintain the sanctions. Although the Senate attempted to overturn the president's decision, the House, led by Solarz, upheld it.[34]

In April 1979, U.S. Ambassador to the UN Andrew Young was forced to resign because of news leaked that he had met with an official from the Palestinian Liberation Organization, a terrorist group that sought the destruction of Israel, a close U.S. ally. The loss of Young, who had proven central to U.S. Africa policy, combined with the onset of the presidential campaign season, prompted the administration to devote less attention to southern Africa. It was thus up to Britain to resolve matters. In August, at a conference of Commonwealth nations, Thatcher and Carrington, working closely with the presidents of Tanzania and Zambia, Julius Nyerere and Kenneth Kaunda, respectively, arranged a new plan for Rhodesia. The following month, Thatcher hosted a conference in London to secure a final settlement. There was no official U.S. representation; rather, Carrington was in charge. The Smith government by this time was ready to accept a settlement. Rhodesia's civil war had shown no sign of ending, South Africa had displayed no willingness to finance Smith's effort to remain in power, and the Rhodesian economy had suffered badly. Through terrific management, Carrington convinced the warring parties to sign an agreement in December 1979. Two months later, elections were held in Rhodesia, with Mugabe's party winning a majority of the seats in Parliament, and ending a war that had killed as many as 50,000 people. Still viewing blacks' desire for majority rule as part of a communist conspiracy, a bitter Smith years later charged that the British settlement "played into the hands of communist aggression in Africa."[35]

Efforts to bring an end to the fighting in Namibia bore less fruit. In part, it was because of South Africa's determination not to permit the South-West Africa People's Organization (SWAPO), which had ties to the communist-controlled government in Angola, to take control of Namibia. Poor relations between South Africa and the United States also had an impact. American university students urged their schools to divest themselves of interests in South Africa. While not all of these efforts were successful, Columbia University, Tufts University, and Boston College were among those schools that divested all or some of their holdings in companies with investments in South Africa. Facing growing economic pressure, Pretoria turned to other nations, including Taiwan and Israel, for financial or, despite the UN arms embargo, military support. Meanwhile, ties between the governments in Pretoria and Washington worsened. In September 1978, Prime Minister John Vorster resigned amid reports that he had overseen several secret programs to use public money to buy influence abroad. In April of the following year, his successor, Pieter W. Botha, kicked all but one of the U.S. military attaches in Pretoria out of the country, charging that they had secretly placed a camera in the U.S. ambassador's plane to take pictures of South Africa's military installations. The Carter administration retaliated by expelling two South African officials in Washington. In October, the White House released information to the press on what appeared to have been a test by South Africa of a nuclear device in the South Atlantic Ocean the month before. Polemics between the two countries continued through the end of Carter's term in office. Still, the administration remained reluctant to impose additional sanctions, particularly as East-West Cold War tensions grew and the White

House increasingly determined that it could not completely alienate the anticommunist government in Pretoria. Combined, though, South Africa's fear of SWAPO and the tensions in U.S.–South African relations made Pretoria unwilling to cooperate on Namibia through the rest of the Carter administration.[36]

Revolutions in Nicaragua . . .

Troubling as well to the White House was the situation in Nicaragua. That nation's new leadership, which called itself the Government of National Reconstruction, was made up of both members of the leftist Sandinista National Liberation Front (FSLN) as well as more centrist business and political leaders who had opposed Anastasio Somoza. But it rapidly became clear, to the dismay of the moderates, that power rested in the hands of the Sandinistas. Two of these more moderate, non-Sandinistas in the leadership, Violeta Chamorro and Alfonso Robelo, quit because of the FSLN's determination to consolidate power in its hands.[37]

Questions about what the United States should do caused a debate within the Carter administration. The Defense Department was especially apprehensive about the Sandinista victory. Defense officials dreaded the idea of more radical elements in the new Nicaraguan government gaining power. Furthermore, Cuba and the Soviet Union might offer more help to revolutionary movements elsewhere in Central America in an attempt to replicate what had happened in Nicaragua. State shared these concerns, but it, along with the president, believed it possible to moderate the new government's attitude through aid. The White House asked Nicaragua's neighbors, such as Guatemala and Honduras, not to use military force against the Sandinista regime, for fear that it might "'radicalize the revolutionary process in Nicaragua,' . . . undermine the already precarious position of the 'moderates' in the new regime," and destabilize the region. Rather, the administration urged Latin American nations to provide Nicaragua with both economic and military assistance, while the White House proposed offering the FSLN–led government $75 million in economic aid. Conservatives in Congress succeeded in obstructing approval of that assistance by insisting that the administration first prove that Nicaragua was neither Marxist-led nor aiding insurrectionary movements elsewhere in the region, especially in El Salvador.[38]

The troubles in El Salvador traced themselves to widespread poverty, a problem endemic throughout much of Latin America. In the cities, members of the center-left Christian Democratic Party joined with rural peasants organized by Catholic priests against the ruling military junta. The military and members of the elite fought back with repression, ranging from kidnapings to murder. Among those targeted were priests. In response, in 1975 the United States embargoed arms to the El Salvadoran government.[39]

The same month as Carter's inauguration, General Carlos Humberto Romero won a fraudulent election in El Salvador and intensified the repression. Although Assistant Secretary for Inter-American Affairs Terence Todman insisted that Romero needed U.S. help against "terrorists," Carter maintained the arms embargo and refused to endorse a loan from the Inter-American Development Bank. When Romero ended martial law, the White House resumed economic aid, seeing it as a way to reward the general and to suggest what further leniency on his part could bring. Instead, government-supported death squads continued their operations, while the regime's opponents acquired more support. Both Viron Vaky, who assumed Todman's post in 1978, and William Bowdler, who was then trying to bring an end to Nicaragua's bloody civil war, secretly traveled to El Salvador to try to convince Romero to resign and hold elections that would, as they hoped to do in Nicaragua, bring to power a moderate alternative to military rule and repression.[40]

In October 1979, a group of young Salvadoran military officers, frightened that they might suffer the same fate as Somoza and the Nicaraguan National Guard if the Salvadoran government did not institute reforms, overthrew Romero and promised a government with civilian membership. It soon became clear, though, that power rested in less-reformist-minded elements of the military. Angry, the civilian members of the government quit, the reformist-minded military leaders fled, violations by hard-line elements in the armed forces continued, and the opposition grew ever more in strength.[41] Despite the repression of the El Salvadoran government, it was that opposition on which conservatives on Capitol Hill focused their attention, charging that it was receiving help from Nicaragua. In turn, those lawmakers determined to add conditions to any economic aid offered to the Sandinista regime succeeded for the time being in fending off the White House's effort to provide the assistance.

. . . and Iran

But what was to draw the greatest amount of White House attention as 1979 ended was the situation in the Middle East. The fall of the shah already had had an impact upon regional U.S. policy, marked by the provisioning of military aid to North Yemen. The White House now followed up by lifting miliary sanctions against Morocco. Carter originally had curbed arms sales to the Moroccan government of King Hassan for a couple of reasons. For one, Morocco had designs on a portion of the western Sahara claimed by the Popular Front for the Liberation of Saguia el Hamra and Rio de Oro (Polisario) and had used weapons sold to it by the United States against rebels there. As Washington did not recognize Moroccan sovereignty over the western Sahara, the use of American-supplied arms was a violation of U.S. law. Additionally, Carter concluded that any effort by Morocco to assume control of the western Sahara would anger Algeria. Not only did the White House not want to have to worry about a conflict in northwest Africa, but it wanted to cultivate closer ties with Algeria, which produced a lot of oil and gas and had influence in the Third World. While the administration did not cut off all military sales to Morocco, the White House did reject Moroccan requests for OV-10 "Bronco" turboprop attack aircraft and Cobra helicopter gunships.[42]

Carter shifted gears following the overthrow of the shah in 1979. The president deemed it vital to improve ties with America's traditional allies in the Third World, among them Morocco. Furthermore, Polisario had begun a new offensive, and the CIA contended that if the United States did not do something, King Hassan might fall. Therefore, in January 1979, the White House, over the objections of a few remaining new internationalists (such as Representative Solarz) lifted the arms curbs and offered over $200 million in military equipment, including the aforementioned Broncos and Cobras.[43]

But it would be Iran that would prove of the greatest concern to the White House. Earlier in 1979, Carter had offered refuge to the shah, Muhammad Reza Pahlavi, in the United States, but instead Pahlavi had traveled to Egypt, followed by Morocco. At the end of March, however, King Hassan ordered Pahlavi to leave. The shah thus contacted Carter and asked to come to America. The president was reluctant, as he knew admitting the deposed leader could endanger any effort to restore normalcy to U.S.–Iranian relations. The White House quickly came under pressure from Pahlavi's allies, most notably Kissinger and Nelson Rockefeller, the president of Chase Manhattan Bank. Kissinger succeeded in finding temporary asylum for the shah in the Bahamas and then Mexico, but Pahlavi insisted on coming to the United States, asserting his safety was in danger. Carter still resisted. "I'm not going to welcome him when he has other places where he'll be safe." Nor did he want the former Iranian leader "here playing tennis while Americans in Tehran were being kidnaped or even killed."[44]

New information changed Carter's mind. Since 1973, the shah had suffered from lymphoma but had kept his illness secret, asserting that knowledge of it would embolden his opponents and convince the United States to give up its support of him. By the late summer of 1979, his condition had become serious. In August, the shah's sister, Princess Ashraf, wrote to Carter, informing him of her brother's infirmity. One of Rockefeller's aides added that Pahlavi could only get treatment in a U.S. hospital. After Undersecretary of State Warren Christopher verified the veracity of these reports, the president began to reconsider. Brzezinski, Mondale, Jordan, and members of both parties of Congress joined the chorus. "[I]f the Shah dies in Mexico," commented Jordan, "can you imagine the field day Kissinger will have with that? He'll say that first you caused the Shah's downfall and now you've killed him." Kissinger's support for a SALT II agreement was vital to its success, and failure to help the former Iranian leader might move Kissinger to retaliate by withdrawing his endorsement of SALT. Even Vance was willing to admit the shah. His subordinates in Iran and State's Iran desk officer, Henry Precht, though, urged the president to stand firm, warning that letting the shah in would generate a "violent reaction" in Iran.[45]

There was good reason for cautiousness. Ever since the revolution in Iran had ended with the shah's departure and the Ayatollah Ruhollah Khomeini's accession to power, many Iranians assumed that the United States would attempt to undermine the revolution, as it had in 1953 when it overthrew then–Prime Minister Muhammad Mossadegh. Washington, the Iranian press declared, was spreading lies about the new government as a first step to staging an uprising and then intervening militarily.[46] That the president would admit the shah into the United States rather than send him back to Tehran to be tried for crimes Iranians accused him of committing while he was leader of that nation would only increase their suspicion of American motives.

Carter found such arguments unconvincing. He could not abandon a long-time ally of the United States. He assumed that the shah would not be in the country very long. And there were encouraging signs in Iran. In February 1979, Iranian militants had taken over the U.S. embassy in Tehran, only to find themselves forced by the Iranian provisional government (PG) to return it to American control; the PG's leader, Prime Minister Mehdi Bazargan, had promised that he would protect the embassy against a future attack. Consequently, both Vance and Brzezinski were confident that moderate elements in the Khomeini government would assume control of the nation and keep in check fundamentalists in the Khomeini regime, even if the shah was allowed into the United States. Thus, in October, the president gave permission for the deposed leader to come to America.[47]

At first, it looked like Carter's decision would have no deleterious impact upon U.S.–Iranian relations. Iran's military had declared itself neutral toward the Khomeini regime, but because its equipment came from the United States, it needed American spare parts. Talks therefore began in October between the two governments and included a November 1 meeting in Algeria that included Brzezinski, Bazargan, Provisional Foreign Minister Ibrahim Yazdi, and Iranian Defense Minister Mustapha Ali Chamran. Following that particular session, the NSC adviser returned home relatively confident that the two nations could restore some sense of normalcy to U.S.–Iranian relations. This, despite his own observation that Iranians were furious with Carter's decision to permit the shah into the United States.[48]

"Furious" was an accurate assessment. Among the most irate were university students, who made up the core of the protesters. While some were left-wing supporters of democracy and others reactionary pro-Islamists, they all criticized Pahlavi's presence in America. The U.S. embassy in Tehran became the target of their anger.[49]

By this time, the U.S. ambassador, William Sullivan, had resigned in protest of the administration's Iran policy. The White House had appointed Robert Cutler to replace him, but the Iranian government refused to permit Cutler to take up his post. This left the chargé d'affaires, Bruce Laingen, in charge. Laingen felt increasingly uneasy. While he did not expect the provisional government to cause trouble, "it remains quite possible that it will be pushed into a posture it might not otherwise adopt if revolutionary radicals, unsophisticated clergymen and the generally irresponsible capture the momentum on the issue of the shah's presence in the U.S."[50]

He was both more wrong and more right than he could have known. In truth, the provisional government had little power. Khomeini had only allowed it to oversee the affairs of the country while he and his allies set the foundation for turning Iran into an Islamist state. Laingen, though, was correct that the momentum would shift into the hands of the radicals. It was the students who struck first. On November 2, a group of them held a meeting and devised a plan to take over the U.S. embassy. They studied the facility, walking around it, drawing up maps, and looking for weaknesses. They also asked one of Khomeini's advisers to inform the cleric of their intentions. He never got the message. But a public statement he delivered on November 3 honoring students who partook in a 1978 protest convinced the plotters that they had his approval.[51]

The following day, about 150 students, calling themselves the Muslim Students Following the Line of the Imam, struck. They anticipated that some of their number might die. Instead, they encountered little resistance from the Iranian policemen guarding the embassy grounds and headed toward the main gate. Many of the civilian personnel fled to the most secure part of the embassy complex, the second floor of the chancery, which was guarded by a steel door. Laingen had ordered the Marines not to fire, so they laid down smoke and retreated to the chancery as well. Despite security protocols, the students succeeded in finding some documents and grabbing a number of embassy employees, blindfolding them and binding their hands together.[52]

The militants then arrived at the chancery, banging on the doors and threatening to kill their American hostages if they were not opened. The threat worked. By the end of the day, they had sixty-three Americans in their hands (though the militants later released thirteen African-American and women hostages, hoping that it would draw support for their cause from blacks and women in the United States).[53]

In addition to Laingen's orders to the Marines, the lack of bloodshed resulted from a feeling among the Americans in the embassy that the current crisis would be a repeat of the one that had occurred in February and ended within a day. U.S. officials in Washington shared that sentiment. In fact, if handled properly, the crisis could bring political points to a president who at that point lagged behind Senator Edward Kennedy for the Democratic nomination. "Don't forget the press will be looking at this in the context of the campaign," Jordan wrote to Carter the afternoon news arrived of the hostage-taking. "It'll be over in a few hours, but it could provide a nice contrast between Carter and our friend from Massachusetts in how to handle a crisis."[54]

The chief of staff had reason for optimism, for the crisis had rallied Americans around Carter. The president's approval rating surged to over 60 percent. Kennedy, who announced his candidacy on November 7, helped Carter even more, seeming unable to answer questions asked of him by CBS correspondent Roger Mudd, denouncing the shah as having led "one of the most violent regimes in the history of mankind," and attacking the decision to allow Pahlavi into the country. Replied an angry Carter, "The issue is that American hostages, fifty of them, are being held by kidnappers," not the shah.[55]

But as the crisis continued, Jordan realized that the president's renewed popularity might not last. Presciently, he told Carter that while the American people had rallied around him, they "will soon begin to sour on the situation and we will see increased support for extreme measures from giving the Shah back to wiping Iran off the face of the earth." Moreover, the longer the crisis lasted, the greater the chance of injury to the hostages, of the Senate rejecting SALT, and of Carter failing in his bid for reelection. For these reasons, it was important for the president to implement "a measured punative [sic] act," including possibly some form of military retaliation.[56]

Carter knew he was in a predicament. The Iranians "have us by the balls," he commented. He was not ready to use force, afraid that the hostages' captors might retaliate by injuring or killing some of them. He imposed a number of sanctions during the first two weeks following the seizure of the embassy, including a ban on the shipment of spare parts to Iran, an embargo on Iranian oil imports (which First Lady Rosalynn Carter had proposed), the deportation of Iranian students whose visas had expired, and the freezing of $6 billion in Iranian assets in the United States, and asked America's allies to follow Washington's lead. Additionally, on Jordan's recommendation, the president canceled a trip to Canada; to have gone to Canada, the chief of staff had commented, would make it seem like Carter did not care about the hostages.[57]

Furthermore, the president, who officially announced his campaign on December 4, decided to stay in the White House and monitor the events in Iran. "While this crisis continues," he told the country, "I must be present to define and lead our response to an ever-changing situation of the greatest security, sensitivity, and importance."[58] Rather, he had others, particularly Rosalynn, stump for him around the country.

Others took matters further—at times, much further. Some lawmakers demanded that the government throw every Iranian student out of the country, longshoremen refused to put cargo on ships headed for Iran, and in Los Angeles, a mob wielding baseball bats injured several Iranian protesters. In New Jersey, an Iranian named valedictorian of her high school was forced to back out. For Ted Koppel, the journalist who expected that the crisis would not last, these events and the Americans still held captive in Iran became the subject of a new nightly program he hosted called "America Held Hostage." The show, which later became known as *Nightline*, had an average viewership of 12 million Americans during its early months on the air. Indeed, the hostage crisis received more media coverage "than any other event since World War II, including the Vietnam war."[59]

There was no indication that American pressure would end the crisis any time soon. Khomeini repudiated efforts by Bazargan and Yazdi to have the hostages released, prompting both of them to resign and bringing an end to the provisional government. The ayatollah turned all authority over to the theocrat-dominated Revolutionary Council. Seeing these events as proof that Khomeini supported the embassy takeover, the students announced that they would not release the hostages until Carter returned the shah. When the president attempted to send two emissaries, William Miller, the staff director of the Senate Committee on Intelligence, and Ramsey Clark, President Lyndon Johnson's attorney general, to hold talks with Khomeini, the cleric refused to see them.[60]

It is even possible that Iran's refusal to release the hostages was influenced by U.S. policy toward Chile. In October 1979, the Chilean Supreme Court refused to extradite to the United States three Chilean officials whom the U.S. government charged were behind a car bombing in 1976 in Washington that killed Orlando Letelier, Chile's former ambassador to the United States, and his assistant, Ronni Moffit, a U.S. citizen. A furious Carter imposed new sanctions on Santiago, including a complete cutoff of Export-Import Bank assistance. Prior to the president's decision, Pastor wrote Brzezinski, "There is no question that if we choose to announce harsh, punitive sanctions against Chile for their failure to extradite [the officials], the Iranians, clutching desperately for any justification for their action, will link our action to theirs." Brzezinski wrote back, "This is a good point."[61]

In late November, the Iranian government issued a series of demands to end the crisis. First, the United States had to return the shah and his wealth to Iran. Second, Washington had to "recognize all the harm it has done to Iran," which would necessarily require the White House to issue an apology for its past Iran policies. Finally, America had to stay out of Tehran's affairs. The Carter administration had no problem with the last of these demands. An apology, though, was out of the question, as was returning the shah.[62]

The White House reasoned it could make at least some headway by getting the shah out of the country as soon as his medical condition stabilized. This way, it could no longer claim responsibility for harboring him. Despite an earlier promise to allow the shah to return, Mexico's president, José López Portillo, now said he did not want him back. "I was outraged," Carter later wrote; the incident only added to an already poor U.S.–Mexican relationship. Carter therefore sent Jordan to Panama, hoping that nation's leader, General Omar Torrijos, would take the shah in. Torrijos was not happy with the request, but he was indebted to Carter for the Panama Canal treaties and invited the shah to come. Nor was Khomeini pleased, charging that the president still could send the shah home if he so desired. Far more excited were the Panamanians assigned to protect the shah and his wife. The shahbanou, who was particularly attractive, enjoyed swimming topless. "Her dips in the ocean," Jordan observed, "were major events for the security guards."[63]

As the Pahlavis bided their time, the administration received word that the Iranian government was thinking of putting the hostages on trial, which could ultimately lead to their execution. The White House sent warnings to Iran that it would use force if harm came to any of the captives. The United States would "blast the hell out of Iran," the president notified his advisers. To make clear he was serious, Carter ordered warships to the Arabian Sea.[64] The show of force had no effect: the Americans remained in captivity.

The Soviet Invasion of Afghanistan

As it confronted the hostage crisis, the White House had to contend with a new emergency when the Soviet Union invaded Iran's neighbor, Afghanistan. The Soviet decision to intervene in Afghanistan dated prior to the February 1979 murder of the U.S. ambassador to that country, Adolph Dubs. In December 1978, Afghanistan's president, Nur Muhammad Taraki, and Deputy Prime Minister Hafizullah Amin returned to Kabul from Moscow, convinced they had the Kremlin's support for their effort to secularize and communize their nation. Amin subsequently requested 20 million rubles in assistance "to cover the expenses of the organs of security and intelligence services." Moscow agreed to look into greater military and economic aid for its ally.[65]

An uprising in the Afghan city of Herat, which left 5,000 people dead, among them government troops and Soviet advisers, moved the Kremlin to boost assistance to Afghanistan. Moscow, though, rejected a new appeal from the Afghan president, that of a commitment of Soviet troops; such a measure, explained Soviet Premier Alexei Kosygin, could drag the Soviet Union into a war similar to that which the United States had faced in Vietnam and would bring international condemnation upon the Kremlin.[66]

By the end of the spring of 1979, the uprising in Herat had devolved into civil war. Not only Islamic fundamentalists but others disaffected with the government took up arms against Taraki. These included thousands of government troops, who changed sides and joined the rebels. Moscow determined to shore up its ally through more military and economic aid and advisers. It also decided to get rid of Amin, seeing him as power-hungry, untrustworthy, and a threat to Taraki's leadership.[67]

By the end of August, Taraki had come to share with the Kremlin the need to remove his potentially problematic subordinate. In September, he attempted to have Amin assassinated but failed. Amin, who had gotten wind of the assassination plot and had rallied troops to his cause, made no such mistake. He overthrew Taraki, killed many of the now-ex-leader's supporters and then, on October 9, had his former superior executed.[68]

What the Soviets had not wanted to happen had occurred, and the Islamic revolution made them even more anxious. As Taraki and Amin literally took shots at one another, Afghan guerrillas had pushed their way toward Kabul. To the Kremlin, it appeared that militant Islam, which had taken control of Iran, and which also spurred an attack in November 1979 on the holiest of Islamic sites, the Grand Mosque in Saudi Arabia, had spread to and was on the verge of capturing Afghanistan. Reports from Soviet advisers in Afghanistan that the situation was serious made the Kremlin wonder how much longer the government in Kabul might survive.[69]

Adding to the Kremlin's trepidation were reports that Amin, who had every reason to distrust his Soviet ally, had sent feelers to the United States. In the early 1970s, President Anwar Sadat of Egypt had turned away from the Soviet Union and to the United States. It looked like Amin was about to do the same thing. Not only would that prove highly embarrassing to the Soviet-supported worldwide communist movement, but it would give Washington a place to put intelligence facilities along the Soviet border, replacing those it had earlier had to close down in Iran.[70] Not wanting to lose Afghanistan to Islamic fundamentalism or to a pro–U.S. regime, Moscow gave more serious thought about a direct intervention.

Furthermore, the Soviets had a tendency to overestimate outside assistance to the Afghan rebels. As early as August 1978, *Pravda* charged the United States, China, Saudi Arabia, Pakistan, and India with providing help to the Kabul government's enemies. Such accusations became even more commonplace after Herat. While it was the case that Egypt, Pakistan, and Saudi Arabia were giving help to Taraki's opponents following Herat, U.S. assistance prior to the Soviet intervention was nonmilitary in nature.[71]

What might also have influenced the discussions in the Kremlin over what to do about Afghanistan was the state of the arms control talks. By the end of 1979, SALT's ratification looked highly unlikely. And NATO had accepted the deployment of Pershing and cruise missiles to counter the Soviets' SS-20s. With SALT likely to die in the upper house of Congress, and with NATO apparently prepared to heat up the arms race, the Soviets may have felt less restrained to take more aggressive action in Afghanistan.[72]

If the Soviet Union was to intervene, however, Brezhnev and the Politburo would have to approve it. Leading the pro-intervention lobbying effort were Defense Minister Dmitri Ustinov and KGB chief Yuri Andropov. On December 8, the two of them presented their case to Brezhnev and Gromyko. Emphasizing in particular the threat a pro–U.S. Afghanistan would pose to the Soviet Union, they convinced the foreign and general secretaries to endorse a full-scale intervention. Four days later, the Politburo gave its endorsement. Though Dobrynin was anxious about the possible impact of a Soviet attack on Afghanistan upon U.S.–Soviet relations, Brezhnev assured him not to fret: "It'll be over in three to four weeks."[73]

On Christmas Day the Soviets launched their attack. It was the first time the Soviet Union had militarily intervened in a neighboring country since 1968—when Moscow toppled a reformist-minded government in Czechoslovakia—and the first effort by Moscow to conquer an Asian nation since 1925, when Mongolia became a Soviet satellite. The invasion came as a surprise to the United States. Although U.S. intelligence for months had kept tabs on the Kremlin's increasing involvement in Afghanistan and Soviet military movements along the Afghan border, there was widespread doubt that Moscow would engage in a large-scale assault. In fact, it was not until a few days after Christmas before the White House understood exactly what was happening in Afghanistan.[74]

Using the hotline to Moscow, Carter issued what he called "the sharpest message of my Presidency," proclaiming the invasion "a clear threat to the peace" which "could mark a fundamental and long-lasting turning point in our relations." In fact, it was a turning point, recognized all too well by the *Washington Post*. "Detente," its front page headline read a few days after the attack, "is Dead."[75]

★   The last six months of 1979 witnessed an administration on a roller coaster. It started with the high of the signing of SALT but was soon followed by attacks on that same treaty from both members of Congress and European allies. In an attempt to shore up domestic and international support, the White House authorized development of the MX missile—despite Carter's own misgivings—and the RDF and sought to redress LRTNF in Europe. These concessions did not guarantee ratification of SALT, and the administration's inept handling of the Soviet brigade in Cuba did not help matters. The president's proposals to provide aid to the Sandinista government and lift military sanctions on Morocco raised questions on Capitol Hill, both from conservatives and liberals. On top of all of this, the administration had to face what appeared likely to become a long hostage crisis in Iran and the presence of Soviet troops in Afghanistan. Yet as the year ended, the White House could point to success in Rhodesia, even if the credit had to go primarily to the British, and Americans had rallied around the president as a result of events in the Middle East and central Asia.

Still, there was every likelihood that the roller coaster could continue. Carter was riding a wave of support, but there was no telling how long it might last. If the Soviets refused to leave Afghanistan, it might raise questions about the president's ability to face up to the communist threat. So might the hostage crisis if it continued. While a Gallup poll in mid-January 1980 found that 62 percent of Americans approved of the president's handling of the hostage crisis, that was 15 points lower than in December. Another poll, taken around the same time, determined that if the hostages were still in captivity as of the middle of February, 53 percent of Americans would regard Carter's Iran policy a failure.[76] For a president desirous of reelection, these were not encouraging signs.

A CRISIS *of* CONFIDENCE

Eight

★   "I come to you this evening," President Jimmy Carter told a national audience on January 4, 1980, "to discuss the extremely important and rapidly changing circumstances in Southwest Asia. . . . Fifty thousand heavily armed Soviet troops have crossed the border and are now dispersed throughout Afghanistan, attempting to conquer the fiercely independent Muslim people of that country." The world had to face up to this new crisis. Otherwise, as history had taught, "aggression, unopposed, becomes a contagious disease."[1]

In its last year, the Carter administration found itself on the defensive. The Soviet presence in Afghanistan, coming on top of the economy, the hostage crisis, and a failed attempt to rescue the Americans being held captive in Iran, all raised questions about the president's competence as a leader. To punish the Soviets, to show himself as strong and capable, and to win his bid for reelection, the president adopted a tough response to the Afghan invasion. To make that response effective, he sought to rally world support; as a consequence, he largely abandoned his human rights, nuclear nonproliferation, and conventional arms transfer policies.

Carter's efforts failed to shore up his political standing at home. The never-ending hostage crisis, the economy, and anger over his handling of two separate refugee crises moved Americans to opt for the Republican candidate, Ronald Reagan. Though disappointed, Carter maintained his efforts to get the hostages out of Iran. His anti-Sovietism, meanwhile, continued to make itself apparent in his reaction to a threatened Soviet invasion of Poland and his preparedness to offer military assistance to the government of El Salvador, despite widespread repression in that nation.

The Never-ending Hostage Crisis

By early 1980, the economy was in dire straits. Unemployment continued to rise, hitting 6.2 percent in January. Inflation was 1.4 percent in January and 1.5 percent in February, for an annual rate of nearly 20 percent. By spring, the United States was in the midst of a recession. An opinion poll in February found 48 percent of Americans considered inflation their greatest concern, an increase of 9 points in just one month.[2]

The president was still riding the wave of support he had garnered as a result of the Iran hostage crisis and the invasion of Afghanistan, but his chief of staff, Hamilton Jordan, realized it might not last. "[I]t seems to me that we must have two very high priorities over the next 30–45 days," Jordan wrote in January. The first was "to eliminate [Massachusetts Senator Edward] Kennedy from the political race so that you will not be preoccupied with the campaign nor restrained politically from doing whatever is necessary to meet the Soviet challenge." The second was "to find some way to resolve the hostage situation in the next 30–45 days so that we can build a relationship—however tenuous—with the Iranian government."[3]

It became clear within a matter of months that neither goal would be easy to achieve. Around the same time he sent his memorandum to Carter, Jordan received a message from the Panamanian government. The chief of staff had gotten to know officials in that country during the negotiations that led to the Panama Canal treaties. It is also likely Panama's president, General Omar Torrijos, unhappy with hosting the shah, wanted to find a way to end the hostage crisis. The Torrijos government offered to put Jordan in touch with a French lawyer, Christian Bourget, and Argentine businessman Hector Villalon. These two men had close connections with the people in Iran who had replaced Prime Minister Mehdi Bazargan and Foreign Minister Ibrahim Yazdi: President Abolhassan Bani-Sadr and Foreign Minister Sadegh Ghotbzadeh. The U.S. government had also developed another connection to Ghotbzadeh via Professor Richard Cottam, an expert on Iran who had known the new foreign minister for many years.[4]

In mid-January, Jordan, along with Henry Precht, the head of the State Department's Iran desk, and Assistant Secretary of State for Near Eastern and South Asian Affairs Harold Saunders traveled to London to meet Villalon and Bourget. Both Bani-Sadr and Ghotbzadeh, like Bazargan and Yazdi, wanted to see the hostages released and some semblance of normality restored to U.S.–Iranian relations. But the Iranians could not say so publicly, as the government was firmly under the control of Khomeini and his radical supporters. Worse, the Iranian president and foreign minister did not like one another, making coordination between them difficult. Still, based upon his talks with Bani-Sadr and Ghotbzadeh, Bourget proposed that the United States return the shah to Iran, something Jordan flatly rejected. The Frenchman then raised the matter of an apology and suggested as well that the United States endorse a United Nations commission to look into the shah's crimes.[5]

Jordan refused an outright apology. But it was possible, he surmised, to find language that amounted to an apology without actually using the word; in turn, Iran could claim a victory and Carter could avoid political embarrassment at home. A commission was another matter. UN Secretary General Kurt Waldheim had been the first to float the idea, yet Jordan wanted its establishment only after Iran freed the hostages; the White House had seconded that scenario. Now, he joined Saunders in suggesting a reversal of the chronology, with a commission established prior to the hostages' release. They believed that Ghobzadeh and Bani-Sadr could use the commission to convince Khomeini and the Revolutionary Council that the American captives had served their purpose and then release them. While the commission would give the Iranians the opportunity to chastize the United States, getting the hostages out, Jordan and Saunders judged, would make up for any domestic political fallout Iran's statements might cause. Carter accepted this reasoning and, in February, announced his preparedness to support a UN commission of inquiry to investigate the shah's past activities.[6]

This effort did not bear fruit. When the UN commissioners arrived in Tehran in February, Khomeini refused to allow them to see the hostages. After two and a half weeks of frustration, the visitors left. Further negotiations got nowhere, and Americans grew increasingly impatient, with those who considered Carter's handling of the crisis a failure outpacing those who did not by sixteen points (47% to 31%). On April 24, Cottam reported that Ghotbzadeh had told him that "[t]here was little prospect . . . [of] a resolution of the crisis." The foreign minister had suggested the United States try "something more dramatic" and request that other Arab nations—he specifically mentioned Algeria and Syria—intervene as mediators.[7]

The administration had indeed decided on something more dramatic, and it took place that same day: a rescue mission by U.S. commandos. From almost the very beginning of the hostage crisis, the White House and U.S. military had discussed the idea of employing soldiers to free the American captives, but Carter had demurred. He wanted to see if negotiations could work; there were concerns, even among members of the armed forces, about the feasibility of such a mission; and the president worried that if attempted, it could lead to the injury or death of some of the hostages. As the weeks progressed, though, Carter reconsidered. His inability to curb inflation or unemployment, questions as to why he left it up to his wife, Rosalynn, to campaign for his reelection, and his falling poll numbers all took their toll.

Other news added to the president's woes. While condemning Iran's hostage-taking, U.S. allies demonstrated reluctance to follow suit with sanctions of their own. West Germany and Italy refused, and Canada wanted first to discuss additional measures with other countries. Even America's closest ally, Great Britain, was standoffish.[8]

Then there was the matter of a miscast UN vote. In March, the international organization considered a resolution calling upon Israel to remove its settlements in the occupied territories as well as Jerusalem. Both the president and Vance were of the opinion that these settlements endangered the Middle East peace process and that the United States should support the resolution. However, they insisted that the UN first had to remove the reference to Jerusalem. When Carter received word from Vance that the UN had complied, the United States voted in favor.[9]

It was only after the vote that Carter learned that because of an error, the United Nations had not deleted the offensive wording. The president quickly admitted the mistake but added that the White House still would have supported the resolution had those words been excised. That they had not been deleted angered Jewish voters who already had lost a great deal of trust in the administration; making them even more upset was the willingness of the White House to support a "cleaned" resolution which, to American Jews, was still anti-Israel.[10]

The combination of the hostage crisis, the economy, and the UN vote played into Kennedy's hands. The Massachusetts senator scored victories in the Connecticut and the even more important New York primaries. While Kennedy still lagged behind Carter for the nomination, his campaign had a new lease on life, and a poll taken around the same time now found the senator leading the president by 3 points. Even worse, the Republican front-runner, former California Governor Ronald Reagan, again moved ahead of Carter.[11] Thus, even if the president won the nomination, his chances for reelection looked shaky.

Fiasco—The Rescue Mission

On April 7, the White House announced the breaking of relations with Iran and urged its allies to follow suit. But the president was on the verge of going significantly further. In his January memorandum suggesting things Carter could do to shore up his chances for reelection, Jordan had urged his boss "to at least consider taking some risks" to get the hostages released. While he did not specifically mention it, one possibility Jordan might have had in the back of his mind was a rescue mission. Carter had permitted planning for such a mission to proceed, but he had remained reluctant to give the green light. Now, with the hostage crisis continuing, with the failure of America's allies to come through, and with his political future at risk, the president gave a rescue operation a harder look. Vance had opposed that option from the start, maintaining, as Carter had earlier, that negotiations might work and that trying to rescue the hostages could end up in the death of some of them. Brzezinski just as consistently contested those conclusions, contending that the nation risked the humiliation of an unending crisis. Powell, Jordan, Vice President Walter Mondale, and Mrs. Carter also favored a rescue attempt, emphasizing the political consequences of inaction. Brown added his voice, pointing out that the Iranians could at any time start killing the hostages. In that case, "we'll have to take punitive measures, and God only knows where that would lead."[12]

On the 11th, Carter gave the go-ahead for a rescue operation. Vance, who was on vacation in Florida at the time, did not learn of the president's decision until his return to Washington three days later. When the secretary of state found out, recalled Undersecretary of State Warren Christopher, his "reaction was volcanic—the angriest I'd ever seen him. Not only did the idea of a rescue mission infuriate him, but also the matter of such moment had been raised and decided in his absence." Vance attempted but failed to convince the president to give diplomacy more time.[13]

The story of the rescue mission is today fairly well known. The plan called for eight helicopters to depart from the aircraft carrier *Nimitz* in the Gulf of Oman and fly to a landing area, called Desert One, located south of Tehran. Six C-130 transports would then touch down, bringing fuel, supplies, and a ninety-member team of Delta Force commandos. Having deposited their cargo, the transports would depart. Meanwhile, the helicopters would fly to a location about 100 miles from Iran and make final preparations. The following night, the rescuers would gather aboard trucks obtained by U.S. agents and drive into the city. Supported by AC-130 gunships, Delta Force would attack both the U.S. embassy and the foreign ministry building—to which Washington had learned some of the hostages had been moved—and then overpower the guards, and free the captives. The helicopters would fly in, gather everyone, and head to an airstrip near the city, where two C-141 transports would take everyone to Saudi Arabia. The helicopters would be destroyed so they would not fall into enemy hands.[14]

Things did not go as intended when the operation got underway on April 24. Before arriving at Desert One, the commandos had to abandon one helicopter because of mechanical problems. Electrical difficulties forced a second to return to the *Nimitz*. After arriving at the landing zone, yet another suffered mechanical problems and could not take off. As the plan called for a minimum of six helicopters, the commander of the team decided to call off the mission.[15]

Delta Force's bad luck only got worse. As the would-be rescuers embarked onto one of the C-130s, a helicopter in the process of taking off clipped the airplane, veered to its left and cut into the C-130s fuselage. Eight soldiers died and another four suffered injuries. The survivors departed, leaving behind the four remaining helicopters and the dead. Upon learning the news via telephone from General David Jones, chairman of the Joint Chiefs of Staff, Carter went pale. "Are there any dead?" When told yes, he said quietly, "I understand" and hung up. A few hours later, the president announced to the nation what had happened. While some administration officials, led by Brzezinski, proposed a second rescue attempt, questions about the survivability of the helicopters, plus the certainty that the Iranians would have made preparations to thwart another U.S. effort, killed the idea.[16]

The rescue mission was a disaster for the administration. For one, Vance resigned in protest. The secretary of state had decided to leave his post after Carter had decided, over Vance's objections, to give the rescue mission the green light. He waited, though, until after the operation had taken place to make his announcement. Carter replaced Vance with Democratic Senator Edmund Muskie of Maine. Muskie had little knowledge of foreign affairs, but he was well respected in the capital and, unlike many lawmakers, had developed a good working relationship with the president. The choice disappointed Christopher, not because he did not like Muskie, but because he had hoped to receive the appointment. Although he considered resigning himself, he concluded that he had agreed to serve the administration as undersecretary and should abide by that promise, no matter what his personal feelings.[17]

Furthermore, while a majority of Americans supported Carter's decision to try to rescue the hostages, they disapproved of his handling of the hostage crisis. Many members of Congress shared that sentiment, realizing that the president had the welfare of fellow Americans at heart but furious that he had once again failed to consult them in advance. Combined with Vance's resignation, this convinced a large number of observers that Carter's entire foreign policy was a failure. *Newsweek* magazine commented, "As things now stand, the President's uncertain diplomatic strategy has left allies perplexed, enemies unimpressed and the nation as vulnerable as ever in an increasingly dangerous world."[18]

Whether the failed rescue mission hurt Carter's political future must remain a matter of debate. The president suggested it did, commenting years later that if he had the chance to do it over again, "I would have [sent] one more helicopter. If we could have rescued the hostages in April 1980, I have no doubt that I would have been a hero, that our country would have been gratified, [and] that I would have been reelected president." Jordan was less certain, pointing out that even with a successful rescue of the American captives, the administration would still have had to deal with the economy and divisions within the Democratic Party.[19]

Yet the fact was that the mission had failed. Facing criticism, the president took a couple of steps. He abandoned his Rose Garden strategy and went out onto the stump. He also knew he had to demonstrate that he was a strong leader who could face up to America's challenges worldwide. This meant not only continuing his effort to get the hostages out of Iran but adopting a tough stand against the Soviet invasion of Afghanistan. Consequently, he finally and completely rejected his earlier effort to move U.S. policy in a new, non–Soviet-centric direction and all but abandoned his previous commitments to promote human rights and nuclear nonproliferation and to curb conventional arms transfers.

Punishing the Soviets

In an interview with a French newspaper in 1998, Brzezinski commented that the Carter administration knew its aid to rebels fighting the Soviet-sponsored Afghan government "increased the probability" of Soviet intervention. "That secret operation was an excellent idea," he commented. "It had the effect of drawing the Russians into the Afghan trap." He even went so far as to claim that it was because of their success at provoking the Kremlin that communism collapsed in the Soviet Union: "[F]or almost 10 years, Moscow had to carry on a war unsupportable by the government, a conflict that brought about the demoralization and finally the breakup of the Soviet empire."[20]

Not only was Brzezinski's statement an example of self-ingratiation run amuck, but there is no evidence to substantiate it. Indeed, that President Carter endorsed measures designed to provoke an attack by any country upon another is preposterous. With so many strikes against SALT, Carter no doubt would have realized that trying to draw the Kremlin into a fight in Afghanistan would prove even more to SALT's opponents that Moscow could not be trusted; it would have been the death knell to a treaty that was already in serious trouble. Furthermore, as he made clear in his memoir, the Soviet attack was a direct threat to U.S. security. "A successful takeover of Afghanistan," he later wrote, "would give the Soviets a deep penetration between Iran and Pakistan, and pose a threat to the rich oil fields of the Persian Gulf area and to the crucial waterways through which so much of the world's energy supplies had to pass."[21] Why provoke an invasion of a country that would jeopardize U.S. interests abroad?

Having pointed to the danger posed by the attack on Afghanistan, Carter determined to make the Soviets pay and, hopefully, get them to withdraw their forces. On December 29, he expanded the covert aid program to the Afghan resistance, instructing the CIA to add ammunition and weapons to the nonlethal assistance it was already providing. Five days later, he asked the Senate to shelve SALT II. The following day, he announced the United States would no longer ship high technology to the Soviet Union and imposed a grain embargo on Moscow, and urged other countries to follow America's lead. He suggested as well that the United States might boycott the summer Olympics, which were to be held in Moscow. On January 23, in his State of the Union Address, he issued what became known as the "Carter Doctrine," in which he warned that the United States would use "any means necessary, including military force," to prevent Soviet domination of the Persian Gulf. The president even stripped Soviet Ambassador Anatoly Dobrynin's right to use the State Department's underground parking garage.[22]

The Soviets were dumbfounded by Carter's response. Why, they wondered, would the president take such strong measures in response to the invasion of Afghanistan, which in any case involved the Kremlin assisting a fellow communist state? Some in Moscow deduced that the reason was Carter himself, who previously had shown a lack of consistency in policy and who had been critical of the way the Soviet Union treated its people. Others placed the blame on Brzezinski, whom they concluded had defeated those favoring a more accommodationist Soviet policy and, subsequently, who had gained the president's ear. No matter what, the Kremlin had no intention of giving in to American pressure. When Carter wrote to Leonid Brezhnev that the invasion was "a clear threat to the peace," the secretary general replied that his nation had acted in response to a request for help from the Afghan government, a claim that Carter refused to accept.[23]

Reaction to the president's measures varied. "Good God," said an administration official following Carter's imposition of sanctions against the Soviets. "[T]his is Cold War in the most classic, extreme form." George Kennan, the father of the policy of containment, commented, "Never since World War II has there been so far-reaching a militarization of thought and discourse in the capital." Most Americans, however, did not share such sentiment. Whereas in September 1979, just a few months before the invasion of Afghanistan, a bare plurality of Americans favored an increase in defense spending, by December, just prior to the invasion, over half did. Widespread domestic approval thus met the administration's new sanctions against Moscow.[24]

Ironically, Brzezinski, while using the invasion to fully convert Carter to his thinking, felt that the president had gone overboard. He told his boss that "before you are a President Wilson you have to be for a few years a President Truman." By showing himself as tough with the Soviets, Brzezinski surmised, the president could then hold out his hand in peace—a repeat of the NSC adviser's long-held belief in negotiating with the Soviets from a position of strength.[25] Taking so many strong measures, the NSC adviser concluded, could disrupt the possibility of future dialogue with the Kremlin.

In fact, the president had not done a good job of thinking through these measures. Carter, always the trustee, had hoped that by doing what he felt was right, others would follow. He expected, for instance, that U.S. allies would join the ban on high technology shipments to the Soviet

Union. But the evidence suggests that some of those countries, especially France and Germany, stepped in to provide goods to Moscow that Washington refused to supply.[26]

The grain embargo also proved problematic. At home, it risked angering farmers, which could cost the president votes in the upcoming and politically important Iowa caucuses and hand the state over to Kennedy. "Food is not, in my opinion, an appropriate weapon to use in the international political arena," Domestic Policy Staff chair Stuart Eizenstat wrote to Carter. Vice President Walter Mondale shared this concern, warning that Republicans might use the embargo to turn farmers against Democrats. To try to assuage Eizenstat and Mondale, Jordan raised the idea of having the government buy up the grain, but Mondale cautioned that storing farmers' crops would not have any impact upon grain prices, which were likely to fall if agriculturalists could not sell their goods. The president refused to budge, contending that a U.S. embargo, particularly if joined by other countries, would create severe problems for the Soviet Union, which already faced a grain shortage. He also indicated his preparedness to financially compensate farmers for any losses the embargo might cause them.[27]

The embargo did not have the impact that had worried Eizenstat and Mondale. The president's January 4 speech received a strongly positive reaction and made itself felt when Iowa held its caucuses on January 21. Carter won all but one county in the state and even earned the support of blue-collar workers and Catholics, who were expected to have voted for Kennedy. The president also received the ardent approval of farmers, whose patriotism trumped any trepidation they had about the embargo.[28]

International support for the embargo was another matter. Australia and Canada, two of the world's biggest producers of grain, agreed to restrict their exports to the Soviet Union. But then there was Argentina, which annually produced a large grain surplus. Here, the president's effort to get Buenos Aires behind the embargo became part of a larger shift in U.S. policy toward Latin America, particularly on the issue of human rights.

Following the Soviet invasion of Afghanistan, the United States altered its policy toward Latin America, especially South America. There, right-wing governments in Argentina, Brazil, Chile, and Uruguay had been angered by the decision of the administration to reduce or completely cut military and economic aid to them for their human rights violations. In light of the new crisis in U.S.–Soviet relations, the White House deemed it necessary to reexamine its relations with its neighbors to the south. In May, Carter specifically asked about the state of Soviet relations with the countries of the Southern Cone (Argentina, Chile, and Uruguay) as well as Brazil and Peru. Christopher replied that the Kremlin had been providing Peru with military and economic assistance, and it was seeking to establish commercial relations with the other four nations, which could

expand Soviet influence there. The administration's "overriding objec-
tive," Christopher wrote, was "to reinforce the traditional and fundamental pro-Western and anti-Soviet attitudes" of those countries. Realizing the
impact the human rights initiative had had, he added that while the
United States would continue to promote that policy, it must do so "in a
way that minimizes adverse effects on our other interests." Carter found
the memo "very good."[29]

Of these countries in South America, Argentina was particularly important. Without Argentine support for the grain embargo, punishing the Soviet Union for its invasion of Afghanistan would become less effective. A
few months before Christopher wrote his memorandum, the president
sent Andrew J. Goodpaster, the U.S. Military Academy's superintendent, to
Buenos Aries to convince Argentina's president, General Jorge Videla, to
join the embargo. The effort failed. Shaken, the administration sought to
improve its ties with the Argentine government, which included, as
Muskie put it in May, "end[ing] our official criticism of the regime." Arguing that the human rights situation in Argentina had improved, and desirous to get the Videla government not to send grain to the Soviet Union,
the United States approved over $79 million in Export-Import Bank loans to
Argentina, more than double what it voted for in 1979. This attempt to encourage Argentine cooperation failed. Buenos Aires saw it could economically benefit from providing grain to Moscow at a time when other countries refused. And rejecting the embargo offered Argentina a means of
exacting revenge for past U.S. treatment of it. Expressed one Argentine official, "Just how does the Carter administration expect to get support from
us, [when] it practically ostracized us during its first three years of office?"[30]

The decision to alter U.S. policy toward Latin America, and especially
Argentina, infuriated Assistant Secretary for Human Rights and Humanitarian Affairs Patricia Derian. Since receiving her appointment in 1977,
she had grown frustrated with what she regarded as the administration's
lack of commitment to the human rights policy. Iran, South Korea, and the
Philippines, just to name a few nations, had repressive governments, yet,
over her objections and those of the Bureau of Human Rights, the United
States had continued to provide them with economic and military assistance. The decision to improve relations with Argentina became too much
for her, particularly when some in the administration suggested providing
the Videla regime with military aid. In May 1980, she told the *New York
Times* that if the White House did not change its mind on military assistance, she would resign, "and I won't say it's for personal reasons."[31]

The human rights secretary did not leave; the administration chose not
to provide military aid to the Argentine government. Whether her threat
had any impact upon that decision is not certain. What is clear is that her
resignation, had she gone through with it, would have hurt the adminis-

tration. President Carter had already angered feminists with his opposition to federal funding of abortions, and Derian's resignation would have been seen as further proof of the administration's lack of concern for women. Furthermore, the president had yet to lock up the nomination against Kennedy. Derian's resignation because of what she regarded as insufficient support for human rights could have allowed Carter's opponents to charge him with failure to back what the president himself had always purported was one of his major policy initiatives.[32] Yet the fact remained that the White House had begun to limit its human rights policy in Latin America, the one area of the world where even the administration had admitted was the primary focus of that initiative.

If the White House had not anticipated the resistance it would find to the grain embargo, it also had not adequately prepared for the Olympic boycott. Rather than have them go to Moscow, the administration sought to convince the world's athletes to opt for so-called alternate games, which the White House sought to put together. The proposal found intense resistance from Olympic athletes worldwide, including those on the American team, who argued that a boycott would politicize the Games. Furthermore, athletes who partook in alternate games risked sanction from the international federations that oversaw amateur athletics and could punish those persons who took part in non-sanctioned events. Lastly, governments legally had no authority over the decision making of their Olympic committees. The administration finally convinced the U.S. team not to attend, but only after it threatened legal action. Formal alternative games were never held. Meanwhile, just over eighty teams, or about half of those sanctioned to take part in the Olympics, refused to take part. Brzezinski himself admitted that the White House had achieved "only partial success."[33] While some countries, including West Germany, China, and Japan endorsed the boycott, other allies, among them Great Britain and France, sent athletes to compete.

Allied Discord

West German Chancellor Helmut Schmidt's willingness to cooperate with the boycott and Britain's decision to send athletes to the Olympics suggested that the animosities between the German and American leaders had subsided and that a tense relationship existed between Carter and Britain's new prime minister, Margaret Thatcher. This was not entirely the case. Though she believed him a poor politician, Thatcher liked Carter as a person and considered it important to join the United States in punishing the Soviets. Schmidt and French President Giscard d'Estaing felt otherwise. Not only did they judge Carter's response to the invasion of Afghanistan a case of overkill, but they concluded it was driven by his desire to win reelection as opposed to any anger he felt toward the Soviets. Schmidt even went so far as to blame Carter's "inept leadership" for the Soviet decision to take a chance and invade Afghanistan.[34]

Yet while Britain went further than France or West Germany in reproving the Soviets, London continued to trade with Moscow. The same was true with both Bonn and Paris. While U.S.–Soviet trade fell by 60 percent in 1980, West Germany and France increased their commerce with the Soviet Union by 65 and 100 percent, respectively.[35]

Still, of America's allies, it was West Germany that was the most problematic. The negotiations with the Soviet Union to restrict the size of the long-range theater nuclear forces (LRTNF) of the North Atlantic Treaty Organization (NATO) and the Soviet-led Warsaw Pact was a case in point. Following the Soviet invasion of Afghanistan, the White House had become clearly less supportive of Schmidt's desire for talks with Moscow than it had been when the chancellor had broached them in early 1979. However, Schmidt sought to keep his initiative alive. In April 1980, he asked that "both sides, for a number of years, give up installation of new or additional intermediate range missiles and use this time for negotiations." What Schmidt was trying to do was to get the Soviets back to the bargaining table. But to many observers, including Carter, it appeared he was trying to renege on his agreement to accept some of the 572 Pershing II and cruise missiles NATO had decided the previous year to deploy in Europe.[36]

Then, over U.S. objections, Schmidt announced his intention to travel to Moscow in the hopes of keeping the talks going, if not reviving détente. The chancellor's junket seemed to the White House another attempt to forego LRTNF deployment. Brzezinski, Muskie, and Brown together drafted for Carter a message he sent to the German head of state "expressing our concern about the confusion generated by Schmidt's statements." The letter then made its way into the press, an act that the chancellor later called an act of "pure spite." Charging that Brzezinski's handiwork was somehow involved, he added, "To all appearances it was someone eager to vent his spleen—someone who had never been able to decide whether the Germans or the Russians were the archenemy of the Polish people, from whom he was descended."[37]

Franco–American relations were not much better. In addition to criticizing the U.S. response to Afghanistan, d'Estaing challenged U.S. Middle East policy, which he deemed too pro–Israel and, as a consequence, jeopardized the West's access to oil. In May, without giving advance notice to the United States, d'Estaing met with Brezhnev. Worse, there were reports that the French president and other European officials wanted to use the upcoming Venice economic summit to insist that the Palestine Liberation Organization have the right to take part in future Middle East talks and that the reference in UN Resolution 242 to the Palestinians as "refugees" be removed. News of the d'Estaing-Brezhnev meeting and of the reported European plans on the Middle East infuriated Muskie, who earlier had been chastised by France's foreign minister, Jean Francois-Poncet, for America's failure to consult with its allies. "I'm concerned that when I was being given a lecture on consultation," the secretary of state told journalists, "the lecturer was not inclined to practice what he was preaching."[38]

The disputes between the United States on the one hand and its West German and French allies on the other placed a pall over the Venice economic summit, held that June. In what the president later called "the most unpleasant personal exchange I ever had with a foreign leader," Schmidt charged Carter with having "insulted" him and insisted that he (the German leader) "had never reneged on any of his pledges." Muskie then intervened, telling Schmidt of the importance of avoiding confusion about NATO's plans on LRTNF deployment. When Schmidt promised to take to Moscow "an accurate, firm message" and asked Carter for a public statement of confidence, the president responded affirmatively. The dispute, wrote Carter, quickly became "a thing of the past," and the following day, Schmidt "was very friendly, as though nothing had happened."[39]

Indeed, the summit proved much more of a success than observers had anticipated. Carter secured a promise from the attendees to condemn the Soviet invasion of Afghanistan in return for assurances that the United States would not impose new sanctions upon the Soviet Union and was willing to hold future talks with the Kremlin. Economically, Carter and his fellow leaders announced their intention to curtail their importation of oil and "double the use of coal by the end of the decade."[40]

Yet Venice did not resolve the serious problems facing the United States and its allies. A month before the summit, the government of Masayoshi Ohira had fallen following a no-confidence vote. His replacement, Zenko Suzuki, a hard-line protectionist, made it clear that he would curb the importation of "cheap American products." That position made him highly popular in Japan and dashed any hope of a trade agreement beneficial to American interests.[41]

Nor had the United States and its allies come to grips on defense matters. In the post–Afghanistan environment, talk of superpower cooperation to curb the arms race all but vanished. The comprehensive test ban treaty talks stalled. The same was true of the discussions on demilitarizing the Indian Ocean. Rather, Washington boosted its naval and air forces in the region and expanded its military facilities at Diego Garcia in the Indian Ocean. This was part of a larger defense effort. Under pressure from Congress, including members of his own party, Carter requested $1.2 trillion in military spending over the next half decade, including $146.2 billion for fiscal year 1980, an increase of 12 percent over the previous year.[42]

Then, in July, Carter signed Presidential Directive 59 (PD-59), which instituted the largest arms buildup in decades. Since the 1960s, both the United States and Soviet Union had built up their intercontinental ballistic missile (ICBM) capability. This led Washington to adopt a doctrine known as mutual assured destruction, which assumed that the ability of the superpowers to use their nuclear arsenals to destroy each other would keep both from attempting to launch a first strike. But both Brzezinski and Brown believed that because of the improved accuracy of their nuclear missiles, the Soviets might launch a more limited nuclear attack against U.S. military targets. This placed Washington in the unenviable position of having to respond to such an attack with either a massive nuclear strike against Soviet military and civilian targets—thus resulting in a full-scale Soviet response and mutual assured destruction—"or giving in to nuclear blackmail." The purpose of PD-59 was to find a way of allowing the United States to meet a limited Soviet atomic strike with a similar response, thereby giving America the ability to deter the Kremlin.[43]

While PD-59 was really an adjustment to existing U.S. nuclear doctrine as opposed to a new policy, news that Carter had signed the document aroused new complaints against the White House. Domestically, critics charged that Brzezinski had intentionally leaked information about PD-59 in the hopes of embarrassing Muskie—who was furious when he learned about the directive only after the media got wind of it. Others insisted the White House was trying to combat Republican charges that its nuclear warfare strategy prior to PD-59 offered "a Hobson's choice between mass mutual suicide and surrender" and had increased the likelihood of Moscow launching a first strike. Internationally, the Soviets berated the new policy, calling it "nuclear blackmail." With the deployment of U.S. LRTNF in Europe, the MX missile system, and the decision to shelve SALT, the Kremlin wondered whether Washington had rejected détente's call for parity in favor of nuclear superiority.[44]

The president had no intention of allowing internal or external criticism of PD-59 to deter the arms buildup, which he and his top advisers regarded as a necessary step in light of events overseas. To buttress its own military efforts, the Carter administration urged its allies to follow suit and increase their own defense spending. The White House found resistance. When Washington asked Tokyo to bump its defense outlays by 9.7 percent, Suzuki replied that such a figure might force him to cut spending elsewhere, such as on social programs; to do that "could turn the Japanese people against future defense increases." (The issue of Japanese appropriations on defense remained unresolved at the time Carter left office.) Nor were the West Germans fully cooperative. Schmidt, as he had promised, gave a tough speech during his visit to Moscow at the end of June, urging the Soviets to withdraw from Afghanistan and to start discussions, without preconditions, on both sides' LRTNF. (Although the Soviets indicated their willingness to talk, discussions had not gotten underway before the end of Carter's term.) Yet Schmidt's preparedness to join the United States in challenging the Soviet presence in Afghanistan did nothing to improve the relationship between himself and Carter. In November 1980, Schmidt announced that his country would not increase its defense spending by 3 percent, as it earlier had promised. When he came to Washington later that month, recalled Brzezinski, the visit "was chilly and thoroughly nonsubstantive."[45]

South Asia—A Change in the Wind

Chilliness also applied to U.S.–Pakistani relations. Seeking to bolster its position in and around the Indian Ocean and Persian Gulf, Carter sought to restore ties with the government of Muhammad Zia-ul-Haq. Citing human rights violations by Islamabad as well as Pakistan's apparent effort to develop nuclear weapons, the Carter administration in 1977 had suspended economic aid to Pakistan, withdrawn an offer to sell A-7 fighter jets to that nation, and put pressure on France not to proceed with the sale to Pakistan of a nuclear reprocessing plant. France indefinitely suspended its contract with Pakistan in 1978; early the following year, the White House decided to resume economic aid. But the administration changed its mind shortly thereafter. Congress earlier had added the Glenn-Symington amendment to the 1977 Foreign Assistance Act, which required the U.S. government not to provide economic or military aid to any nation seeking nuclear equipment outside of international safeguards. News that Pakistan had secretly been trying to get such equipment so it could build a uranium enrichment plant moved the White House in April 1979 to cut all aid to Pakistan. This is not to say that U.S.–Pakistani cooperation came to an end. The growth of Soviet influence in a fellow, and in this case, neighboring, Muslim country made Islamabad willing to help funnel U.S. assistance to the Afghan rebels.[46]

In light of the Soviet invasion, the United States reconsidered its earlier decision to cut aid to Pakistan. Glenn-Symington permitted a presidential waiver in the event that the White House believed cutting aid to a nation violating the amendment's provisions would endanger U.S. interests. Michel Oksenberg, an East Asian specialist on the NSC, probably had this in mind when he wrote to Brzezinski on December 28, "The President's nuclear non-proliferation and arms restraint policies must take second place to a concerted effort to teach Moscow that aggression does not pay." The president agreed, and in January 1980 the White House offered $400 million in economic and military assistance over a two-year period, including A-7 fighter jets. However, he refused Pakistan's request for the more advanced F-16 fighter, fearing that it would upset India. Zia rejected the package as "peanuts," contending that it was not "commensurate with the size of the threat" posed by the Soviet Union.[47] Concluding that Zia had not completely rejected the U.S. proposal, Carter sent Brzezinski and Christopher to Islamabad. Neither was able to persuade the Pakistani leader to reconsider, even after they said that the $400 million could be increased by another $100 million. In October 1980, Carter, against the wishes of the State Department, finally offered the F-16s, but Zia remained aloof. He realized that if Carter won the following month's election, then he could expect the U.S. president to present his earlier offer of assistance (plus, now, the F-16s). But if Reagan won, then Carter's offer would become a nonissue.[48]

Attempts to improve ties with Pakistan did not please that country's neighbor, India. Relations between the United States and the government of Morarji Desai, while cordial, had been strained prior to the invasion of Afghanistan because of India's nuclear program. Although Carter had shipped nuclear fuel to India's atomic plant at Tarapur, he had continued to urge New Delhi to accept International Atomic Energy Agency (IAEA) safeguards; otherwise, the United States, under the 1977 Nuclear Non-Proliferation Act (NNPA), would in late 1979 have to stop all shipments of fuel to Tarapur. Desai refused to accept the safeguards, which he saw as an infringement of India's sovereignty. Furthermore, while promising not to use his nation's nuclear technology to develop atomic weapons, he rebuffed a firm commitment on that score until the world's nuclear powers made large cuts in their nuclear arsenals.[49]

The tensions in U.S.–Indian relations grew worse after Desai's coalition government collapsed in June 1979. His successor, Charan Singh, lasted less than six months in office; in January 1980, Indira Gandhi, Desai's predecessor, returned to power. While Gandhi denounced the Soviet presence in Afghanistan, she was even more concerned by the U.S. offer of military aid to Pakistan, charging that Washington and China—another Pakistani ally—were turning India's old enemy "into an arsenal." Indeed, when the United Nations voted by a wide margin in favor of condemning the Soviet invasion, India abstained, offsetting moderate disapprobation of Moscow's action with criticism of the United States.[50]

The attitude of the Gandhi government annoyed Carter, but he wanted to avoid angering the new Indian leader. The president expected that Gandhi could influence the Kremlin. Accordingly, later in January, he sent his roving ambassador, Clark Clifford, to New Delhi to explain U.S. policy toward Pakistan and reassure India of America's intentions. Washington also offered military aid to New Delhi. But the most significant indication of Carter's desire to maintain cordial relations with India came in May. That month, the National Regulatory Commission (NRC), pointing to the

NNPA and India's failure to accept IAEA safeguards, unanimously voted against New Delhi's request to license a shipment of fuel to the Tarapur plant. Carter overturned the NRC's decision and approved the license. The president knew that he would receive flak for his decision, and in fact he faced condemnation from both the *New York Times* and *Washington Post*, which accused him of violating his own nonproliferation policy.[51]

But it was in Congress that the battle was most strongly waged. The House of Representatives, infuriated by Gandhi's failure to condemn the Soviet invasion of Afghanistan, and determined to uphold the NNPA, voted by an overwhelming 298–98 margin against Carter's approval of the license. To successfully override the president's decision, however, a majority in the Senate would have to uphold the vote in the House. The White House engaged in intense lobbying, asserting that failure to approve the shipment would undercut U.S. efforts to get India to apply IAEA safeguards to Tarapur; furthermore, if the United States stopped supplying the fuel to the plant, the Soviet Union would surely step in. "Approval of these exports," Carter insisted, "will help strengthen ties with a key South Asian democracy at a time when it is particularly important for us to do so." In September, by a vote of 48 to 46, the Senate voted in favor of the president.[52]

By the fall of 1980, therefore, the president's nuclear nonproliferation policy was even more in shambles than it had been at the start of his administration. Carter had not realized upon taking office how difficult it would be to get U.S. allies to stop developing their own nuclear energy programs or shipping their technology to other nations. Furthermore, the president had chosen to deliver nuclear fuel to India despite a consistent unwillingness of that nation to accept IAEA safeguards and in the face of strong congressional opposition. In the end, the United States had not only failed to stop the proliferation of nuclear technology, but it had strained relations with its allies and upset nations such as India with which it had wanted closer ties.

Binding the Ties—China and Somalia

While the U.S. relationship with Pakistan and India remained largely standoffish, that with China grew closer. This process had actually begun several months earlier, following the loss of the Iranian intelligence stations the United States had used to monitor the Soviet Union. To make up for the Iranian facilities, the Defense Department and CIA between August and December 1979 established similar monitoring equipment in the PRC; furthermore, the CIA taught members of China's military intelligence to use the equipment, thus allowing the two nations to share the information gathered.[53]

Carter at first refused to go further than this. Despite the urging of Brzezinski, Brown, and Mondale during 1979 that the United States develop closer military relations with the People's Republic, the president had demurred. Instead, he sided with American specialists on both China and the Soviet Union, as well as Vance, who warned that tighter Sino–American strategic ties would not bring the White House any benefits in its relations with Beijing and would anger the Kremlin, to the detriment of U.S.–Soviet relations. But the president did veto Vance's request that he postpone a planned trip by Secretary of Defense Brown to Beijing. The secretary of state contended that with the dispute over the Soviet brigade in Cuba still raging, Brown's visit would be perceived by the Soviets as designed to pressure them. Brzezinski and Brown convinced Carter to give the trip the go-ahead for that very reason.[54] In short, prior to late December, Carter had sought something of a middle ground, wanting to send the Soviets a message that the United States would not stand for their actions around the world but reluctant to tighten Sino–American military relations so much that it might undermine any hope of restoring détente. What he failed to consider was that sending none other than the U.S. secretary of defense to China would surely be taken as a sign by the Kremlin that the United States was building the very security relationship that Carter desired to avoid.

The Soviet invasion of Afghanistan made such considerations about endangering détente moot. Now, Brown received instructions to offer Beijing nonlethal military items, including transport planes, a station with which it could receive information from Landsat satellites—which took detailed images of the Earth—and communications equipment. This set the stage for a series of trips by military officials of each nation to the other during 1980.[55]

The types of matériel the United States offered China expanded as 1980 progressed. Washington had long imposed the same restrictions on China and the Soviet Union with regard to the shipment of military equipment. In April, however, the limitations on the People's Republic were removed, thereby allowing Beijing to buy military helicopters, transport planes, trucks, and air defense radar. (As it turned out, the Chinese could not afford these weapons, but to scare the Soviets, it pressed Washington to say that the United States was *willing* to sell them to Beijing.) In September, a delegation led by William Perry, the White House's expert on military technology, traveled to the People's Republic and looked over that nation's defense plants. Upon his return, he suggested additional ways in which the United States could help China militarily, including the sale of missiles and antisubmarine technology. However, no action was taken on his report before Carter's defeat in the 1980 election.[56]

Lastly, the two nations improved coordination of some aspects of their security policies. They talked about ways to increase their aid to Pol Pot, the former leader of Cambodia whose Khmer Rouge continued to resist Vietnamese forces that had invaded Cambodia in November 1978. Additionally, Washington encouraged Beijing to provide arms to the mujahidin in Afghanistan and offered to reimburse China for some of the cost of shipping those weapons. There were still disagreements between them; for instance, the Chinese reportedly refused to allow U.S. planes bringing military equipment to Pakistan to fly over their airspace. But in general, 1980 had seen greater congruity in Sino–American defense and security relations.[57]

The same was true with U.S. ties with Somalia. Following the attack on Afghanistan, Washington decided to get access to the Somali port of Berbera, which the Soviet Union had built prior to its fallout with the Somali government. Berbera would be a perfect location for the administration to base the Rapid Deployment Force (RDF) it had decided to put together to contend with crises in the Persian Gulf region. The United States had found that relying too much upon regional powers, like Iran, to defend Washington's interests was not a good idea. Saudi Arabia, concerned about upsetting fundamentalist elements—such as those which had already attacked the Great Mosque—was less than enthusiastic about giving the United States an expanded military presence on its soil. Other possible base locations, such as Diego Garcia in the Indian Ocean, Mombasa in Kenya, and Bahrain were too far away or too small to meet U.S. needs. Berbera, however, met the prerequisites for size and location. While the United States realized that tightening these ties with Somalia would likely kill any hope of drawing Ethiopian President Mengistu Haile Mariam away from the Soviet Union, it accepted that cost in the existing climate.[58]

Somalia's leader, General Muhammad Siad Barre, was more than prepared to cooperate, assuming he could demand a lot in return. He requested $1 billion in aid in 1980. This the United States refused, and talks dragged on for half a year. Finally, in June, the White House told Somalia that it would offer $40 million in defensive security assistance over a two-year period; however, the administration made clear, it would not recognize Somalia's claims to the Ogaden, and Mogadishu had to promise in writing that it would not use U.S.–supplied weaponry in Ethiopia. Importantly, Washington nowhere stated that Somalia had to give up its claim to the Ogaden or stop aiding Somali insurgents in Ethiopia. For these reasons, and because he ascertained that rejecting this offer would mean no U.S. aid whatsoever, Siad Barre accepted it. Thus, on August 22, the two nations inked a ten-year agreement by which the United States received the right to use Berbera. This pact was significant in that it once again represented a decision by the United States to emphasize security concerns over what had earlier been two key initiatives, those of curtailing conventional arms transfers and of punishing countries that violated human rights. As Paul Henze, the NSC's specialist on intelligence coordination, noted, the agreement reached with Somalia "helped prolong an odious regime which has killed—*proportionately*—as many of its citizens as Mengistu's regime has and has forced even larger numbers—*proportionately* —to flee."[59] The Soviets countered by building up their military presence in South Yemen and strengthening their naval forces in the Red Sea and Indian Ocean.

Billygate, Refugees, Hostages, and the 1980 Election

While working to develop closer relations with countries he had once denounced, the president continued his campaigning at home. By June he had won enough delegates to capture his party's nomination. Securing reelection was another matter. In July, the "Billygate" affair exploded. Americans learned that Billy Carter, the president's brother, had accepted a $220,000 "loan" from the country of Libya in return for getting a Florida company to buy more Libyan oil. According to U.S. law, anyone representing a foreign country had to register as that nation's agent. Billy had refused, saying he was not a Libyan representative. It was only after news of the loan that he had registered. The question for investigators, Congress, and the U.S. public was whether Billy had used his connections in the White House to attempt to garner the president's favor. President Carter denied any such thing ever happened, and there was no evidence to suggest otherwise. But the whole affair did not help his political future. By late July, Carter's approval rating had fallen to 21 percent, even lower than Nixon's at the height of the Watergate crisis. "This damn Billy Carter stuff is killing us!," exclaimed Pat Caddell, the president's pollster.[60]

So did news that Rosalynn Carter had convinced her husband to try to use Billy's Libyan connection to get the hostages out. The president's brother had in fact set up meetings between Libya's representative in Washington, Ali Houderi, and Brzezinski, though the connection had done no good in freeing the hostages. For many Americans, this use of a questionable means of diplomacy did not sit well.[61]

The same month Billygate made the headlines, the shah died in Egypt, having traveled there several months earlier from Panama. His death, though, did not bring the hostages' release. Billy's machinations, the hostage crisis, the failure to complete the Camp David peace process, and economic problems at home, including double-digit inflation, took their toll. By the middle of July, Ronald Reagan, who had just obtained the Republican nomination, had what seemed an overwhelming 28 point lead over the incumbent.[62]

In September, the Democratic Party formally gave Carter the nomination, and it soon looked like the president might win reelection after all. Carter depicted his Republican contender as a "trigger-happy" person who might lead the country into World War III. A series of gaffes by Reagan, such as a statement that the explosion of the Mt. St. Helens volcano in May 1980 had expelled more sulphur than humans had "in the last ten years of auto driving or things of that kind"—and which the Environmental Protection Agency promptly proved incorrect—hurt the Republican candidate as well. Carter began a resurgence in the polls. And there was more good news in the form of some new demands issued by Khomeini in September. They included "release of all of Iran's frozen assets, cancellation of all claims by Americans against Iran, and return of the shah's wealth to Iran." Significantly, he had dropped an earlier stipulation that Washington apologize for its past Iranian policy. It had been the requirement for an apology that had been a sticking point; now, it looked like a resolution to the crisis was possible. The Republicans knew that securing the hostages' release would all but guarantee Carter's reelection. They therefore warned of an "October surprise"—an announcement by the White House that the hostage crisis was about to end even though there was no guarantee of it.[63]

But not all of the news was good. In addition to continued economic woes, the White House had to contend with two separate refugee crises. One originated in Cuba, where economic difficulties and a lack of democratic institutions had bred dissent. The island's rate of economic growth had slowed down substantially, from 9.4 percent in 1978 to less than one-third of that in 1980. Food and housing became short in supply. Meanwhile, to bring in much-needed revenue, the Cuban government permitted tens of thousands of exiles to return to Cuba, where the visitors spent $100 million on the island just in 1979. Their visible affluence and the stories they told of their lives in the United States served to add to the disaffection felt by many Cubans.[64]

In April 1980, six Cubans crashed a bus through the gate of Peru's embassy in Havana, killing a Cuban guard in the process. They then requested asylum. The Cuban government immediately demanded that Lima turn their men over to be tried for the guard's death, but Peru refused. An angry Fidel Castro responded by removing the other guards. Wayne Smith, who worked at the interests section in Havana, recalled that one Cuban official bet him "five pesos that not more than several hundred people, and probably considerably fewer, would take advantage of the guards' absence." Smith did not accept the bet. It turned out he made the right decision, as Castro then declared that all Cubans who wanted to leave Cuba could head to the embassy. To the shock of both Peru and Cuba, about 10,000 Cubans packed into the embassy grounds within three days.[65]

Upset with the clear indication of discontent with his government, Castro decided to take the opportunity to get rid of the disaffected. He announced that he would permit any of his countrypersons, including those at the Peruvian embassy, to leave Cuba via the port of Mariel. Furthermore, he would allow Cuban exiles living in the United States to come to Mariel and retrieve their friends and family members. Viewing it as wrong to deny entrance to asylum-seekers, Carter announced that America would "provide an open heart and open arms for the tens of thousands of refugees seeking common freedom from Communist domination."[66]

Carter likely believed that he was demonstrating his opposition to a repressive government that he, along with numerous fellow Americans, had come to see as a threat to U.S. interests. However, Cuban-Americans saw his statement as opening the door to proceed with what became known as the Mariel boatlift. Dozens of boats of all sizes sailed to Mariel, bringing back an average of 3,000 people a day during the month of May. A stunned and unprepared administration found itself in a difficult situation. Not only was Washington caught up in numerous other matters, including the Iran hostage crisis, the invasion of Afghanistan, and the domestic economy, but there was no single agency in the government with the capability, let alone authority, to handle the cases of the thousands of persons arriving in the United States. This latter issue of who had the authority to handle the arrivals prompted the White House to assume responsibility for them, but there were few people within the executive branch who had an extensive knowledge of U.S.–Cuban relations or refugee policy. Indeed, there were questions about whether these people were refugees at all. According to the Refugee Act, passed earlier in the year, the United States could accept only 19,500 Cubans annually, and each of those individuals entering the country had to go through a review process before receiving refugee status. Additionally, according to the law, only those persons who refused to go home "because of political, racial, religious, or other persecutions" would receive such a status. Since many of those Cubans coming to the United States did not meet those qualifications, they were not refugees but undocumented aliens.[67]

Castro announced that he would take steps to curb the number of arrivals if Carter assented to discussing matters such as the U.S. embargo against Cuba or overflights of Cuba by Americans planes. The White House refused, and Cubans continued to arrive. It was not until September, when Havana realized that the size of the boatlift was proving more of an embarrassment than beneficent, that it finally closed Mariel harbor. By then, 125,000 Cubans had entered the United States. Unable to document so many people quickly, the White House set up tent cities in Florida, shipped others to military facilities as far away as Wisconsin and Arkansas, and imprisoned others for offenses they had committed back home. News that some of the entrants were criminals, that others had mental disabilities, and that still others had destroyed federal property while waiting to be processed inflamed U.S. public opinion, with almost 60 percent of Americans opposed to the new arrivals.[68]

The Mariel boatlift did not bode well for the administration. The anger among Floridians—Dade County, where Miami was located, was spending $50,000 daily to handle the refugees—concerned White House aides Gene Eidenberg and John White, who knew how important it was to win that state in the 1980 election. Although by September the administration had sped up the process of documenting the arrivals, Eidenberg and White cautioned the president that "the perception, aided by a negative Miami press, that we have 'dumped' this problem on the taxpayers of Florida is widespread." Carter, ever the manager, simply wrote in the margin, "Do something about this."[69]

Carter and his advisers could have avoided many of these problems had they looked at the handling of a similar situation in 1965, the Camarioca boatlift. It was true that Castro gave then-President Lyndon Johnson time to prepare by announcing his intention to open the port of Camarioca before actually doing so. Castro did not give Carter such a luxury. But Carter and his advisers made a bad situation worse by not, as had Johnson, providing immediate and large-scale financial help to those states affected.[70] As a result, he left state officials, and voters, angry.

And the influx of Indochinese refugees also cost the president votes. By the end of 1979, Thailand had accepted some 150,000 refugees and sought help from the world community. In November of that year, Mrs. Carter traveled to Thailand and visited the refugee camps. "Nothing," she later wrote, "had prepared me for the human suffering I saw in the refugee camps when I arrived." The smell of human excrement and the sight of people living in shelters made of plastic bags and dying from illness and malnutrition made a powerful impression upon her. "I felt momentarily paralyzed by the magnitude of the suffering," she later wrote. Upon her return home, both she and the president issued an international call for donations, while the president himself promised the U.S. government would provide financial help. In the end, nearly $500 million was raised, over half of it from foreign nations.[71]

But there were limits to the number of refugees Thailand could accept. While Carter offered to take many in, he asked two of the nearest major powers, Japan and China, to do their part. The Japanese were reluctant to admit a large number of foreigners who would endanger the homogeneity of Japan's population, and, in turn, upset voters; Tokyo thus announced it would limit its help primarily to financial assistance. The Chinese insisted that they were doing all they could. This left the United States. While many Americans shared Carter's concern for the refugees' plight, they considered the number allowed into the country, which by July 1979 had reached 17,000 a month, as going too far. Americans already had concerns about the state of the economy and the problem of illegal immigrants coming into the country and taking jobs from legal citizens; they did not want hundreds of thousands of additional foreigners allowed into the United States. By July, as many as 66 percent of Americans opposed the White House's program to aid Indochina's refugees.[72]

Such sentiment made itself felt on Capitol Hill. A September 1980 meeting between Attorney General Benjamin Civiletti and U.S. Coordinator for Refugee Affairs Victor Palmieri on the one hand, and Representatives Peter Rodino (D-New Jersey), Elizabeth Holtzman (D-New York), and Hamilton Fish, Jr. (R-New York), on the other, "did not go well," explained Eizenstat and White House congressional liaison Frank Moore in a legislative report. "Rodino expressed grave concern over the numbers of Indochinese refugees, the cost to U.S. citizens who are growing resentful over the U.S. footing the refugee bill, and the fact that relatives from other regions face delay and difficulty in reaching the U.S." Holtzman charged other countries with curtailing the number of refugees they admitted while "Fish picked up similar themes." "This is all very disturbing," Carter wrote in the report's margin. But he had no intention of changing his position on what he felt would otherwise be a humanitarian disaster. "We'll just have to minimize losses."[73]

The White House could minimize its losses by securing the hostages' release. In mid-September, Christopher and four other officials headed to Bonn, West Germany, to hold discussions with Sadegh Tabatabai, one of Khomeini's relatives. They expressed their willingness to meet the Iranian leader's demands, and Tabatabai headed home with their message. However, not long after he returned to Tehran, Iraq attacked Iran, beginning a war that would last eight years. Tabatabai could not return to Bonn until the following month. With the sanctions finally having an effect, with Iran now at war against Iraq, and with Soviet troops next door in Afghanistan, Tehran wanted to end the crisis. Thus, when he arrived in Bonn, Tabatabai brought with him news that the American response had "fallen on fertile ground."[74]

As it turned out, that news was not enough to win Carter reelection. Not only was the economy still in a weak state—one poll found that 77 percent of voters considered the economy the most important issue facing the country—and not only did observers believe Carter lost his one and only debate with Reagan on October 28, but at about the same time, the president publicly suggested the hostage crisis was nearly over. Carter's aides knew that Republicans had warned of an "October surprise," but Jordan had suggested the president make such a statement to appeal to the Iranian government. Americans, though, saw it as a last-gasp attempt to get their vote. On November 4, election day, they voted Reagan into office.[75]

In 1989, Barbara Honegger, who had worked on the 1980 Reagan campaign, charged that officials assisting the Republican candidate's bid for

A Crisis of Confidence   **227**

the presidency had secretly met with Iranian officials and convinced them
to hold on to the hostages until after the election so as to guarantee a Reagan victory. What became known as the "October surprise" was later
picked up by other authors, among them Gary Sick, who worked for the
NSC during Carter's term.[76] No evidence has ever been found to substantiate such claims. A 1993 investigation by the Senate judged the allegation
without merit, and others who have looked into the issue shared this conclusion. Mark Bowden, a journalist who interviewed both Iranian officials
and some of the hostage takers, discovered that while there were indeed
approaches made by Reagan campaign officials, those overtures "had little
bearing on Iran's decision to hang on to the hostages." Rather, "[a]ll of the
hostage takers I interviewed said that the decision to wait until Carter officially left office was deliberate, a final insult to the man they had propped
up as the representative of the devil on earth."[77]

Carter was disappointed with his defeat, but he could not dwell on it,
as Iran had yet to release the hostages. The signs were promising. Khomeini
had the militants turn the Americans over to the Iranian government in
preparation for their return to the United States once the crisis ended.
Tehran also appointed a commission, led by Prime Minister Muhammad
Ali Rajai, to hold talks with Washington, using Algeria as an intermediary.[78]

Coming to agreement on the remaining issues took several weeks. At issue was some $10 billion in assets, including gold, money in U.S. banks,
and securities. There were also hundreds of millions of dollars Iran still
owed U.S. companies from the shah's days in power. Carter legally could
neither seize nor return the shah's wealth. Likewise, he could not automatically give up the claims against Iran or unfreeze Tehran's assets. It was
not until January 18, two days before the inauguration, that the two sides
agreed that Washington would turn over $9 billion in assets once Tehran
released the hostages. Carter hoped to see the completion of the final matters before Reagan took the oath of office, but they were not finished until
a few minutes after he officially became president.[79]

Crises in Poland and El Salvador

During this time, the White House had to contend with a new crisis,
in Poland. Following the Second World War, the Soviet Union had imposed
communism on the nations of Eastern Europe, including Hungary, Czechoslovakia, Romania, East Germany, Bulgaria, and Poland. This did not mean, however, that these countries did everything Moscow demanded of them. Over
time, they had achieved some level of independence from the Kremlin. In September 1977, the administration determined to further divide the Soviet
Union from Eastern Europe by giving favorable concessions to those Eastern

European nations that had shown the greatest level of independence from Moscow or that had human rights records better than that of the Kremlin.[80]

Poland was one of the countries selected. Not only were there signs of liberalization there, but Brzezinski had a personal connection to that nation, having been born there. In December 1977, Carter traveled to Poland, and while there, he placed a wreath at a monument built in honor of the Poles who had risen up against Nazi Germany in the Warsaw Uprising of 1944. "Thus," Brzezinski later wrote, "Carter identified himself with the Polish thirst for independence, a gesture which was much appreciated by the Polish people." During his term the president also increased economic aid to Poland to help it combat its economic problems, particularly its shortage of food.[81]

It was because of its economic difficulties that the Polish government announced in July that it was raising the price of food and other goods; the cost of meat, for instance, rose as much as 90 percent. A walkout by angry workers spread throughout the country, reaching the port of Gdansk, where employees had been enraged not just by the rise in prices but by the firing of a fellow laborer. Led by Lech Walesa, the Gdansk workers formed a union in September called Solidarity. Its members received assistance from the AFL-CIO, which sent tens of thousands of dollars as well as communications and printing equipment. The White House's response was less straightforward. Administration officials expressed their approval of Solidarity, but they resisted steps that might provoke a Soviet response. In fact, the White House attempted to convince AFL-CIO head Lane Kirkland not to send assistance to Solidarity; when that failed, it assured Moscow that it did not endorse what Kirkland's organization was doing.[82]

The Soviets were split on what to do. On the one hand, with 85,000 of its soldiers tied down in Afghanistan, Moscow was not keen on invading yet another country, particularly if doing so could lead to resistance there as well. On the other, many in the Kremlin viewed Solidarity as part of a broader Western conspiracy to bring down Poland's communist government. The West's success in Poland could engender uprisings elsewhere in Eastern Europe and undermine communist domination of the entire region. These considerations in mind, the issue for the U.S. government was what path the Soviets might choose. The Central Intelligence Agency (CIA) speculated that Moscow would withhold doing anything for the time being. If the Kremlin ordered the Polish government to crack down on the protests, it was possible that part or all of the Polish military would resist; there were also indications that the Poles would resist if the Soviets themselves intervened. But, added the CIA, if it decided it had no choice, Moscow would take that step.[83]

Indeed, as the fall continued, U.S. intelligence estimates took note of Soviet military activity that suggested Moscow was preparing to use force. The Kremlin, the CIA now judged, could not allow the Solidarity movement to succeed, as it would open a Pandora's box that might bring down communism not just in Poland but elsewhere in Eastern Europe. Reported Brzezinski in early December, "gathering clouds over Poland are getting darker."[84]

Although Muskie and Brzezinski oftentimes did not get along, they worked well together in handling the Polish crisis. On December 3, the secretary of state and NSC adviser, seconded by Brown and CIA Director Stansfield Turner, decided to have Carter send a letter to Brezhnev, which the administration made sure to publicize. Declaring that the Soviets should not undermine Polish self-determination, the president warned, "Foreign military intervention in Poland would have most negative consequences for East-West relations in general and U.S.–Soviet relations in particular." Intelligence reports, however, suggested that the warning had done no good: rather, the Soviets were continuing preparations for attack. On December 7, the White House informed a number of its allies that "entry into Poland by a substantial Soviet force, possibly under the guise of a joint maneuver, may be imminent." NATO cautioned the Soviets that if they invaded Poland, it would impose economic sanctions against Moscow.[85]

Within a week, intelligence estimates showed that Soviet military forces had begun to stand down and to return to their barracks. Brzezinski later commented that American pressure was key. The United States had brought international attention to the Soviets' intentions and had taken the element of surprise away from Moscow, giving the Poles an opportunity to prepare for resisting a Soviet intervention. Soviet documents, though, suggest that the reason for the change of heart on the Kremlin's part was not the result of American machinations but instead a concern that it could not expect the full support of the Polish government if it took military action.[86]

Just as the Polish crisis wound down, the White House found its attention turning back to Central America and the countries of Nicaragua and El Salvador. The White House, arguing that providing assistance to the Sandinista (FSLN) government in Nicaragua could moderate the behavior of that country's leadership and keep it from turning to the Soviet Union for all of its aid, fought to obtain congressional approval of a $75 million package in assistance it had proposed for Managua. While some lawmakers, such as Clement Zablocki (D-Wisconsin), the chair of the House Foreign Affairs Committee, endorsed the aid package, conservatives, among them Representatives Robert Bauman (R-Maryland) and Edward Derwinski (R-Illinois), denounced it, viewing it as a waste of money that would have no impact upon the Sandinista regime. The legislation barely made its way through Congress by the end of the spring, but to have the funds disbursed, Carter had to assure lawmakers that the Sandinistas were not aiding guerrillas in El Salvador. U.S. intelligence was split, with the CIA seeing a connection between the FSLN and the Salvadoran rebels and the State Department's

Bureau of Intelligence and Research less convinced. Meanwhile, State Department officials averred that the aid, if approved, would moderate the Sandinistas' behavior. In September, the president certified that there was no such connection, and Congress approved the assistance.[87]

In fact, the money made little difference. While the FSLN did not abolish capitalism or oppose political parties prior to the end of Carter's term, it was not because of the U.S. aid. Determined to prevent Washington's renewed interference, the Sandinistas had no intention of allowing the White House to determine the course of events in Nicaragua.[88] Rather, the Sandinistas' decision making was based upon what they regarded as being in their own best interests.

The desire to promote moderate governments in Central America also prompted the White House to stand behind the new right-wing regime in El Salvador, despite clear signs it had no intention of enacting reforms. In an effort to avoid being seen as too hard-line, the military leaders in that country convinced two members of the Christian Democratic Party, including Napoleon Duarte, to join the government. The White House was accordingly able to depict the Salvadoran leadership as centrist in nature, under attack from extremists on both sides of the political spectrum. In early 1980 Carter thus offered $5.7 million in nonlethal military assistance, notwithstanding pleas from Archbishop Oscar Romero, a critic of the Salvadoran government and a nominee for the 1979 Nobel Peace Prize, not to do so.[89]

In March 1980, unidentified assailants killed Romero while he gave mass. Though angered, the White House, determined to stem the tide of revolution, offered the Salvadoran military $5 million in military aid and counterinsurgency training. The White House then suspended this and economic aid following the killing of four American nuns, although some $64 million in assistance in the pipeline remained untouched. But after the military government, including the few moderates who remained, promised new reforms, the president on December 17—less than two weeks after the nuns were murdered—offered to resume the assistance to El Salvador.[90]

In early January, the Farabundo Martí Front for National Liberation (FMLN), a coalition of several insurgent groups formed in early 1980 and supported by the FSLN, launched an insurrection against the Salvadoran government. The rebels, however, were too weak, and by the middle of the month, their offensive had fallen apart. The United States had earlier insisted that the Salvadoran government investigate the murder of the nuns and give Duarte more authority over his country's military affairs; on January 19, believing that El Salvador was attempting to meet those conditions and that the government needed protection from the FMLN and its Sandinista allies, and over the objections of some lawmakers, the

White House approved $5.9 million in lethal military aid to the Salvadoran regime. Simultaneously, now charging that there was indeed a connection between the FMLN and FSLN, Carter cut off the remaining $15 million in economic aid that the White House had yet to give Nicaragua.[91] These moves marked the beginning of larger programs of punishing the Sandinista government and assisting the regime in San Salvador that the Reagan administration would undertake.

★   The last year of the Carter administration marked, at least until the second half of the 1980s, the end of détente and a full-scale resurgence of Cold War anti-Sovietism. Although prior to 1980 the president had been returning to the Soviet-centric foreign policy of his predecessors, he had retained elements of his original foreign policy, which called for reviving détente, if not ending the Cold War, and giving more attention to North-South issues. After the Soviet invasion of Afghanistan, the White House looked at all aspects of its foreign policy through the prism of its relationship with Moscow. Consequently, the Carter administration deemphasized human rights, nuclear nonproliferation, and the control of conventional arms transfers to the point that all three policies became virtually nonexistent. Instead, the White House attempted to restore its relations with countries such as Argentina, Somalia, and Pakistan, which it had earlier berated; tried to get U.S. allies to increase their defense spending; tightened its strategic relationship with China; warned of serious consequences in the event of a Soviet invasion of Poland; and, despite clear signs of repression, offered lethal military aid to El Salvador.

The Soviet Union deserved its share of the blame for this turn of events. The Kremlin, adhering to a definition of détente that permitted it to assist fellow communist governments, convinced Carter through its invasion of Afghanistan that it could not be trusted; the White House accordingly sought to punish Moscow for its transgression. Yet the Kremlin had its own reasons for doubting the president's commitment to détente, based upon Carter's toughened rhetoric and actions starting in early 1978. It was "tragic," wrote Soviet ambassador to the United States Anatoly Dobrynin, as "both Brezhnev and Carter personally favored the principles of detente and slowing the arms race. But things developed in a such way that the Kremlin failed to see in Carter a potential American counterpart who shared that goal." Rather, adhering to the old communist ideology, which envisioned communism and capitalism in a constant state of conflict, Soviet officials "viewed the administration's contradictory course in foreign affairs as a plot against Soviet interests. And Carter himself was no great help in the unpredictable and emotional way he conducted foreign policy."[92]

If Carter assumed that by punishing the Soviets he could appeal to a U.S. public that had grown wary of the Kremlin, he was wrong. His attempt to show himself a strong and determined leader could not overcome frustration with the never-ending hostage crisis and, maybe even more important, the economy. While many Americans did indeed have concerns about Reagan's anti-Soviet rhetoric, they were willing to take that risk rather than keep in office a president they had determined was ineffective, inconsistent, and weak, and who never adequately explained to them what the larger purpose of his foreign policy was.

CONCLUSION

★   In his January 1981 Farewell Address to the nation, Jimmy Carter returned to two issues he had made central to the foreign policy he planned to pursue if reelected. One was controlling the spread of weaponry, especially nuclear weapons. Without some way to check the proliferation of atomic technology, he said, "it may only be a matter of time before madness, desperation, greed, or miscalculation lets loose this terrible force." The other was human rights. "Those who hunger for freedom, who thirst for human dignity, and who suffer for the sake of justice," he told the audience, were "the patriots of this cause." It was America's duty to "stand for these basic rights at home and abroad."[1]

Five days later, the now ex-president, at Reagan's request, went to West Germany to welcome the hostages home. He explained to the former captives his diplomatic effort to free them and took questions. Recalled Bruce Laingen, who had been the chargé d'affaires in the U.S. embassy in Tehran and the highest-level official taken hostage, "Carter identified with every one of us. He knew all of us by name, knew our backgrounds, our families. It was obviously an emotional moment for him."[2]

Returning home to Plains, the president and his wife, Rosalynn, prepared for post–White House life. They had to confront a variety of issues, some of them serious. They had to fix up their home, which they had not lived in continuously since Carter had become governor of Georgia. The family's main asset, a peanut warehouse business that Carter's father had established, was $1 million in debt. Furthermore, the president had to write his memoirs and plan his presidential library.

Gradually, the Carters made headway. The home got fixed up, the Carters sold the business—minus 2,000 acres of land—and both the former president and first lady signed lucrative contracts for their memoirs. As for the library, neither of the Carters wanted it to become simply "a lifeless memorial" devoted to Jimmy's presidency but a center with a larger purpose. Following a restless night's sleep in 1982, Carter came up with that purpose: "We're going to make it a place to resolve conflicts," he told his wife. With financial support from a variety of individuals, corporations, and private foundations, the Carter Center opened its doors in 1986.[3]

Yet Carter did not allow his personal and professional concerns to keep him from speaking out about subjects of importance to him. He traveled to the Middle East in 1983 in pursuit of a peace agreement. In the meantime, he charged the Reagan administration with opposing a Middle East peace settlement; with fomenting war in Nicaragua by giving military aid to the contras, a group opposed to that country's Sandinista government; and with overlooking South Africa's apartheid system.[4]

Carter's barrages on the White House had little effect. Although Republicans gained control of the Senate in 1980, Democrats maintained their majority in the House of Representatives. Even so, Reagan was able to convince both houses to endorse his calls for a 25 percent tax cut, reductions in welfare programs, and an increase in military spending, thereby suggesting what a president could accomplish if he was willing to play the game of Washington politics. Indeed, if anything, Democrats distanced themselves from Carter. Most notably, when Carter's former vice president, Walter Mondale, ran against Reagan in 1984, he did not ask his former boss to endorse his candidacy. The Democratic Party only reluctantly invited Carter to speak at its national convention that year and then made sure to schedule his talk for a time when it received little media coverage.[5]

In the mid-1980s, however, Carter's reputation began to show signs of rejuvenation. Observers praised his work with Habitat for Humanity (building homes for impoverished individuals), his attempts to promote peace in Central America and the Middle East, and the effort of the Carter Center to monitor elections and fight disease. Whereas Mondale had shunned Carter in 1984, Senator Joseph Biden of Delaware requested Carter's endorsement when Biden sought the Democratic Party nomination in 1988. Commented *Nation* magazine in 1990, "It is as if Carter had decided to take the most liberal and successful policies of his failed administration—human rights, peacemaking and concern for the poor—and make them the centerpiece of a campaign for his own political resurrection."[6]

Still, Carter could not avoid, and to this day has not avoided, controversy. He has been criticized for denouncing President George H. W. Bush's decision to go to war against Iraq in 1990–1991, for taking part in negotiations with Serbian officials accused of ethnic cleansing in Kosovo in the 1990s, for condemning George W. Bush's invasion of Iraq in 2003, for his 2006 book *Palestine: Peace Not Apartheid*—which assailed Israeli treatment of the Palestinians, for calling the second President Bush's presidency "the worst in history," and for charging that Vice President Dick Cheney was "a disaster for our country." For example, the *New Republic* lambasted Carter for meeting with Radovan Karazdic, one of those who oversaw the killing of thousands of people in Kosovo. The ex-president, declared the magazine's editors, "provides tyrants with the thing that tyranny cannot provide, which is legitimacy." While some observers contended that *Palestine: Peace Not Apartheid* rightly addressed a matter that they felt was oftentimes ignored, many Jews spoke out against it, calling Carter antisemitic; fourteen members of the Carter Center's advisory board resigned in protest, while the *Washington Post* assailed the former president for glossing over Palestinian violence against Israel. "God, unlike Carter," wrote *Post* reviewer Jeffrey Goldberg, "does not manufacture sins to hang around the necks of Jews when no sins have actually been committed." Vice President Cheney's wife, Lynne, defended her husband against Carter's charges, asserting that the ex-president only made his statement so as to sell books.[7]

Despite the criticisms, there has clearly been a reconsideration of Carter's presidency. A study of 78 presidential scholars taken in 2000 ranked Carter as one of America's ten worst presidents. Yet that same survey rated him as one of the nation's ten most underrated chief executives. In June 2006, Quinnipiac University found that Carter ranked among the five best *and* worst presidents since the end of World War II.[8]

There are a couple of likely explanations for the dichotomy in these surveys. One is Carter's post-presidential efforts to fight disease and promote peace around the world; in turn, Americans have come to see him in a more positive light. Another is an opportunity to compare the Carter administration's policies with those of the current president, George W. Bush. Bush's inability to achieve passage of major initiatives, such as the partial privatization of Social Security; questions surrounding his education policy, particularly that of No Child Left Behind; uncertainty over how to pay for his prescription drug program; and a debt of $9 billion as of October 2007, fed in part by spending on a highly unpopular war in Iraq, have given Carter's earlier critics reason for pause. In its June 2006 poll, Quinnipiac University found that a plurality (34%) of respondents listed Bush as the worst postwar chief executive, twice as much as the individual in second place, Richard Nixon. Likewise, 65 percent of those polled by *USA Today* and Gallup asserted that Carter would go down in history as an average or above average president; meanwhile, 54 percent believed future generations would view Bush as below average or poor. Fifty-one percent of respondents to another poll, taken in May 2007, agreed with Carter's assessment that the Bush presidency was the worst in U.S. history.[9]

Looking back, it is clear that Carter tried to change the world in a way that he believed would make it better. In so doing, he tackled an enormous number of foreign policy matters. Sometimes he did so out of personal interest. In other cases, precedent (such as negotiations already underway), congressional pressure, or unforeseen circumstance had an impact. The president attempted to control both conventional and nuclear weapons, promote human rights, withdraw U.S. forces from South Korea, advance the locomotive strategy, get a law of the sea treaty signed, and solve regional disputes around the world. He looked at normalizing relations with Cuba, China, and Vietnam. He confronted revolutions in Nicaragua, Grenada, Iran, and El Salvador. And he faced both the Soviet invasion of Afghanistan and a threatened attack on Poland. One could easily compare the number of foreign policy initiatives Carter proposed or confronted with the New Deal programs Franklin Roosevelt sent to Congress in his first year in the Oval Office.[10]

Carter registered several diplomatic successes, of which even his contemporaries took note. The two most significant were the Panama Canal treaties and the Camp David Accords. Yet Carter also successfully brought the Iranian hostages home unharmed, restored access to the Turkish military bases, normalized relations with China, and increased defense spending. At the same time, he did not run up the massive debt left behind by the Reagan administration, nor was his term in office marred by extralegal scandals like those of Nixon or Reagan.[11] But the issue that has brought Carter the most praise by far was his human rights initiative. Although Congress started the effort to make human rights a component of U.S. foreign policy, Carter joined that endeavor and used a broad range of methods to bring attention to, as well as combat, human rights abuses abroad. In the process, he restored America's reputation as a worldwide defender of the rights of others around the world. Robert Gates, who worked for the Central Intelligence Agency during the Carter years, further contends that by "challenging the legitimacy of Soviet authority," the president set the foundation for the downfall of communism in the Soviet Union and Eastern Europe. Still others credit Carter with saving numerous lives worldwide. There is, though, a debate to this day regarding whether the downfall of the Soviet system and the improvement in human rights conditions in several countries was due more to internal rather than external forces. Even the administration admitted that in "many cases," positive changes "reflected dramatic internal political developments."[12]

Furthermore, Carter may have been the victim of forces beyond his control. He faced a Congress that was reasserting itself. Without jeopardizing America's relations with its allies or using some form of force—which, in some cases, could lead to a superpower war—the president had only a limited ability to influence events in places like Nicaragua, the Horn of Africa, Iran, and Afghanistan. He also had to deal with a Soviet Union that defined détente differently than the United States. Washington asserted that détente required the maintenance of the status quo; Moscow contended that it permitted the placement of advanced SS-20 missiles in Europe, aid to communists abroad, and the spread of communist ideology. Though he did a poor job in confronting these challenges, could someone else have done any better?[13]

Whether a Ronald Reagan or Gerald Ford could have been more successful is impossible to know. What is clear are two things. First, Carter did not handle his foreign policy well. Second, Carter himself had set a standard of getting at least 95 percent of what he wanted. He got far less.

One reason why Carter ended up having a mediocre foreign policy was his view of himself as a political outsider. He did not believe he owed anything to members of Congress, even to members of his own party, as they did not help get him elected. Simultaneously, he regarded himself as a trustee of the people who knew what was right for them and that they would see the wisdom of his proposals for the nation. This was not the formula for a successful politician. Even the president's wife, Rosalynn, all but admitted this. "Jimmy was never really a politician," she commented years after leaving Washington. "My definition of a politician is you let the people guide you. Jimmy is more of a leader who wants people to follow him."[14]

Carter had difficulty understanding, and was even irritated by, those who did not see the righteousness of his cause. When Vernon Jorden, the head of the Urban League, told Carter that the White House was not doing enough to help those living in poverty, the president "took him aside" and admonished him against making "erroneous or demagogic statements" that could undermine government assistance, which Carter called "the last hope of the poor." Likewise, when labor leader George Meany challenged one of Carter's policies, the president replied, "If you can't support me, I'd rather not talk," and left the room.[15]

Carter exhibited the same attitude with respect to Congress. Vice President Walter Mondale stated years after leaving the White House that his boss was "apt to define what he, as President, wanted done and then expect and hope that the Congress would respond." This was a major mistake, particularly at a time when Capitol Hill had made clear its determination to place more power in its hands. Carter thus created serious difficulties for his administration, as seen in the cases of the Strategic Arms Limitation Treaties (SALT II), normalization of relations with China, the Middle East peace process, the Turkish arms embargo, the B-1 bomber, the neutron bomb, the call to withdraw U.S. troops from South Korea, and the Iran hostage rescue mission. "Washington hates it," commented Anthony Lake, the head of the State Department's Policy Planning Staff during Carter's term, "when presidents don't treat it with the respect it *believes* it deserves." Mondale seconded Lake. "Carter's anti-political attitudes used to drive me nuts, because you couldn't get him to grapple with a political problem."[16]

Carter's perception of himself as a trustee appeared in his relations with other countries. He ignored repeated warnings from the Soviet Union that it would not accept deep cuts; when it rejected that proposal, the White House was forced to go back to the drawing board and lost precious time arranging an arms agreement that ultimately was very similar to Vladivostok. While West German Chancellor Helmut Schmidt early on came to dislike Carter, the U.S. president's decisions on such matters as the neutron bomb, long-range theater forces, and punishment of the Soviets following their invasion of Afghanistan only reinforced Schmidt's impressions of his American colleague.

Carter showed that he was capable of using persuasion. He convinced lawmakers to vote in favor of the Panama Canal treaties and to give Saudi Arabia F-15 fighter jets. He took part in several economic summits that proved more successful than observers had anticipated. Had he shown a willingness to consult with lawmakers more often, he could have avoided the uproar that ensued when he suddenly announced his decisions on the neutron bomb or the B-1 bomber. He would have realized that withdrawing U.S. troops from South Korea was virtually impossible and have avoided expending so much political capital on that goal. A combination of consultation with the signing of a Vladivostok-style pact early on might have allowed the president to overcome resistance from both the Committee on the Present Danger and Senator Henry Jackson (D-Washington); the ratification of such an agreement would have given Carter an early foreign policy success and possibly set the foundation for a more far-reaching arms control agreement. When asked a decade after his resignation whether the president's demeanor toward lawmakers made his job as secretary of state more vexatious, Cyrus Vance replied, "Yes."[17]

Carter only compounded his problems by undertaking too many initiatives. Trained as an engineer, the president saw himself as a problem solver. William Quandt, a Middle East specialist on the National Security Council (NSC), commented that if Carter "saw a problem, he wanted to solve it, and that was all there was to it." Quandt recalled, "[W]e would send lists to the president and say, 'Here are twenty issues or so that are of concern, that need attention. You can devote attention to only two or three of them and really hope to do very much. Which two are three are the most important to you?' And the checklist would come back with a note to do all twenty of them." Concluded Quandt, "President Carter did not have the inclination or capacity to make the grand strategic trade-offs."[18]

Trying to do so much on the diplomatic front in addition to the numerous domestic initiatives the president put forth—hospital cost containment, a comprehensive energy program, welfare and social security reform, and environmental legislation, just to name a few—was bound to cause trouble. For one, it overburdened the congressional schedule and forced the White House to delay some policies in favor of others. The president decided to hold off on normalization of relations with China until after the Panama Canal treaties were signed; normalization of relations with China interfered with the timing of SALT II. By the time SALT II came up for ratification, the political climate in Washington had changed, complicating the president's efforts to get it ratified.[19]

Moreover, taking on so many initiatives limited the amount of time members of the White House could devote to each one. Not only were top administration officials unable to keep fully informed on each and every initiative, but the president did not take care to set priorities or to address the possibility that one policy might interfere with another.[20] He reasoned the Soviet Union would not link public attacks on the treatment of its citizens to arms control. Yet the Kremlin did just that, delaying an arms agreement and forcing the president to choose either arms control or human rights. Had Carter not broken the long-standing principle of publicly denouncing the Soviets for their human rights violations—instead, using quiet, behind-the-scenes pressure—he could have met calls for making human rights a component of America's foreign policy while at the same time avoiding the trouble with Moscow that ended up postponing the signing of an arms control pact. Indeed, Carter was willing elsewhere to compromise his human rights initiative when he realized that it interfered with the maintenance of good relations with countries such as Iran, South Korea, the Philippines, Cambodia, China, and South Africa. The president had to make exceptions as well to the policy of nuclear nonproliferation in the cases of Japan, India, and West Germany. Trying to separate the issue of normalization of relations with Cuba and Vietnam from other matters also proved impossible. National Security Adviser Zbigniew Brzezinski acknowledged that Carter "did become overloaded." Vance pointed out the difficulty of getting Carter "to focus on some of the broader aspects of the problem in a way that a Cabinet officer who was charged with responsibility in that area would like them to have been dealt with." Even the president later admitted that "perhaps we tried to do too much."[21]

Trying to do so much at once raised another problem. A successful politician needs to express individual policies in the context of a larger vision. The elements were there, but no one, either at the time or today, agrees about what those elements amounted to. Did the president see arms control, human rights, nuclear nonproliferation, normalization of relations with communist countries, the withdrawal of U.S. troops from South Korea, the resolution of the Greco-Turkish dispute over Cyprus, the locomotive strategy, and a successful outcome to the law of the sea negotiations as parts of a larger plan of making America more secure? Were they designed to create a global community, where all nations would share responsibility in developing a stable, safer world? It was not clear.[22] As noted earlier, Brzezinski commented on the lack of vision. Donald McHenry, who succeeded Andrew Young as U.S. ambassador to the United Nations, seconded the NSC adviser. Carter's "attention to detail tended to carry over to the way in which he discussed policy matters with the public. The public doesn't want, in my view, to hear a recitation of the detailed complications of foreign policy. . . . The public tends to want to know how you, as president, are going to act."[23]

Then there was Carter's managerial style. The president issued orders, expecting each member of the cabinet, who was largely given autonomy over his or her agency, to carry them out. This, however, led to bureaucratic battles over such matters as human rights, which pitted the State Department's Bureau of Human Rights against both rival geographic bureaus and other agencies of government. The result was a human rights initiative that became watered down and that, by Carter's second year in office, had come to focus almost entirely on Latin America.

But the most damaging aspect of Carter's managerial style was his inability or unwillingness to stop the internecine warfare between the State Department and the National Security Council. "Cy Vance and Zbig Brzezinski were fighting all the time," recalled Mondale. The secretary of state and NSC adviser, as well as their subordinates, disagreed on such matters as policy toward Nicaragua, Iran, China, the Soviet Union, the Horn of Africa, and elsewhere. The president compounded matters when he paper-clipped the advice given him by Vance and Brzezinski. He neither rejected nor accepted the Salisbury Plan for Rhodesia, angering both sides on the issue. He used the language of cooperation and criticism in reference to relations with the Soviet Union, confusing observers there and in the United States as to what his policy was. He never made it clear to the shah how much support he had in the White House. Vance wrote that the dispute between himself and Brzezinski, combined with the lack of guidance from the president, "became a political liability, leaving the Congress and foreign governments with the impression that the administration did not know its mind."[24]

Over time, it was Brzezinski and the NSC that came out on top in the struggle with Vance and State. In 1977 and into 1978, Carter had leaned largely in Vance's favor. The president discarded Brzezinski's call for linkage, emphasized SALT over normalization of relations with China, and viewed communist machinations in places like the Horn of Africa as local crises unrelated to the broader East-West struggle. But the president grew increasingly frustrated with Soviet and Cuban activities in Africa and moved in the direction of a more hard-nosed Soviet-centric foreign policy similar to that of his Cold War predecessors. While he still held out hope for some kind of accommodation with the Soviets, that ended with the invasion of Afghanistan. From that point, the president fully joined the Brzezinski camp.

The move to a hard-line, Soviet-centric policy had an impact on numerous Carter administration initiatives. Normalization of relations with Cuba and Vietnam was tabled. Demilitarization of the Indian Ocean, Mutual Balanced Force Reduction, the comprehensive test ban treaty, and SALT died. The human rights policy, which had already been watered down, was largely set aside as the White House sought to restore ties with countries in Latin America, such as Argentina and Uruguay. The policies of controlling the spread of nuclear technology and conventional weaponry, which also had been compromised prior to 1979, were pushed aside in the name of containing the Soviet threat. In fact, instead of declining, U.S. foreign arms sales increased nearly $4.5 billion during Carter's term, reaching $17.1 billion in 1980.[25]

Meanwhile, other initiatives were either dead or floundering. The Cyprus negotiations had fallen apart. The withdrawal of U.S. troops from South Korea was put in abeyance. The locomotive strategy was not working. The law of the sea negotiations were at a standstill. A comprehensive Middle East peace settlement looked stillborn.

Had Carter not tried to do so much, had he worked harder to consult with both foreign officials and members of Congress, had he not adopted a managerial style that was bound to lead to turf wars, and had he provided the nation a vision of where he planned to lead it, he might easily have gone down as a more successful president. It was true that there were internal and external limits to what Carter could do; every president faces such limits. A successful president, though, understands those limitations and then finds a way to work within them, if not take advantage of them. That was not Jimmy Carter.

NOTES

Abbreviations Used

AL	Allen Library, University of Washington, Seattle, Washington
AMSC	Anthony M. Solomon Collection
BM	Brzezinski Material
CF	Country File
COS	Chief of Staff
CWIHP	*Cold War International History Project*
DHM	Donated Historical Material
FE	Far East
GI	Global Issues
H/S	Horn/Special
JCL	Jimmy Carter Library, Atlanta, Georgia
MCPOHP	Miller Center Presidential Oral History Program, Miller Center, University of Virginia
N/S	North/South
NatSA	National Security Archive, George Washington University, Washington, D.C.
NSA	National Security Affairs
OSS	Office of Staff Secretary
PCFLF	Presidential Correspondence with Foreign Leaders File
PF	Plains File
PHF	Presidential Handwriting File
PPPUS	*Public Papers of the Presidents of the United States*
SF	Subject File

SM   Staff Material

SO   Staff Offices

VF   Vertical File

WHCF   White House Central File

WM   Walter Mondale

ZB   Zbigniew Brzezinski

Prelude

1. Terence Smith, "Experts See '76 Victory as Carter's Big Achievement," *New York Times,* January 8, 1981; Steven V. Roberts, "Analysts Give Carter Higher Marks in Foreign Affairs Than in Domestic Policy," *New York Times,* January 19, 1981.

2. See, for example, Gaddis Smith, *Morality, Reason, and Power: American Diplomacy in the Carter Years* (New York: Hill and Wang, 1986); Alexander Moens, *Foreign Policy Under Carter: Testing Multiple Advocacy Decision Making* (Boulder: Westview, 1990); Richard Thornton, *The Carter Years: Toward a New Global Order* (New York: Paragon House, 1992); Burton I. Kaufman and Scott Kaufman, *The Presidency of James Earl Carter, Jr.,* 2nd ed. (Lawrence: University Press of Kansas, 2006); Jerel A. Rosati, *The Carter Administration's Quest for Global Community: Beliefs and Their Impact on Behavior* (Columbia: University of South Carolina Press, 1987); Raymond Garthoff, *Détente and Confrontation: American-Soviet Relations from Nixon to Reagan,* rev. ed. (Washington, D.C.: Brookings Institution, 1994); A. Glenn Mower, *Human Rights and American Foreign Policy: The Carter and Reagan Experiences* (New York: Greenwood, 1987); Lars Schoultz, *Human Rights and U.S. Policy towards Latin America* (Princeton: Princeton University Press, 1981); Victor S. Kaufman, "The Carter Administration and the Human Rights Bureau," *Historian* 61 (Fall 1998): 51–66.

3. Such works include David W. Engstrom, *Presidential Decision Making Adrift: The Carter Administration and the Mariel Boatlift* (Lanham, Md.: Rowman and Littlefield, 1997); Michael Ledeen and William Lewis, *Debacle: The American Failure in Iran* (New York: Alfred A. Knopf, 1981); Timothy P. Maga, *The World of Jimmy Carter: U.S. Foreign Policy, 1977–1981* (Westhaven, Conn.: University of New Haven Press, 1994); Richard A. Melanson, *Reconstructing Consensus: American Foreign Policy since the Vietnam War* (New York: St. Martin's, 1991).

4. Charles O. Jones, *The Trusteeship President: Jimmy Carter and the United States Congress* (Baton Rouge: Louisiana State University Press, 1988). See also Richard E. Neustadt, *Presidential Power and the Modern Presidents: The Politics of Leadership from Roosevelt to Reagan* (New York: Free Press, 1990); Betty Glad, *Jimmy Carter: In Search of the Great White House* (New York: Norton, 1980).

5. A fairly extensive list includes David Skidmore, *Reversing Course: Carter's Foreign Policy, Domestic Politics, and the Failure of Reform* (Nashville: Vanderbilt University Press, 1996); Joanna Spear, *Carter and Arms Sales: Implementing the Carter Administration's Arms Transfer Restraint Policy* (New York: St. Martin's, 1995); William F. Grover, *The President as Prisoner: A Structural Critique of the Carter and Reagan Years* (Albany: State University of New York Press, 1989); Morris H. Morley, *Washington, Somoza, and the Sandinistas: State and Regime in U.S. Policy toward Nicaragua, 1969–1981* (New York: Cambridge University Press, 1994); Odd Arne Westad, "The Fall of Détente and the Turning Tides of History," in *The Fall of Détente: Soviet-American Relations during the Carter Years,* ed. Odd Arne Westad (Boston: Scandinavian University Press, 1997); Robert J. McMahon, *The Cold War: A Very Short Introduction* (New York: Oxford Univer-

sity Press, 2003); Ralph B. Levering, *The Cold War, 1945–1987,* 2nd ed. (Arlington Heights, Ill.: Harland Davidson, 1988); Ronald E. Powaski, *The Cold War: The United States and the Soviet Union, 1917–1991* (New York: Oxford University Press, 1998); Joseph L. Nogee and John Spanier, *Peace Impossible—War Unlikely: The Cold War Between the United States and the Soviet Union* (Glenview, Ill.: Scott, Foresman/Little, 1988); James A. Bill, *The Eagle and the Lion: The Tragedy of American-Iranian Relations* (New Haven: Yale University Press, 1988); William Stivers, *America's Confrontation with Revolutionary Change in the Middle East, 1948–83* (New York: St. Martin's, 1986); Maya Chadda, *Paradox of Power: The United States in Southwest Asia, 1973–1984* (Santa Barbara, Calif.: ABC-Clio, 1986).

6. See Erwin C. Hargrove, *Jimmy Carter as President: Leadership and the Politics of the Public Good* (Baton Rouge: Louisiana State University Press, 1988); John Dumbrell, *The Carter Presidency: A Re-evaluation,* 2nd ed. (New York: Manchester University Press, 1995); Robert A. Strong, *Working in the World: Jimmy Carter and the Making of American Foreign Policy* (Baton Rouge: Louisiana State University Press, 2000); Friedbert Pflüger, "Human Rights Unbound: Carter's Human Rights Policy Reassessed," *Presidential Studies Quarterly* 19 (Fall 1989): 705–16; David F. Schmitz and Vanessa Walker, "Jimmy Carter and the Foreign Policy of Human Rights: The Development of a Post-Cold War Foreign Policy," *Diplomatic History* 28 (January 2004): 113–43; Harold Molineau, "Carter and Human Rights: Administrative Impact of a Symbolic Policy," *Policy Studies Journal* 8 (Summer 1980): 879–85; Douglas Brinkley, "The Rising Stock of Jimmy Carter: The 'Hands on' Legacy of Our Thirty-ninth President," *Diplomatic History* 20 (Fall 1996): 505–29.

1—Continuity or Change?

1. Jimmy Carter, *Keeping Faith: Memoirs of a President* (Fayetteville: University of Arkansas Press, 1995), 19; Haynes Johnson, "Carter is Sworn in as President," *Washington Post,* January 21, 1977.

2. Carter, *Keeping Faith,* 20; Johnson, "Carter is Sworn in as President."

3. Kaufman and Kaufman, *Presidency of James Earl Carter,* 26.

4. Bruce J. Schulman, *The Seventies: The Great Shift in American Culture, Society, and Politics* (New York: Free Press, 2001), 103.

5. Ibid., 194–205.

6. James T. Patterson, *Restless Giant: The United States from Watergate to Bush v. Gore* (New York: Oxford University Press, 2005), 133.

7. Garthoff, *Détente and Confrontation,* 280–81.

8. Nogee and Spanier, *Peace Impossible—War Unlikely,* 94.

9. John Lewis Gaddis, *Strategies of Containment: A Critical Appraisal of American National Security Policy during the Cold War,* rev. ed. (New York: Oxford University Press, 2005), 312.

10. Nogee and Spanier, *Peace Impossible—War Unlikely,* 92–95.

11. Quoted in Gaddis, *Strategies of Containment,* 310.

12. Schulman, *Seventies,* 199.

13. Dale Carter, "The Crooked Path: Continuity and Change in American Foreign Policy, 1968–1981," in *The Lost Decade: America in the Seventies,* ed. Elsebeth Hurup (Oakville, Conn.: Aarhus University Press, 1996), 112.

14. Olav Njølstad, "Keys of Keys? Salt II and the Breakdown of Détente," in *Fall of Détente,* ed. Wested, 37.

15. Thomas G. Paterson, et al., *American Foreign Relations: A History,* 2 vols. (Boston: Houghton Mifflin, 2006), 2:256.

16. Dana H. Allin, *Cold War Illusions: America, Europe, and Soviet Power, 1969–1989* (New York: St. Martin's, 1995), 57.

17. George D. Moffett III, *The Limits of Victory: The Ratification of the Panama Canal Treaties* (Ithaca: Cornell University Press, 1985), 54–55.

18. Schoultz, *Human Rights and United States Policy,* 194–95.

19. Patterson, *Restless Giant,* 84.

20. Peter G. Bourne, *Jimmy Carter: A Comprehensive Biography from Plains to Post-Presidency* (New York: Scribner, 1997), 33, 412; Kenneth E. Morris, *Jimmy Carter: American Moralist* (Athens: University of Georgia Press, 1996), 99; Zbigniew Brzezinski, *Power and Principle: Memoirs of the National Security Adviser, 1977–1981* (New York: Farrar, Straus, Giroux, 1983), 22.

21. Charles Bussey, "Jimmy Carter: Hope and Memory versus Optimism and Nostalgia," in *The Lost Decade: America in the Seventies,* ed. Elsebeth Hurup (Oakville, Conn.: Aarhus University Press, 1996), 92–93; Kaufman and Kaufman, *Presidency of James Earl Carter,* 11–12.

22. Gerry Argyris Andrianopoulos, *Kissinger and Brzezinski: The NSC and the Struggle for Control of U.S. National Security Policy* (New York: St. Martin's, 1991), 137.

23. Kaufman and Kaufman, *Presidency of James Earl Carter,* 44–45; Mower, *Human Rights and American Foreign Policy,* 14–15; Joshua Muravchik, *The Uncertain Crusade: Jimmy Carter and the Dilemmas of Human Rights Policy* (Lanham, Md.: Hamilton Press, 1986), 2–4.

24. Andrianopoulos, *Kissinger and Brzezinski,* 136. Carter quoted in Smith, *Morality, Reason, and Power,* 29.

25. Smith, *Morality, Reason, and Power,* 61–62.

26. Powaski, *Cold War,* 205; Shai Feldman, "Superpower Nonproliferation Policies: The Case of the Middle East," in *The Soviet-American Competition in the Middle East,* ed. Steven L. Spiegel, Mark A. Heller, and Jacob Goldberg (Lexington, Mass.: Lexington Books, 1988), 96; J. Michael Martinez, "The Carter Administration and the Evolution of American Nuclear Nonproliferation Policy, 1977–1981," *Journal of Policy History* 14 (2002): 264.

27. Powaski, *Cold War,* 205; *PPPUS, Jimmy Carter,* 1977, I:956–57.

28. *The Presidential Campaign, 1976,* 3 vols. (Washington, D.C.: Government Printing Office, 1978), 1:268.

29. Smith, *Morality, Reason, and Power,* 134.

30. Ibid., 30–31; Tad Szulc, "Carter's Foreign Policy," *New Republic,* July 17, 1976, 16; "Carter and the Arms Race," *The Progressive,* October 1976, 5–6.

31. Skidmore, *Reversing Course,* 90, 93; Jerry W. Sanders, *Peddlers of Crisis: The Committee on the Present Danger and the Politics of Containment* (Boston: South End Press, 1983), 266–67.

32. Stephanie Slocum-Schaffer, *America in the Seventies* (Syracuse: Syracuse University Press, 2003), 63.

33. Lawrence X. Clifford, "An Examination of the Carter Administration's Selection of Secretary of State and National Security Adviser," in *Jimmy Carter: Foreign Policy and Post-Presidential Years,* ed. Herbert D. Rosenbaum and Alexej Ugrinsky (Westport, Conn.: Greenwood, 1994), 7. Vance quoted in David Harris, *The Crisis: The President, the Prophet, and the Shah—1979 and the Coming of Militant Islam* (New York: Little, Brown and Co., 2004), 61.

34. Cyrus Vance, *Hard Choices: Critical Years in American Foreign Policy* (New York: Simon and Schuster, 1983), 441; Melchiore J. Laucella, "A Cognitive-Psychodynamic Perspective to Understanding Secretary of State Cyrus Vance's Worldview," *Presidential Studies Quarterly* 34 (June 2004): 244.

35. David S. McLellan, *Cyrus Vance* (Totowa, N.J.: Rowman and Allanheld, 1985), 34.

36. Harris, *Crisis,* 62.

37. Moffett, *Limits of Victory,* 55.

38. Andrianopoulos, *Kissinger and Brzezinski*, 40, 44; Smith, *Morality, Reason, and Power*, 36; Zbigniew Brzezinski, "Peace and Power," *Military Review* 49 (July 1969): 37; Zbigniew Brzezinski, "The Deceptive Structure of Peace," *Foreign Policy* no. 14 (Spring 1974): 41–43.

39. Zbigniew Brzezinski and Samuel P. Huntington, *Political Power: USA/USSR* (New York: Viking Press, 1964), 436; Smith, *Morality, Reason, and Power*, 37.

40. Brezinski, *Power and Principle*, 147, 149; McLellan, *Cyrus Vance*, 35.

41. Brzezinski, *Power and Principle*, 148.

42. Clark Clifford, with Richard Holbrooke, *Counsel to the President: A Memoir* (New York: Random House, 1991), 621.

43. Vance, *Hard Choices*, 30.

44. Hamilton Jordan, *Crisis: The Last Year of the Carter Presidency* (New York: Putnam, 1982), 47; Smith, *Morality, Reason, and Power*, 39–40.

45. Andrianopoulos, *Kissinger and Brzezinski*, 138.

46. Dumbrell, *Carter Presidency*, 196; Vance, *Hard Choices*, 37.

47. McLellan, *Cyrus Vance*, 24.

48. Clifford, "An Examination," 6; Smith, *Morality, Reason, and Power*, 38.

49. Carter, *Keeping Faith*, 56, 57; Kenneth W. Thompson, ed., *The Carter Presidency: Fourteen Intimate Perspectives of Jimmy Carter* (Lanham, Md.: University Press of America, 1990), 8.

50. Smith, *Morality, Reason, and Power*, 45; Ezer Weizman, *The Battle for Peace* (New York: Bantam, 1981), 239.

51. Brzezinski, *Power and Principle*, 47.

52. Scott Kaufman, *Rosalynn Carter: Equal Partner in the White House* (Lawrence: University Press of Kansas, 2006), 29; Carter, *Keeping Faith*, 34; "Second Most Powerful Person," *Time*, May 7, 1979, 22; Martin Tolchin, "Rosalynn Carter: An Adviser in Her Own Right," *New York Times*, May 30, 1978.

53. Interview with Zbigniew Brzezinski, with Madeline K. Albright, Leslie G. Denend, and William Odom, MCPOHP, February 18, 1982; Harris, *Crisis*, 64. Muskie replaced Vance as secretary of state in 1980 upon Vance's resignation.

54. Finlay Lewis, *Mondale: Portrait of an American Politician* (New York: Harper and Row, 1980), 48.

55. Andrianopoulos, *Kissinger and Brzezinski*, 143; Lewis, *Mondale*, 247; Smith, *Morality, Reason, and Power*, 47; Thompson, *Carter Presidency*, 244.

56. Smith, *Morality, Reason, and Power*, 47.

2—The Human Rights, Arms Control, and Nonproliferation Conundrums

1. Carter quote from Thompson, *Carter Presidency*, 229.

2. *PPPUS, Jimmy Carter*, 1977, I:2.

3. Schoultz, *Human Rights and United States Policy*, 111–12; "Human Rights, Chilean Wrongs," *Washington Post*, June 27, 1976; Edward S. Maynard, "The Bureaucracy and Implementation of U.S. Human Rights Law," *Human Rights Quarterly* 11 (May 1989), 178 n. 1, 179; John P. Salzberg, "A View from the Hill: U.S. Legislation and Human Rights," in *The Diplomacy of Human Rights*, ed. David D. Newsom (Lanham, Md.: University Press of America/Georgetown University Institute for the Study of Diplomacy, 1986), 19.

4. Anthony Lake, *Somoza Falling* (Boston: Houghton Mifflin, 1989), 21.

5. Dale R. Herspring, *The Pentagon and the Presidency: Civil-Military Relations from FDR to George W. Bush* (Lawrence: University Press of Kansas, 2005), 239; Alexander L. George and Eric Stern, "Presidential Management Style and Models," in *Presidential Personality and Performance*, ed. Alexander L. George and Juliette L. George, 219 (Boulder: Westview, 1998); Thompson, *Carter Presidency*, 141.

6. Kaufman, "The Carter Administration and the Human Rights Bureau," 52–54.

7. Ibid., 56–57.

8. Caleb Rossiter and Anne-Marie Smith, "Human Rights: The Carter Record, the Reagan Reaction," *International Policy Report* (September 1984): 7–10.

9. Ibid., 18.

10. Lincoln Bloomfield, "The Carter Human Rights Policy: A Provisional Appraisal," January 11, 1981, DHM, ZB, SF, Box 34, JCL.

11. Kaufman, "Bureau of Human Rights," 58–59; Robert Gordon Kaufman, *Henry M. Jackson: A Life in Politics* (Seattle: University of Washington Press, 2000), 369–71.

12. Bernard Gwertzman, "Vance Says the U.S. Won't Be Strident Over Rights Abroad," *New York Times*, February 1, 1977; I. M. Destler, Leslie Gelb, and Anthony Lake, *Our Own Worst Enemy: The Unmaking of American Foreign Policy* (New York: Simon and Schuster, 1984), 72.

13. Virginia S. Capulong-Hallenberg, *Philippine Foreign Policy toward the U.S., 1972–1980: Reorientation?* (Stockholm: Department of Political Science, University of Stockholm, 1987), 111, 120–21; Raymond Bonner, *Waltzing with a Dictator: The Marcoses and the Making of American Policy* (New York: Vintage, 1988), 206–7.

14. Bonner, *Waltzing with a Dictator,* 108, 220, 249–50, 258–62.

15. Ibid., 205; Capulong-Hallenberg, *Philippine Foreign Policy toward the U.S.,* 109.

16. Bonner, *Waltzing with a Dictator,* 207, 210–11.

17. "Philippine Base Negotiations," October 22, 1977, NSA, SM, FE, Box 5, JCL.

18. Far East to Brzezinski, January 16, 1978, NSA, SM, FE, Box 1, and Vice President to President, April 26, 1978, NSA, SM, FE, Box 7, JCL; Bonner, *Waltzing with a Dictator,* 226–30.

19. Amy Blitz, *The Contested State: American Foreign Policy and Regime Change in the Philippines* (Lanham, Md.: Rowman and Littlefield, 2000), 132.

20. Far East to Brzezinski, March 23, 1978, NSA, SM, FE, Box 1, JCL; Bonner, *Waltzing with a Dictator,* 232.

21. Blitz, *Contested State,* 132–33; "Counting the Losses in Manila," *New York Times,* April 11, 1978; "'Thrillah in Manila,'" *Washington Post,* April 11, 1978.

22. Vice President to President, April 26, 1978.

23. Bonner, *Waltzing with a Dictator,* 243–48; Vice President to President, April 26, 1978; Marcos to Carter, May 3, 1978; and Carter to Marcos, June 2, 1978, NSA, SM, FE, Box 7, JCL. Although Mondale later wrote Carter that he did not bring up the issue of compensation, the administration did raise its offer to $450 million. Ultimately, a base agreement was signed, in which Marcos received $500 million. See Vice President to President, May 15, 1978, DHM, WM, Box 205, JCL; Bonner, *Waltzing with a Dictator,* 253.

24. Lake to Secretary, January 16, 1978, WHCF, Box HU-1, JCL.

25. Kaufman, *Rosalynn Carter,* 62–74.

26. Kaufman, "Human Rights," 54; Rossiter and Smith, "Human Rights," 15; Harold Molineau, *U.S. Policy toward Latin America: From Regionalism to Globalism* (Boulder: Westview, 1986), 139.

27. Patrick J. Flood, "U.S. Human Rights Initiatives Concerning Argentina," in *Diplomacy of Human Rights,* ed. Newsom, 137.

28. Schoultz, *Human Rights and United States Policy,* 259–60.

29. Brzezinski, *Power and Principle,* 49, 128.

30. Ibid., 149; Cathal J. Nolan, *Principled Diplomacy: Security and Rights in U.S. Foreign Policy* (Westport, Conn.: Greenwood, 1993), 142; Powell to President, February 21, 1977, Stuart Eizenstat Papers, Box 208, JCL.

31. Quoted in David Mayers, *The Ambassadors and America's Soviet Policy* (New York: Oxford University Press, 1995), 230, 231.

32. Kaufman and Kaufman, *Presidency of James Earl Carter,* 47–48.

33. Strobe Talbott, *Endgame: The Inside Story of SALT II* (New York: Harper and Row, 1979), 24–29.

34. Talbott, *Endgame,* 34–35.

35. Kaufman and Kaufman, *Presidency of James Earl Carter,* 50; Burton I. Kaufman, *Presidential Profiles: The Carter Years* (New York: Facts on File, 2006), 508; Strong, *Working in the World,* 21–22; "Record of the Conversation with A. Harriman," December 1, 1976, VF, Box 117, JCL.

36. Talbott, *Endgame,* 51–52; Vance, *Hard Choices,* 51.

37. Talbott, *Endgame,* 32; Grover, *President as Prisoner,* 143; Brezhnev to Carter, February 4 and 25, 1977, and Carter to Brezhnev, February 14, 1977, PF, SF, Box 17, JCL.

38. Talbott, *Endgame,* 36–37; "Record of the Conversation with Z. Brzezinski," March 5, 1977, VF, Box 117; and Brezhnev to Carter, March 15, 1977, PF, SF, Box 17, JCL.

39. "Record of the Conversation with the Secretary of State of the USA, C. Vance," March 21, 1977, VF, Box 117; Talbott, *Endgame,* 60–61.

40. Talbott, *Endgame,* 62; Strong, *Working in the World,* 38; "Record of the Conversation with the Secretary of State of the USA, C. Vance," March 21, 1977, VF, Box 117, JCL.

41. Talbott, *Endgame,* 67.

42. Carter quoted in Nolan, *Principled Diplomacy,* 142–43. Dobrynin, in Westad, *Fall of Détente,* 16.

43. Svetlana Savranskaya and David A. Welch, eds., *Global Competition and the Deterioration of U.S.–Soviet Relations, 1977–1980* (Providence, R.I.: Center for Foreign Policy Development, Thomas J. Watson Jr. Institute for International Studies, 1995), 170–74, VF, Box 117, JCL.

44. Oral history interview with Jimmy Carter, November 29, 1982, MCPOHP.

45. Talbott, *Endgame,* 83–84; Brzezinski Memorandum re SALT, April 23, 1977, VF, Box 116, JCL.

46. Talbott, *Endgame,* 85–86, 88, 92–93; Brzezinski to President, June 7, 1977, VF, Box 116, JCL.

47. Talbott, *Endgame,* 101–2.

48. Ibid., 104, 106–8; Nick Kotz, *Wild Blue Yonder: Money, Politics, and the B-1 Bomber* (New York: Pantheon, 1988), 154, 166, 194; Vance, *Hard Choices,* 58.

49. Talbott, *Endgame,* 111–12.

50. Jackson to President, August 22 and September 22, 1977, Papers of Henry M. Jackson, Box 2, AL.

51. Tip O'Neill, with William Novak, *Man of the House: The Life and Political Memoirs of Speaker Tip O'Neill* (New York: Random House, 1987), 302; Dan Caldwell, "The Carter Administration, the Senate, and SALT II," in *Jimmy Carter: Foreign Policy and Post-Presidential Years,* ed. Herbert D. Rosenbaum and Alexej Ugrinsky (Westport, Conn.: Greenwood, 1994), 333.

52. Jackson to President, September 22, 1977. Lance quoted in Oral History Interview with T. Bertram Lance, Peter Petkas, interviewer, May 12, 1982, MCPOHP. Vance quoted in Slocum-Schaffer, *America in the Seventies,* 64.

53. Memoranda of Conversation, September 22 and 23, 1977, VF, Box 117, JCL.

54. Vance, *Hard Choices,* 107.

55. Robert M. Gates, *From the Shadows: The Ultimate Insider's Story of Five Presidents and How They Won the Cold War* (New York: Simon and Schuster, 1996), 115–16.

56. Carter to Brezhnev, January 26, 1977, PF, SF, Box 17, JCL; Garthoff, *Détente and Confrontation,* 832–33.

57. Garthoff, *Détente and Confrontation,* 833–35.

58. Alan Neidle, "Nuclear Test Bans: History and Future Prospects," in *U.S.–Soviet Security Cooperation: Achievements, Failures, Lessons,* ed. Alexander George, Philip J. Farley, and Alexander Dallin (New York: Oxford University Press, 1988), 196–99.

59. Garthoff, *Détente and Confrontation,* 135, 844–45.

60. Richard N. Haass, "Arms Control at Sea: The United States and the Soviet Union in the Indian Ocean, 1977–78," in *U.S.–Soviet Security Cooperation: Achievements, Failures, Lessons,* ed. Alexander George, Philip J. Farley, and Alexander Dallin (New York: Oxford University Press, 1988), 524–26.

61. Ibid., 527–28.

62. Ibid., 528.

63. Ibid., 528–29.

64. Ibid., 529–33.

65. Janne E. Nolan, "The U.S.–Soviet Conventional Arms Transfer Negotiations," in ibid., 510.

66. Ibid., 513.

67. Ibid., 513–15.

68. Ibid., 515–16.

69. Ibid., 516–17.

70. Sherri L. Wasserman, *The Neutron Bomb Controversy: A Study in Alliance Politics* (New York: Praeger, 1983), chap. 2.

71. Ibid., 38–42; Kaufman, *Henry M. Jackson,* 357; Kaufman and Kaufman, *Presidency of James Earl Carter,* 115.

72. Wasserman, *Neutron Bomb Controversy,* 54–55.

73. Carter to Stennis, July 12, 1977, NSA, BM, SF, Box 16, JCL; Wasserman, *Neutron Bomb Controversy,* 42, 48–52.

74. Kaufman and Kaufman, *Presidency of James Earl Carter,* 59; Goronwy Jones, *The Rise, Breakdown, and Future of the East-West Detente Process* (New York: Vantage, 1987), 94; Wasserman, *Neutron Bomb Controversy,* 69–70.

75. Wasserman, *Neutron Bomb Controversy,* 78–79, 81–82, 96.

76. Ibid., 111–13; Carter oral history, November 29, 1982; Kaufman and Kaufman, *Presidency of James Earl Carter,* 115; Memorandum of Conversation, October 5, 1978, NSA, BM, SF, Box 33, JCL.

77. Martinez, "The Carter Administration and the Evolution of American Nuclear Nonproliferation Policy," 262.

78. Bourne, *Jimmy Carter,* 74–75; *PPPUS, Jimmy Carter,* 1977, I:960.

79. Robert F. Goheen, "U.S. Policy toward India During the Carter Presidency," in *The Hope and the Reality: U.S.–Indian Relations from Roosevelt to Reagan,* ed. Harold A. Gould and Sumit Ganguly (Boulder: Westview, 1992), 127.

80. Shirin Tahir-Kheli, *The United States and Pakistan: The Evolution of an Influence Relationship* (New York: Praeger, 1982), 116.

81. Ibid., 123, 126–27.

82. Goheen, "U.S. Policy toward India," 123; M. Srinivas Chary, *The Eagle and the Peacock: U.S. Foreign Policy toward India since Independence* (Westport, Conn.: Greenwood, 1995), 149.

83. Dennis Kux, *The United States and Pakistan, 1947–2000: Disenchanted Allies* (Washington, D.C.: Woodrow Wilson Center Press, 2001), 231, 235–36.

84. Goheen, "U.S. Policy toward India," 127, 128; Robert L. Beckman, *Nuclear Non-Proliferation, Congress and the Control of Peaceful Nuclear Activities* (Boulder: Westview, 1985), 357–58; *Congressional Record,* 95th Cong., 2nd sess., 12005–6, 12113–4; "Continuing Burlesque," *Wall Street Journal,* May 1, 1978.

85. Henry F. Carey, "Free Elections Based on Human Rights Protection: The Carter Contribution," in *Jimmy Carter: Foreign Policy and Post-Presidential Years,* ed. Herbert D. Rosenbaum and Alexej Ugrinsky (Westport, Conn.: Greenwood, 1994), 80.

86. Brzezinski, *Power and Principle*, 57.
87. Skidmore, *Reversing Course*, 134.

3—Negotiating Peace . . .

1. Carter, *Keeping Faith*, 182.
2. Lawrence S. Kaplan, *NATO Divided, NATO United: The Evolution of an Alliance* (Westport, Conn.: Praeger, 2004), 74.
3. Ibid., 74.
4. Vance, *Hard Choices*, 447; Clifford, *Counsel to the President*, 625–27.
5. Memorandum of Conversation, August 22, 1977, VF, Box 40, and Henze to Brzezinski, August 3, 1977, NSA, SM, H/S, Box 1, JCL.
6. Henze to Brzezinski, November 21, 1977, NSA, SM, H/S, Box 1, JCL; Theodore A. Couloumbis, *The United States, Greece, and Turkey: The Troubled Triangle* (New York: Praeger, 1983), 158.
7. Bernard Gwertzman, "President, in Shift, Will Try to End Ban on Arms for Turkey," *New York Times*, April 2, 1978.
8. *Congressional Record*, 95th Cong., 2nd sess., 1978: 8875, 9036; Memoranda of Conversation, May 31, 1978, NSA, SM, H/S, Box 2, JCL.
9. Ian Douglas Smith, *The Great Betrayal: The Memoirs of Ian Douglas Smith* (London: Blake, 1997), 326.
10. Gerald Horne, *From the Barrel of a Gun: The United States and the War against Zimbabwe, 1965–1980* (Chapel Hill: University of North Carolina Press, 2001), 162.
11. Smith, *Morality, Reason, and Power*, 139–40; Vance, *Hard Choices*, 259.
12. Sabina Ann Fischer, *Namibia Becomes Independent: The U.S. Contribution to Regional Peace* (Zurich: Forschungsstelle fur Sicherheitspolitik und Konfliktanalyse, Eidgenossische Technische Hochschule, 1992), 29.
13. Vance, *Hard Choices*, 262; Mordechai Tamarkin, "Kissinger, Carter, and the Rhodesian Conflict—From the Art of the Possible to Mission Impossible," *Asian and African Studies* 26 (1992): 159.
14. Tamarkin, "Kissinger, Carter, and the Rhodesian Conflict," 170; Smith, *Morality, Reason, and Power*, 135–36, 141; Richard E. Bissell, *South Africa and the United States: The Erosion of an Influence Relationship* (New York: Praeger, 1982), 128–30.
15. Brzezinski, *Power and Principle*, 139–40.
16. Ibid., 139; Peter J. Schraeder, *United States Foreign Policy toward Africa: Incrementalism, Crisis, and Change* (New York: Cambridge University Press, 1994), 215; Smith, *Morality, Reason, and Power*, 134–35.
17. Fischer, *Namibia Becomes Independent*, 28; Andrew DeRoche, *Black, White, and Chrome: The United States and Zimbabwe, 1953 to 1998* (Trenton, N.J.: Africa World Press, 2001), 246.
18. Brzezinski, *Power and Principle*, 140; Solomon to Blumenthal, February 8, 1977, DHM, AMSC, Box 1, JCL.
19. DeRoche, *Black, White, and Chrome*, 250–52; Vance, *Hard Choices*, 269.
20. Memoranda of Conversation, May 19 and 20, 1977, DHM, WM, Box 13, JCL; Bissell, *South Africa and the United States*, 17.
21. Benjamin Kline, *Profit, Principle, and Apartheid, 1948–1994: The Conflict of Economic and Moral Issues in the United States–South African Relations* (Lewiston, N.Y.: Edwin Mellen, 1997), 100, 110; Thornton to Aaron, June 5, 1978, WHCF, Box CO-67, JCL; Bissell, *South Africa and the United States*, 32. Bergsten quote in Bissell, 80.
22. Christopher Coker, *The United States and South Africa, 1968–1985: Constructive Engagement and Its Critics* (Durham: Duke University Press, 1986), 148–49; Schraeder, *United States Foreign Policy toward Africa*, 216–17.

23. DeRoche, *Black, White, and Chrome,* 253.

24. Vance, *Hard Choices,* 267, 270.

25. DeRoche, *Black, White, and Chrome,* 256–57; Kema Irogbe, *The Roots of United States Foreign Policy toward Apartheid South Africa, 1969–1985* (Lewiston, N.Y.: Edwin Mellen, 1997), 90; Kline, *Profit, Principle, and Apartheid,* 109; Coker, *United States and South Africa,* 149–50.

26. Jeffrey Davidow, *Dealing with International Crises: Lessons from Zimbabwe* (Muscatine, Iowa: Stanley Foundation, 1983), 7–8; DeRoche, *Black, White, and Chrome,* 260–62; Vance, *Hard Choices,* 91–92, 285; Brzezinski, *Power and Principle,* 140–41.

27. DeRoche, *Black, White, and Chrome,* 262–63.

28. Vance to President, December 28, 1977, NLC-7-19-4-2-8, RAC Program, JCL.

29. Fischer, *Namibia Becomes Independent,* 30, 33–36.

30. Kwang-il Baek, *Korea and the United States: A Study of the ROK–US Security Relationship within the Conceptual Framework of Alliance between Great and Small Powers* (Seoul: Research Center for Peace and Unification, 1988), 141.

31. Chae-jin Lee and Hideo Sato, *U.S. Policy toward Japan and Korea: A Changing Influence Relationship* (New York: Praeger, 1982), 104–5; Kaufman and Kaufman, *Presidency of James Earl Carter,* 56; "Mondale Says U.S. Will Keep Some Forces in Korea," *New York Times,* February 1, 1977.

32. Lee and Sato, *U.S. Policy toward Japan and Korea,* 109–10.

33. Memorandum of Conversation, February 1, 1977, WHCF, Box CO-37, JCL.

34. Carter to Park, February 14, 1977, NSA, BM, PCFLF, Box 12, and SecState to White House, February 28, 1977, NSA, SM, FE, Box 2, JCL.

35. Armacost to Brzezinski, February 9, 1977, NSA, SM, FE, Box 1, JCL; Kaufman and Kaufman, *Presidency of James Earl Carter,* 57; Lee and Sato, *U.S. Policy toward Japan and Korea,* 108–9.

36. PRC minutes, April 21, 1977, DHM, ZB, SF, Box 24, JCL.

37. NSC Meeting, April 27, 1977, NSA, SM, FE, Box 3, JCL.

38. Sneider to Secretary of State, May 25, 1977, NSA, BM, CF, Box 43, and Memoranda of Conversation, May 21, 1977, NSA, SM, FE, Box 3, JCL.

39. Baek, *Korea and the United States,* 152–53.

40. Kaufman and Kaufman, *Presidency of James Earl Carter,* 57.

41. Lee and Sato, *U.S. Policy toward Japan and Korea,* 73–80.

42. Ibid., 80; Brzezinski to the President, July 21, 1977, NSA, BM, CF, Box 43, JCL.

43. Lee and Sato, *U.S. Policy toward Japan and Korea,* 80–81; Sneider to Secretary of State, August 30 and 31, 1977, NSA, BM, CF, Box 45, JCL.

44. Lee and Sato, *U.S. Policy toward Japan and Korea,* 81; Minutes of Cabinet Meeting, January 9, 1978, SO, OSS, PHF, Box 67, JCL.

45. Lee and Sato, *U.S. Policy toward Japan and Korea,* 81; Far East to Brzezinski, January 24, 1978, NSA, SM, FE, Box 1, JCL.

46. Nicholas M. Horrock, "Tongsun Park, in Seoul Testimony, Linked K.C.I.A. Tie to Private Gain," *New York Times,* March 1, 1978; Charles R. Babcock, "Park Whets Hill Probers' Appetite for Kim," *Washington Post,* March 6, 1978.

47. Richard Halloran, "Jaworski Differs with 2 Agencies in Korea Inquiry," *New York Times,* February 6, 1978; Armacost to Brzezinski, February 10, 1978, NSA, SM, FE, Box 6, JCL.

48. Brzezinski to President, April 19, 1978, NSA, BM, CF, Box 43; Letter, Carter to Park, undated (ca. May 16, 1978), NSA, BM, PCFLF, Box 12, JCL.

49. Lee and Sato, *U.S. Policy toward Japan and Korea,* 83–84.

50. Armacost to Brzezinski, January 25, 1977, NSA, SM, FE, Box 1; Memorandum of Conversation, March 21, 1977, NSA, SM, FE, Box 2; Memorandum of Conversation, October 27, 1978, NSA, SM, FE, Box 65, JCL.

51. Quoted in G. Harvey Summ and Tom Kelly, eds., *The Good Neighbors: America, Panama, and the 1977 Canal Treaties* (Athens: Ohio University Center for International Studies, 1988), 60.

52. John Major, *Prize Possession: The United States and the Panama Canal, 1903–1979* (New York: Cambridge University Press, 1993), 345; William L. Furlong and Margaret E. Scranton, *The Dynamics of Foreign Policymaking: The President, the Congress, and the Panama Canal Treaties* (Boulder: Westview, 1984), 85; Memorandum of Conversation, May 18, 1977, NSA, BM, SF, Box 33, JCL.

53. Brzezinski, *Power and Principle*, 136; Vance, *Hard Choices*, 141.

54. Walter LaFeber, *The Panama Canal: The Crisis in Historical Perspective*, updated ed. (New York: Oxford University Press, 1989), 157.

55. Robert A. Pastor, *Whirlpool: U.S. Foreign Policy toward Latin America and the Caribbean* (Princeton: Princeton University Press, 1992), 45–46.

56. Major, *Prize Possession*, 346–47.

57. Carter, *Keeping Faith*, 162; Major, *Prize Possession*, 347–48; William J. Jorden, *Panama Odyssey* (Austin: University of Texas Press, 1984), 420, 425.

58. Furlong and Scranton, *Dynamics of Foreign Policymaking*, 143; Skidmore, *Reversing Course*, 113, 116, 118–19; J. Michael Hogan, *The Panama Canal in American Politics: Domestic Advocacy and the Evolution of Policy* (Carbondale: Southern Illinois University Press, 1986), 120–28; Larry Grubbs, "'Hands on Presidency' or 'Passionless Presidency'?: Jimmy Carter and Ratification of the Panama Canal Treaties," *Society for Historians of American Foreign Relations Newsletter* 30 (December 1999): 3.

59. Kaufman and Kaufman, *Presidency of James Earl Carter*, 108; Carter, *Keeping Faith*, 164, 176.

60. Kaufman and Kaufman, *Presidency of James Earl Carter*, 107; LaFeber, *Panama Canal*, 174–75.

61. Jorden, *Panama Odyssey*, 613–14.

62. Kaufman and Kaufman, *Presidency of James Earl Carter*, 53–54.

63. H. W. Brands, *Into the Labyrinth: The United States and the Middle East, 1945–1993* (New York: McGraw-Hill, 1994), 146–47; Kaufman and Kaufman, *Presidency of James Earl Carter*, 53; Kathleen Christison, *Perceptions of Palestine: Their Influence on U.S. Middle East Policy* (Berkeley: University of California Press, 1999), 160.

64. Joe Stork, "U.S. Policy and the Palestine Question," in *The United States and the Middle East: A Search for New Perspectives*, ed. Hooshang Amirahmadi (Albany: State University of New York Press, 1993), 136–37; Christison, *Perceptions of Palestine*, 163–67.

65. Paul Charles Merkley, *American Presidents, Religion, and Israel: The Heirs of Cyrus* (Westport, Conn.: Praeger, 2004), 93; Herbert Druks, *The Uncertain Alliance: The U.S. and Israel from Kennedy to the Peace Process* (Westport, Conn.: Greenwood, 2001), 165–66; Kaufman and Kaufman, *Presidency of James Earl Carter*, 54–55.

66. Abraham Ben-Zvi, *The United States and Israel: The Limits of the Special Relationship* (New York: Columbia University Press, 1993), 109.

67. Alfred M. Lilienthal, *The Zionist Connection II: What Price Peace?* (New Brunswick, N.J.: North American, 1982), 685; Kaufman and Kaufman, *Presidency of James Earl Carter*, 55.

68. William B. Quandt, *Camp David: Peacemaking and Politics* (Washington, D.C.: Brookings Institution, 1986), 62; Melvin A. Friedlander, *Sadat and Begin: The Domestic Politics of Peacemaking* (Boulder: Westview, 1983), 13, 16.

69. Kenneth W. Stein, *Heroic Diplomacy: Sadat, Kissinger, Carter, Begin, and the Quest for Arab-Israeli Peace* (New York: Routledge, 1999), 25; Brands, *Into the Labyrinth*, 147.

70. Carter, *Keeping Faith*, 297; Kaufman and Kaufman, *Presidency of James Earl Carter*, 56; Ben-Zvi, *The United States and Israel*, 109–10.

71. Lilienthal, *The Zionist Connection II*, 691.

72. Vance, *Hard Choices*, 190, 191; Brzezinski, *Power and Principle*, 110; Abraham Ben-Zvi, *The American Approach to Superpower Collaboration in the Middle East, 1973–1986* (Boulder: Westview, 1986), 47–48, 50; Ben-Zvi, *United States and Israel*, 113; Friedlander, *Sadat and Begin*, 58.

73. Steven L. Spiegel, *The Other Arab-Israeli Conflict: Making America's Middle East Policy, from Truman to Reagan* (Chicago: University of Chicago Press, 1985), 338; Dan Tschirgi, *The American Search for Mideast Peace* (New York: Praeger, 1989), 112; Kaufman and Kaufman, *Presidency of James Earl Carter*, 104; Abraham Ben-Zvi, *Alliance Politics and the Limits of Influence: The Case of the US and Israel, 1975–1983* (Boulder: Westview, 1984), 30; Merkley, *American Presidents, Religion, and Israel*, 107–8; Mideast Peace Initiative Provokes Criticism in U.S.," *New York Times*, October 3, 1977; Robert Slater, *Warrior Statesman: The Life of Moshe Dayan* (New York: St. Martin's, 1991), 401.

74. Bernard Reich, "Israel in US Perspective: Political Design and Pragmatic Practices," in *Superpowers and Client States in the Middle East: The Imbalance of Influence*, ed. Moshe Efrat and Jacob Berkovitch (New York: Routledge, 1991), 66; Quandt, *Camp David*, 81; William B. Quandt, *Peace Process: American Diplomacy and the Arab-Israeli Conflict since 1967* (Washington, D.C.: Brookings Institution, 1993), 267; Druks, *Uncertain Alliance*, 171; Tschirgi, *American Search for Mideast Peace*, 115; Merkley, *American Presidents, Religion, and Israel*, 109.

75. Stein, *Heroic Diplomacy*, 3–5.

76. Rachel Bronson, *Thicker than Oil: America's Uneasy Partnership with Saudi Arabia* (New York: Oxford University Press, 2006), 142; Kaufman and Kaufman, *Presidency of James Earl Carter*, 105; Memorandum of Conversation, December 5, 1977, NSA, BM, SF, Box 33, JCL.

77. Brezhnev to Carter, December 16, 1977, Brzezinski to Toon, December 21, 1977, Brezhnev to President, January 12, 1978, and Carter to President, January 25, 1978, PF, SF, Box 17; Memorandum of Conversation, January 26, 1978, VF, Box 117; Savranskaya and Welch, *Global Competition*, 101–2, VF, Box 117, JCL.

78. Kaufman and Kaufman, *Presidency of James Earl Carter*, 106.

79. Richard H. Curtiss, *A Changing Image: American Perceptions of the Arab-Israeli Dispute* (Washington, D.C.: American Educational Trust, 1982), 108; David Howard Goldberg, *Foreign Policy and Ethnic Interest Groups: American and Canadian Jews Lobby for Israel* (New York: Greenwood, 1990), 64–65; Spiegel, *Other Arab-Israeli Conflict*, 347; Bourne, *Jimmy Carter*, 401; Kaufman and Kaufman, *Presidency of James Earl Carter*, 107.

80. Thompson, *Carter Presidency*, 231; Rosalynn Carter, *First Lady from Plains* (Boston: Houghton Mifflin, 1984), 226.

81. Wolf Blitzer, *Between Washington and Jerusalem: A Reporter's Notebook* (New York: Oxford University Press, 1985), 218–19, 222.

82. "Questions and Answers," in *Jimmy Carter: Foreign Policy and Post-Presidential Years*, ed. Herbert D. Rosenbaum and Alexej Ugrinsky (Westport, Conn.: Greenwood, 1994), 186.

83. Spiegel, *Other Arab-Israeli Conflict*, 353, 354.

84. Carter, *Keeping Faith*, 364.

85. Spiegel, *Other Arab-Israeli Conflict*, 355–56.

86. Ibid., 356–58; Joseph Finklestone, *Anwar Sadat: Visionary Who Dared* (London: Frank Cass, 1996), 247–49.

87. Spiegel, *Other Arab-Israeli Dispute*, 358–60.

88. Ibid., 360–61.

89. Kaufman and Kaufman, *Presidency of James Earl Carter*, 153.

90. "Supplementary Material," *New York Times*, September 19, 1978; "Supplementary Material," *New York Times*, September 20, 1978.

91. Tschirgi, *American Search for Mideast Peace*, 126–27; Thornton, *Carter Years*, 216–17; Smith, *Morality, Reason, and Power*, 166–67; Kaufman and Kaufman, *Presidency of James Earl Carter*, 152–53; "Supplementary Material," *New York Times*, September 20, 1978; Christison, *Perceptions of Palestine*, 185–87.

92. Andrew J. Pierre, *The Global Politics of Arms Sales* (Princeton: Princeton University Press, 1982), 157, 159, 168.

4— . . . and Prosperity

1. "Steel's Sea of Troubles," *Business Week*, September 19, 1977, 69; "A Push for Protection," *Newsweek*, October 17, 1977, 81.

2. Skidmore, *Reversing Course*, 58.

3. Lee and Sato, *U.S. Policy toward Japan and Korea*, 169, 171; Kaufman and Kaufman, *Presidency of James Earl Carter*, 25.

4. Kaufman and Kaufman, *Presidency of James Earl Carter*, 37; "U.S. Shows Trade Deficit for Last Year of $5.9 Billion," *New York Times*, January 29, 1977.

5. Kaufman and Kaufman, *Presidency of James Earl Carter*, 25, 37.

6. W. Carl Biven, *Jimmy Carter's Economy: Policy in an Age of Limits* (Chapel Hill: University of North Carolina Press, 2002), 117.

7. Ibid., 96, 97–98.

8. Ibid., 97, 98.

9. Kaufman and Kaufman, *Presidency of James Earl Carter*, 33; "Flare-up at Yawning Gap," *Time*, August 8, 1977, 66.

10. Biven, *Jimmy Carter's Economy*, 98–101; Robert D. Schulzinger, *U.S. Diplomacy since 1900*, 5th ed. (New York: Oxford University Press, 2002), 130.

11. Memorandum of Conversation, January 31, 1977, NSA, SM, FE, Box 2, and Memorandum of Conversation, February 1, 1977, WHCF, Box CO-37, JCL; Edward D. Berkowitz, *Something Happened: A Political and Cultural Overview of the Seventies* (New York: Columbia University Press, 2006), 121.

12. SecState to AmEmbassy Bonn, and Sec State to AmEmbassy Tokyo, February 12, 1977, NSA, BM, PCFLF, Box 6, and Memorandum of Conversation, March 21, 1977, NSA, SM, FE, Box 2, JCL.

13. Lee and Sato, *U.S. Policy toward Japan and Korea*, 171; Frederick L. Shiels, *Tokyo and Washington: Dilemmas of a Mature Alliance* (Lexington, Mass.: Lexington Books, 1980), 150.

14. Lee and Sato, *U.S. Policy toward Japan and Korea*, 171.

15. Kaufman and Kaufman, *Presidency of James Earl Carter*, 34, 35–36.

16. Ibid., 38–39.

17. Ibid., 38.

18. Karen DeYoung, "Latin Americans Hurry to Catch Up on Nuclear Power," *Washington Post*, June 8, 1977.

19. Hans W. Gatzke, *Germany and the United States: A "Special Relationship"* (Cambridge, Mass.: Harvard University Press, 1980), 232; Kaufman and Kaufman, *Presidency of James Earl Carter*, 59; Carter to Schmidt, undated (ca. February 1977), and Brzezinski to the President, February 25, 1977, NSA, BM, PCFLF, Box 6; Carter, *First Lady from Plains*, 194; "Carter Spins the World," *Time*, August 8, 1977, 23–24.

20. "Japan: Will the Meters Run on Nuclei?," *New York Times*, January 3, 1977; Memorandum of Conversation, February 1, 1977, WHCF, Box CO-37, JCL.

21. Henry Kamm, "Tokyo Aide Hints Bad Faith by U.S. in Nuclear Talks," *New York Times*, May 18, 1977; Vance to the President, March 20, 1977, NSA, BM, CF, Box 40, and Memoranda of Conversation, March 21 and 22, 1977, NSA, SM, FE, Box 2, JCL.

22. Armacost to Brzezinski, April 18, 1977, NSA, BM, CF, Box 40, JCL.

23. "Putting the Brakes on the Fast Breeder," *Time*, April 18, 1977, 57; Edward Cowan, "Senator Church Urges President to Reverse Position on Plutonium," *New York Times*, May 3, 1977; Brzezinski to President, August 13, 1977, NSA, BM, VIP Visit File, Box 40, JCL.

24. Kaufman and Kaufman, *Presidency of James Earl Carter*, 60; James Callaghan, *Time and Chance* (London: Collins, 1987), 483.

25. Biven, *Jimmy Carter's Economy*, 112.

26. Charles S. Costello III, "Nuclear Nonproliferation: A Hidden but Contentious Issue in US–Japan Relations During the Carter Administration (1977–1981)," *Asia Pacific: Perspectives* 3 (May 2003): 4.

27. Brzezinski to President, August 13, 1977; Brzezinski to Secretary of State, August 23, 1977, NSA, SM, FE, Box 4, JCL.

28. Kaufman and Kaufman, *Presidency of James Earl Carter*, 70; Beckman, *Nuclear Non-Proliferation, Congress and the Control of Peaceful Nuclear Activities*, 352–53.

29. Berkowitz, *Something Happened*, 121; Shiels, *Tokyo and Washington*, 151; William R. Nester, *Power Across the Pacific: A Diplomatic History of American Relations with Japan* (Washington Square: New York University Press, 1996), 328–29; "The U.S. Trade Balance—Recent Trends and Outlook," undated (ca. July 1977), DHM, AMSC, Box 1, JCL.

30. Kaufman and Kaufman, *Presidency of James Earl Carter*, 85–86.

31. Quoted in ibid., 86.

32. Biven, *Jimmy Carter's Economy*, 120–21.

33. Owen to President, November 15, 1977, NSA, BM, CF, Box 40, and "Priority Policy Areas for Japanese Balance of Payments Management," undated (circa November 4, 1977), NSA, SM, FE, Box 5, JCL.

34. AmEmbassy Tokyo to SecState, November 9, 1977, and Armacost to Brzezinski, November 9, 1977, NSA, BM, CF, Box 40, JCL.

35. Far East to Brzezinski, November 10, 1977, and Brzezinski to President, undated (ca. November 10, 1977), NSA, BM, CF, Box 40, JCL.

36. Owen to President, November 15 and December 2, 1977, Memorandum to Dr. Brzezinski with the President's Party, author unknown, undated (ca. December 29, 1977), and AmEmbassy Tokyo to SecState, December 29, 1977, NSA, BM, CF, Box 40, JCL.

37. Kaufman and Kaufman, *Presidency of James Earl Carter*, 64, 91; Biven, *Jimmy Carter's Economy*, 112–13, 120; Youssef Ibrahim, "$26.7 Billion Trade Deficit Fed by Oil Imports, is Nation's Biggest," *New York Times*, January 31, 1978; Clyde H. Farnsworth, "Trade Gap for 1978 a Record," *New York Times*, January 31, 1979.

38. Nester, *Power Across the Pacific*, 329; Strauss to the President, January 26, 1978, NSA, BM, CF, Box 40, JCL.

39. Aaron to President, December 23, 1977, and Carter to Schmidt, December 28, 1977, NSA, BM, PCFLF, Box 6, and Owen to the Vice President, February 2, 1978, WHCF, Box CO-26, JCL; Andrianopoulos, *Kissinger and Brzezinski*, 141; Biven, *Jimmy Carter's Economy*, 146.

40. Kenneth O. Morgan, *Callaghan: A Life* (New York: Oxford University Press, 1997), 589–91, 602–3.

41. Biven, *Jimmy Carter's Economy*, 147, 149; Kaufman and Kaufman, *Presidency of James Earl Carter*, 100; Owen to President, February 8, 1978, Carter to Schmidt, April 11, 1978, NSA, BM, PCFLF, Box 6, JCL.

42. Vance, et al., to President, June 7, 1978, SO, OSS, HF, Box 90, JCL.

43. Biven, *Jimmy Carter's Economy*, 166.

44. Ibid., 167–68.

45. Ibid., 160.

46. Ibid., 150–51; Kaufman and Kaufman, *Presidency of James Earl Carter,* 116–17.

47. Bernhard May, "The World Economic Summits: A Difficult Learning Process," trans. Tradukas, in *The United States and Germany in the Era of the Cold War, 1945–1990,* vol. 2, *1968–1990,* ed. Detlef Junker (New York: Cambridge University Press, 2004), 2:251; Kaufman and Kaufman, *Presidency of James Earl Carter,* 116–17; Biven, *Jimmy Carter's Economy,* 167.

48. Robert Jones Shafer and Donald Mabry, *Neighbors—Mexico and the United States: Wetbacks and Oil* (Chicago: Nelson-Hall, 1981), 98–99; Lester D. Langley, *Mexico and the United States: The Fragile Relationship* (Boston: Twayne, 1991), 89; George W. Grayson, *The United States and Mexico: Patterns of Influence* (New York: Praeger, 1984), 146.

49. Pastor, *Whirlpool,* 51.

50. Lawrence Jada, *International Law and Ocean Use Management: The Evolution of Ocean Governance* (New York: Routledge, 1996), 187–88.

51. Ibid., 188–89.

52. Ibid., 192; James B. Morell, *The Law of the Sea: An Historical Analysis of the 1982 Treaty and Its Rejection by the United States* (Jefferson, N.C.: McFarland and Company, 1992), 4–5.

53. R. R. Churchill and A. V. Lowe, *The Law of the Sea* (Manchester, UK: Manchester University Press, 1985), 14.

54. Draft PRM, undated (ca. January 27, 1977), NSA, SM, GI, Box 12, JCL; Ann L. Hollick, *U.S. Foreign Policy and the Law of the Sea* (Princeton: Princeton University Press, 1981), 359.

55. Glad, *Jimmy Carter,* 418.

56. Presidential Directive/NSC-4, March 8, 1977, NSA, SM, GI, Box 38, JCL; Morell, *Law of the Sea,* 47–48; George Patrick Smith, *Restricting the Concept of Free Seas: Modern Maritime Law Re-evaluated* (Huntington, N.Y.: R. E. Krieger, 1980), 100.

57. Smith, *Restricting the Concept of Free Seas,* 100; Hollick, *U.S. Foreign Policy and the Law of the Sea,* 361; Ralph B. Levering and Miriam Levering, *Citizen Action for Global Change: The Neptune Group and the Law of the Sea* (Syracuse: Syracuse University Press, 1999), 109; Brzezinski to President, April 25, 1977, NSA, SM, GI, Box 37, JCL; "U.N. Sea Talks Resume; U.S. Presses Domestic Laws," *New York Times,* March 20, 1979.

58. Richardson to Aldrich, June 16, 1978, and Aldrich to Richardson, July 12, 1978, NSA, SM, GI, Box 38, JCL.

59. Smith, *Restricting the Concept of Free Seas,* 99, 100.

5—Hardening

1. *PPPUS, Jimmy Carter,* 1978, I:531–32.

2. Njølstad, "Keys of Keys?," 54–55. Caddell quoted in Dan Caldwell, "US Domestic Politics and the Demise of Détente," in *The Fall of Détente,* ed. Wested, 101–2.

3. Carter, *Keeping Faith,* 188; Robert David Johnson, *Congress and the Cold War* (New York: Cambridge University Press, 2006), 240–41; Peter C. Stuart, "Human Rights: New, Low Profile," *Christian Science Monitor,* January 29, 1979; Kaufman and Kaufman, *Presidency of James Earl Carter,* 139; Caldwell, "The Carter Administration, the Senate, and SALT II," 332.

4. Ermias Abebe, "The Horn, the Cold War, and Documents from the Former East Bloc: An Ethiopian View," *CWIHP* 8/9 (Winter 1996/97): 40.

5. David A. Korn, *Ethiopia, the United States, and the Soviet Union* (Carbondale: Southern Illinois University Press, 1986), 29.

6. Bereket H. Selassie, "The American Dilemma on the Horn," in *African Crisis Areas and U.S. Foreign Policy,* ed. Gerald J. Bender, James S. Coleman, and Richard L. Sklar (Berkeley: University of California Press, 1985), 174.

7. Abebe, "The Horn," 41–42, 43.

8. Ibid., 43–44; McLellan, *Cyrus Vance,* 49; Vance, *Hard Choices,* 73.

9. Vance, *Hard Choices,* 73.

10. Jeffrey Alan Lefebvre, *Arms for the Horn: U.S. Security Policy in Ethiopia and Somalia, 1953–1991* (Pittsburgh: University of Pittsburgh Press, 1991), 182.

11. PRC Meeting, April 11, 1977, DHM, ZB, SF, Box 24, JCL.

12. Vance, *Hard Choices,* 73.

13. Ibid., 73–74; Lefebvre, *Arms for the Horn,* 184; PRC Meeting, August 25, 1977, and Brzezinski to President, August 26, 1977, DHM, ZB, SF, Box 24; Fred Marte, *Political Cycles in International Relations: The Cold War and Africa, 1945–1990* (Amsterdam, Netherlands: VU University Press, 1994), 242.

14. Lefebvre, *Arms for the Horn,* 189; Bernard Gwertzman, "U.S., in Policy Shift, Now Willing to Sell Sudan Combat Jets," *New York Times,* December 23, 1977.

15. Vance, *Hard Choices,* 74–75.

16. Quoted in Donna R. Jackson, "The Carter Administration and Somalia," *Diplomatic History* 31 (September 2007): 716–17.

17. Brzezinski, *Power and Principle,* 180; "Core of Presidential Message to Heads of State of Sudan, Saudi Arabia, Iran and Egypt," undated (ca. January 1978), NSA, SM, H/S, Box 1, JCL.

18. "Core of Presidential Message."

19. Henze to Brzezinski, January 16, 1978, NSA, SM, H/S, Box 1, JCL.

20. Andrianopoulos, *Kissinger and Brzezinski,* 268.

21. Henze to Brzezinski, January 24 and 26, 1978, and Circular Telegram from Vance, January 24, 1978, NSA, SM, H/S, Box 1, and Henze to Brzezinski, January 24, 1978, NSA, BM, CF, Box 2, JCL.

22. Memorandum of Conversation, February 14, 1978, VF, Box 117, JCL; Brzezinski, *Power and Principle,* 182–83; Lefebvre, *Arms for the Horn,* 19; SCC Meeting, February 22, 1978, in Westad, *Fall of Détente,* 254, 256.

23. *PPPUS, Jimmy Carter,* 1978, I:442.

24. Bernard Gwertzman, "Top Carter Aides Seen in Discord on How to React to Soviet Actions," *New York Times,* March 3, 1978; Memorandum of Conversation, March 3, 1978, VF, Box 117, JCL.

25. Memorandum of Conversation, March 8, 1978, VF, Box 117; and Henze to Brzezinski, March 10, 1978, NSA, SM, H/S, Box 2, JCL.

26. Henze to Brzezinski, March 27, 1978, NSA, BM, CF, Box 3, JCL.

27. Marte, *Political Cycles in International Relations,* 242; Memorandum of Conversation, March 16, 1978, VF, Box 117, JCL.

28. Quoted in Garthoff, *Détente and Confrontation,* 657–58.

29. Brzezinski to Mondale, December 14, 1978, NSA, SM, H/S, Box 3, and Memorandum of Conversation, May 27, 1978, VF, Box 117, JCL.

30. Piero Gleijeses, "Havana's Policy in Africa, 1959–76: New Evidence from Cuban Archives," *CWIHP* 8/9 (Winter 1996/97): 7–9.

31. Ibid., 8–10.

32. Ibid., 10–11; Odd Arne Westad, "Moscow and the Angolan Crisis, 1974–1976: A New Pattern of Intervention," *CWIHP* 8/9 (Winter 1996/97): 26–27.

33. George Wright, *The Destruction of a Nation: United States Policy toward Angola since 1945* (Chicago: Pluto Press, 1997), 78.

34. Ibid., 79.

35. Ibid., 78–79.

36. Ibid., 79–80.

37. Ibid., 80–81; Vance, *Hard Choices,* 90; Smith, *Morality, Reason, and Power,* 149. Brzezinski quoted in Garthoff, *Détente and Confrontation,* 692.

38. *PPPUS, Jimmy Carter,* 1978, I:972.

39. *PPPUS, Jimmy Carter,* 1978, I:1053, 1056, 1057; Murrey Marder, "President Challenges Soviet Leaders; Two Different Speeches," *Washington Post,* June 8, 1978; Mary McGrory, "Did Carter Leave Them All Baffled with Annapolis Speech?" *Washington Star,* June 12, 1978; Thompson, *Carter Presidency,* 166; "Political Letter of Soviet Ambassador to the United States Anatoly F. Dobrynin, 11 July 1978," *CWIHP* 8/9 (Winter 1996/97): 120.

40. Powaski, *Cold War,* 228; Nolan, "The U.S.–Soviet Conventional Arms Transfer Negotiations," 518–19; Spear, *Carter and Arms Sales,* 127–28.

41. Robert S. Ross, *Negotiating Cooperation: The United States and China, 1969–1989* (Stanford: Stanford University Press, 1995), 81; Michael Schaller, *The United States and China in the Twentieth Century,* 2nd ed. (New York: Oxford University, 1990), 203.

42. James Mann, *About Face: A History of America's Curious Relationship with China from Nixon to Clinton* (New York: Alfred Knopf, 1999), 82; Memoranda of Conversation, December 21, 1976, and February 8, 1977, VF, Box 40, and Memorandum of Conversation, March 22, 1977, NSA, SM, FE, Box 2, JCL; Carter, *Keeping Faith,* 195, 196.

43. Qingxin Ken Wang, *Hegemonic Cooperation and Conflict: Postwar Japan's Policy and the United States* (Westport, Conn.: Praeger, 2000), 201.

44. Harry Harding, *A Fragile Relationship: The United States and China since 1972* (Washington, D.C.: Brookings Institution, 1992), 70–71.

45. Ibid., 71–72.

46. Ibid., 72–73.

47. Ibid., 73.

48. Mann, *About Face,* 79; Vance, *Hard Choices,* 79; Carter to Vance, undated (ca. August 16, 1977), NSA, SM, FE, Box 4, JCL.

49. Roy Medvedev, *China and the Superpowers,* trans. Harold Shukman (New York: Oxford University Press, 1986), 112–14; Robert A. Garson, *The United States and China since 1949: A Troubled Affair* (Madison: Fairleigh Dickinson Press, 1994), 159; Ross, *Negotiating Cooperation,* 98.

50. Memorandum of Conversation, August 23, 1977, VF, Box 40, JCL.

51. Vance, *Hard Choices,* 79; Harding, *Fragile Relationship,* 74; Memoranda of Conversation, August 24, 1977, VF, Box 40, JCL.

52. Brzezinski to President, August 25, 1977, NSA, SM, FE, Box 4, JCL; Harding, *Fragile Relationship,* 75.

53. Carter, *Keeping Faith,* 197.

54. Brzezinski, *Power and Principle,* 202–4, 206; Oksenberg to Brzezinski, November 2, 1977, NSA, BM, CF, Box 8, JCL; Ross, *Negotiating Cooperation,* 128; Vance, *Hard Choices,* 114–15.

55. Carter to Vice President and Vance, March 16, 1978, VF, Box 116, JCL; Carter, *Keeping Faith,* 198.

56. Vance, *Hard Choices,* 115; Memorandum of Conversation, April 11, 1978, NSA, SM, FE, Box 7, JCL.

57. Carter to Brzezinski, May 17, 1978, VF, Box 117, JCL; Vance, *Hard Choices,* 115.

58. Memoranda of Conversation, May 22 and 25, 1978, VF, Box 40, JCL; Brzezinski, *Power and Principle,* 218.

59. Ross, *Negotiating Cooperation,* 131; Nancy Bernkopf Tucker, ed., *China Confidential: American Diplomats and Sino–American Relations, 1945–1996* (New York: Columbia University Press, 2001), 324.

60. Anatoly Dobrynin, *In Confidence: Moscow's Ambassador to America's Six Cold War Presidents (1962–1986)* (New York: Times Books, 1995), 398–99, 409–10; Memoranda of Conversation, May 27 and 31, 1978, and "Record of the Main Content of the

Conversation between A.A. Gromyko and the U.S. Secretary of State C. Vance, May 31, 1978," Box 117, VF, JCL; Garthoff, *Détente and Confrontation,* 779–81.

61. Brzezinski, *Power and Principle,* 224; Mann, *About Face,* 89.

62. Tucker, *China Confidential,* 329; Sadako N. Ogata, *Normalization with China: A Comparative Study of U.S. and Japanese Processes* (Berkeley: Institute of East Asian Studies, University of California, 1988), 65.

63. Memorandum of Conversation, September 7, 1978, VF, Box 40, and Oksenberg to Brzezinski, September 12, 1977, and Memorandum of Conversation, September 19, 1978, VF, Box 41, JCL; Harding, *Fragile Relationship,* 80.

64. East Asia to Brzezinski, October 26, 1978, NSA, SM, FE, Box 1, JCL.

65. Harding, *Fragile Relationship,* 80; Ross, *Negotiating Cooperation,* 127–28; Gong Li, "The Difficult Path to Diplomatic Relations: China's U.S. Policy, 1972–1978," in *Normalization of U.S.–China Relations: An International History,* ed. William C. Kirby, Robert Ross, and Gong Li (Cambridge: Harvard University Asia Center, 2006), 140–41.

66. Memorandum of Conversation, December 15, 1978, VF, Box 41, and Woodcock to Vance and Brzezinski, December 15, 1978, VF, Box 40, JCL; Ross, *Negotiating Cooperation,* 137.

67. "No Other Purpose Than This—Peace," "U.S. to Normalize Ties with Peking, End Its Defense Treaty with Taiwan," and "China, Revealing Ties, Says Move Not Aimed at Anyone," all in *Washington Post,* December 16, 1978.

68. Quandt, *Peace Process,* 305–6; Ross, *Negotiating Cooperation,* 137; Warren Christopher, *Chances of a Lifetime* (New York: Scribner, 2001), 90.

69. Garthoff, *Détente and Confrontation,* 799; Memoranda of Conversation, July 12, 1978, and undated (circa October 1, 1978), VF, Box 117, and Memorandum of Conversation, September 27, 1978, VF, Box 41, JCL.

70. Talbott, *Endgame,* 234–36.

71. Gates, *From the Shadows,* 115–16; Savranskaya and Welch, *Global Competition,* 147, 152, VF, Box 117, JCL.

72. Schaller, *United States and China in the Twentieth Century,* 207–8; Leonard A. Kusnitz, *Public Opinion and Foreign Policy: America's China Policy, 1949–1979* (Westport, Conn.: Greenwood, 1984), 143–45; Ross, *Negotiating Cooperation,* 141–42. Helms quoted in Harding, *Fragile Relationship,* 83–84.

73. Ross, *Negotiating Cooperation,* 142–43.

74. Christopher, *Chances of a Lifetime,* 91–94.

75. Ross, *Negotiating Cooperation,* 74, 152; Memorandum of Conversation, January 31, 1979, VF, Box 41, JCL; Robert G. Sutter, *The China Quandary: Domestic Determinants of U.S. China Policy, 1972–1982* (Boulder: Westview, 1983), 133–34.

76. Qingshan Tan, *The Making of U.S. China Policy: From Normalization to the Post–Cold War Era* (Boulder: Lynne Rienner, 1992), 74–75; Carter, *Keeping Faith,* 213; Ross, *Negotiating Cooperation,* 153–54; Sutter, *China Quandary,* 135.

77. Ross, *Negotiating Cooperation,* 146; Harding, *Fragile Relationship,* 89, 90–91.

78. PRM, undated (circa February 1977), NSA, SM, FE, Box 1, JCL; Steven Hurst, *The Carter Administration and Vietnam* (New York: St. Martin's, 1996), 27–30.

79. Armacost to Brzezinski, February 4, 1977, NSA, BM, CF, Box 85, JCL.

80. Hurst, *Carter Administration and Vietnam,* 35; Memorandum of Conversation, June 10, 1977, NSA, SM, FE, Box 3, JCL.

81. Vance to President, November 29, 1977; Brzezinski to President, and Brzezinski to Secretary of State, December 1, 1977, NSA, BM, CF, Box 85, JCL.

82. Hurst, *Carter Administration and Vietnam,* 70; Holbrooke to Secretary, August 21, 1978, NSA, SM, FE, Box 65, and Oksenberg to Brzezinski, September 22, 1978, NSA, BM, CF, Box 85, JCL.

83. Christopher to President, September 27, 1978, PF, SF, Box 39, and Oksenberg to Brzezinski, September 28, 1978, NSA, BM, CF, Box 85, JCL; Brzezinski, *Power and Principle,* 228.

84. Zbigniew Brzezinski Exit Interview, February 20, 1981, JCL.

85. Robert D. Schulzinger, *A Time for Peace: The Legacy of the Vietnam War* (New York: Oxford University Press, 2006), 13–14.

86. Pastor to Brzezinski, March 8, 1977, NSA, BM, CF, Box 13, JCL.

87. McGovern to President, April 19, 1977, in ibid.

88. Vance to President, April 23, 1977, and Brzezinski to President, April 27, 1977, in ibid.

89. Pastor, *Whirlpool*, 52.

90. Brzezinski to President, August 5, 1977, DHM, ZB, SF, Box 24, JCL.

91. Church to President, August 12, 1977, NSA, BM, CF, Box 13, and Vance to President, undated (ca. January 1979), PF, SF, Box 39, JCL.

92. McMahon, *Cold War*, 141–42.

6—The Problems of Peace and Prosperity

1. William H. Sullivan, *Mission to Iran* (New York: Norton, 1981), 258; David Farber, *Taken Hostage: The Iran Hostage Crisis and America's First Encounter with Radical Islam* (Princeton: Princeton University Press, 2005), 112–13.

2. Sullivan, *Mission to Iran*, 258–63.

3. Christopher to President, July 18, 1978, SO, OSS, HF, Box 96, JCL.

4. *Congressional Quarterly Almanac, 1978* (Washington, D.C.: Congressional Quarterly News Features, 1978), 416–24; Graham Hovey, "Senate Acts to Lift Arms Ban on Turks, but Adds Warning," *New York Times*, July 26, 1978.

5. Christopher to President, October 6, 1978, PF, SF, Box 39, JCL.

6. Bernard Gwertzman, "U.S. Offers New Cyprus Plan in an Effort to Revive Talks," *New York Times*, November 29, 1978; "U.S. Plans for Cyprus Encounter Objections of Greeks and Turks," *New York Times*, December 10, 1978; Vance to President, January 25, 1979, PF, SF, Box 39, JCL.

7. Brzezinski to President, undated (ca. May 1979), NSA, SM, N/S, Box 3, JCL.

8. T. G. Fraser, *The USA and the Middle East since World War Two* (New York: St. Martin's 1989), 154–55.

9. Quandt, *Peace Process*, 309; Spiegel, *Other Arab-Israeli Conflict*, 369–70.

10. Fraser, *USA and the Middle East since World War II*, 156; Kaufman and Kaufman, *Presidency of James Earl Carter*, 154; Quandt, *Peace Process*, 300–301; Vance, *Hard Choices*, 249–50; Bernard Reich, *The United States and Israel: Influence in the Special Relationship* (New York: Praeger, 1984), 75–76.

11. Memorandum of Conversation, June 28, 1979, NSA, SM, FE, Box 67, JCL; Kaufman and Kaufman, *Presidency of James Earl Carter*, 154–55; Thomas W. Lippman, "Economic Boycott of Egypt Imposed by Arab Countries, Arab States Unite in Boycott of Egypt," *Washington Post*, March 31, 1979.

12. Kaufman and Kaufman, *Presidency of James Earl Carter*, 184; Fraser, *USA and the Middle East since World War II*, 157.

13. Ledeen and Lewis, *Debacle*, 59; Said Amir Arjomand, *The Turban for the Crown: The Islamic Revolution in Iran* (New York: Oxford University Press, 1988), 106–7.

14. Amin Saikal, *The Rise and Fall of the Shah* (Princeton: Princeton University Press, 1980), 186; Ledeen and Lewis, *Debacle*, 62–63.

15. Mark Bowden, *Guests of the Ayatollah: The First Battle in America's War with Militant Islam* (New York: Atlantic Monthly Press, 2006), 120; Ledeen and Lewis, *Debacle*, 79.

16. Bill, *Eagle and the Lion*, 219–22.

17. Vance, *Hard Choices*, 314; Brzezinski, *Power and Principle*, 354.

18. Bill, *Eagle and the Lion*, 227; Barry M. Rubin, *Paved with Good Intentions: The American Experience in Iran* (New York: Penguin, 1981), 198.

19. Bill, *Eagle and the Lion*, 229; Ofira Seliktar, *Failing the Crystal Ball Test: The*

Carter Administration and the Fundamentalist Revolution in Iran (Westport, Conn.: Praeger, 2000), 59–60; Rubin, *Paved with Good Intentions,* 198; Benson Lee Grayson, *United States–Iranian Relations* (Washington, D.C.: University Press of America, 1981), 155–56.

20. SecState to AmEmbassy Tehran, May 24, 1977, PF, SF, Box 23, JCL; Christos P. Ionnides, *America's Iran: Injury and Catharsis* (Lanham, Md.: University Press of American, 1984), 16; Rubin, *Paved with Good Intentions,* 196; Pierre, *Global Politics of Arms Sales,* 148–49.

21. Rubin, *Paved with Good Intentions,* 200. Carter quoted in Harris, *Crisis,* 70–71.

22. Harris, *Crisis,* 72; *PPPUS, Jimmy Carter,* 1977, II:2221, 2222.

23. Mark J. Gasiorowski, *U.S. Foreign Policy and the Shah: Building a Client State in Iran* (Ithaca: Cornell University Press, 1991), 215.

24. Arjomand, *Turban for the Crown,* 101; Bill, *Eagle and Lion,* 235; Gasiorowski, *U.S. Foreign Policy and the Shah,* 216, 217; Seliktar, *Failing the Crystal Ball Test,* 81.

25. Farber, *Taken Hostage,* 92–93; Gasiorowski, *U.S. Foreign Policy and the Shah,* 218.

26. Gary Sick, *All Fall Down: America's Tragic Encounter with Iran* (New York: Random House, 1985), 29, 35–36.

27. Ibid., 41, 46, 66; Seliktar, *Failing the Crystal Ball Test,* 68; Harris, *Crisis,* 66–67; Rubin, *Paved with Good Intentions,* 210.

28. Quoted in Gates, *From the Shadows,* 141.

29. Peter L. Hahn, "Jimmy Carter and the Central Intelligence Agency," in *The Presidency and Domestic Policies of Jimmy Carter,* ed. Herbert D. Rosenbaum and Alexej Ugrinsky (Westport, Conn.: Greenwood, 1994), 329–33; "Assessment of the Political Situation in Iran," undated (ca. September 1, 1978), *Iran: The Making of U.S. Policy, 1977–1980,* NatSA, Microfiche; Stansfield Turner, *Burn Before Reading: Presidents, CIA Directors, and Secret Intelligence* (New York: Hyperion, 2005), 180, 186–88.

30. Smith, *Morality, Reason, and Power,* 46; Hahn, "Jimmy Carter and the Central Intelligence Agency," 327; Gates, *From the Shadows,* 141–42. Even Brzezinski admitted that "the CIA was effectively supervised by the NSC." Yet he also commented that despite "my repeated efforts, and for reasons which I could never understand, I was unable to prevail on the President to include Turner" in the weekly breakfast held between Carter and his advisers. See Brzezinski, *Power and Principle,* 68, 73.

31. William H. Blanchard, *Neocolonialism American Style, 1960–2000* (Westport, Conn.: Greenwood, 1996), 41; Harris, *Crisis,* 85.

32. Christopher to President, October 24, 1978, PF, SF, Box 39, and Vance to President, October 30, and November 10 and 30, 1978, PF, SF, Box 39, JCL; Rubin, *Paved with Good Intentions,* 224; Farber, *Taken Hostage,* 95; Gasiorowski, *U.S. Foreign Policy and the Shah,* 220.

33. Rubin, *Paved with Good Intentions,* 226; Harris, *Crisis,* 103.

34. Harris, *Crisis,* 95–96; Pierre Salinger, *America Held Hostage: The Secret Negotiations* (Garden City, NY: Doubleday, 1981), 38; Sick, *All Fall Down,* 88.

35. Salinger, *America Held Hostage,* 39; Blanchard, *Neocolonialism American Style,* 42–44; Bill, *Eagle and the Lion,* 253.

36. AmEmbassy Tehran to SecState, September 21 and November 9, 1978, and Precht to Saunders, December 19, 1978, *Iran: The Making of U.S. Policy, 1977–1980,* NatSA, Microfiche; Christopher to President, December 11, 1978, PF, SF, Box 39, JCL.

37. Memorandum of Conversation, December 11, 1978, VF, Box 41, JCL; Brzezinski, *Power and Principle,* 355; Bill, *Eagle and the Lion,* 249.

38. Sick, *All Fall Down,* 69, 137; Kaufman and Kaufman, *Presidency of James Earl Carter,* 157–58.

39. Sick, *All Fall Down,* 131; Farber, *Taken Hostage,* 97–98; AmEmbassy Tehran to SecState, January 10, 1979, PF, SF, Box 23, JCL; Oral history interview with Jimmy Carter, MCPOHP, November 29, 1982; Seliktar, *Failing the Crystal Ball Test,* 116; Robert

E. Huyser, *Mission to Tehran* (New York: Harper and Row, 1986), 46; Jordan, *Crisis*, 94; *PPPUS, Jimmy Carter*, 1978, II:2172.

40. Kaufman and Kaufman, *Presidency of James Earl Carter*, 158.

41. Seliktar, *Failing the Crystal Ball Test*, 111.

42. Harris, *Crisis*, 151.

43. Kaufman and Kaufman, *Presidency of James Earl Carter*, 156; Seliktar, *Failing the Crystal Ball Test*, 126.

44. "Iran: Khomeini's Prospects and Views," January 19, 1979, *Iran: The Making of U.S. Policy, 1977–1990*, NatSA, Microfiche; Seliktar, *Failing the Crystal Ball Test*, 151–53.

45. Sick, *All Fall Down*, 151; Farber, *Taken Hostage*, 112–14; Rubin, *Paved with Good Intentions*, 281.

46. Fraser, *USA and the Middle East since World War II*, 155; Harvey Sicherman, *Palestinian Autonomy, Self-Government, and Peace* (Boulder: Westview, 1993), 41–43; Spiegel, *Other Arab-Israeli Conflict*, 373; "The Question of Who's in Charge," *Time*, September 3, 1979, 14.

47. Douglas MacEachin, "Predicting the Soviet Invasion of Afghanistan: The Intelligence Community's Record," https://www.cia.gov/library/center-for-the-study-of-intelligence/csi-publications/books-and-monographs/predicting-the-soviet-invasion-of-afghanistan-the-intelligence-communitys-record.html#link2.

48. Smith, *Morality, Reason, and Power*, 220–21; Brzezinski, *Power and Principle*, 427; Steve Coll, *Ghost Wars: The Secret History of the CIA, Afghanistan, and Bin Laden, from the Soviet Invasion to September 10, 2001* (New York: Penguin, 2004), 46; Bronson, *Thicker than Oil*, 149.

49. Brzezinski, *Power and Principle*, 181, 447; Carol R. Saivetz, "Superpower Competition in the Middle East and the Collapse of Détente," in *Fall of Détente*, ed. Wested, 84; Garthoff, *Détente and Confrontation*, 723.

50. Garthoff, *Détente and Confrontation*, 724–25.

51. "The Crescent of Crisis," *Time*, January 15, 1979, 18.

52. Schulzinger, *A Time for Peace*, 14.

53. *PPPUS, Jimmy Carter*, 1978, I:767; Michael Haas, *Cambodia, Pol Pot, and the United States: The Faustian Pact* (New York: Praeger, 1991), 15; Memorandum of Conversation, February 1, 1979, NSA, SM, FE, Box 66, JCL; Kenton J. Clymer, *The United States and Cambodia, 1969–2000: A Troubled Relationship* (New York: Routledge, 2004), 114–15.

54. Carter, *Keeping Faith*, 211; Brzezinski, *Power and Principle*, 409; Gates, *From the Shadows*, 121.

55. Carter, *Keeping Faith*, 211; Memorandum of Conversation, February 1, 1979, and Abramowitz to the Vice President and Brzezinski, February 2, 1979, NSA, SM, FE, Box 66, JCL.

56. NSC Meeting, February 16, 1979, NSA, SM, FE, Box 46, and Brezhnev to Carter, February 18, 1979, PF, SF, Box 17, JCL; Dobrynin, *In Confidence*, 418; Garthoff, *Détente and Confrontation*, 905; Vitaly Kozyrev, "Soviet Policy toward the United States and China," in *Normalization of U.S.–China Relations: An International History*, ed. William C. Kirby, Robert Ross, and Gong Li (Cambridge: Harvard University Press, 2006), 282; Mann, *About Face*, 100.

57. Jay Mathews and Lee Lescaze, "China Announces End of Invasion," *Washington Post*, March 6, 1979; Jay Mathews, "Hanoi Will Talk after Withdrawal," *Washington Post*, March 7, 1979; SCC Meeting, February 18, 1979, NSA, SM, FE, Box 46, JCL; "Invasion by Chinese Threatens World Peace, Moyhihan Says," *Washington Post*, February 19, 1979.

58. Lee and Sato, *U.S. Policy toward Japan and Korea*, 84–85; East Asia to Brzezinski, October 5, 1978, NSA, SM, FE, Box 1, JCL.

59. Lee and Sato, *U.S. Policy toward Japan and Korea*, 122; William H. Gleysteen,

Jr., *Massive Entanglement, Marginal Influence: Carter and Korea in Crisis* (Washington, D.C.: Brookings Institution, 1999), 28; George C. Wilson, "Troop Withdrawal from South Korea Too Risky at Present, Senators Say," *Washington Post,* January 24, 1979; Brzezinski to President, undated (ca. January 17, 1979), and Memorandum of Conversation, January 23, 1979, NSA, SM, FE, Box 66, JCL.

60. *PPPUS, Jimmy Carter,* 1979, I:247; Memorandum of Conversation, July 5, 1979, and Park to Carter, July 31, 1979, NSA, SM, FE, Box 67, and SecDef to SSO DIA, October 22, 1979, NSA, BM, CF, Box 41, JCL; Lee and Sato, *U.S. Policy toward Japan and Korea,* 123–24; *PPPUS, Jimmy Carter,* 1979, II:1275.

61. Dennis Gilbert, *Sandinistas: The Party and the Revolution* (New York: Basil Blackwell, 1988), 3; William M. LeoGrande, *Our Own Backyard: The United States in Central America, 1977–1992* (Chapel Hill: University of North Carolina Press, 1998), 14.

62. Robert Kagan, *A Twilight Struggle: American Power and Nicaragua, 1977–1990* (New York: Free Press, 1996), 29–30.

63. Lake, *Somoza Falling,* 22, 203–5; Karl Bermann, *Under the Big Stick: Nicaragua and the United States since 1848* (Boston: South End Press, 1986), 262–63; Alex Roberto Hybel, *How Leaders Reason: US Intervention in the Caribbean Basin and Latin America* (Cambridge, Mass.: Basil Blackwell, 1990), 237.

64. Kagan, *Twilight Struggle,* 41–42.

65. Lake, *Somoza Falling,* 82–83.

66. Ibid., 84–88; Robert A. Pastor, *Condemned to Repetition: The United States and Nicaragua* (Princeton: Princeton University Press, 1987), 67–68; Anastasio Somoza, as told to Jack Cox, *Nicaragua Betrayed* (Boston: Western Islands, 1980), 137–38.

67. Lake, *Somoza Falling,* 83.

68. Robert A. Pastor, *Not Condemned to Repetition: The United States and Nicaragua,* rev. ed. (Boulder: Westview, 2002), 50, 102; Strong, *Working in the World,* 91.

69. Kagan, *Twilight Struggle,* 53, 56–57, 58; Morley, *Washington, Somoza, and the Sandinistas,* 116, 122.

70. Gilbert, *Sandinistas,* 10–11.

71. Morley, *Washington, Somoza, and the Sandinistas,* 113–14; Kagan, *Twilight Struggle,* 60–62.

72. Kagan, *Twilight Struggle,* 63–64.

73. Kagan, *Twilight Struggle,* 65–68; Harkin quoted in Gaddis Smith, *The Last Years of the Monroe Doctrine, 1945–1993* (New York: Hill and Wang, 1994), 155.

74. Kagan, *Twilight Struggle,* 70–71, 73–74; Hybel, *How Leaders Reason,* 244.

75. Kagan, *Twilight Struggle,* 74–75. State Department official quoted in Morley, *Washington, Somoza, and the Sandinistas,* 166.

76. Ibid., 164; Kagan, *Twilight Struggle,* 85–87, 90–91; "A Billion Dollars to Give Away Panama Canal?," *U.S. News and World Report,* March 5, 1979, 46.

77. Hybel, *How Leaders Reason,* 248–49.

78. Ibid., 249.

79. Ibid., 250.

80. Kagan, *Twilight Struggle,* 91–92.

81. Ibid., 92–96; Morley, *Washington, Somoza, and the Sandinistas,* 187–88.

82. LeoGrande, *Our Own Backyard,* 26; Kagan, *Twilight Struggle,* 96–97; Graham Hovey, "Carter Officials Assert Bill in House Violates Panama Canal Treaty," *New York Times,* April 5, 1979; Steven V. Roberts, "Carter Wins House Vote on Canal But Loses on Aid Grant to Turkey," *New York Times,* June 22, 1979.

83. Morley, *Washington, Somoza, and the Sandinistas,* 192–93.

84. Walter LaFeber, *Inevitable Revolutions: The United States in Central America,* expanded ed. (New York: Norton, 1984), 237.

85. Langley, *Mexico and the United States,* 84; Carter to Schmidt, August 2, 1978,

NSA, BM, PCFLF, Box 6, Fukuda to Carter, September 2, 1978, NSA, BM, PCFLF, Box 11, and Memorandum of Conversation, October 27, 1978, NSA, SM, FE, Box 65, JCL.

86. William Chapman, "Japan Accepts Boost in Imported American Beef, Citrus Products," *Washington Post,* December 5, 1978; Maga, *World of Jimmy Carter,* 50.

87. Platt to Brzezinski and Aaron, April 3, 1979, NSA, BM, CF, Box 41, JCL.

88. Memorandum of Conversation, May 2, 1979, NSA, SM, FE, Box 66, JCL.

89. Memorandum of Conversation, June 27, 1979, NSA, SM, FE, Box 67, JCL; Hugo Dobson, *Japan and the G7/8: 1975–2002* (New York: Routledge, 2004), 36–37.

90. Biven, *Jimmy Carter's Economy,* 177; Kaufman and Kaufman, *Presidency of James Earl Carter,* 170–71.

91. Ronald Koven and J. P. Smith, "The OPEC Decision," *Washington Post,* June 29, 1979; Kaufman and Kaufman, *Presidency of James Earl Carter,* 186; Rouhollah K. Ramazani, *United States and Iran: The Patterns of Influence* (New York: Praeger, 1982), 135; Steven F. Hayward, *The Real Jimmy Carter: How Our Worst Ex-President Undermines American Foreign Policy, Coddles Dictators, and Created the Party of Clinton and Kerry* (Washington, D.C.: Regnery, 2004), 141, 143–44; Berkowitz, *Something Happened,* 130. Eizenstat quoted in Berkowitz, 126.

92. Hollick, *U.S. Foreign Policy and the Law of the Sea,* 365.

93. Ibid., 370–71; George P. Smith II, *Restricting the Concept of Free Seas: Modern Maritime Law Re-Evaluated* (Huntington, N.Y.: R. E. Krieger, 1980), 101, 108–9.

94. "Approval of Carter Falls to 37% Low, Poll Finds," *New York Times,* May 31, 1979; Andrew Z. Katz, "Public Opinion and the Contradictions of Jimmy Carter's Foreign Policy," *Presidential Studies Quarterly* 30 (December 2000): 664.

95. "New Poll Gives Kennedy Big Lead over President," *New York Times,* June 24, 1979; Adam Clymer, "Carter is Edged in Poll by Reagan and Ford; Kennedy Leads Both," *New York Times,* July 1, 1979.

7—"Detente Is Dead"

1. John Giuffo, "Nightline Is Spawned Out of the Hostage Crisis," *Columbia Journalism Review* 40 (November–December 2001), http://findarticles.com/p/ articles/ mi_qa3613/is_200111/ai_n8976166.

2. Vance to the President, undated (ca. January 1979), PF, SF, Box 39, JCL; *PP-PUS, Jimmy Carter,* 1979, I:305.

3. Talbott, *Endgame,* 236–38, 242–44, 257–63, 271–72; *Arms Control and National Security: An Introduction* (Washington, D.C.: Arms Control Association, 1989), 55.

4. Moens, *Foreign Policy under Carter,* 82–83; Dobrynin, *In Confidence,* 393.

5. Wilfried Loth, *Overcoming the Cold War: A History of Détente, 1950–1991,* trans. Robert F. Hogg (New York: Palgrave, 2002), 141; Dobrynin, *In Confidence,* 425–26; "Interview with Leslie H. Gelb," http://www.gwu.edu/~nsarchiv/coldwar/ interviews/episode-19/gelb2.html; Zbigniew Brezinski, *Power and Principle: Memoirs of the National Security Adviser, 1977–1981* (New York: Farrar, Straus, Giroux, 1983), 343.

6. Loth, *Overcoming the Cold War,* 141–42.

7. Samuel P. Huntington, "Renewed Hostility," in *The Making of America's Soviet Policy,* ed. Joseph S. Nye, Jr. (New Haven: Yale University Press, 1984), 277–78.

8. Skidmore, *Reversing Course,* 137–38; Sanders, *Peddlers of Crisis,* 254–55; Kaufman and Kaufman, *Presidency of James Earl Carter,* 187.

9. Skidmore, *Reversing Course,* 138–41.

10. Joseph J. Kruzel, "Verification and SALT II," in *Verification and SALT: The Challenge of Strategic Deception,* ed. William C. Potter (Boulder: Westview, 1980), 97; Erik Beukel, *American Perceptions of the Soviet Union as a Nuclear Adversary: From Kennedy to Bush* (New York: Pinter, 1989), 99.

11. Kruzel, "Verification and SALT II," 108. Humphrey quoted in Johnson, *Congress and the Cold War,* 243.

12. Kaufman and Kaufman, *Presidency of James Earl Carter,* 187–88.

13. Ibid., 188; Johnson, *Congress and the Cold War,* 243.

14. Sanders, *Peddlers of Crisis,* 259.

15. Carter, *Keeping Faith,* 247; Stansfield Turner, *Secrecy and Democracy: The CIA in Transition* (Boston: Houghton Mifflin, 1985), 134; Brzezinski, *Power and Principle,* 336.

16. Charles Mohr, "Arms Pact Foes Pose Dilemma for Carter," *New York Times,* June 25, 1979; *PPPUS, Jimmy Carter,* 1979, I:903.

17. Robert A. Hoover, *The MX Controversy: A Guide to Issues and References* (Claremont, Calif.: Regina, 1982), 18–19; Lauren H. Holland and Robert A. Hoover, *The MX Decision: A New Direction in U.S. Weapons Procurement Policy?* (Boulder: Westview, 1985), 88–89, 165, 166, 167–68; Grover, *President as Prisoner,* 150; Kaufman and Kaufman, *Presidency of James Earl Carter,* 187–88.

18. Kaufman and Kaufman, *Presidency of James Earl Carter,* 188–89; Albert R. Hunt, "In the SALT Debate, Sen. Sam Nunn's Role Could Prove Decisive," *Wall Street Journal,* March 22, 1979.

19. Kaufman and Kaufman, *Presidency of James Earl Carter,* 189.

20. Wayne S. Smith, *The Closest of Enemies: A Personal and Diplomatic Account of U.S.–Cuban Relations since 1957* (New York: Norton, 1987), 163–64.

21. Smith, *Morality, Reason, and Power,* 117–18; Strong, *Working in the World,* 212–13.

22. Garthoff, *Détente and Confrontation,* 920–21; Kaufman and Kaufman, *Presidency of James Earl Carter,* 189.

23. Garthoff, *Détente and Confrontation,* 913, 921; Carter, *Keeping Faith,* 268; Savranskaya and Welch, *Global Competition,* 306, 308–9, Box 117, VF, JCL; Brzezinski, *Power and Principle,* 349; Kaufman and Kaufman, *Presidency of James Earl Carter,* 190.

24. Savranskaya and Welch, *Global Competition,* 287–88; Garthoff, *Détente and Confrontation,* 923–24; Kaufman and Kaufman, *Presidency of James Earl Carter,* 190; Clifford, *Counsel to the President,* 636, 637–38.

25. Kaufman and Kaufman, *Presidency of James Earl Carter,* 190–91.

26. Ibid., 191; Robert G. Kaiser, "Senate Committee Says SALT Not in America's Best Interest," *Washington Post,* December 21, 1979.

27. Robert M. Hathaway, *Great Britain and the United States: Special Relations since World War II* (Boston: Twayne, 1990), 115; Wolfgang Krieger, "German-American Security Relations, 1968–1990," trans. Tradukas, in *The United States and Germany in the Era of the Cold War, 1945–1990,* vol. 2, *1968–1990,* ed. Detlef Junker (New York: Cambridge University Press, 2004), 120.

28. Jonathan Carr, *Helmut Schmidt: Helmsman of Germany* (New York: St. Martin's 1985), 126–27; Garthoff, *Détente and Confrontation,* 943.

29. Carr, *Helmut Schmidt,* 127.

30. Ibid., 130; Garthoff, *Détente and Confrontation,* 945–48; Morgan, *Callaghan,* 605.

31. Loth, *Overcoming the Cold War,* 153, 154; Garthoff, *Détente and Confrontation,* 949–53; C. J. Bartlett, *'The Special Relationship': A Political History of Anglo-American Relations since 1945* (New York: Longman, 1992), 144; Carr, *Helmut Schmidt,* 131, 132; Andrianopoulos, *Kissinger and Brzezinski,* 256, 257.

32. DeRoche, *Black, White, and Chrome,* 266–68.

33. Ibid., 268–71; Francis Njubi Nesbitt, *Race for Sanctions: African Americans against Apartheid, 1946–1994* (Bloomington: Indiana University Press, 2001), 103, 109.

34. DeRoche, *Black, White, and Chrome,* 274–76, 278–80; Horne, *From the Barrel of a Gun,* 165; Diggs, Collins, and Gray to President, April 25, 1979, NSA, SM, N/S, Box 119, JCL.

35. Bissell, *South Africa and the United States,* 41; Davidow, *Dealing with International Crises,* 7, 9; Smith, *The Great Betrayal,* 328.

36. Kline, *Profit, Principle, and Apartheid,* 112–14, 117; Martin Meredith, *In the Name of Apartheid: South Africa in the Postwar Period* (New York: Harper and Row, 1988), 168; Don Oberdorfer, "U.S. Suspects South Africans of Detonating Nuclear Bomb," *Washington Post,* October 26, 1979; Bissell, *South Africa and the United States,* 41; Schraeder, *United States Foreign Policy toward Africa,* 219–20; Fischer, *Namibia Becomes Independent,* 38–41.

37. Gilbert, *Sandinistas,* 13; Morley, *Washington, Somoza, and the Sandinistas,* 294.

38. Morley, *Washington, Somoza, and the Sandinistas,* 221–25, 249; Bermann, *Under the Big Stick,* 277; Johnson, *Congress and the Cold War,* 249.

39. Kyle Longley, *In the Eagle's Shadow: The United States and Latin America* (Wheeling, Ill.: Harlan Davidson, 2002), 282–83.

40. Ibid., 283; LaFeber, *Inevitable Revolutions,* 247; Martha L. Cottam, *Images and Intervention: U.S. Policies in Latin America* (Pittsburgh: University of Pittsburgh Press, 1994), 107.

41. Martin Diskin and Kenneth Sharpe, *The Impact of U.S. Policy in El Salvador, 1979–1985* (Berkeley: Institute of International Studies, University of California, 1986), 10; LaFeber, *Inevitable Revolutions,* 250.

42. Tony Hodges, "At Odds with Self-Determination: The United States and Western Sahara," in *African Crisis Areas and U.S. Foreign Policy,* ed. Gerald J. Bender, James S. Coleman, and Richard L. Sklar (Berkeley: University of California Press, 1985), 265–66.

43. Ibid., 266–67.

44. Farber, *Taken Hostage,* 120–25.

45. Ibid., 91–92, 125; Jordan, *Crisis,* 31; William Shawcross, *The Shah's Last Ride: The Fate of an Ally* (New York: Simon and Schuster, 1988), 153; Seliktar, *Failing the Crystal Ball Test,* 162, 163.

46. Rubin, *Paved with Good Intentions,* 294.

47. Carter, *First Lady from Plains,* 292–93.

48. Farber, *Taken Hostage,* 119–20.

49. Ibid., 128.

50. Seliktar, *Failing the Crystal Ball Test,* 143–44; AmEmbassy Tehran to SecState, October 28, 1979, *Iran: The Making of U.S. Policy, 1977–1990,* NatSA, Microfiche.

51. Farber, *Taken Hostage,* 127–30.

52. Ibid., 130–32; Bowden, *Guests of the Ayatollah,* 32–35; Harris, *Crisis,* 205.

53. Farber, *Taken Hostage,* 133–36; Bowden, *Guests of the Ayatollah,* 198–99.

54. Jordan, *Crisis,* 19.

55. Kaufman and Kaufman, *Presidency of James Earl Carter,* 194, 195–96.

56. Jordan to Carter, undated (ca. November 8, 1979), COS-Jordan, Box 34, JCL.

57. Jordan to Carter, November 8, 1979, in ibid.; Sick, *All Fall Down,* 209; Farber, *Taken Hostage,* 148; Carter, *Keeping Faith,* 471.

58. PPPUS, *Jimmy Carter,* 1979, II:2194.

59. Farber, *Taken Hostage,* 151–52; Melani McAlister, *Epic Encounters: Culture, Media, and U.S. Interests in the Middle East* (Berkeley: University of California Press, 2001), 205; Smith, *Morality, Reason, and Power,* 198.

60. Farber, *Taken Hostage,* 142, 144.

61. "U.S. Cuts Nearly All Ties with Chile, Accuses Regime of Condoning Terrorism," *Los Angeles Times,* December 1, 1979; Pastor to Brzezinski, November 19, 1979, NSA, SM, N/S, Box 9, JCL.

62. Salinger, *America Held Hostage,* 54, 165.

63. Farber, *Taken Hostage,* 160–61; Langley, *Mexico and the United States,* 85; Carter, *Keeping Faith,* 477; Jordan, *Crisis,* 206.

64. Farber, *Taken Hostage,* 162; Sick, *All Fall Down,* 214–15; George C. Wilson, "A Powerful U.S. Flotilla is Steaming in Mideast," *Washington Post,* November 28, 1979.

65. Odd Arne Westad, "The Road to Kabul: Soviet Policy on Afghanistan, 1978–1979," in Wested, *The Fall of Détente,* 124.

66. Ibid., 125–26.

67. Ibid., 127–28.

68. Ibid., 129–30.

69. Ibid., 130–31.

70. Ibid., 132.

71. Andrew Bennett, *Condemned to Repetition?: The Rise, Fall, and Reprise of Soviet-Russian Military Interventionism, 1973–1996* (Cambridge, Mass.: MIT Press, 1999), 201–2.

72. Westad, *The Fall of Détente,* 133.

73. Ibid., 135–36; Dobrynin, *In Confidence,* 440.

74. Nancy Peabody Newell and Richard S. Newell, *The Struggle for Afghanistan* (Ithaca: Cornell University Press, 1981), 109; MacEachin, "Predicting the Soviet Invasion of Afghanistan: The Intelligence Community's Record."

75. Carter, *Keeping Faith,* 481; Peter Osnos, "Detente is Dead, Arms Race Resumes," *Washington Post,* December 30, 1979.

76. "Carter Slips in Poll on Handling of Iran," *Washington Post,* January 11, 1980; Farber, *Taken Hostage,* 164.

8—A Crisis of Confidence

1. *PPPUS, Jimmy Carter,* 1980–81, I:21–22, 24.

2. Kaufman and Kaufman, *Presidency of James Earl Carter,* 205, 206; Art Pine, "Major Banks Raise Prime to 17 3/4 Pct," *Washington Post,* March 8, 1980.

3. Jordan to Carter, January 22, 1980, COS-Jordan, Box 34, JCL.

4. Salinger, *America Held Hostage,* 103–4, 122–23; Sick, *All Fall Down,* 239.

5. Bowden, *Guests of the Ayatollah,* 291–92; Sick, *All Fall Down,* 253.

6. Salinger, *America Held Hostage,* 131, 165–66; Christopher Hemmer, *Which Lessons Matter?: American Foreign Policy Decision Making in the Middle East, 1979–1987* (Albany: State University of New York Press, 2000), 67; Bowden, *Guests of the Ayatollah,* 364, 365.

7. Farber, *Taken Hostage,* 168; Rubin, *Paved with Good Intentions,* 327; "Cottam/Ghotbzadeh Conversation, 0800," April 24, 1980, COS-Jordan, Box 35, JCL.

8. Bowden, *Guests of the Ayatollah,* 407–8.

9. Kaufman and Kaufman, *Presidency of James Earl Carter,* 208–9.

10. Ibid., 209.

11. Ibid.

12. Jordan to Carter, January 22, 1980; Hemmer, *Which Lessons Matter?,* 72–73, 75–76; Bowden, *Guests of the Ayatollah,* 410.

13. Christopher, *Chances of a Lifetime,* 100; Kaufman and Kaufman, *Presidency of James Earl Carter,* 211–12.

14. Kaufman and Kaufman, *Presidency of James Earl Carter,* 212; Bowden, *Guests of the Ayatollah,* 231.

15. Kaufman and Kaufman, *Presidency of James Earl Carter,* 212; Bowden, *Guests of the Ayatollah,* 450.

16. Kaufman and Kaufman, *Presidency of James Earl Carter,* 212–13; Jordan, *Crisis,* 272–73; David Patrick Houghton, *US Foreign Policy and the Iran Hostage Crisis* (New York: Cambridge University Press, 2001), 136–39.

17. Christopher, *Chances of a Lifetime,* 105–7; Kaufman and Kaufman, *Presidency of James Earl Carter,* 224.

18. Kaufman and Kaufman, *Presidency of James Earl Carter,* 213.

19. "Jimmy Carter Conference—High School Colloquium," and "Discussant: Hamilton Jordan," in *Jimmy Carter: Foreign Policy and Post-Presidential Years,* ed. Herbert D. Rosenbaum and Alexej Ugrinsky (Westport, Conn.: Greenwood, 1994), 238, 468.

20. "Zbigniew Brzezinski: How Jimmy Carter and I Started the Mujahideen," *Counterpunch,* http://www.counterpunch.org/brzezinski.html.

21. Carter, *Keeping Faith,* 481.

22. Kux, *United States and Pakistan,* 251–52; Kaufman and Kaufman, *The Presidency of James Earl Carter,* 197; *PPPUS, Jimmy Carter,* 1980–81, I:197; Gabriella Grasselli, *British and American Responses to the Soviet Invasion of Afghanistan* (Brookfield, Vt.: Dartmouth, 1996), 159.

23. Dobrynin, *In Confidence,* 452; Carter to Brezhnev, December 28, 1979, and Brezhnev to President, December 29, 1979, PF, SF, Box 17, JCL.

24. Ben-Zvi, *American Approach to Superpower Collaboration,* 65; Peter C. Stuart, "US Gets Tough against Soviet Aggression," *Christian Science Monitor,* January 25, 1980; Don Oberdorfer and Barry Sussman, "Tough New Carter Stands Win Overwhelming Popular Support," *Washington Post,* February 3, 1980. Administration official quoted in Bernard A. Weisberger, *Cold War, Cold Peace: The United States and Russia since 1945* (New York: American Heritage, 1984), 291–92. Kennan quoted in McMahon, *Cold War,* 144.

25. Brzezinski, *Power and Principle,* 432.

26. Grasselli, *British and American Responses,* 156.

27. Eizenstat to the President, January 3, 1980, Staff Offices, Lloyd Cutler, Presidential Papers of Jimmy Carter, Box 76, JCL; NSC Meeting, January 2, 1980, in Wested, *The Fall of Détente,* 348; Kaufman and Kaufman, *Presidency of James Earl Carter,* 197.

28. Kaufman and Kaufman, *Presidency of James Earl Carter,* 197–98.

29. Christopher to President, June 19, 1980, NSA, SM, N/S, Box 27, JCL.

30. Juan de Onis, "Argentines Expect Soviet to Buy Grain," *New York Times,* February 1, 1980; "4 Years After Coup, Argentina is Regaining Favor," *New York Times,* March 26, 1980; Joseph Tulchin, *Argentina and the United States: A Conflicted Relationship* (Boston: Twayne, 1990), 150; Ann Crittenden, "Human Rights and Mrs. Derian," *New York Times,* May 31, 1980; *Statistical Abstract of Latin America,* vol. 28 (Los Angeles: UCLA Center Publications, 1990), 1092; James Nelson Goodsell, "Argentina: 'No' to Embargo," *Christian Science Monitor,* January 28, 1980.

31. Crittenden, "Human Rights and Mrs. Derian," *New York Times,* May 31, 1980.

32. Kaufman, "The Carter Administration and the Human Rights Bureau," 65; Kaufman and Kaufman, *Presidency of James Earl Carter,* 135–36.

33. NSC Meeting, January 2, 1980, in Westad, *Fall of Détente,* 342; Kane and Miller to Carter, January 3, 1980, SO, OSS, PHF, Box 166, and Scott to Onek, February 15, 1980, SO, Counsel—Cutler, Box 101, JCL; Neil Amdur, "Carter Speech Dashes Last Hope for U.S. Olympic Role," *New York Times,* April 12, 1980; Steven R. Weisman, "U.S. Olympic Group Votes to Boycott the Moscow Games," *New York Times,* April 13, 1980; Brzezinski, *Power and Principle,* 434.

34. Margaret Thatcher, *The Downing Street Years* (New York: Harper Collins, 1993), 68–69, 88; Frank Costigliola, *France and the United States: The Cold Alliance since World War II* (New York: Twayne, 1992), 184; Maga, *World of Jimmy Carter,* 145.

35. Minton F. Goldman, "President Carter, Western Europe, and Afghanistan in 1980: Inter-Allied Differences over Policy toward the Soviet Invasion," in *Jimmy Carter: Foreign Policy and Post-Presidential Years,* ed. Herbert D. Rosenbaum and Alexej Ugrinsky (Westport, Conn.: Greenwood, 1994), 22; Andrianopoulos, *Kissinger and Brzezinski,* 270.

36. Carr, *Helmut Schmidt,* 134; Carter, *Keeping Faith,* 544–45.

37. Garthoff, *Détente and Confrontation*, 955; Carter, *Keeping Faith*, 545; Helmut Schmidt, *Men and Powers: A Political Retrospective* (New York: Random House, 1989), 210.

38. Kaufman and Kaufman, *Presidency of James Earl Carter*, 223–24.

39. Carter, *Keeping Faith*, 546–47.

40. Kaufman and Kaufman, *Presidency of James Earl Carter*, 225.

41. Maga, *World of Jimmy Carter*, 51.

42. Lloyd Jensen, *Negotiating Nuclear Arms Control* (Columbia: University of South Carolina Press, 1988), 40–41; NSC Meeting, January 2, 1980, in Westad, *Fall of Détente*, 336; McMahon, *Cold War*, 144; Herspring, *The Pentagon and the Presidency*, 251.

43. Kaufman and Kaufman, *Presidency of James Earl Carter*, 230–31.

44. Ibid., 231; Michael Dobbs, *Madeleine Albright: A Twentieth-Century Odyssey* (New York: Henry Holt, 1999), 278–79.

45. SecState to AmEmbassy Tokyo, February 16, 1980, NSA, BM, PCFLF, Box 11, and SecState to AmEmbassy Tokyo, December 3, 1980, and Tokyo to White House, December 12, 1980, NSA, BM, CF, Box 41, JCL; John Dumbrell, *American Foreign Policy: Carter to Clinton* (New York: St. Martin's, 1997), 27–28; Carr, *Helmut Schmidt*, 136; Brzezinski, *Power and Principle*, 311.

46. Tahir-Kheli, *United States and Pakistan*, 132–34; Kux, *United States and Pakistan*, 242.

47. Tahir-Kheli, *United States and Pakistan*, 132; Oksenberg to Brzezinski, December 28, 1979, NSA, BM, CF, Box 1; Kux, *United States and Pakistan*, 249; Chadda, *Paradox of Power*, 85.

48. Kux, *United States and Pakistan*, 250–51, 254.

49. Norman D. Palmer, *The United States and India: The Dimensions of Influence* (New York: Praeger, 1984), 85.

50. Gandhi quote in ibid., 88; Goheen, "U.S. Policy toward India," 132.

51. Goheen, "U.S. Policy toward India," 132; Dennis Kux, *India and the United States: Estranged Democracies, 1941–1991* (Washington, D.C.: National Defense University Press, 1992), 371–72.

52. Kux, *India and the United States*, 372–73; PPPUS, *Jimmy Carter*, 1980–81, II:1138.

53. Patrick Tyler, *A Great Wall: Six Presidents and China, An Investigative History* (New York: Public Affairs, 1999), 284–85.

54. Mann, *About Face*, 109–10; Brzezinski, *Power and Principle*, 423; Vance, *Hard Choices*, 390; Ross, *Negotiating Cooperation*, 145.

55. Harding, *Fragile Relationship*, 92.

56. Brzezinski, *Power and Principle*, 424; Mann, *About Face*, 111–13; Ross, *Negotiating Cooperation*, 149–50; Schaller, *United States and China in the Twentieth Century*, 212–13.

57. Harding, *Fragile Relationship*, 93.

58. Lefebvre, *Arms for the Horn*, 205–7, 209–11.

59. Ibid., 200–201; Paul B. Henze, *The Horn of Africa: From War to Peace* (New York: St. Martin's, 1991), 4.

60. Jordan, *Crisis*, 313; Burton Kaufman, *The Presidency of James Earl Carter, Jr.* (Lawrence: University Press of Kansas, 1993), 189–91, 193.

61. Kaufman, *Presidency of James Earl Carter*, 191.

62. Kaufman and Kaufman, *Presidency of James Earl Carter*, 219.

63. Ibid., 240–42, 244.

64. Engstrom, *Presidential Decision Making Adrift*, 46–47.

65. Felix Roberto Masud-Piloto, *From Welcomed Exiles to Illegal Immigrants: Cuban Migration to the U.S., 1959–1995* (Lanham, Md.: Rowman and Littlefield, 1996), 78–79; Smith, *The Closest of Enemies*, 207.

66. Masud-Piloto, *From Welcomed Exiles to Illegal Immigrants,* 83.

67. Engstrom, *Presidential Decision Making Adrift,* 69–70; Masud-Piloto, *From Welcomed Exiles to Illegal Immigrants,* 83–84.

68. Smith, *The Closest of Enemies,* 231; Engstrom, *Presidential Decision Making Adrift,* 114; Masud-Piloto, *From Welcomed Exiles to Illegal Immigrants,* 85–86.

69. Eidenberg and White to the President, September 5, 1980, SO, OSS, HF, JCL; Engstrom, *Presidential Decision Making Adrift,* 141.

70. Engstrom, *Presidential Decision Making Adrift,* 19–31, 63, 199.

71. R. Sean Randolph, *The United States and Thailand: Alliance Dynamics, 1950–1985* (Berkeley: Institute of East Asian Studies, University of California, 1986), 212; Carter, *First Lady from Plains,* 279; "Discussant: Kathryn E. Cade," in *The Presidency and Domestic Policies of Jimmy Carter,* ed. Herbert D. Rosenbaum and Alexej Ugrinsky (Westport, Conn.: Greenwood, 1994), 533.

72. AmEmbassy Beijing to SecState, July 9, 1979, NSA, SM, FE, Box 67, Memorandum of Conversation, May 2, 1979, NSA, SM, FE, Box 66, and Memorandum of Conversation, January 30, 1979, VF, Box 41, JCL; Vance, *Hard Choices,* 126; Engstrom, *Presidential Decision Making Adrift,* 76–77.

73. Moore and Eizenstat to the President, September 19, 1980, SO, OSS, PHF, Box 206, JCL.

74. Kaufman and Kaufman, *Presidency of James Earl Carter,* 242; Bowden, *Guests of the Ayatollah,* 548–49.

75. Melanson, *Reconstructing Consensus,* 121; Kaufman and Kaufman, *Presidency of James Earl Carter,* 244–45.

76. Barbara Honegger, *October Surprise* (New York: Tudor Publishing Co., 1989); Gary Sick, *October Surprise: America's Hostages in Iran and the Election of Ronald Reagan* (New York: Times Books, 1991); Robert Perry, *Trick or Treason: The October Surprise Mystery* (New York: Sheridan Square Press, 1993).

77. Harris, *Crisis,* 399–400; Russell Leigh Moses, *Freeing the Hostages: Reexamining U.S.–Iranian Negotiations and Soviet Policy, 1979–1981* (Pittsburgh: University of Pittsburgh Press, 1996), 285–89, 353–66; Bowden, *Guests of the Ayatollah,* 627–29.

78. Kaufman and Kaufman, *Presidency of James Earl Carter,* 246.

79. Ibid., 247; Bowden, *Guests of the Ayatollah,* 556–57.

80. Brzezinski, *Power and Principle,* 296–97.

81. Ibid., 297, 298–99; Arthur R. Rachwald, *In Search of Poland: The Superpowers' Response to Solidarity, 1980–1989* (Stanford: Hoover Institution Press, 1990), 48.

82. Douglas J. MacEachin, *U.S. Intelligence and the Confrontation in Poland, 1980–81* (University Park: Pennsylvania State University Press, 2002), 17–19; Rachwald, *In Search of Poland,* 50, 51; Thomas M. Cynkin, *Soviet and American Signalling in the Polish Crisis* (New York: St. Martin's, 1988), 46, 48.

83. Patrick G. Vaughan, "Beyond Benign Neglect: Zbigniew Brzezinski and the Polish Crisis of 1980," *The Polish Review* 44 (1999): 11; MacEachin, *U.S. Intelligence and the Confrontation in Poland,* 27, 35–38.

84. MacEachin, *U.S. Intelligence and the Confrontation in Poland,* 29–30, 34–35, 44–47; Gates, *From the Shadows,* 164.

85. Madeleine Albright, with Bob Woodward, *Madam Secretary* (New York: Miramax, 2003), 89–90; MacEachin, *U.S. Intelligence and the Confrontation in Poland,* 50–51, 55, 57–58, 69; Brzezinski, *Power and Principle,* 465–66; John Vinocur, "NATO Warns Soviet Invasion of Poland Would End Detente," *New York Times,* December 13, 1980.

86. MacEachin, *U.S. Intelligence and the Confrontation in Poland,* 61, 71–72; Brzezinski, *Power and Principle,* 467–68.

87. Pastor, *Not Condemned to Repetition,* 172; LeoGrande, *Our Own Backyard,* 31.

88. LeoGrande, *Our Own Backyard*, 32.

89. Ibid., 42–43, 44; LaFeber, *Inevitable Revolutions*, 250.

90. Jan Knippers Black, *Sentinels of Empire: The United States and Latin American Militarism* (New York: Greenwood, 1986), 150, 151–52, 153; LeoGrande, *Our Own Backyard*, 62–63.

91. Pastor, *Not Condemned to Repetition*, 186, 328, n. 36; Aucoin, et al., to Carter, January 16, 1981, VF, (No Box Number), JCL; Bermann, *Under the Big Stick*, 277–78.

92. Dobrynin, *In Confidence*, 476.

Conclusion

1. *PPPUS, Jimmy Carter*, 1980–81, III:2892.

2. Douglas Brinkley, *The Unfinished Presidency: Jimmy Carter's Journey Beyond the White House* (New York: Penguin, 1998), 41.

3. Ibid., 64–65, 76, 78, 210.

4. Kaufman and Kaufman, *Presidency of James Earl Carter*, 252.

5. Ibid., 252–53; Brinkley, *Unfinished Presidency*, 129–30, 231–35.

6. Morris, *Jimmy Carter*, 300–301; Kai Bird, "Citizen Carter: The Very Model of an Ex-President," *Nation*, November 12, 1990, 545.

7. "Carter Criticizes Bush and Blair on War in Iraq," *New York Times*, May 20, 2007; Michael Abramowitz and Peter Baker, "Genocide and Diplomatic Policy," *Washington Post*, October 15, 2007; "Merry Christmas, Mr. Karadzić," *New Republic*, January 9 and 15, 1995, 7; Drew Christiansen, "Of Many Things," *America*, March 5, 2007, 2; Josh Getlin, "Carter's Frontal Attack," *Los Angeles Times*, December 4, 2006; Pam Belluck, "At Brandeis, Carter Responds to Critics," *New York Times*, January 24, 2007; Jeffrey Goldberg, "What Would Jimmy Do?," *Washington Post*, December 10, 2006.

8. James Lindgren, "Ranking Our Presidents," http://falcon.arts.cornell.edu/Govt/courses/F04/PresidentialRankings.pdf; "Bush Tops List As U.S. Voters Name Worst President, Quinnipiac University National Poll Finds," http://www.quinnipiac.edu/x1295.xml?ReleaseID=919.

9. Peter Baker, "Bush Stands His Ground on Budget; Opponents in Congress Appear Equally Prepared to Fight," *Washington Post*, October 16, 2007; "Bush Tops List As U.S. Voters Name Worst President"; Polling Report.com, "Presidents and History," http://www.pollingreport.com/wh-hstry.htm; Mark Fitzgerald, "'National Focus Group' Claim: Half of Americans Agree with Carter about Bush," *Editor and Publisher*, May 2, 2007.

10. Smith, *Morality, Reason, and Power*, 8.

11. See Brinkley, "The Rising Stock of Jimmy Carter," 505–29; Dumbrell, *Carter Presidency;* Schmitz and Walker, "Jimmy Carter and the Foreign Policy of Human Rights," 113–43.

12. Gates, *From the Shadows*, 175–76, 177, 179; Daniel C. Thomas, "Human Rights Ideas, the Demise of Communism, and the End of the Cold War," *Journal of Cold War Studies* 7 (Spring 2005): 110–41; Pierre, *Global Politics of Arms Sales*, 252; Tony Smith, *America's Mission: The United States and the Worldwide Struggle for Democracy in the Twentieth Century* (Princeton: Princeton University Press, 1994), 261; Abraham F. Lowenthal, "Jimmy Carter and Latin America: A New Era or Small Change?," in *Eagle Entangled: U.S. Foreign Policy in a Complex World*, ed. Kenneth A. Oye, Donald Rothchild, and Robert J. Lieber (New York: Longman, 1979), 293; David D. Newsom, "The Diplomacy of Human Rights: A Diplomat's View," in *Diplomacy of Human Rights*, ed. Newsom, 11; Kathryn Sikkink, "The Effectiveness of US Human Rights Policy, 1973–1980," in *The International Dimensions of Democratization: Europe and the Ameri-*

cas, ed. Laurence Whitehead (New York: Oxford University Press, 1996), 100–2; Dumbrell, *Carter Presidency*, 184–85, 194; Brinkley, "Rising Stock of Jimmy Carter," 523; Roberta Cohen, "Human Rights Diplomacy: The Carter Administration and the Southern Cone," *Human Rights Quarterly* 4 (Spring 1982): 237–38; Katherine Metres, "U.S. and U.N. Human Rights Policy toward Argentina, 1977–1980," *Michigan Journal of Political Science*, no. 19 (1995): 136–37; Molineau, "Carter and Human Rights," 879–85; Pflüger, "Human Rights Unbound," 709–10; Inderfurth to Brzezinski, December 1, 1978, NLC-11-3-7-10-8, JCL.

13. Powaski, *Cold War*, 230; Dobrynin, *In Confidence*, 430; Gaddis, *Strategies of Containment*, 347.

14. "True Believer," *People*, June 12, 2000, 155.

15. Glad, *Jimmy Carter*, 496.

16. Thompson, *Carter Presidency*, 147, 240–41; Bourne, *Jimmy Carter*, 419.

17. Thompson, *Carter Presidency*, 140.

18. "Discussant: William B. Quandt," in *Jimmy Carter: Foreign Policy and Post-Presidential Years*, ed. Herbert D. Rosenbaum and Alexej Ugrinsky (Westport, Conn.: Greenwood, 1994), 61–62.

19. Jean A. Garrison, *Games Advisors Play: Foreign Policy in the Nixon and Carter Administrations* (College Station: Texas A&M University Press, 1999), 98.

20. Glad, *Jimmy Carter*, 441.

21. Michael Charlton, "The President's Men at the NSC, Part II: The Struggle Under Carter," *National Interest*, no. 21 (Fall 1990): 103; Thompson, *Carter Presidency*, 139; John Whiteclay Chambers II, "The Agenda Continued: Jimmy Carter's Postpresidency," in *The Carter Presidency: Policy Choices in the Post–New Deal Era*, ed. Gary M. Fink and Hugh Davis Graham (Lawrence: University Press of Kansas, 1998), 268.

22. Skidmore, *Reversing Course*, 90, 93; Melanson, *Reconstructing Consensus*, 91, 114; Rosati, *Carter Administration's Quest for Global Community*, 40–44; Katz, "Public Opinion," 674–83.

23. Thompson, *Carter Presidency*, 171.

24. Ibid., 242; Vance, *Hard Choices*, 36.

25. Skidmore, *Reversing Course*, 49.

WORKS CITED

Archival Sources

Allen Library, University of Washington, Seattle, Washington
Papers of Henry M. Jackson
Jimmy Carter Library, Atlanta, Georgia
Chief of Staff File
Donated Historical Materials Collection
Papers of Zbigniew Brzezinski
Papers of Walter Mondale
Papers of Anthony M. Solomon
Exit Interviews
Zbigniew Brzezinski
President's Files
Office of Staff Secretary File
Plains File
RAC Program
Staff Office Files
National Security Affairs File
Papers of Lloyd Cutler
Papers of Stuart Eizenstat
Vertical File
White House Central File
Miller Center Oral History Program, Miller Center, University of Virginia
Jimmy Carter
T. Bertram Lance
National Security Archive, George Washington University, Washington, D.C.
Iran: The Making of U.S. Policy, 1977–1980 (Microfiche)

Newspapers and Popular Magazines

America
Business Week
Christian Science Monitor
Editor and Publisher
Los Angeles Times

New Republic
Newsweek
New York Times
People
Time
U.S. News and World Report
Wall Street Journal
Washington Post
Washington Star

Books and Articles

Abebe, Ermias. "The Horn, the Cold War, and Documents from the Former East Bloc: An Ethiopian View." *Cold War International History Project* 8/9 (Winter 1996/97): 40–45.

Albright, Madeleine, with Bob Woodward, *Madam Secretary.* New York: Miramax, 2003.

Allin, Dana H. *Cold War Illusions: America, Europe, and Soviet Power, 1969–1989.* New York: St. Martin's, 1995.

Andrianopoulos, Gerry Argyris. *Kissinger and Brzezinski: The NSC and the Struggle for Control of U.S. National Security Policy.* New York: St. Martin's, 1991.

Arjomand, Said Amir. *The Turban for the Crown: The Islamic Revolution in Iran.* New York: Oxford University Press, 1988.

Arms Control Association. *Arms Control and National Security: An Introduction.* Washington, D.C.: Arms Control Association, 1989.

Baek, Kwang-il. *Korea and the United States: A Study of the ROK–US Security Relationship within the Conceptual Framework of Alliance between Great and Small Powers.* Seoul: Research Center for Peace and Unification, 1988.

Bartlett, C. J.'*The Special Relationship': A Political History of Anglo-American Relations since 1945.* New York: Longman, 1992.

Beckman, Robert. *Nuclear Non-Proliferation, Congress and the Control of Peaceful Nuclear Activities.* Boulder: Westview, 1985.

Ben-Zvi, Abraham. *Alliance Politics and the Limits of Influence: The Case of the US and Israel, 1975–1983.* Boulder: Westview, 1984.

———. *The American Approach to Superpower Collaboration in the Middle East, 1973–1986.* Boulder: Westview, 1986.

———. *The United States and Israel: The Limits of the Special Relationship.* New York: Columbia University Press, 1993.

Bennett, Andrew. *Condemned to Repetition? The Rise, Fall, and Reprise of Soviet-Russian Military Interventionism, 1973–1996.* Cambridge, Mass.: MIT Press, 1999.

Berkowitz, Edward D. *Something Happened: A Political and Cultural Overview of the Seventies.* New York: Columbia University Press, 2006.

Bermann, Karl. *Under the Big Stick: Nicaragua and the United States since 1848.* Boston: South End Press, 1986.

Beukel, Erik. *American Perceptions of the Soviet Union as a Nuclear Adversary.* New York: Pinter, 1989.

Bill, James A. *The Eagle and the Lion: The Tragedy of American-Iranian Relations.* New Haven: Yale University Press, 1988.

Bissell, Richard E. *South Africa and the United States: The Erosion of an Influence Relationship.* New York: Praeger, 1982.

Biven, W. Carl. *Jimmy Carter's Economy: Policy in an Age of Limits.* Chapel Hill: University of North Carolina Press, 2002.

Black, Jan Knippers. *Sentinels of Empire: The United States and Latin American Militarism.* New York: Greenwood, 1986.

Blanchard, William. *Neocolonialism American Style, 1960–2000.* Westport, Conn.: Greenwood, 1996.

Blitz, Amy. *The Contested State: American Foreign Policy and Regime Change in the Philippines.* Lanham, Md.: Rowman and Littlefield, 2000.

Blitzer, Wolf. *Between Washington and Jerusalem: A Reporter's Notebook.* New York: Oxford University Press, 1985.

Bonner, Raymond. *Waltzing with a Dictator: The Marcoses and the Making of American Policy.* New York: Vintage, 1988.

Bourne, Peter. *Jimmy Carter: A Comprehensive Biography from Plains to Post-Presidency.* New York: Scribner, 1997.

Bowden, Mark. *Guests of the Ayatollah: The First Battle in America's War with Militant Islam.* New York: Atlantic Monthly Press, 2006.

Brands, H. W. *Into the Labyrinth: The United States and the Middle East, 1945–1993.* New York: McGraw-Hill, 1994.

Brinkley, Douglas. "The Rising Stock of Jimmy Carter: The 'Hands on' Legacy of Our Thirty-ninth President." *Diplomatic History* 20 (Fall 1996): 505–29.

———. *The Unfinished Presidency: Jimmy Carter's Journey Beyond the White House.* New York: Penguin, 1998.

Bronson, Rachel. *Thicker than Oil: America's Uneasy Partnership with Saudi Arabia.* New York: Oxford University Press, 2006.

Brzezinski, Zbigniew. "The Deceptive Structure of Peace." *Foreign Policy* no. 14 (Spring 1974): 35–55.

———. "How Jimmy Carter and I Started the Mujahideen." *Counterpunch.* http://www.counterpunch.org/brzezinski.html (accessed February 16, 2007).

———. "No Regrets: How Jimmy Carter and I Started the Mujahideen," http://www.counterpunch.org/brzezinski.html.

———. "Peace and Power." *Military Review* 49 (July 1969): 31–43.

———. *Power and Principle: Memoirs of the National Security Adviser, 1977–1981.* New York: Farrar, Straus, Giroux, 1983.

———, and Samuel Huntington. *Political Power: USA/USSR.* New York: Viking Press, 1964.

"Bush Tops List As U.S. Voters Name Worst President, Quinnipiac University National Poll Finds." Quinnipiac University. http://www.quinnipiac.edu/x1295.xml?ReleaseID=919 (accessed May 3, 2007).

Bussey, Charles. "Jimmy Carter: Hope and Memory Versus Optimism and Nostalgia." In *The Lost Decade: America in the Seventies,* edited by Elsebeth Hurup, 89–102. Oakville, Conn.: Aarhus University Press, 1996.

Caldwell, Dan. "The Carter Administration, the Senate, and SALT II." In *Jimmy Carter: Foreign Policy and Post-Presidential Years,* edited by Herbert D. Rosenbaum and Alexej Ugrinsky, 331–55. Westport, Conn.: Greenwood, 1994.

———. "US Domestic Politics and the Demise of Détente." In *Fall of Détente,* edited by Westad, 95–117. Boston: Scandinavian University Press, 1997.

Callaghan, James. *Time and Chance.* London: Collins, 1987.

Capulong-Hallenberg, Virginia S. *Philippine Foreign Policy toward the U.S., 1972–1980: Reorientation?* Stockholm: Department of Political Science, University of Stockholm, 1987.

Carey, Henry F. "Free Elections Based on Human Rights Protection: The Carter Contribution." In *Jimmy Carter: Foreign Policy and Post-Presidential Years,* edited by Herbert D. Rosenbaum and Alexej Ugrinsky, 77–87. Westport, Conn.: Greenwood, 1994.

Carr, Jonathan. *Helmut Schmidt: Helmsman of Germany.* New York: St. Martin's, 1985.

Carter, Dale. "The Crooked Path: Continuity and Change in American Foreign Policy, 1968–1981." In *The Lost Decade: America in the Seventies,* edited by Elsebeth Hurup, 103–32. Oakville, Conn.: Aarhus University Press, 1996.

Carter, Jimmy. *Keeping Faith: Memoirs of a President.* Fayetteville: University of Arkansas Press, 1995.

Carter, Rosalynn. *First Lady from Plains.* Boston: Houghton Mifflin, 1984.

Chadda, Maya. *Paradox of Power: The United States in Southwest Asia, 1973–1984.* Santa Barbara: ABC-Clio, 1986.

Chambers, John Whiteclay, II. "The Agenda Continued: Jimmy Carter's Postpresidency." In *The Carter Presidency: Policy Choices in the Post–New Deal Era,* edited by Gary M. Fink and Hugh Davis Graham, 267–85. Lawrence: University Press of Kansas, 1998.

Charlton, Michael. "The President's Men at the NSC, Part II: The Struggle Under Carter." *National Interest* 21 (Fall 1990): 100–8.

Chary, M. Srinivas. *The Eagle and the Peacock: U.S. Foreign Policy toward India since Independence.* Westport, Conn.: Greenwood, 1995.

Christison, Kathleen. *Perceptions of Palestine: Their Influence on U.S. Middle East Policy.* Berkeley: University of California Press, 1999.

Christopher, Warren. *Chances of a Lifetime.* New York: Scribner, 2001.

Churchill, R. R., and A. V. Lowe. *The Law of the Sea.* Manchester, UK: Manchester University Press, 1985.

Clifford, Clark, with Richard Holbrooke. *Counsel to the President: A Memoir.* New York: Random House, 1991.

Clifford, Lawrence X. "An Examination of the Carter Administration's Selection of Secretary of State and National Security Adviser." In *Jimmy Carter's Foreign Policy and Post-Presidential Years,* edited by Herbert D. Rosenbaum and Alexej Ugrinsky, 5–15. Westport, Conn.: Greenwood, 1994.

Clymer, Kenton J. *The United States and Cambodia, 1969–2000: A Troubled Relationship.* New York: Routledge, 2004.

Cohen, Roberta. "Human Rights Diplomacy: The Carter Administration and the Southern Cone." *Human Rights Quarterly* 4 (Spring 1982): 212–42.

Coker, Christopher. *The United States and South Africa, 1968–1985: Constructive Engagement and Its Critics.* Durham: Duke University Press, 1986.

Coll, Steve. *Ghost Wars: The Secret History of the CIA, Afghanistan, and Bin Laden, from the Soviet Invasion to September 10, 2001.* New York: Penguin, 2004.

Congressional Quarterly Almanac, 1978. Washington, D.C.: Congressional Quarterly News Features, 1978.

Costello, Charles S., III. "Nuclear Nonproliferation: A Hidden but Contentious Issue in US–Japan Relations during the Carter Administration (1977–1981)." *Asia Pacific: Perspectives* 3 (May 2003): 1–6.

Costigliola, Frank. *France and the United States: The Cold Alliance since World War II.* New York: Twayne, 1992.

Cottam, Martha L. *Images and Intervention: U.S. Policies in Latin America.* Pittsburgh: University of Pittsburgh Press, 1994.

Couloumbis, Theodore A. *The United States, Greece, and Turkey: The Troubled Triangle.* New York: Praeger, 1983.

Curtiss, Richard H. *A Changing Image: American Perceptions of the Arab-Israeli Dispute.* Washington, D.C.: American Educational Trust, 1982.

Cynkin, Thomas M. *Soviet and American Signalling in the Polish Crises.* New York: St. Martin's, 1988.

Davidow, Jeffrey. *Dealing with International Crises: Lessons from Zimbabwe.* Muscatine, Iowa: Stanley Foundation, 1983.

DeRoche, Andrew. *Black, White, and Chrome: The United States and Zimbabwe, 1953–1998.* Trenton, N.J.: Africa World Press, 2001.

Destler, I. M., Leslie H. Gelb, and Anthony Lake. *Our Own Worst Enemy: The Unmaking of American Foreign Policy.* New York: Simon and Schuster, 1984.

Diskin, Martin, and Kenneth Sharpe. *The Impact of U.S. Policy in El Salvador, 1979–1985.* Berkeley: Institute of International Studies, University of California, 1986.

Dobbs, Michael. *Madeleine Albright: A Twentieth-Century Odyssey.* New York: Henry Holt, 1999.

Dobrynin, Anatoly. *In Confidence: Moscow's Ambassador to America's Six Cold War Presidents (1962–1986).* New York: Times Books, 1995.

Dobson, Hugo. *Japan and the G7/8, 1975–2002.* New York: Routledge, 2004.

Druks, Herbert. *The Uncertain Alliance: The U.S. and Israel from Kennedy to the Peace Process.* Westport, Conn.: Greenwood, 2001.

Dumbrell, John. *American Foreign Policy: Carter to Clinton.* New York: St. Martin's, 1997.

———. *The Carter Presidency: A Re-evaluation,* 2nd ed. New York: Manchester University Press, 1995.

Engstrom, David W. *Presidential Decision Making Adrift: The Carter Administration and the Mariel Boatlift.* Lanham, Md.: Rowman and Littlefield, 1997.

Farber, David. *Taken Hostage: The Iran Hostage Crisis and America's First Encounter with Radical Islam.* Princeton: Princeton University Press, 2005.

Feldman, Shai. "Superpower Nonproliferation Policies: The Case of the Middle East." In *The Soviet-American Competition in the Middle East,* edited by Steven L. Spiegel, Mark A. Heller, and Jacob Goldberg. Lexington, Mass.: Lexington Books, 1988.

Finklestone, Joseph. *Anwar Sadat: Visionary Who Dared.* London: Frank Cass, 1996.

Fischer, Sabina Ann. *Namibia Becomes Independent: The U.S. Contribution to Regional Peace.* Zurich: Forschungsstelle fur Sicherheitspolitik und Konfliktanalyse, Eidgenossische Technische Hochschule, 1992.

Flood, Patrick J. "U.S. Human Rights Initiatives Concerning Argentina." In *The Diplomacy of Human Rights,* edited by David D. Newsom, 129–39. Lanham, Md.: University Press of America, 1986.

Fraser, T. G. *The USA and the Middle East since World War II.* New York: St. Martin's, 1989.

Friedlander, Melvin A. *Sadat and Begin: The Domestic Politics of Peacemaking.* Boulder: Westview, 1983.

Furlong, William L., and Margaret E. Scranton. *The Dynamics of Foreign Policymaking: The President, the Congress, and the Panama Canal Treaties.* Boulder: Westview, 1984.

Gaddis, John Lewis. *Strategies of Containment: A Critical Appraisal of American National Security Policy during the Cold War,* rev. ed. New York: Oxford University Press, 2005.

Garrison, Jean. *Games Advisors Play: Foreign Policy in the Nixon and Carter Administrations.* College Station: Texas A&M Press, 1999.

Garson, Robert A. *The United States and China since 1949: A Troubled Affair.* Madison: Fairleigh Dickinson Press, 1994.

Garthoff, Raymond L. *Détente and Confrontation: American-Soviet Relations from Nixon to Reagan,* rev. ed. Washington, D.C.: Brookings Institution, 1994.

Gasiorowski, Mark J. *U.S. Foreign Policy and the Shah: Building a Client State in Iran.* Ithaca: Cornell University Press, 1991.

Gates, Robert M. *From the Shadows: The Ultimate Insider's Story of Five Presidents and How They Won the Cold War.* New York: Simon and Schuster, 1996.

Gatzke, Hans W. *Germany and the United States: A "Special Relationship."* Cambridge, Mass.: Harvard University Press, 1980.

George, Alexander L., and Eric Stern. "Presidential Management Style and Models." In *Presidential Personality and Performance,* edited by Alexander L. George and Juliette L. George, 199–280. Boulder: Westview, 1998.

Gilbert, Dennis. *Sandinistas: The Party and the Revolution*. New York: Basil Blackwell, 1988.

Giuffo, John. "Nightline Is Spawned Out of the Hostage Crisis." *Columbia Journalism Review* 40 (November–December 2001). http://findarticles.com/p/articles/mi_qa3613/is_200111/ai_n8976166 (accessed October 14, 2007).

Glad, Betty. *Jimmy Carter: In Search of the Great White House*. New York: Norton, 1980.

Gleijeses, Piero. "Havana's Policy in Africa, 1959–76: New Evidence from Cuban Archives." *Cold War International History Project* 8/9 (Winter 1996/97): 5–18.

Gleysteen, William H., Jr. *Massive Entanglement, Marginal Influence: Carter and Korea in Crisis*. Washington, D.C.: Brookings Institution, 1999.

Goheen, Robert F. "U.S. Policy toward India during the Carter Presidency." In *The Hope and the Reality: U.S.–Indian Relations from Roosevelt to Reagan*, edited by Harold A. Gould and Sumit Ganguly, 121–37. Boulder: Westview, 1992.

Goldberg, David Howard. *Foreign Policy and Ethnic Interest Groups: American and Canadian Jews Lobby for Israel*. New York: Greenwood, 1990.

Goldman, Minton F. "President Carter, Western Europe, and Afghanistan in 1980: Inter-Allied Differences over Policy toward the Soviet Invasion." In *Jimmy Carter: Foreign Policy and Post-Presidential Years*, edited by Herbert D. Rosenbaum and Alexej Ugrinsky, 19–34. Westport, Conn.: Greenwood, 1994.

Gong, Li. "The Difficult Path to Diplomatic Relations: China's U.S. Policy, 1972–1978." In *Normalization of U.S.–China Relations: An International History*, edited by William C. Kirby, Robert Ross, and Gong Li, 116–46. Cambridge: Harvard University Asia Center, 2006.

Grasselli, Gabriella. *British and American Responses to the Soviet Invasion of Afghanistan*. Brookfield, Vt.: Dartmouth, 1996.

Grayson, Benson Lee. *United States-Iranian Relations*. Washington, D.C.: University Press of America, 1981.

Grayson, George W. *The United States and Mexico: Patterns of Influence*. New York: Praeger, 1984.

Grover, William F. *The President as Prisoner: A Structural Critique of the Carter and Reagan Years*. Albany: State University of New York Press, 1989.

Grubbs, Larry. "'Hands on Presidency' or 'Passionless Presidency'?: Jimmy Carter and Ratification of the Panama Canal Treaties." *Society for Historians of American Foreign Relations Newsletter* 30 (December 1999): 1–17.

Haas, Michael. *Cambodia, Pol Pot, and the United States: The Faustian Pact*. New York: Praeger, 1991.

Haass, Richard N. "Arms Control at Sea: The United States and the Soviet Union in the Indian Ocean, 1977–78." In *U.S.–Soviet Security Cooperation: Achievements, Failures, Lessons*, edited by Alexander George, Philip J. Farley, and Alexander Dallin, 524–39. New York: Oxford University Press, 1988.

Hahn, Peter L. "Jimmy Carter and the Central Intelligence Agency." In *The Presidency and Domestic Policies of Jimmy Carter*, edited by Herbert D. Rosenbaum and Alexej Ugrinsky, 323–51. Westport, Conn.: Greenwood, 1994.

Harding, Harry. *A Fragile Relationship: The United States and China since 1972*. Washington, D.C.: Brookings Institution, 1992.

Hargrove, Erwin C. *Jimmy Carter as President: Leadership and the Politics of the Public Good*. Baton Rouge: Louisiana State University Press, 1988.

Harris, David. *The Crisis: The President, the Prophet, and the Shah—1979 and the Coming of Militant Islam*. New York: Little, Brown and Company, 2004.

Hathaway, Robert M. *Great Britain and the United States: Special Relations since World War II*. Boston: Twayne, 1990.

Hayward, Steven F. *The Real Jimmy Carter: How Our Worst Ex-President Undermines American Foreign Policy, Coddles Dictators, and Created the Party of Clinton and Kerry*. Washington, D.C.: Regnery, 2004.

Hemmer, Christopher. *Which Lessons Matter?: American Foreign Policy Decision Making in the Middle East, 1979–1987*. Albany: State University of New York Press, 2000.

Henze, Paul B. *The Horn of Africa: From War to Peace*. New York: St. Martin's, 1991.

Herspring, Dale R. *The Pentagon and the Presidency: Civil-Military Relations from FDR to George W. Bush*. Lawrence: University Press of Kansas, 2005.

Hodges, Tony. "At Odds with Self-Determination: The United States and Western Sahara." In *African Crisis Areas and U.S. Foreign Policy*, edited by Gerald J. Bender, James S. Coleman, and Richard L. Sklar, 257–76. Berkeley: University of California Press, 1985.

Hogan, J. Michael. *The Panama Canal in American Politics: Domestic Advocacy and the Evolution of Policy*. Carbondale: Southern Illinois University Press, 1986.

Holland, Lauren H., and Robert A. Hoover. *The MX Decision: A New Direction in U.S. Weapons Procurement Policy?* Boulder: Westview, 1985.

Hollick, Ann L. *U.S. Foreign Policy and the Law of the Sea*. Princeton: Princeton University Press, 1981.

Honegger, Barbara. *October Surprise*. New York: Tudor Publishing Co., 1989.

Hoover, Robert A. *The MX Controversy: A Guide to Issues and References*. Claremont, Ca.: Regina, 1982.

Horne, Gerald. *From the Barrel of a Gun: The United States and the War against Zimbabwe, 1965–1980*. Chapel Hill: University of North Carolina Press, 2001.

Houghton, David Patrick. *US Foreign Policy and the Iran Hostage Crisis*. New York: Cambridge University Press, 2001.

Huntington, Samuel. "Renewed Hostility." In *The Making of America's Soviet Policy*, edited by Joseph S. Nye, Jr., 265–89. New Haven: Yale University Press, 1984.

Hurst, Steven. *The Carter Administration and Vietnam*. New York: St. Martin's, 1996.

Huyser, Robert E. *Mission to Tehran*. New York: Harper and Row, 1986.

Hybel, Alex Roberto. *How Leaders Reason: US Intervention in the Caribbean Basin and Latin America*. Cambridge, Mass.: Basil Blackwell, 1990.

"Interview with Leslie H. Gelb." National Security Archive. http://www.gwu.edu/~nsarchiv/coldwar/interviews/episode-19/gelb2.html (accessed December 5, 2006).

Ionnides, Christos P. *America's Iran: Injury and Catharsis*. Lanham, Md.: University Press of America, 1984.

Irogbe, Kema. *The Roots of United States Foreign Policy toward Apartheid South Africa*. Lewiston, N.Y.: Edwin Mellen, 1997.

Jackson, Donna R. "The Carter Administration and Somalia." *Diplomatic History* 31 (September 2007): 703–21.

Jada, Lawrence. *International Law and Ocean Use Management: The Evolution of Ocean Governance*. New York: Routledge, 1996.

Jensen, Lloyd. *Negotiating Nuclear Arms Control*. Columbia: University of South Carolina Press, 1988.

Johnson, Robert David. *Congress and the Cold War*. New York: Cambridge University Press, 2006.

Jones, Charles O. *The Trusteeship Presidency: Jimmy Carter and the United States Congress*. Baton Rouge: Louisiana State University Press, 1988.

Jones, Goronwy. *The Rise, Breakdown, and Future of the East-West Detente Process*. New York: Vantage, 1987.

Jordan, Hamilton. *Crisis: The Last Year of the Carter Presidency*. New York: Putnam, 1982.

Jorden, William J. *Panama Odyssey*. Austin: University of Texas Press, 1984.

Kagan, Robert. *A Twilight Struggle: American Power and Nicaragua, 1977–1990*. New York: Free Press, 1996.

Kaplan, Lawrence S. *NATO Divided, NATO United: The Evolution of an Alliance*. Westport, Conn.: Praeger, 2004.

Katz, Andrew Z. "Public Opinion and the Contradictions of Jimmy Carter's Foreign Policy." *Presidential Studies Quarterly* 30 (December 2000): 662–87.

Kaufman, Burton I. *The Presidency of James Earl Carter, Jr.* Lawrence: University Press of Kansas, 1993.

———. *Presidential Profiles: The Carter Years.* New York: Facts on File, 2006.

———, and Scott Kaufman. *The Presidency of James Earl Carter, Jr.,* 2nd ed. Lawrence: University Press of Kansas, 2006.

Kaufman, Robert Gordon. *Henry M. Jackson: A Life in Politics.* Seattle: University of Washington Press, 2000.

Kaufman, Victor S[cott]. "The Carter Administration and the Human Rights Bureau." *Historian* 61 (Fall 1998): 51–66.

———. *Rosalynn Carter: Equal Partner in the White House.* Lawrence: University Press of Kansas, 2006.

Kline, Benjamin. *Profit, Principle, and Apartheid, 1948–1994: The Conflict of Economic and Moral Issues in the United States–South African Relations.* Lewiston, N.Y.: Edwin Mellen, 1997.

Korn, David A. *Ethiopia, the United States, and the Soviet Union.* Carbondale: Southern Illinois University Press, 1986.

Kotz, Nick. *Wild Blue Yonder: Money, Politics, and the B-1 Bomber.* New York: Pantheon, 1988.

Kozyrev, Vitaly. "Soviet Policy toward the United States and China." In *Normalization of U.S.–China Relations: An International History,* edited by William C. Kirby, Robert Ross, and Gong Li, 252–86. Cambridge: Harvard University Press, 2006.

Krieger, Wolfgang. "German-American Security Relations, 1968–1990." Translated by Tradukas. In *The United States and Germany in the Era of the Cold War, 1945–1990,* vol. 2, *1968–1990,* edited by Detlef Junker, 111–25. New York: Cambridge University Press, 2004.

Kruzel, Joseph J. "Verification and SALT II." In *Verification and SALT: The Challenge of Strategic Deception,* edited by William C. Potter, 95–110. Boulder: Westview, 1980.

Kusnitz, Leonard A. *Public Opinion and Foreign Policy: America's China Policy, 1949–1979.* Westport, Conn.: Greenwood, 1984.

Kux, Dennis. *India and the United States: Estranged Democracies, 1941–1991.* Washington, D.C.: National Defense University Press, 1992.

———. *The United States and Pakistan, 1947–2000: Disenchanted Allies.* Washington, D.C.: Woodrow Wilson Center Press, 2001.

LaFeber, Walter. *Inevitable Revolutions: The United States in Central America,* expanded ed. New York: Norton, 1984.

———. *The Panama Canal: The Crisis in Historical Perspective,* updated ed. New York: Oxford University Press, 1989.

Lake, Anthony. *Somoza Falling: A Case Study of Washington at Work.* Boston: Houghton Mifflin, 1989.

Langley, Lester D. *Mexico and the United States: The Fragile Relationship.* Boston: Twayne, 1991.

Laucella, Melchiore J. "A Cognitive-Psychodynamic Perspective to Understanding Secretary of State Cyrus Vance's Worldview." *Presidential Studies Quarterly* 34 (June 2004): 227–71.

Ledeen, Michael, and William Lewis. *Debacle: The American Failure in Iran.* New York: Alfred A. Knopf, 1981.

Lee, Chae-jin, and Hideo Sato. *U.S. Policy toward Japan and Korea: A Changing Influence Relationship.* New York: Praeger, 1982.

Lefebvre, Jeffrey Alan. *Arms for the Horn: U.S. Security Policy in Ethiopia and Somalia, 1953–1991.* Pittsburgh: University of Pittsburgh Press, 1991.

LeoGrande, William M. *Our Own Backyard: The United States in Central America, 1977–1992.* Chapel Hill: University of North Carolina Press, 1998.

Levering, Ralph B. *The Cold War, 1945–1987,* 2nd ed. Arlington Heights, Ill.: Harland Davidson, 1988.

———, and Miriam Levering. *Citizen Action for Global Change: The Neptune Group and the Law of the Sea.* Syracuse: Syracuse University Press, 1999.

Lewis, Finlay. *Mondale: Portrait of an American Politician.* New York: Harper and Row, 1980.

Lilienthal, Alfred M. *The Zionist Connection II: What Price Peace?* New Brunswick, N.J.: North American, 1982.

Lindgren, James. "Ranking Our Presidents." http://falcon.arts.cornell.edu/Govt/courses/F04/PresidentialRankings.pdf (accessed May 3, 2007).

Longley, Kyle. *In the Eagle's Shadow: The United States and Latin America.* Wheeling, Ill.: Harlan Davidson, 2002.

Loth, Wilfried. *Overcoming the Cold War: A History of Détente, 1950–1991.* Translated by Robert F. Hogg. New York: Palgrave, 2002.

Lowenthal, Abraham F. "Jimmy Carter and Latin America." In *Eagle Entangled: U.S. Foreign Policy in a Complex World,* edited by Kenneth A. Oye, Donald Rothchild, and Robert J. Lieber, 290–303. New York: Longman, 1979.

MacEachin, Douglas. "Predicting the Soviet Invasion of Afghanistan: The Intelligence Community's Record." Central Intelligence Agency. https://www.cia.gov/library/center-for-the-study-of-intelligence/csi-publications/books-and-monographs/predicting-the-soviet-invasion-of-afghanistan-the-intelligence-communitys-record.html#link2 (accessed October 1, 2005).

MacEachin, Douglas J. *U.S. Intelligence and the Confrontation in Poland, 1980–1981.* University Park: Pennsylvania State University Press, 2002.

Maga, Timothy. *The World of Jimmy Carter: U.S. Foreign Policy, 1977–1981.* West Haven, Conn.: University of New Haven Press, 1994.

Major, John. *Prize Possession: The United States and the Panama Canal, 1903–1979.* New York: Cambridge University Press, 1993.

Mann, James. *About Face: A History of America's Curious Relationship with China from Nixon to Clinton.* New York: Alfred Knopf, 1999.

Marte, Fred. *Political Cycles in International Relations: The Cold War and Africa, 1945–1990.* Amsterdam, Netherlands: VU University Press, 1994.

Martinez, J. Michael. "The Carter Administration and the Evolution of American Nuclear Nonproliferation Policy, 1977–1981." *Journal of Policy History* 14 (Summer 2002): 261–92.

Masud-Piloto, Felix Roberto. *From Welcomed Exiles to Illegal Immigrants: Cuban Migration to the U.S., 1959–1995.* Lanham, Md.: Rowman and Littlefield, 1996.

May, Bernhard. "The World Economic Summits: A Difficult Learning Process." Translated by Tradukas. In *The United States and Germany in the Era of the Cold War, 1945–1990,* vol. 2, *1968–1990,* edited by Detlef Junker, 249–55. New York: Cambridge University Press, 2004.

Mayers, David. *The Ambassadors and America's Soviet Policy.* New York: Oxford University Press, 1995.

Maynard, Edward S. "The Bureaucracy and Implementation of US Human Rights Policy." *Human Rights Quarterly* 11 (May 1989): 175–248.

McAlister, Melani. *Epic Encounters: Culture, Media, and U.S. Interests in the Middle East.* Berkeley: University of California Press, 2001.

McLellan, David S. *Cyrus Vance.* Totowa, N.J.: Rowman and Allanheld, 1985.

McMahon, Robert J. *The Cold War: A Very Short Introduction.* New York: Oxford University Press, 2003.

Medvedev, Roy. *China and the Superpowers.* Translated by Harold Shukman. New York: Oxford University Press, 1986.

Melanson, Richard A. *Reconstructing Consensus: American Foreign Policy since the Vietnam War.* New York: St. Martin's, 1991.

Meredith, Martin. *In the Name of Apartheid: South Africa in the Postwar Period.* New York: Harper and Row, 1988.

Merkley, Paul Charles. *American Presidents, Religion, and Israel: The Heirs of Cyrus.* Westport, Conn.: Praeger, 2004.

Metres, Katherine. "U.S. and U.N. Human Rights Policy toward Argentina, 1977–1980." *Michigan Journal of Political Science,* no. 19 (1995): 93–153.

Moens, Alexander. *Foreign Policy under Carter: Testing Multiple Advocacy Decision Making.* Boulder: Westview, 1990.

Moffett, George D., III. *The Limits of Victory: The Ratification of the Panama Canal Treaties.* Ithaca: Cornell University Press, 1985.

Molineau, Harold. "Carter and Human Rights: Administrative Impact of a Symbolic Policy." *Policy Studies Journal* 8 (Summer 1980): 879–85.

———. *U.S. Policy toward Latin America: From Regionalism to Globalism.* Boulder: Westview, 1986.

Morell, James B. *The Law of the Sea: An Historical Analysis of the 1982 Treaty and Its Rejection by the United States.* Jefferson, N.C.: McFarland and Company, 1992.

Morgan, Kenneth O. *Callaghan: A Life.* New York: Oxford University Press, 1997.

Morley, Morris H. *Washington, Somoza, and the Sandinistas: State and Regime in U.S. Policy toward Nicaragua, 1969–1981.* New York: Cambridge University Press, 1994.

Morris, Kenneth E. *Jimmy Carter: American Moralist.* Athens: University of Georgia Press, 1996.

Moses, Russell Leigh. *Freeing the Hostages: Reexamining U.S.–Iranian Negotiations and Soviet Policy, 1979–1981.* Pittsburgh: University of Pittsburgh Press, 1996.

Mower, A. Glenn. *Human Rights and American Foreign Policy: The Carter and Reagan Experiences.* New York: Greenwood, 1987.

Muravchik, Joshua. *The Uncertain Crusade: Jimmy Carter and the Dilemmas of Human Rights Policy.* Lanham, Md.: Hamilton Press, 1986.

Neidle, Alan. "Nuclear Test Bans: History and Future Prospects." In *U.S.–Soviet Security Cooperation: Achievements, Failures, Lessons,* edited by Alexander George, Philip J. Farley, and Alexander Dallin, 175–214. New York: Oxford University Press, 1988, 196–99.

Nesbitt, Francis Njubi. *Race for Sanctions: African Americans against Apartheid, 1946–1994.* Bloomington: Indiana University Press, 2001.

Nester, William R. *Power Across the Pacific: A Diplomatic History of American Relations with Japan.* Washington Square: New York University Press, 1996.

Neustadt, Richard E. *Presidential Power and the Modern Presidents: The Politics of Leadership from Roosevelt to Reagan.* New York: Free Press, 1990.

Newell, Nancy Peabody, and Richard S. Newell. *The Struggle for Afghanistan.* Ithaca: Cornell University Press, 1981.

Newsom, David D. "The Diplomacy of Human Rights: A Diplomat's View." In *The Diplomacy of Human Rights,* edited by David D. Newsom, 3–12. Lanham, Md.: University Press of America/Georgetown University Institute for the Study of Diplomacy, 1986.

Njølstad, Olav. "Keys of Keys? Salt II and the Breakdown of Détente." In *Fall of Détente,* edited by Westad, 34–71. Boston: Scandinavian University Press, 1997.

Nogee, Joseph L., and John Spanier. *Peace Impossible—War Unlikely: The Cold War Between the United States and the Soviet Union.* Glenview, Ill.: Scott, Foresman/Little, 1988.

Nolan, Cathal J. *Principled Diplomacy: Security and Rights in U.S. Foreign Policy.* Westport, Conn.: Greenwood, 1993.

Nolan, Janne E. "The U.S.–Soviet Conventional Arms Transfer Negotiations." In *U.S.–Soviet Security Cooperation: Achievements, Failures, Lessons,* edited by Alexander George, Philip J. Farley, and Alexander Dallin, 510–23. New York: Oxford University Press, 1988.

Ogata, Sadako. *Normalization with China: A Comparative Study of U.S. and Japanese Processes.* Berkeley: Institute of East Asian Studies, University of California, 1988.

O'Neill, Tip, with William Novak. *Man of the House: The Life and Political Memoirs of Speaker Tip O'Neill.* New York: Random House, 1987.

Palmer, Norman D. *The United States and India: The Dimensions of Influence.* New York: Praeger, 1984.

Pastor, Robert. *Condemned to Repetition: The United States and Nicaragua.* Princeton: Princeton University Press, 1987.

———. *Not Condemned to Repetition: The United States and Nicaragua,* rev. ed. Boulder: Westview, 2002.

———. *Whirlpool: U.S. Foreign Policy toward Latin America and the Caribbean.* Princeton: Princeton University Press, 1992.

Paterson, Thomas G., J. Garry Clifford, Shane J. Maddock, Deborah Kisatsky, and Kenneth J. Hagan. *American Foreign Relations: A History,* 2 vols. Boston: Houghton Mifflin, 2006.

Patterson, James T. *Restless Giant: The United States from Watergate to Bush v. Gore.* New York: Oxford University Press, 2005.

Perry, Robert. *Trick or Treason: The October Surprise Mystery.* New York: Sheridan Square Press, 1993.

Pflüger, Friedbert. "Human Rights Unbound: Carter's Human Rights Policy Reassessed." *Presidential Studies Quarterly* 19 (Fall 1989): 705–16.

Pierre, Andrew J. *The Global Politics of Arms Sales.* Princeton: Princeton University Press, 1982.

"Political Letter of Soviet Ambassador to the United States Anatoly F. Dobrynin, 11 July 1978." *CWIHP* 8/9 (Winter 1996/97): 119–22.

Polling Report.com. "Presidents and History." http://www.pollingreport.com/whhstry.htm (accessed May 3, 2007).

Powaski, Ronald E. *The Cold War: The United States and the Soviet Union, 1917–1991.* New York: Oxford University Press, 1998.

The Presidential Campaign 1976, 3 vols. Washington, D.C.: Government Printing Office, 1978.

Public Papers of the Presidents of the United States: Jimmy Carter. 9 vols. Washington, D.C.: Government Printing Office, 1977–1981.

Quandt, William. *Camp David: Peacemaking and Politics.* Washington, D.C.: Brookings Institution, 1986.

———. *Peace Process: American Diplomacy and the Arab-Israeli Conflict since 1967.* Washington, D.C.: Brookings Institution, 1993.

Rachwald, Arthur R. *In Search of Poland: The Superpowers' Response to Solidarity, 1980–1989.* Stanford: Hoover Institution Press, 1990.

Ramazani, Rouhollah K. *United States and Iran: The Patterns of Influence.* New York: Praeger, 1982.

Randolph, R. Sean. *The United States and Thailand: Alliance Dynamics, 1950–1985.* Berkeley: Institute of East Asian Studies, University of California, 1986.

Reich, Bernard. "Israel in US Perspective: Political Design and Pragmatic Practices." In *Superpowers and Client States in the Middle East: The Imbalance of Influence,* edited by Moshe Efrat and Jacob Berkovitch, 55–91. New York: Routledge, 1991.

———. *The United States and Israel: Influence in the Special Relationship.* New York: Praeger, 1984.

Rosati, Jerel A. *The Carter Administration's Quest for Global Community: Beliefs and Their Impact on Behavior.* Columbia: University of South Carolina Press, 1987.

Rosenbaum, Herbert D., and Alexj Ugrinsky, eds. *Jimmy Carter: Foreign Policy and Post-Presidential Years.* Westport, Conn.: Greenwood, 1994.

Ross, Robert S. *Negotiating Cooperation: The United States and China, 1969–1989.* Stanford: Stanford University Press, 1995.

Rossiter, Caleb, and Anne-Marie Smith. "Human Rights: The Carter Record, the Reagan Reaction." *International Policy Report* (September 1984): 1–27.

Rubin, Barry M. *Paved with Good Intentions: The American Experience in Iran.* New York: Penguin, 1981.

Saikal, Amin. *The Rise and Fall of the Shah.* Princeton: Princeton University Press, 1980.

Saivetz, Carol R. "Superpower Competition in the Middle East and the Collapse of Détente." In *Fall of Détente,* edited by Westad, 72–94. Boston: Scandinavian University Press, 1997.

Salinger, Pierre. *America Held Hostage: The Secret Negotiations.* Garden City, N.Y.: Doubleday, 1981.

Salzberg, John P. "A View from the Hill: U.S. Legislation and Human Rights." In *The Diplomacy of Human Rights,* edited by David D. Newsom, 13–20. Lanham, Md.: University Press of America/Georgetown University Institute for the Study of Diplomacy, 1986.

Sanders, Jerry W. *Peddlers of Crisis: The Committee on the Present Danger and the Politics of Containment.* Boston: South End Press, 1983.

Savranskaya, Svetlana, and David A. Welch, eds. *Global Competition and the Deterioration of U.S.–Soviet Relations, 1977–1980.* Providence, R.I.: Center for Foreign Policy Development, Thomas J. Watson Jr. Institute for International Studies, 1995.

Schaller, Michael. *The United States and China in the Twentieth Century,* 2nd ed. New York: Oxford University, 1990.

Schmidt, Helmut. *Men and Powers: A Political Retrospective.* Trans. Ruth Hein. New York: Random House, 1989.

Schmitz, David F., and Vanessa Walker. "Jimmy Carter and the Foreign Policy of Human Rights: The Development of a Post–Cold War Foreign Policy." *Diplomatic History* 28 (January 2004): 113–43.

Schoultz, Lars. *Human Rights and United States Policy toward Latin America.* Princeton: Princeton University Press, 1981.

Schraeder, Peter J. *United States Foreign Policy toward Africa: Incrementalism, Crisis, and Change.* New York: Cambridge University Press, 1994.

Schulman, Bruce J. *The Seventies: The Great Shift in American Culture, Society, and Politics.* New York: Free Press, 2001.

Schulzinger, Robert D. *A Time for Peace: The Legacy of the Vietnam War.* New York: Oxford University Press, 2006.

———. *U.S. Diplomacy since 1900,* 5th ed. New York: Oxford University Press, 2002.

Selassie, Bereket H. "The American Dilemma on the Horn." In *African Crisis Areas and U.S. Foreign Policy,* edited by Gerald J. Bender, James S. Coleman, and Richard L. Sklar, 163–77. Berkeley: University of California Press, 1985.

Seliktar, Ofira. *Failing the Crystal Ball Test: The Carter Administration and the Fundamentalist Revolution in Iran.* Westport, Conn.: Praeger, 2000.

Shafer, Robert Jones, and Donald Mabry. *Neighbors—Mexico and the United States: Wetbacks and Oil.* Chicago: Nelson-Hall, 1981.

Shawcross, William. *The Shah's Last Ride: The Fate of an Ally.* New York: Simon and Schuster, 1988.

Shiels, Frederick L. *Tokyo and Washington: Dilemmas of a Mature Alliance.* Lexington, Mass.: Lexington Books, 1980.

Sicherman, Harvey. *Palestinian Autonomy: Self-Government and Peace*. Boulder: Westview, 1993.

Sick, Gary. *All Fall Down: America's Tragic Encounter with Iran*. New York: Random House, 1985.

———. *October Surprise: America's Hostages in Iran and the Election of Ronald Reagan*. New York: Times Books, 1991.

Sikkink, Kathryn, "The Effectiveness of US Human Rights Policy, 1973–1980." In *The International Dimensions of Democratization: Europe and the Americas*, edited by Laurence Whitehead, 93–124. New York: Oxford University Press, 1996.

Skidmore, David. *Reversing Course: Carter's Foreign Policy, Domestic Politics, and the Failure of Reform*. Nashville: Vanderbilt University Press, 1996.

Slater, Robert. *Warrior Statesman: The Life of Moshe Dayan*. New York: St. Martin's, 1991.

Slocum-Schaffer, Stephanie. *America in the Seventies*. Syracuse: Syracuse University Press, 2003.

Smith, Gaddis. *The Last Years of the Monroe Doctrine, 1945–1993*. New York: Hill and Wang, 1994.

———. *Morality, Reason, and Power: American Diplomacy in the Carter Years*. New York: Hill and Wang, 1986.

Smith, George Patrick. *Restricting the Concept of Free Seas: Modern Maritime Law Reevaluated*. Huntington, N.Y.: R. E. Krieger, 1980.

Smith, Ian Douglas. *The Great Betrayal: The Memoirs of Ian Douglas Smith*. London: Blake, 1997.

Smith, Tony. *America's Mission: The United States and the Worldwide Struggle for Democracy in the Twentieth Century*. Princeton: Princeton University Press, 1994.

Smith, Wayne S. *The Closest of Enemies: A Personal and Diplomatic Account of U.S.–Cuban Relations since 1957*. New York: Norton, 1987.

Somoza, Anastasio, as told to Jack Cox. *Nicaragua Betrayed*. Boston: Western Islands, 1980.

Spear, Joanna. *Carter and Arms Sales: Implementing the Carter Administration's Arms Transfer Restraint Policy*. New York: St. Martin's, 1995.

Spiegel, Steven L. *The Other Arab-Israeli Conflict: Making America's Middle East Policy, from Truman to Reagan*. Chicago: University of Chicago Press, 1985.

Statistical Abstract of Latin America, vol. 28. Los Angeles: UCLA Center Publications, 1990.

Stein, Kenneth. *Heroic Diplomacy: Sadat, Kissinger, Carter, Begin, and the Quest for Arab-Israeli Peace*. New York: Routledge, 1999.

Stivers, William. *America's Confrontation with Revolutionary Change in the Middle East, 1948–83*. New York: St. Martin's, 1986.

Stork, Joe. "U.S. Policy and the Palestine Question." In *The United States and the Middle East: A Search for New Perspectives*, edited by Hooshang Amirahmadi, 125–48. Albany: State University of New York Press, 1993.

Strong, Robert A. *Working in the World: Jimmy Carter and the Making of American Foreign Policy*. Baton Rouge: Louisiana State University Press, 2000.

Sullivan, William. *Mission to Iran*. New York: Norton, 1981.

Summ, G. Harvey, and Tom Kelly, eds. *The Good Neighbors: America, Panama, and the 1977 Canal Treaties*. Athens: Ohio University Center for International Studies, 1988.

Sutter, Robert G. *The China Quandary: Domestic Determinants of U.S. China Policy, 1972–1982*. Boulder: Westview, 1983.

Tahir-Kheli, Shirin. *The United States and Pakistan: The Evolution of an Influence Relationship*. New York: Praeger, 1982.

Talbott, Strobe. *Endgame: The Inside Story of SALT II*. New York: Harper and Row, 1979.

Tamarkin, Mordechai. "Kissinger, Carter, and the Rhodesian Conflict—From the Art of the Possible to Mission Impossible." *Asian and African Studies* 26 (1992): 153–72.

Tan, Qingshan, *The Making of U.S. China Policy: From Normalization to the Post–Cold War Era*. Boulder: Lynne Rienner, 1992.

Thatcher, Margaret. *The Downing Street Years*. New York: Harper Collins, 1993.

Thomas, Daniel C. "Human Rights Ideas, the Demise of Communism, and the End of the Cold War." *Journal of Cold War Studies* 7 (Spring 2005): 110–41.

Thompson, Kenneth W., ed. *The Carter Presidency: Fourteen Intimate Perspectives of Jimmy Carter*. Lanham, Md.: University Press of America, 1990.

Thornton, Richard. *The Carter Years: Toward a New Global Order*. New York: Paragon House, 1991.

Tschirgi, Dan. *The American Search for Mideast Peace*. New York: Praeger, 1989.

Tucker, Nancy Bernkopf, ed. *China Confidential: American Diplomats and Sino–American Relations, 1945–1996*. New York: Columbia University Press, 2001.

Tulchin, Joseph. *Argentina and the United States: A Conflicted Relationship*. Boston: Twayne, 1990.

Turner, Stansfield. *Burn Before Reading: Presidents, CIA Directors, and Secret Intelligence*. New York: Hyperion, 2005.

———. *Secrecy and Democracy: The CIA in Transition*. Boston: Houghton Mifflin, 1985.

Tyler, Patrick. *A Great Wall: Six Presidents and China, An Investigative History*. New York: Public Affairs, 1999.

Vance, Cyrus. *Hard Choices: Critical Years in America's Foreign Policy*. New York: Simon and Schuster, 1983.

Vaughan, Patrick. "Beyond Benign Neglect: Zbigniew Brzezinski and the Polish Crisis of 1980." *Polish Review* 64 (1999): 3–28.

Wang, Qingxin Ken. *Hegemonic Cooperation and Conflict: Postwar Japan's China Policy and the United States*. Westport, Conn.: Praeger, 2000.

Wasserman, Sherri L. *The Neutron Bomb Controversy: A Study in Alliance Politics*. New York: Praeger, 1983.

Weisberger, Bernard A. *Cold War, Cold Peace: The United States and Russia since 1945*. New York: American Heritage, 1984.

Weizman, Ezer. *The Battle for Peace*. New York: Bantam, 1981.

Westad, Odd Arne, ed. *The Fall of Détente: Soviet-American Relations during the Carter Years*. Boston: Scandinavian University Press, 1997.

Wright, George. *The Destruction of a Nation: United States Policy toward Angola since 1945*. Chicago: Pluto Press, 1997.

INDEX

Ortiz, Frank, 173
Ottinger, Richard, 54
Owen, David, 63–64, 65, 190
Owen, Henry, 109, 110–11, 172

Pahlavi, Muhammad Reza, 10, 151–61,
194–95, 197, 198–99, 204, 222
Pahlavi, Reza Muhammad, 151, 152
Pakistan, 14, 52–54, 103, 163, 200, 209,
217–18, 221, 231
Palestinians. *See* Middle East peace
process
Palmieri, Victor, 226
Panama, 17, 199; and canal treaties, 4,
27, 56, 72–76, 79, 85, 86, 118, 131,
133, 134, 169, 172, 174, 178, 181,
183, 185, 186, 199, 204, 236, 238, 239
Papandreou, Andreas, 58
Pardo, Arvid, 113–14
Park Chung-hee, 67, 68, 69, 70–71, 166, 167
Park Tong-jin, 166
Park Tong-sun, 70–71
Pastor, Robert, 171, 172, 186, 198
People's Republic of China, 6–7, 8, 14,
20, 27, 29, 35, 60, 118–19, 129–42,
143, 146, 147, 164–66, 177, 200, 213,
218, 219–21, 225, 231, 236, 237, 239,
240–41
Pérez, Carlos Andrés, 170
Perry, William, 220
Peru, 35, 78, 211, 223
Pezzullo, Lawrence, 174
Phan Hien, 142
Philippines, 10, 29, 32–35, 142, 157
Pincus, Walter, 49
Pinochet Ugarte, Augusto, 10, 29
Platt, Nicholas, 137, 175
Pol Pot, 164–65, 178, 220–21
Poland, 19, 203, 227–29, 231, 236
Portugal, 126–27
Powell, Jody, 27, 37, 186, 207
Precht, Henry, 159, 160, 161, 195, 204
Proxmire, William, 183, 184

Quandt, William, 77, 78, 82, 238

Rabin, Yitzhak, 77–78
Rajai, Muhammad Ali, 227
Rapid Deployment Force, 183–84, 201, 221
Reagan, Ronald, 3, 73, 163, 178, 203,
206, 218, 222–23, 226–27, 232, 233,
234, 236, 237

Rhodes, John, 71
Rhodesia, 59–67, 86, 146, 157, 179,
189–91, 202, 240
Richardson, Elliot, 114–16, 176–77
Robelo, Alfonso, 170, 172, 192
Roberto, Holden, 126
Rockefeller, David, 19
Rockefeller, Nelson, 194
Rodino, Peter, 226
Rolvaag, Karl, 26
Romania, 60, 227
Romero, Carlos Humberto, 193
Romero, Archbishop Oscar, 230
Roosevelt, Franklin, 12, 186, 236
Rosen, Barry, 147
Rosenthal, Benjamin, 58
Rossiter, Caleb, 31
Rostow, Walt, 8
Rusk, Dean, 186
Ryan, Leo, 153

Sadat, Anwar, 77, 80–84, 119–20, 135,
149–50, 162, 200
Sakharov, Andrei, 37
Saleh, Ali Abdullah, 163
SALT, 9, 20, 37–46, 47, 55, 73, 85,
118–19, 121, 124–25, 126, 131, 132,
133, 134, 135, 136, 138–39, 141, 146,
147, 151, 157, 165–66, 169, 172, 173,
177, 179–87, 189, 194–95, 197,
200–201, 209, 216, 237, 238, 239,
240, 241
Samrin, Hang, 164
Sandino, Augusto, 168
Sarbanes, Paul, 58
Saudi Arabia, 35, 77, 80, 81–82, 129, 163,
200, 207, 221, 238
Saunders, Harold, 204–5
Savimbi, Jonas, 126
Schlesinger, James, 8, 103
Schmidt, Helmut, 50–51, 101, 103, 104,
105, 109–12, 188, 213–14, 215,
216–17, 238
Schultze, Charles, 103, 109
Selassie, Haile, 119, 120, 121
Serbia, 234
Sharif-Emami, Jafar, 157
Sharon, Ariel, 84
Shriver, Sargent, 22
Shulman, Marshall, 42
Siad Barre, Muhammad, 119–23,
125–26, 221

Sick, Gary, 159, 227
Simpson, Alan, 118
Singh, Charan, 218
Singlaub, John K., 69–70
Sithole, Ndibaningi, 65, 66
Smith, Hedrick, 84
Smith, Ian, 59–60, 61, 63, 65, 66, 67, 189–90, 191
Smith, Wayne, 223
Sneider, Richard, 70
Solarz, Stephen, 190, 194
Solaun, Mauricio, 171, 174
Somalia. *See* Horn of Africa
Somoza, Anastasio Debayle, 168–75, 177, 192, 193
Somoza, Luis, 168
Somoza García, Anastasio, 168
South Africa, 35, 60–61, 62, 64–67, 86, 127, 145, 189, 191–92, 234
South Korea, 29, 35, 67–72, 79, 86, 129, 142, 147, 166–67, 177, 178, 236, 237, 238, 239, 241
South Yemen, 163–64
Soviet Union, 3, 4, 5, 14, 15, 16, 18, 35, 60, 73, 142, 144, 145, 152, 154; and Afghanistan, 162–63, 199–201, 203, 204, 209–11, 212, 213–15, 216–18, 219–21, 226, 228, 231, 236, 238; and Angola, 126–28; and arms control and disarmament, 7–8; and Bulgaria, 227; and comprehensive test ban treaty negotiations, 46–47, 48, 129, 215; and conventional arms transfer negotiations, 48–49, 118, 129; and Cuba, 48, 62, 127, 144, 192, 201; and Czechoslovakia, 227; and détente, 6–9, 145, 231, 236–37; and East Germany, 227; and Horn of Africa, 48, 117, 119–26, 129, 134, 181; and Hungary, 227; and Indian Ocean, demilitarization of, 47–48, 215; and Iran, 151; and Middle East peace process, 79–80, 81; and Mutual Balanced Force Reduction negotiations, 47; and North Yemen, 163–64; and People's Republic of China, 6–7, 8, 120, 130, 131, 135, 137, 166, 200; and Poland, 227–29, 236; and Rhodesia, 60, 62; and Romania, 227; and SALT, 9, 37–46, 47, 48, 125, 132, 135, 138–39, 179–82, 186–88, 200–201; and South Yemen, 163; and Vietnam, 7, 137, 142, 143, 164. *See also* Human rights, Soviet Union and
Spain, 36, 171
Stalin, Josef, 130
Stennis, John, 44, 50, 51
Stevens, Ted, 184
Stewart, Bill, 174
Stone, Richard, 185
Strategic Arms Limitations Treaty. *See* SALT
Strauss, Robert, 102, 108, 109, 162
Studds, Gerry, 153
Sudan, 119, 120, 122, 128
Sullivan, William, 147, 156, 158–59, 160, 196
Suzuki, Zenko, 215, 216
Syria, 76, 77, 81, 123, 205

Tabatabai, Sadegh, 226
Taiwan, 129–41, 166, 177, 191
Tanzania, 62, 63, 119, 191
Taraki, Nur Muhammad, 162–63, 199, 200
Thailand, 49, 144, 225
Thatcher, Margaret, 190, 191, 213
Thornton, Thomas, 64
Thurmond, Strom, 118
Todman, Terence, 30, 36, 144–45, 168, 169, 171, 193
Togo, 128
Toon, Malcolm, 37
Torrijos, Omar, 73–74, 75, 199, 204
Tower, John, 185, 187
Track, Juan, 72
Trilateral Commission, 13, 15, 18, 19, 23, 62, 74, 100
Truman, Harry, 8, 21, 57, 186, 210
Tsongas, Paul, 11
Turkey, 18, 56–59, 147, 148–49, 177, 178, 236, 237, 239
Turner, Stansfield, 45, 46, 68–69, 156–57, 163, 184, 229

Uganda, 128, 165
Ullman, Al, 102
Unger, Leonard, 140
United Nations, 57, 60, 61, 62, 65, 76–77, 80, 127, 204–5, 206, 218
Uruguay, 10, 36, 211, 241
Ustinov, Dmitri, 201